THE SECRET WORLD

It is a city within the city of Moscow. The KGB community has a separate power plant, separate communications system, its own farms and slaughterhouses, a small army of plumbers, electricians, doctors, cooks, valets, handymen, and almost every variety of professional service, including prostitutes.

Information supplied by informers is stored in exhaustive files, kept on people from all walks of life, from the factory worker to the artist, from the politician to members of the intelligence establishment itself. The information is seldom verified and is used by the government against its own people . . .

THE SECRET WORLD

Peter Deriabin and Frank Gibney

BALLANTINE BOOKS • NEW YORK

ACKNOWLEDGMENTS

This book grew out of a two-part series of articles in *Life* magazine, published on March 23 and 30, 1959. The authors would like to thank Edward K. Thompson, Managing Editor, and the Editors of *Life* for their help and co-operation in preparing it. We are particularly indebted to John K. Jessup, Chief Editorial Writer, for his advice during the book's early stages.

It would be impossible to cite individually all who helped with the book's preparation, but some names stand out. Miss Jean Nicholas of *Life* was of literally invaluable assistance throughout the course of an involved writing and research program. Mrs. Frank Gibney was not only kind and encouraging to the authors, as good wives are in such a situation; she contributed a wealth of excellent editorial suggestions. Finally, we should like to thank our good friends George Mitchell and Walter Benson for their unstinting guidance in planning this book and bringing it to the light of day. Without them it could not have been written.

CONTENTS

INTRODUCTION

LIKE OLD CONS who have learned exactly what accommodations to expect in any jail, seasoned spies and veteran intelligence officers know that safehouses run to form. In the kitchen, the sink will be filled with scarcely rinsed glasses, grimy coffee cups, and stainless steel cutlery that has been wiped clean, not washed. The refrigerator will be empty except for a few cans of beer, a stick of vintage butter, half a loaf of rock-solid pumpernickel, a bit of cheese gone green, and a bottle of stuffed olives. In the living room, nary a plant or flower offsets the ingrained fragrance of stale air and unwashed ashtrays.

This place was special. As safehouses go, it was a mansion. Perhaps because it was in the Washington area and provided the first glimpse of the United States that certain rather exceptional immigrants were to have, there was a live-in housekeeper and the accommodations were big, airy, and comfortable. Extra care had been taken to find a place isolated and spacious enough to permit the guest a walk. This safehouse had a wooded garden. Still, even after a few days of confinement, however comfortable, everyone needs a break, a change of pace.

That Saturday night someone had the idea of screening a few Soviet documentary films on World War II. The war had been over for almost a decade, but no one had forgot the impression the films had made when first released by the Russians. Soviet cameramen had shot some of the best battle footage in history. The movies would be a welcome change from the evening routine of TV and chess.

Before the room darkened, a short, dark-haired man took a seat. He walked with a slight limp, his leg a throbbing testimony to the effectiveness of the Wehrmacht artillery along the front west of Moscow.

Hunched forward, the man remained motionless as "The Battle For Stalingrad" began to roll. Only when the camera panned slowly around the shattered ruin of a schoolhouse in which a Soviet mortar platoon had hunkered down did he start with surprise.

When the camera lingered for a moment on a crudely painted sign above a makeshift table, scattered mounds of rugs, and torn greatcoats that served as beds, he laughed aloud. In Russian, the sign read: "Here Lt. P. Deriabin's mortar men stood fast." It was an ironic reminder of his survival.

In the hours the Soviet editors had spent splicing thousands of feet of combat film together, and despite the presumably lengthy discussions with the censors, no Soviet official could have had the foresight to spot the name on the sign and to snip the frames taken in the improvised shelter. Eleven years after Stalingrad, a court martial, presided over by a Soviet Lieutenant General, had found Major Peter Sergeyevich Deriabin a traitor to the fatherland and sentenced him to death.

In the crowded years that followed Stalingrad, Peter Deriabin had not thought of the sign the proud private soldier had painted. He had never forgotten, however, that his regiment had gone into the cauldron of Stalingrad with 2800 men. He could only hope that the painter-private was among the 151 still on their feet when the last German units surrendered.

Deriabin had a lot to remember. His war had not ended at Stalingrad—months later he was so gravely wounded that his comrades were forced to leave him behind the German lines on the Bug river in the Ukraine. It was not until a German soldier started to remove the prized American combat boots Deriabin had been issued a week earlier that the tough Siberian regained consciousness. Surprised to find that the "corpse" had moved, the German pumped another round into Deriabin's chest and scuttled away—

with the boots. Deriabin is not sure how, in his delirium, he regained his feet and struggled barefoot back to the Soviet lines, but that incident was the end of *his* war. And the war is only the prologue to the story Deriabin and his coauthor Frank Gibney tell so well in the pages that follow.

Today, twenty some years after the book was first published, *The Secret World* is still required reading in Western intelligence training schools. It is an insider's view of the Soviet intelligence and security forces. The information on Soviet intelligence methods and the personnel behind KGB operations is as vital and fresh today as when it was first put to paper.

In fact, this book is a troika of stories. The first is that of a precocious country boy from a remote corner of Siberia whose early ambition was to make a career in the Communist Party, and also as a teacher. He would exalt the enlightened rule of Comrade Stalin and spread the gospel of revolution and the wisdom of Lenin. The message of Soviet education was powerful stuff for an ambitious schoolboy.

The second story, the biography of a *starshiy operupolnomochennyy*—a Senior Case Officer—in the counterintelligence arm of the Soviet secret police, is a veritable textbook on KGB operations in the USSR and abroad.

Intertwined with these narratives is the history of the growing disillusionment, the loss of faith, and finally the rebellion of a man who had served the Soviet state as a Party official, a soldier, and an intelligence officer.

Deriabin is a uniquely qualified observer of the Soviet scene. As a young Party activist, he was as well schooled in Soviet mythology as anyone his age in the USSR. From the October Cubs, a Soviet organization roughly equivalent to the Cub Scouts, Deriabin went on to the Young Pioneers, and then to the Komsomol, the Young Communist League; at seventeen, he was a high-school teacher of history. When he was eighteen, he was given the "supreme honor" of serving on the district Komsomol committee. Finally, at twenty-one, he was admitted to the Communist Party.

The young patriot had studied Stalin's *Short History Of The Communist Party* so thoroughly he could recite large portions of it from memory. Given the opportunity, he might even have talked shop with Mikhail Suslov, Stalin's vicar for ideology.

Not everyone was impressed by Deriabin's enthusiasm for the Communist Party. Perhaps it was fortunate that no police snitch was present to hear his father, when the nine-year-old Peter proudly arrived home wearing the red neckerchief that certified his membership in the Young Pioneers. "Look," his father said, "he has put on a dog's leash and now he's showing off." Years later, in Vienna, when he broke with the Soviet Union, Deriabin had reason to remember his father's words.

Even in Stalin's army, ideology took second place to combat. Although formally assigned to work with the political commissar, Deriabin commanded a mortar company at Stalingrad and later served as an assistant chief of staff at the regimental headquarters. It was after his fourth wound—and five medals and five military orders—that Deriabin was transferred to counterintelligence by a battle commander who knew that the young captain's luck was spent.

By the time Deriabin had left the hospital, completed counterintelligence school, and served a few months in Moscow, his enthusiasm for counterintelligence and Party work had begun to wear thin. The ideals of the revolution, as perceived by a bright young teacher, had little to do with the reality of political life in Moscow. The hordes of self-serving bureaucrats and ambitious Party regulars scarcely troubled to give even lip service to the "truths" Deriabin had so earnestly pressed on his students.

It is a mark of Deriabin's growing political acumen that, after a year of service with State Security in Moscow, he was able to resign from the secret police, then the NKGB. Officers were sometimes cashiered, but few indeed ever simply opted out of the secret police. Like many veterans, Deriabin wanted to go home, to pick up the life he had known before the war. And, like many veterans, he soon found that what he remembered, or thought he remembered, had vanished. No longer could he be content lecturing students and hawking Moscow policies that he did not believe. But Deriabin had no experience to qualify for anything but work in the Party or State Security. Thus, realizing he could not support his wife and help his relatives on the pittance he would make if he began again at the bottom as a teacher, he returned to what was now called the Ministry of State Security, or MGB.

As Deriabin puts it, "The State Security case officer is the cop-on-the-beat in the world's most ruthlessly efficient police force." Assigned to Barnaul in the Altai Kray, a province in Siberia, he soon sickened of the routine surveillance of his fellow citizens, jailing "dissidents," and recruiting agents to spy on suspects whose anti-Sovietism, once it was smoked out, often consisted simply of a belief in God. When his bride of a few months died, Deriabin had had enough. He wrangled a job in Moscow. There, at least, he would be able to spend part of his time in graduate work at a university.

Deriabin's career in State Security—it was not to become the KGB until a few weeks after he had fled—spanned the period in which the postwar Soviet intelligence and security organs took their shape. In a sense, he was present at the creation in a front-row seat. As a senior counterintelligence officer in the elite Kremlin Guard, the unit responsible for the safety of Stalin and the Soviet political hierarchy, he was perfectly placed to watch the political drama unfold and to witness the manuevering of Stalin's henchmen. Beria was his boss.

The six years he spent in Moscow coincided with the last convulsions of Stalin's state. Deriabin's account of the inner workings of the Kremlin Guard and the infighting among Stalin's satraps is illuminated with anecdotes, gossip, and history unwritten elsewhere. It is life observed by a member of the establishment who combined the interests and perspectives of an intelligence officer, a keen student, and a historian.

It was in Moscow that Deriabin began to document his swelling hatred of the Soviet system. As a student at the Institute of Marxism-Leninism and a trusted State Security officer, he had free access to its library of Western newspapers, magazines, and books. He could also read the proscribed works of communist intellectuals and early Party members who had been executed by Stalin. With all that he had once seen as "bright and shining" gone gray, his communist convictions crumbled. Almost unconsciously, he -

became convinced that the only solution was to escape from the USSR.

When faced with a decision that meant committing himself to Stalin's Guard and the lethal power struggles at the summit, he contrived to slip out of the Kremlin and into the foreign intelligence arm of the NKGB. After a year on the German-Austrian desk in Moscow—where he supervised some of the most sensitive NKGB operations in Germany and Austria—Deriabin swung an assignment with the newly appointed Soviet intelligence *rezident* for Austria and was assigned to Vienna. His account of Soviet operations in Germany and Austria is one of the most revealing disclosures of Soviet secret activity by any former operative.

Deriabin has always had a keen technical interest in espionage and counterintelligence operations. If his motivation had remained strong, he would have been a formidable field case officer. Although he took the time to involve CIA in a double-agent operation, his interest in KGB operations flagged as his faith in the Soviet system collapsed. His hasty second marriage to a Moscow girl, who had been a secretary to Lazar Kaganovich, a Politburo member, had gone sour. He was a man alone on the battlefield between two worlds.

Without having made a final decision on his future, Deriabin attempted to establish contact with CIA through an agent. When that failed, he continued to soldier on. Then, halfway through the investigation of the defection of a minor Soviet official in Vienna, Deriabin abruptly made up his mind.

Stopping at an open-air lunch stand in Vienna, he ordered sausages and a bottle of beer and paused to reflect, but for just long enough to finish his meal. Once finished, Deriabin hailed a cab and went directly to an American military police post in Vienna.

It is typical of Deriabin that he casually dismisses the drama of his actual escape from Vienna. In the edition of this book published in 1958, Deriabin says he left Vienna in disguise. Some disguise—he was shipped out as freight on a military train that took him a hundred miles through the Soviet occupation zone surrounding Vienna. With the entire Austria KGB staff and platoons of picked soldiers gunning for him, it was a perilous passage.

But when the train reached the American zone of occupation at Enns, Deriabin had forever closed the door on the USSR, his beloved Siberia, and the only life he had ever known.

The trim house is no different from the dozen others on the neatly kept suburban block. A well-tended lawn and the carefully clipped shrubs offer no hint that the occupant ever lived anywhere but in that development or one of a dozen others just like it in the area. Nor is there any clue in the living room to suggest that the "retired Government employee" might even have traveled abroad.

Any unknowing visitor lucky enough to be invited for dinner might wonder how this former civil servant and his family learned to cook *pel'meni*, the little meat dumplings that are a Siberian speciality. After eating the prescribed two courses—the first with bullion and a few drops of vinegar, the second in sour cream—and swigging a little vodka, he might almost hear the hiss of a sleigh slipping along a snow-packed road in Siberia.

If the visitor is invited into the cellar study, and stumbles over the stacks of *Pravda, Izvestia,* and *Red Star,* the charade is over. The walls are lined with books in Russian, German, and English. Ranged alongside volumes of Russian poetry and military history is a shelf of books on intelligence.

Deriabin retired in 1981 and his employers have drawn a curtain across that period of his life. His approved resumé suggests that he was a researcher and analyst, as indeed he certainly was. After shaking hands with him, and some conversation about what is going on in the world, one may well wonder how anyone quite so tough, quite so engaged politically, could ever have spent all of his time pushing paper. But that's the story and Peter Sergeyevich Deriabin sticks to it.

—May 1982

PROLOGUE

AT SIX O'CLOCK on the evening of February 15, 1954, a Russian-born engineer named Sergey Feoktistov, known to a limited circle by the code name of "Builder," dropped in at his accustomed rendezvous point in the Graben Café, a drab little meeting place of streetwalkers, cheap *Schnapps*-drinkers, and petty Soviet occupation officials on the corner of Vienna's much-traveled shopping street. He began to wait. Although he had once fought with the Whites after the Revolution, the Builder was now a trusted agent of the Soviet spy network in Vienna. The man he sought was a ranking officer of Soviet intelligence in eastern Europe, known to him only by the name of Smirnov.

Several hours before, an attractive French citizen named Irina Kotomkina, secretary to Louis Saillant, Secretary-General of the World Federation of Trade Unions, had begun telephoning a familiar but very private number, U6-1875. She wished to inform her link with the Soviet intelligence network that she could not make a certain appointment on the following day, when she was scheduled to turn in a detailed report on her employer's office conversations at the WFTU's Vienna headquarters. The man she called was a high official of the Soviet High Commissioner's staff, as it appeared, but she knew him only as Korobov. He did not answer.

In the Imperial Hotel offices of the Soviet High Commissioner (soon to become the Soviet Embassy) Counselor Evgeniy Kovalev was waiting in turn. The Counselor was

better known to his Moscow connections by his original
name and title of Colonel Kravtsov. His real position in
Vienna was as Resident of the Soviet State Security's
intelligence apparatus there. Kovalev expected momentarily a report of an extremely confidential nature from his
most valuable subordinate, a man known to Moscow communications officers only as "Konstantin." Konstantin was
in fact Major Peter Sergeyevich Deriabin, the acting chief
of Vienna's SK division, the agency inside every Soviet installation abroad that concerns itself with the surveillance
and counter-intelligence investigation of all Soviet citizens.
Deriabin was due to report on the matter of a Russian recently defected to the West. He had not yet been heard
from.

In the Soviet garage behind the Parkring, Anatoliy Yelfi-
mov, a chauffeur for the High Commission by circum-
stance and a non-commissioned officer in the State Security
by profession, was standing by for orders. His boss, the SK
chief at the Residency, had not yet telephoned him. There
was nothing very extraordinary about this lack of word.
Deriabin was a busy man, chronically given to sudden jour-
neys, hastily switched appointments and all the minutiae of
his job that a State Security "chauffeur" was trained to
anticipate. But it was unusual not to have heard from him
earlier.

Scarcely two hours before his non-arrival became a concern to these various business associates, Peter Sergeyevich
Deriabin, 33 (alias "Smirnov," "Voronov," "Korobov,"
and his code name of "Konstantin"), Section head in the
State Security's intelligence network, veteran Communist
Party secretary, former security official in the Guard Directorate of the Kremlin, veteran of Stalingrad, four times
wounded, holder of five military orders and five medals,
graduate of the Soviet Army Counter-Intelligence School,
the Institute of Marxism-Leninism and fifteen years of un-
interrupted Soviet security checks, had walked into an
American military headquarters on the Mariahilferstrasse
and asked for political asylum.

The story which led to Peter Deriabin's decision on that
February day is not only a singular personal adventure. It
is also, from the nature of Deriabin's position and background, a commentary on the workings and history of the

critical area in Soviet society. It may strike the foreign reader with the force of a window suddenly opened in a long-darkened room. At its heart is the revolt against the Soviet system of a young Siberian who had distinguished himself in the system's three most sensitive areas of command: as a strategically placed member of Soviet foreign intelligence, as a Communist Party secretary, and as a trusted officer of the Kremlin's private security forces.

Deriabin entered the service of the Soviet State Security when he was twenty-three, after distinguished service as a front-line military officer. At that time he was already a Communist Party member of three years' standing and an eight-year veteran of the Party youth organization, the Komsomol. In the next ten years he acquired an almost unique indoctrination in the State Security's methods of controlling the Soviet population. He began as a local "case officer" investigating instances of "anti-Soviet activity" in his home province, the Altai Kray, in Siberia. He later served inside the sacrosanct Guard Directorate in Moscow, transferring from this to work in the Austro-German Section of the Foreign Intelligence Directorate and, ultimately, in Vienna.

All this experience made Deriabin an unusually accomplished Chekist, as the officers of the State Security are still called, although the exact title of their organization has long since changed from Cheka through OGPU through NKVD and MGB to its present intialed designation of KGB. He revolted against his own experience precisely because there had been so much of it, and he had thought deeply about its meaning.

"Having been brought up by the Communist Party," he wrote later, "with a good position in Moscow and the later good fortune of receiving a foreign assignment, I was led to make the acquaintance of a different world. It was a curious world, rich but ugly. Almost from the day in 1947 when I began work inside it, with the Guard Directorate in the Kremlin, a poison of doubt began to work in my soul. What had looked so shining and wonderful on the outside looked very gray now. It grew grayer and grayer, until it ceased to appear as an achievement of any positive nature. An idea took hold of my mind that the very few were dictators and the many forced to live under their oppression. I could not reconcile this with my previous teachings, but I could not suppress it.

"After a long period working for the State Security I was convinced that the police mechanism exists not because of acts committed by enemies of the people, but because of the system itself, the way that the Soviet state is organized."

It took Deriabin many years, understandably, to reach the conclusions which he found so easy to write from the vantage point of his new country. A codified system of terror leaves a far heavier mark on its employees than on its victims. There were many factors in his ultimate decision—a mixture, like most human acts, of the ideal, the practical, and the circumstantial. He is a person of courage, curiosity, and uncompromising honesty, who would be known for these qualities in any society. And when a man such as this makes even a hidden inner decision it is hard for him long to hide it from the world around him. At the time of his escape he had few close relatives to worry about inside the Soviet Union; the war had taken most of them. He could thus dispense with much of the worry about family hostages that remains the most formidable practical obstacle to more "defections" such as his.

In the widest sense, the thinking that led to his conclusions arose also from his upbringing in a remote frontier area of the Soviet Union and his mixed fortune in belonging to a peculiar interim generation of Russians. The generation before him contained the people of the Revolution, who fought one oppression and lived to canonize another. The best among them remained unable to face this fact until the time for correction had long passed, and by this point most of them were already rotting in Stalin's prisons. Many of these people have escaped to the outside world, including some from the State Security itself; but their past lives were generally too scarred by conspiracy and counter-conspiracy for them to evaluate what they left behind.

The generation after Deriabin is the world's great question mark. These are the young people who have known no experience outside of Soviet Communism; but their natual questioning conscience has been paradoxically revived as an inescapable by-product of a mass education that was planned to eliminate will and conscience altogether. Whether the revival will have any fruits no one can predict.

Deriabin's generation has lived in between. It is the generation which operates the Soviet Union, but does not rule it: the managers, the colonels, the school principals. It is almost knowingly a technicians' generation, competent but wary, which has seen more than its share of fear, doubt, and disillusionment.

Peter Deriabin was born in a society where all power and advancement already resided with the Soviets. He wore the red tie of a Young Pioneer when he was nine and laughed at his elders' "superstitions" before he was ten. Yet he was old enough to remember a day when his father Sergey owned his own land and drove the family around the district on Sundays in their cart to pay friendly social calls on the neighbors, rituals that died forever with the coming of the collectives. His family was religious, and he sometimes prayed. His first teachers at school in Siberia considered themselves Russians and Europeans first, and Communists, if at all, a poor second.

Deriabin, in short, was part of the generation colonized by Communism. Like all colonists, its members retained a few glimpses of the motherland they had left; that is to say, they were hardly Czarists, but they remembered a bit of Europe. They fought World War II at a time when Communism had almost seeped into their souls from constant varnishing. The war was enough to reaffirm their ancient faith in Russia, but the war and its aftermath shook to its foundations the Marxist political faith that trades on its peculiar boasts of permanence and prescience. If they maintain a nominal profession of Communism it has been as much as anything for the lack of any visible alternative within their ken.

Such, in brief, were the premises for Peter Deriabin's escape from Soviet society. For a variety of reasons, most of them dealing with the sensitivity of his former intelligence connection, he withheld telling his story until five years after his escape, when his first two articles appeared in *Life*, preliminary to the writing of this book. He is now grateful for the time interval. Without losing touch with developments inside the Soviet Union he has had five years in which to evaluate his experience as a member of the Soviet "New Class" of managers and governors.

His story is fortuitously told at this moment of history, with relations between the United States and the Soviet Union such a weird combination of war and peace, exchange and competition. At no time is it more important to distinguish between the externals of Soviet society and its essence, between the outward change and the continuing permanent factors of its life. Deriabin has witnessed some changes in his society: although a legalist may object there is no essential difference between the use of physical and mental torture, for example, in extracting a confession, to the man who has had to deal with both varieties the change is significant. He does not hold, therefore, with the typical émigré view that "nothing in the system" has changed since the worst days of Stalin. There is some truth in the statements of foreign tourists that the people of the Soviet Union now seem better off and more contented with their life.

Some truth, and no more. What worries Deriabin now is his fear that this tendency to loose the most obvious bonds of a statist society be confused with a fundamental change in its nature. Ten years in the State Security taught Deriabin one unforgettable lesson: the secert police apparatus, with its own foreign and domestic intelligence branches, is the Soviet régime's principal reliance for power. Working directly under the Communist Party Central Committee in Moscow, it is the ultimate executive arm of that Party and the régime. It is the cement that keeps in position the unnatural power structure of the Soviet Union. Its adhesive qualities—a mixture of fear, suspicion, and the actual use of force—are essential to a government which continues to be dedicated not to the well-being of its citizens, nor even to the enrichment of a particular class, but to the preservation and continuity of power among a small vested oligarchy.

Before writing this book, also, Deriabin has had the chance to accustom himself to life in the United States, an experience which has been exciting, surprising, and satisfying, although not without its moments of embarrassment and pain. "It is not hard," as Deriabin says, "to change your country. It *is* hard to change your customs. I use customs in the widest sense of the word. It encompasses the manner in which life is lived, ways of thinking and speaking, the way you argue or read a book or spend your leisure time. The customs of this society in which I now live are all the more puzzling to a one-time Soviet citizen because they are loosely stated and not punitively enforced. The lack of restrictions on a man's thoughts and movements was in itself an absolute and, for a time, bewildering break with everything in my life before."

This line of thought was responsible for our decision to write this book in the third person. Peter Deriabin the Chekist is dead. It would be pointless to exhume him for the sake of the first-person pronoun. This also enabled my own collaboration, for which I am most happy. Deriabin *could* have written his own autobiography. I *could* have written a book about Peter Deriabin, whether cast in that mold or hiding behind that well-used literary drapery, "as told to." We chose instead to synthesize our thoughts and observations on the life and times here narrated, feeling that they demanded a wider perspective than simple personal experience.

I could not close this introduction without explaining the reason why I insisted on writing it alone, without the co-author's participation. As an American and a citizen of what we legitimately call the free world, I would like to thank Peter Deriabin for what he did. It is appallingly common in our society, for all our lip service to "man's struggle against Communist tyranny," to look askance at the men with the courage to escape this tyranny out of honest motives. We call them "defectors," and there is always a bit of suspicion in the air when the subject is introduced. In the same breath that we acknowledge the immorality behind the Soviet system we voice our doubts about someone who has had the courage to leave this immoral society and possesses the knowledge to help ours—too nonconformist, perhaps. I hope that this book may alter this suspicion.

Frank Gibney

CHAPTER I

The Farm In The Altai

PETER DERIABIN WAS born in the tiny farming settlement of Lokot, in southwestern Siberia, on February 13, 1921. It was not a particularly happy moment for a Russian child to begin his life. If Americans born some years later could ever after call themselves "depression babies," Russians of Deriabin's vintage have abundant right to a title like "chaos children." Although the Revolution was three and a half years old, the country remained twisted in its convulsions. The last organized army of the Whites had given up the ghost the previous autumn, when Baron Wrangel loaded some 100,000 of his supporters aboard the remnants of the Czarist navy, anchored off the Crimea, after an earlier-day Dunkirk at Sevastopol. But numerous, if less formidable, White groups kept fighting; and the blood and banditry in the backwash of modern history's worst civil war continued without cease.

"Tens and hundreds of thousands of disbanded soldiers," as Lenin himself admitted, had become brigands. Farms had been wrecked and the life of the cities thrown into wild disorder by the pell-mell ordering of "war Communism." On the day of Deriabin's birth the sailors of the Red Fleet were mutinying at Kronstadt in the first armed rebellion within the new régime. That same month the desperate Bolshevik leaders gingerly put forth the first explanations of the New Economic Policy, designed to give peasants and small shop owners a brief respite from the fury of their own communizing.

17

Deriabin's family background, at least, was able to give him some cushion against the formalized class warfare which, even by the fourth year of Communist rule, was written into the law of the land. It was gratifyingly proletarian. His father, Sergey, who owned a small farm when Peter was born, had behind him a career as a trusty, intelligent, dependable member of what the Old Russia definitely considered respectable lower-class society. He had attended school through the first two years of high school, a fact that insured him a leading position in the councils of Siberian village life, where even literate men were rare. Sergey started working at fifteen, when he got a job as coachman for a wealthy judge in Biysk. In the judge's household he met an attractive servant girl named Stepanida or "Stesha." He courted her and married her in 1907, when they were both nineteen.

The following year Deriabin's father was drafted for service in the Czarist army. He did his duty in the garrison at Russian Island, off Vladivostok, for four years, and reenlisted for a second term in 1912, after he had been promoted to corporal. The small bonus he received for reenlisting he used to bring his wife out on the trans-Siberian railway to join him. In 1916 he was mustered out[1] with the rank of sergeant major. He took his wife and their oldest child back to Biysk, where he made a living for the next three years as a carpenter.

Sergey Deriabin had two brothers and two sisters, all of them workers or simple artisans. The artistic rebel in the family, Peter's Uncle Pavel, was a self-taught painter of religious themes who wandered throughout Russia painting icons and murals for village churches. (After the Revolution, as his specialty became increasingly precarious, the family lost track of him.) The founder of the family, Grandfather Andrey, had come from the vicinity of Moscow. He settled in Biysk in the late 1860s, setting up in business as a small trader, running packhourse caravans into Mongolia and back, over the mountain passes. With the proper breaks he might have turned this enterprise into the beginnings of an

---

[1] Under the Czarist military law, even in time of war, one son in a family was released from military obligations to provide for the support of the household.

impressive family business. Any businessman settling in that half-deserted area at that period was, to put it mildly, getting in on the ground floor. As it happened, he did not, and whatever he left his sons in the way of money or talent they used modestly also.

Biysk, Lokot, and the other towns and farming villages where Peter Deriabin grew up are all part of what is now called the Altai Kray,[2] which was then and remains one of the more out-of-the-way parts of the Soviet Union. The Altai Kray is primarily farming country. Its soil is as fertile as the famous *chernozem* of the Kuban and the Ukraine, and Altai wheat is esteemed by bakers throughout the country. Although there are a few industrial cities—

[2] The word *kray* is derived from the Russian word for frontier. It denotes a large border area containing within itself autonomous national units. Such units are autonomous in cultural matters, but their administration is part of the *kray* responsibility. An *oblast* is a province, the basic territorial division within the U.S.S.R. Although equal in status to a *kray*, an *oblast* is not a frontier area and does not contain any autonomous territory. Both *oblasts* and *krays* are divided into *rayons*, which are the equivalent of counties. There is a difference, however, between urban and rural *rayons*. In a city a *rayon* corresponds to a ward: Moscow has twenty; Barnaul has three.

The word *okrug* was used as a territorial term equivalent to *oblast* until 1929, when the division between *kray* and *oblast* came in. The word is now retained only to describe military territorial commands, e.g. the Odessa Military Okrug, and for national *okrugs*, which are large, sparsely populated territories usually containing the remnants of their indigenous primitive population. They are autonomous, but form posts of individual *krays*.

There are fifteen Union republics in the U.S.S.R. In order to permit the possibility of secession laid down in the constitution of every Union republic (no one has yet attempted to take it literally), a Union republic must be on the borders of the Soviet Union. Thus an act of secession could physically take place by redrawing the border *between* the U.S.S.R. and the departing member. The autonomous republics do not have this requirement. They represent politically and culturally important segments considered worthy of individual representation, and they contain only *rayons*, whereas the Union republics are organized into *krays*, *oblasts*, and *rayons*, in a descending scale of importance.

Barnaul, Biysk, Rubtsovsk and Chesnokovka—the Altai is not heavily peopled. The farmers there have a good deal of elbow-room or, rather, they had before collectivization. The population still numbers only 2,685,000 according to the 1958 census, for an area as large as the British Isles.

The land is generally high but flat. The rugged peaks of the Altai are in the southernmost part of the region. It is there that the river Ob, one of the largest rivers in the Soviet Union, begins its 2500-mile course to the Artic Ocean, winding with its tributaries through every part of the *kray*. Further north the Altai Mountains give way to rolling foothill country and a predominant expanse of plateau land. Birch groves and pine forests are thick over these high-altitude steppes, and the country is traditionally attractive to hunters and fishermen. Bear, deer, beaver, reindeer, mountain goats, and wild boar range the hills and forests. Wolves are still a menace to the farmers' livestock. When Deriabin was a boy they could be heard at night howling everywhere outside the villages. Frequently they left dead calves, colts, and even horses behind them in the morning, when they retreated to the forests.

The whole region lies well to the south of the main line of the trans-Siberian railway. It is rarely visited by tourists, and no one in Moscow has ever given it more than a minimum of official attention either under the Czarist or the Soviet dispensation. As a result, the changes of the Revolution and the civil war, as well as the twists and turns of Soviet policy later in the twenties and the thirties, came slowly to the Altai. For several years after October 25, 1917, governement went on in the provincial capital of Barnaul much as it had gone on before. Officials performed whatever Moscow asked of them, while trying to piece together in their minds some sensible outline of the new Bolshevik régime. The nearest major battles of the civil war, which lasted well into 1921, were fought along the trans-Siberian, and the *kray* thus went through the turmoil of the Revolution and its aftermath with relatively little physical disturbance.

No corner of the country was immune, however, from the fevers spreading out from Moscow and Petrograd. Local soviets were organized, manifestos turned out on town printing presses, pledges of loyalty exacted, shots fired.

Counter-revolutionary movements were not lacking. In February 1918 the local national minority in the Altai proclaimed its autonomy. It was an anti-Communist group and was promptly squashed when the Red Army arrived in force in 1919. In 1920 Party and Komsomol organizations were established in the Altai, but the province was not fully taken over until 1922.

The official Soviet "history" of Siberia gives an illuminating view of the confusions of this time, despite the allowances which must be made for Marxist-Leninist heroic prose:

"Defeated but not completely broken-up *kulak* elements of the Altai and Zaisanyen native tribes, chieftains and their agents, Social Revolutionaries, Mensheviks, counter-revolutionary nationalists, and White Guardist officers hiding in the area[3] began to organize formations in the Altai Mountains. The organization of White bands took place under the instructions of Kolchak émigrés in Mongolia: namely, Baron Ungern and White Guard General Bakich, paid servants of the interventionists. These men were in contact with counter-revolutionary elements lying low in the Altai. As a result, a White Guardist officer called Kaigorodov, equipped by the interventionists, crossed the Soviet border from Mongolia. In the spring of 1922 regular Red Army units and squadrons of troops of special designation finally crushed the White bandit movement in the Altai."

For themselves, the people of the Altai were not massively interested either in furthering the progress of the Revolution or in halting it. There were few intellectuals in southwestern Siberia at that time, no universities, no nuclei of discontented workers, mutinous soldiers, or plotting bureaucrats. The inequities of class and station or the deep-seated problems of the Russian economy did not cause much specific concern in an area which was best compared to the homesteading sections of Wyoming and Colorado in the closing days of last century. For, if almost everybody had it hard in the Altai, at the same time everybody had

---

[3] One wonders whether the Soviet historians presumed these varied opponents to have sought shelter in the same location.

some kind of a future open to him. The land was available to any man who could till it. It was a frontier society.

Exactly what Deriabin's family did during the five years of revolution and civil war he has never found out. One of his uncles may have been killed in either the war or its aftermath, but when and for which side he was fighting has never been said. It is a tribute to the relentless probings of official Soviet questionnaires about "revolutionary backgrounds" and the desperate wish of the people to conceal any potentially "derogatory" information about their pasts that millions of Soviet citizens have grown up similarly unenlightened as to how their parents stood in the Revolution.

He did gather that his parents, along with most of their friends and relatives in the district, were neutral through most of the civil war. Despite the later shouting of Soviet propagandists, the Revolution was the outcome of a struggle between several very small groups, with the great majority of the country looking on as helpless, leaderless outsiders. When the fighting broke out between the Reds and various groups of Whites (there were also some dissident bands of militant noncomformists—anarchists, non-partisan idealists, or bandits—who called themselves the "Greens"), the prudent citizen pledged his allegiance to whatever group happened to be holding his town at the moment. If he were really prudent he avoided making any commitments. For four years the antagonists marched and counter-marched across Siberia with bewildering changes of position. A village that was White today could easily be Red tomorrow and vice versa.

Sergey Deriabin was an exceptionally prudent man in this respect, and his caution may have saved himself and his family. Since he had been a veteran noncom in the Czar's army, both sides were anxious to recruit him, at least as an instructor. He put them off with excuses for a time. Then, as the civil war grew more intense, he fled with his family to Lokot, a straggling collection of homesteads along the upper reaches of the Chumysh River, eighty miles from the nearest railroad connection at Biysk. Sergey built his family a one-room log hut and began the work of digging out a living from the hills alongside the river. There were no Reds or Whites in evidence officially, although groups of alleged "partisans," little more than common bandits, penetrated all sections of the country. They came several times to Lokot. On one occasion Sergey Deriabin was saved from either sure death or "conscription" by hiding for hours in the loft. His wife, displaying a frontier presence of mind, had previously burnt the only ladder which led to the loft. When the "partisans" could not find it they were content to go away, not having expected much, anyway.

Three years after Peter was born his family moved to the larger settlement of Ovsyanikovo, which had the advantage of a village school. The rhythm of life went on much the same as at Lokot. Sergey Deriabin farmed during the summer, and did carpentry work and odd jobs through the winter, sometimes at home, sometimes as far away as Biysk. At one point the Deriabins were, by Siberian standards, rather prosperous. They farmed thirty acres and kept two horses, two cows, fifteen sheep, and some geese and chickens. Their new house, which Deriabin also built himself, had two rooms and a painted floor of split logs and was made entirely of new lumber—something of a monument for Ovsyanikovo. He built in addition several barns and a Russian steam bath. Neighbors were impressed, also, by his possession of a *bayan*, an accordionlike instrument, and a hairy-voiced phonograph, brought up from Biysk, the only such instrument in the vicinty.

Social life was sparse but hearty, often enlivened by the local rivalry between the Russian and the Ukrainian settlers. The prime social, and in a way athletic, event of the week, especially during the long winters, was the Saturday night *sauna*, or Finnish-style steam bath. The Deriabin family and their friends would gather in the bathhouse behind their hut and work themselves over in the steaming interior, beating their bodies with birch twigs and drinking bucketsful of *kvas*, a yeasty beverage that serves as the Russian national soft drink.[4] When they had steamed

---

[4] Many years later, as Peter Deriabin advanced up the rungs of the Soviet social ladder, he found this humble routine considerably improved on. High-ranking Soviet officials preferred a drink of cognac with *kvas* chasers, which sometimes resulted in impressive bathing parties. Mayakovsky, the poet laureate of the early Soviet days, had a little quatrain:

themselves sufficiently they would rush out and throw themselves in the snow for a minute or two as a restorative. Those who survived were very healthy—temperatures of 10° below zero are usual in this region.

But such luxuries were purely relative. The Deriabins rarely pushed themselves far above a level of bare subsistence. Sugar and tea were hard to come by, and the tea was generally made with a mixture of herbs which Stepanida Deriabin picked herself in the forest. Hand-me-downs and homemade materials were the rule. Peter did not possess his own pair of shoes until he was thirteen. Doctors were almost unknown. It makes its own commentary on life in the Altai of those years to note that out of eleven children born to the Deriabins only three survived their childhood.

In this region of sudden hot summers and furiously cold winters, unexpected hardship was a condition of life. Boys of ten and eleven would have to travel five miles to school on homemade skis at the peak of the snow season. Once Peter lost his skis returning home in the middle of a blizzard. Unable to go on without them, he spent the night and half the next day shivering in a haystack, the only available shelter. When the snow stopped he fell out, half frozen, and stumbled home. His mother quickly rubbed snow and alcohol on the frostbitten parts of his body—an old Siberian remedy—and in a week he had recovered.

On another occasion he and his father were followed by a huge pack of wolves as they drove home from town in a horse-drawn sleigh. His father kept the wolves off by lighting bundles of straw and throwing them behind the sleigh, since the wolves feared both light and flame. But they had a narrow escape. The horse was so spent from the desperate flight that it died in the stable the next day.

It was Peter Deriabin's good fortune, nonetheless, to live the first ten years of his life in Lokot and Ovsyanikovo more or less the way other European farm children were living at the same time, in similar circumstances, free from the spread of constant state control and inspection. Not only was southwestern Siberia remote from Moscow's im-

"The (proletarian) *Klass*
Quenches thirst with *kvas*
Nor will it shrink
From stronger drink."

mediate attention, but the New Economic Policy, which Lenin formally announced in March 1921, had stopped the heedless nationalization of the country's resources. The NEP, briefly stated, was Soviet recognition that the economy was too badly battered for any ambitious transfers of methods or control. Private enterprise was allowed to flourish in the wreckage of the war nationalization, and it did for almost ten years. To the farmers of the Altai this meant carrying on as usual with their individual lives, hardly dreaming of the forced collectivizations, the famines, and the mass liquidation of the *kulaks* which were to come with the early thirties.

Peter, in fact, was the first in his family to be touched by the new world which the Soviet Party bosses in Moscow were then preparing. In 1928 he went to school, the result of his father's decision to give at least one of his sons an education. The school was a simple one-room proposition with only one teacher regularly assigned, but it was the channel through which Communists could work most directly on the Russian people. As Moscow tightened its grip on the provinces a parade of Party bosses, Komsomol bosses, and other varieties of youth experts came to visit throughout the school year, giving their very explicit lessons. At the close of the first year that Peter spent in school he was taken into the national Communist organization for the very young, called the October Cubs. A year after, he joined the Pioneers, the feeder youth organization for the Komsomol.

School and Communism came into Deriabin's life together and increased their influence all the more proportionately. On the one hand, there was praise for good work such as he had never received at home and a field of intellectual stimulation he had never suspected. Deriabin liked school and did well with his lessons; mercifully his family put no pressure on him to leave and come back to work the farm—although this was the fate of his older brother. The school readers and geography books produced for him a world he had never thought existed. Wonder and imagination did the rest, helped by one or two good teachers. When he transferred to a larger school in the same town of Ovsyanikovo, he skipped a class.

At the same time, all the praise for the good schoolwork

and the students' enthusiasm were funneled into the service of the Party. This indoctrination had its own changes in emphasis. Deriabin's very first schoolbook began with a noble-looking portrait of Lenin ("our grandfather Ilyich") followed by one of Aleksey Rykov, then Premier of the Soviet Union ("Here is our dear friend, Aleksey Ivanovich Rykov"). Later editions began with a picture of Lenin and Stalin together; then Stalin held the field by himself. Rykov was eliminated from the students' view by 1931, a victim of Stalin's power politics. Seven years later he was eliminated from everyone's view in the executions after the Moscow purge trials, by which time most of the students who had studied their "dear friends'" picture in earlier years were accomplished enough in the ways of Soviet life to vie with each other in coining new vituperative phrases to call Rykov and the other "traitors."

If hindsight could reconstruct the erratic fates of the régime leadership by looking at successive school textbooks, such inconsistencies made no impression on the students themselves. The indoctrination had the weight of new learning behind it, and it took. The first buds of idealism were equally directed into Communism's service. Children glamorized the high-minded talks of their "intelligent and educated" teacher, which contrasted happily with the bread-and butter ruminations of their "illiterate" parents. At an age when the concept of the group first becomes really attractive to the child, Communist instruction pounded home the futility of individual action or individual development. Everything was to be done or thought shoulder to shoulder with the brave workers, collective farmers, Komsomol members, Young Pioneers, or whatever group happened to be pertinent to the occasion.

Deriabin was nine when he ran home with the new red neckerchief that signalized his membership in the Young Pioneers. The movement's organizers had thoughtfully invested the neckerchief with a bit of ritual. It was not to be touched by anyone except the wearer. If anyone did so, the Pioneer leader instructed, the child wearing it was to answer solemnly: "Don't touch proletarian blood; enough of it has been spilled already." When his father asked Peter about his tie and touched it, the son returned the ritual answer. The father laughed. "Ha, look at him," he said.

"He has put on a dog's leash and now is showing off in front of his parents." His father's words had little effect on Peter, who understood their real meaning as cloudily as he understood the formula he had repeated. Since he was not ordered to take it off he continued to wear the neckerchief, which was bright and cheerful.

For the next six years Peter ran with the pack in the Pioneers. Always first in his class in studies, he developed a barely conscious feeling that this position gave him an obligation to work even harder than most at the "political" duties given the Young Pioneers. This feeling was fostered by some of his teachers and the Pioneer leaders and organizers. He received rewards and encouragement for the work he did, even when it was out of context. A good deed for the Pioneers, e.g. informing the teacher about children who still said their prayers, could help a boy's school record as surely as good marks in school. The marks and deeds added up to a prominent position in the "political" group. So early in the game did Deriabin get a feel for the interlockings of Party job and professional job which were to determine the course of his life.

The immediate objectives of the Pioneers reflected the step-by-step Sovietization of Russia. In the late twenties they concentrated on the anti-religious campaign. Although the hierarchy of the Russian Orthodox Church had been killed, imprisoned, or driven into exile, a great many priests remained on the land, carrying on divine worship as they had before. As late as 1923 the villagers of Lokot sank all their available talents and money into the job of rebuilding the church, which had been destroyed by fire. But as the power of the régime consolidated itself the word went out to liquidate all remnants of belief within the country as a holdover from Czarist days. "There is no God," the children learned to sloganize, "and there is no need for a Czar."

The immediate job of the Young Pioneers was to visit each other's homes and report on which families still kept religious images, said prayers, or otherwise behaved in a suspicious manner. Like thousands of other Russian children, Deriabin was told by his teachers that the parents of the village were in error and grossly misled. The Bible was nonsense written by the *popy*—Russian slang for priests—and everything in life could be explained by science. Nei-

ther then nor later in his Soviet existence did Deriabin ever
actually read the Bible. If he had, he once observed, he
would probably not have understood it. But he found a
great deal of childish pleasure in innocently performing his
reportorial duties.

The godless campaign was only a tactic in the basic
strategy of the Soviet school: to detach the children from
the influence of their parents and re-create them as wards
of the state. The Pioneer organizers worked hard to culti-
vate in the children a feeling of scorn for their parents'
beliefs as relics of an outmoded era. They dwelt on the
parents' lack of education, contrasting the rising cultural
level of the children themselves. It was the duty of the
Communist child to re-educate his parents so that they
might assist, in their limited way, in the building of the
shining new Communist society.

The result was a painful period of intra-family war and
bitterness, which has been perpetuated to this day in the
Soviet Union, although its fierceness has markedly lessened. Whether a family disintegrated or stayed together
through this ideological pounding was a matter of personality. Peter and his brother, Vladimir, never lost their respect
for their father, who was strong-willed but kind, with a
rather shrewd perception of the breadth and permanency
of the changes in their world. Sergey Deriabin, however,
kept most of his thoughts to himself, aside from occasional
outbursts of feeling, and it was their mother who bore the
brunt of the children's atheist catechizing. With the exas-
perating persistence of the smart small boy Peter ham-
mered away at his mother for believing in God because the
village "popes" said so, instead of recognizing the truth of
the official Pioneer arguments for His absence.

Shortly after his birth, Peter Deriabin had been baptized.
His mother, worried about the boy's faith as he grew older,
tried counter-propaganda of her own—a step which would
have been dangerous, had her children been serious informers. She took Peter to see a neighbor who had been a
novice nun before the convents were closed by Soviet order.
The nun talked quietly to him, read him simple stories
from the Bible, and told him about the gospel miracles.
But it was no use. The boy only kept repeating the rote
anti-religious answers he had learned at school proving that

it was scientifically impossible for Christ to have fed a multitude with one loaf of bread or to have walked over the water barefooted.

In 1930, Aleksandr Bogatyrev, a clever and intelligent member of the Komsomol and the principal of Deriabin's school, climbed up the belfry of the church at Ovsyanikovo and tossed the bells to the ground to the accompaniment of wild cheers from his students. The priest had already been arrested and deported. The villagers, particularly the women, stood around the smashed bells in horror, alternately cursing Bogatyrev and praying. Women tore their hair and shouted that the end of the world had come. Feeling ran so strongly against the principal thereafter that he was forced to ask for a transfer. But the deed was done. The children made a holiday of the occasion. They ran around the churchyard, clapping their hands and gibing at the weeping women. They had been promised the use of the church as a clubhouse where they could dance and watch films when they grew older.

The personal climax of the anti-religious campaign occured shortly afterwards, in Deriabin's house. When he came home from school one evening Peter found his father sitting at the table drunk, with the family icons smashed in pieces around him. His mother said Sergey had gone mad, smashed all the holy icons, and stamped on them. His father's explanation, however, was far from irrational. "Remember, my son," he told Peter, "it is better to do it this way. It is better to remove the icons and destroy them than to commit sacrilege daily by profaning holy things. I was told at the village meeting what you have been told in your school: that they will be coming to all the houses for a check and those found in possession of icons will be listed as followers of the Faith and the Czar."

Next day Peter noticed a typical family compromise. Those icons not completely destroyed were set up again by his mother, but in the kitchen instead of the living room, in a corner where she did most of her work.

With the church gone and the authority of the family shaken if not, in some homes, completely discredited, life for the children of Ovsyanikovo centered completely and irrevocably on the Pioneer group. A sort of "Socialist morality," as the later generation was taught to call it, was implanted among them by their teachers, the result of Moscow's increasing worry over the vast moral breakdown that had followed the Revolution. Both kissing and handshaking were denounced as insanitary customs of the old régime, not only conducive to spreading diseases but among the last disgraceful heritages of the old landlord and capitalist class.

In this, as in other matters, the war on the parents continued. Fathers called their sons hoodlums, delinquents, or worse. If a child got a beating for disobedience at home he would report his parents to the Komsomol or Pioneer leaders and go back to the attack with their renewed moral support. What positive works the youth groups accomplished—collecting scrap metal and salvage material, teaching illiterate relatives to read, etc.—was largely canceled out by the disruption they brought to their homes.

On a more cosmic level Deriabin and his fellow neckerchief-wearers were introduced to the international Communist slogans of the day. They demanded the surrender of Warsaw or Berlin (as occasion demanded) to Communism and learned to sing formidable little tunes like "We shall join the vanguard of the World Revolution, to the discomfort of all bourgeois."

In January 1928, before Peter Deriabin and his friends in Siberia had learned how to be properly godless, the General Secretary of the Communist Party in Moscow, Josef Stalin, was preparing a more ambitious target for their efforts than foreign anti-Communists or the dwindling number of Orthodox priests. The campaign of forced collectivization was ordered throughout the Soviet Union.

The reasons later given for the collectivization drive were two: the growing insufficiency of food supply for the cities and the need for rapid industrialization. Actually it was done from far more basic motives. Moscow realized that the growing success of the free enterprise allowed under the NEP threatened to bring down the status of Communism to that of an ideology not to be taken seriously. To the men at the head of the Soviet Union this was tantamount to self-destruction. The industrialization to be achieved through this upheaval was planned to provide a more powerful base for the spread of Communism in the world. The Communist rulers, furthermore, steeped in the

Marxist "working-class" theory of Revolution, distrusted and despised the Russian farmer both as a class and individually and saw him as the enemy of their state. Collectivization appeared to offer a solution by turning the independent farmer into an agricultural "worker." He would then, it was hoped, develop a true "working-class" psychology and a necessary loyalty to the régime, because he would be so dependent on it.

In addition, the whole Soviet structure, reeling from political feuds and the grossest economic mismanagement, needed a scapegoat. Scapegoats are the eternal ugly premise of any dictator's power. The Soviet dictators found one in the *kulak*.

Kulak is the Russian word for fist. Originally it was applied to a farmer who was hard-headed, hard-working, and thrifty, although not necessarily stingy. It was a term of simple description, not one of disgust. No one minded being called a *kulak* in Biysk, Ovsyanikovo, or anywhere else where Russian was spoken. The Soviet leadership took this old slang word and made it the blackest term of opprobrium in the official Russian vocabulary. Officially *kulak* was defined as a farmer who owned means of production to the value of 1600 rubles or hired labor for more than fifty days in the year, or the equivalent. As such, the *kulaks* represented perhaps four percent of the entire peasant population. In practice, the term was stretched to mean any reasonably prosperous farmer who could stand on his own feet. Its only interpreters were the local Party boss or propagandists, and from their definitions there was no appeal.

In 1929 the liquidation of the *kulaks* was begun. Along with this went the forced collectivization of the entire Russian peasantry. For the ostensible reason of using the land more efficiently by large-plot farming, Stalin planned to secure a big supply of labor for the new industries and an absolute control of the countryside, the last sizable element in Russian life to avoid Soviet colonization. He gained his real objectives, if not his announced ones (the collectives have rarely been an efficient instrument of farm production), at the cost of more than ten million lives, several diastrous famines, and the worst reign of terror ever visited on a civilized people.

Collectivization marched into Ovsyanikovo in 1930. A delegation of Party members announced that all the families of the settlement would work on the three collective farms which had been set up in the neighborhood. Specific assignments were given, and the Party delegation departed after a tirade against *kulaks* and similar "enemies of the state." There were as yet no Party members in Ovsyanikovo itself. The youth organizations, however, down to the youngest Pioneer, were mobilized for the most intensive kind of local progaganda campaign to join the collectives—known by the soon-to-be-notorious name of *kolkhoz*—and to liquidate the *kulaks*.

"*Kulaks*—parasites, exploiters, bloodsuckers . . ." This was the standard nomenclature for the peasants who refused to join the collectives. The children screamed these names with childish cruelty at their playmates who belonged to the *kulak* families. "That will be enough of your rich life," they yelled threateningly at the others. "We will take everything away from you and live richly ourselves." The children of the reasonably well-to-do farmers were refused admission to the Pioneers and jeered at as "*kulak* progeny." Peter Deriabin joined the mandatory clamor, although it was some years before he understood what *kulak* really meant.

It was hard even for grownups to figure out any reasonable standard for judging who was a *kulak*. There had never been any "classes" at all in their frontier communities, and the gradations of "wealth" were highly relative. It was therefore puzzling to find they had been harboring "class enemies" in their midst. The selection of *kulaks* was even more puzzling. It was at least understandable when Pavel Ivanov, who hired laborers, was carted off at a few minutes' notice for "resettlement," or the Krechetovs, because they had more land than anyone else, or Grigoriy Ivanov, because he had a two-story house. Sergey Deriabin himself only escaped because he had sold off most of his original thirty acres to do more carpentry work. But Nikolay Reutov, a friend of Sergey's and one of the poorest men in the settlement, was taken only because he had refused to join a collective.

The agitation against the *kulaks* long continued. Two years after the Reutovs were taken away Peter became quite friendly with their daughter, Anastasia, a schoolmate of his who had remained in Ovsyanikovo after her parents. He helped her with her lessons, walked her home from school, and on occasion exchanged a childish kiss. When this became known in the village he was teasingly called a *kulak* sympathizer. The teasing got ugly. Although he remained the first student in his class—in Soviet schools virtually a hierarchical post—he was constantly reproved at Pioneer meetings for his friendliness with the daughter of a known *kulak*. He was stubborn enough to continue the friendship. In time the furor passed over without imparing his simon-pure Pioneer standing.

In the famine year of 1932–33 (the direct result of the collectivization drive) the Pioneer organization rewarded Peter by sending him to the Pioneer summer camp, where he had a chance to recuperate and rest and where food was for once plentiful. He came back from camp for the first time an eager propagandist for the movement, telling all the other children about the good things open to good Pioneers. It was his first taste of the material rewards given to faithful members of the Soviet "New Class."

Before the three new collectives had their full complement four of the twenty families in Deriabin's district of Ovsyanikovo had been taken away. Two had fled of their own accord to even more isolated parts of Siberia. The Deriabins had done fairly well. Peter's brother, Vladimir, had already joined the Komsomol. He had the reputation of an activist. In 1935 their father was elected chairman of the nearest *kolkhoz*, the *Krasnoye Znamya*, because of his superior education and his reputation as a good manager. He was not a Party member but was considered to be a sympathizer. With the authority of his new post he became a strenuous propagandist for the virtues of the *kolkhoz* economy.

CHAPTER II

Poets And The Komsomol

WHEN PETER DERIABIN was fifteen he asked to join the Komsomol. His six years of Pioneering had made nothing seem more attractive than the Komsomol membership card reserved for the teen-age Soviet product. In March 1936 his formal application was accepted. He exchanged his red Pioneer tie for the badge lettered KIM (for *Kommunisticheskiy Internatsional Molodezhi*, the Communist International of Youth) and the card with the picture of Lenin on its face.

His motives for joining typified the political puppy love which Lenin and his successors proved so expert at stimulating. "At that time," he wrote later, "no one could have argued me out of joining the Komsomol. My only goal was to join the ranks of those fighting to build Communism in the world. I accepted completely the idea of the class struggle and the creation of the classless society. I was thirsty for knowledge, and I had always tried to be at the top. So I worked hard to be in the front ranks of Communism. I had faith in the bright future, for its signs seemed to be dawning everywhere. The year before, for instance, our village saw its first tractor (an American Fordson, incidentally). When a mobile film team came to show silent pictures of the tractor's use in Soviet agriculture my Komsomol friends and I were tremendously happy. In truth, we said, the light was triumphing over darkness.

"All of this created a feeling of heroic emotion. If there were still snags in the way of our accomplishment they

35

were considered to be only temporary. We felt so strongly that everything was going well and getting better."

The high tide of necessity carried Deriabin, for a time, almost as far as his own enthusiasm had promised. He was graduated from the high school[1] at Ovsyanikovo in 1937 with the highest possible honors. Less than a year later he received a teacher's certificate, after finishing a short correspondence course in pedagogy, and he began to teach classes in history and civics at the Savinovo high school, some 100 miles from Ovsyanikovo, on the other side of Biysk. Good teachers, or any teaching material whatsoever, were scarce all over the Soviet Union, and there was much opportunity for quick advancement. To get the certificate he had had to advance his age two years on the application form, a white lie which was condoned by his Komsomol bosses. Since there were no birth records to check back at Lokot, he ran no danger of exposure in later security checks. He was thus a high school history teacher in good standing at the age of seventeen.

While continuing with his teaching Deriabin took further courses at the Teacher's Institute. Ordinarily his youth and his continuing student status would have made him the lowest-ranking instructor in the school. But this was to overlook his faithful service in the Komsomol. At his own school he had been the Komsomol secretary. He was

---

[1] The average Soviet child enters elementary school at the age of seven and has four years there. At eleven he goes on to high school (Middle High School) and does six more years. At the age of seventeen, if he is bright enough, he can go on to higher education. This is most often provided by the institutes, which offer college-level courses of two, four, or five years, depending on the subject and the person's ability. After two years in a pedagogic institute, for instance, the student is qualified to teach high school, but a higher course may be given. The point to be remembered is that the institute gives "professional" training and, as such, takes the place of the university as understood in the U.S. Universities in the Soviet Union, like those in Europe, concentrate on academic education for those wanting to do research or teach in universities. Their courses last four, five, or six years. A doctor, for example, can qualify through study at a medical institute, but to do advanced medical research he would need to attend a university.

elected secretary of the Komsomol at the Savinovo school almost immediately after he went on the teaching rolls, since that post was open there. Shortly afterward he took over the secretaryship of the *Profsoyuz*, (for *Professionalnyi Soyuzi*), as the Association of Trade Unions was generally abbreviated.

Deriabin was politically "sound" in an area where Party fidelity was still at something of a premium, and as such he could do little wrong. Having glimpsed in his Pioneer days a few rewards of the Communist faithful, he now learned by example what it meant to be a working Communist, or at least an apprentice Communist, in any quarter of Soviet life. At school meetings a good *Komsomolets* could criticize with impunity the conduct and performance of teachers far older and more experienced. They were hesitant about doing the converse. A good *Komsomolets* also could easily arrange for himself a transfer to the school at Forminskoye, where there was a bigger school, with bigger and better opportunities. Deriabin did so.

For he supplemented teaching and his own teacher's courses by a backbreaking burden of extra work. In his late teens Deriabin was a Siberian equivalent to that energy phenomenon in capitalist society, the go-getter president of the Junior Chamber of Commerce who always finds time, somehow, to pump a hand, make a speech, or launch a civic improvement drive. Besides running his school Komsomol unit, he presided over Komsomol activity in the town of Biysk. In addition, he enjoyed the multi-initialed fellowship of the district branch of the "Down with Illiteracy" Association (the ODN), the League of the Militant Godless (the SVB), and the International Society for Helping the Fighters of the Revolution (the MOPR).

Deriabin was too young to vote in the first "general election" of 1937. He was already, however, a local expert on the 1936 Stalin constitution. He saturated his home town with lectures and informal talks contrasting the "real freedoms" of the new constitution with the tyranny disguised by the "so-called constitutions" of capitalist countries. He held forth at the local Komsomol club and at the neighboring *kolkhozes* and organized a special Komsomol group for teaching reading and writing to young men about to be inducted into the Soviet Army. He was also active in the local dramatic circle, acting and directing whenever he had the chance.

All his work outside the school only added to his reputation as one of the best teachers in the district. As an immediate reward he was given a trip to Moscow, his first, in August 1939, to see the Agricultural Fair. As a more lasting expression of confidence he had been entrusted with the job of teaching Party history and the constitution of the U.S.S.R. to third-year students in the high school at Fominskoye. Here again he owed rapid promotion to a combination of his own talents and a desperate shortage of qualified, trusted people, able to fill this especially sensitive post.

Soviet students then as now begin studying the history of the Communist Party in the third grade. They continue up through high school to the institute or university, covering increasingly complex fugal variations of the same theme. Even at its most advanced, Party history is largely à rote exercise: constant repetitions of set questions and answers. The few discussions that occur are aimed not at criticism but respectful elaboration. Deriabin learned his lessons virtually by heart from Stalin's *Short History of the Communist Party* (*Bolsheviks*), the little book which the leader had dashed off for his captive audience in 1938. After six months of teaching he could recite every article in the Soviet constitution from memory. The more standard the recitations, the better mark a student received.

As he became more experienced in teaching the subject Deriabin grew to rely solely on set question-and-answer formulae. It was safer, he discovered. Individual interpretations might easily cause trouble for a teacher or a student, or both. But no Party committee could complain of a teacher who taught Marxism-Leninism straight out of the book. After a time his lessons became so mechanical that he could turn his thoughts elsewhere while he was in the act of droning out the familiar passages, like a tired fundamentalist preacher who has long since memorized his Bible.

It would be a mistake to say that this sort of dull, safety-first routine caused any question in Deriabin's mind about the basic truths of the Soviet system. It was merely a tactical device and not enough to stop the enthusiasm of the hardest-working Komsomol secretary in the district. But his strict Communist education did have its moments of ventilation. The same teacher shortage by which he profited had forced the Soviet Ministry of Education to sanction employment of other teachers highly unreliable by Soviet standards. The principal of the high school at Ovsyanikovo was the nephew of a former high official in the Czarist Ministry of Education, a fact which would have automatically disqualified him from any teaching job a few years later. The science teacher was a former Czarist infantry officer, the German teacher was the daughter of a condemned *kulak*, another instructor the daughter of a priest.

Many such people had come deliberately to the remoteness of the Altai Kray, hoping to put off, if not escape, the inevitable purges that were already fissioning the urban centers of the Soviet Union. Some were exiled there. They brought with them a way of thinking that was not Communist, that retained the standards of the Europe against which the Soviet government declared war. Deriabin learned much from these teachers, both as a high school student and as their later associate. Their presence, in fact, gave some of the remote Siberian schools an educational standard far higher than that of the purged schools in the large cities of European Russia. Some of them were able to bring their libraries. Through his teens the gray enthusiasm of the Komsomol was enlivened for Deriabin by the same classics which teen-agers everywhere were reading at the same time: Mark Twain, Jules Verne, Fenimore Cooper, and Kipling. He was in the habit of borrowing a new book every few days from the house of his ex-officer chemistry teacher and reading it, in Russian Abe Lincoln style, by the light of an improvised oil lamp in the family hut (his father complained violently about the smell) or by winter moonlight when a weird but functional substitute was produced by the moon's reflections on the expanse of Siberian snow.

He had the further advantage of that period of relatively free thought in the Soviet Union which had lasted for more than a decade after the October Revolution. Those were the days of Aleksandr Blok, author of *The Twelve*, the epic poet who tried to combine the new Russia with the old; of Vladimir Mayakovsky and Sergey Esenin, the two spoiled romantic geniuses who used the Revolution, briefly, as a Byronic backdrop for their poetry; of Izaak Babel, the gifted novelist and short-story writer; of Ivan Bunin, the émigré of 1919 and later Nobel Prize winner for literature—not to mention a young poet and critic just returned from studies in Germany named Boris Pasternak.

There was at first no Soviet Union of Writers to discipline these original minds and turn Russian literature into a pablum. Even in the thirties, when the Party lines on art and literature grew tight, it was still possible to discuss their work. So students and faculty alike in the school at Ovsyanikovo could read and criticize one of the most brilliant flowerings of a national literature on record.

Esenin was Deriabin's favorite. He found a book of his poems when he was fourteen and spread them among his classmates. By no stretch of the imagination could Esenin be called a Communist poet. He was born in a peasant village in central Russia, and all his work was the expression of a longing for a pastoral village society. He looked with a messianic eye toward a new primitive Russia, intensely religious and communal, without machines. The Revolution he hailed as the beginning of his own private dream, but he was the first to feel the stringencies of the Soviet censor, who did not take kindly to the goal of a strengthened village society.

Frustrated, he sought solace in drugs, strong drink, and strong women. He consorted with several of the last, including his sometime wife, the dancer Isadora Duncan, in a whirlwind of foreign travel before he returned to his village in despair in 1924. He was driven to suicide, after he saw what the beginnings of Communism had done there to his pastoral dream. On December 27, 1925, he strangled himself in the Hotel Angleterre in Leningrad. He wrote his last poem in his own blood, in the finest romantic tradition:

> ". . . in this life there's nothing new in dying,
> And, in truth, to live is nothing new."

Hundreds of despairing young men throughout the Soviet Union followed his example.

The story of Esenin's protest took a while to get to Si-

beria, but ten years after it happened it was still strong stuff
for a rising young Komsomol leader. Deriabin had appreciated Esenin "uncritically" as his favorite poet through his
schooldays. Now becoming, through his Komsomol work,
more and more identified with the régime's views, Deriabin felt the need of some clarification on why and where
his poet had gone wrong. He raised the question of Esenin's
fitness at several district meetings. He was able, thereafter,
to give his students, if any asked, the Party explanation
that Esenin was the "*kulak*'s poet," interesting only as the
last spoken gasp of the "dying peasant landlord class."
After listening to one particularly convincing Komsomol
lecture on poets and poetry Deriabin went back to the lodgings he shared with a teacher friend and threw their only
volume of Esenin into the fire. His friend managed to res-
cue it and carried it with him until he was killed in 1941,
serving with Deriabin as a platoon commander on the Moscow front.

By the middle of the thirties the literary flowering had
been weeded out. Blok died of starvation at Petrograd in
1921, Babel perished in the purges. Pasternak's poems
were no long read in Soviet schools after 1935. He survived
only as an occasional poet and translator of foreign classics
until he wrote *Dr. Zhivago* after World War II.

Mayakovsky, the six-foot-four exhibitionist of Moscow
literary circles who fancied yellow vests, daubs of paint on
his forehead, and raw carrots in his buttonhole, had tried
energetically to keep his poetry in step with the Party. "I
want the pen," he cried, "to be equal to the bayonet," and
thousands cheered him all over the Soviet Union. When
Esenin committed suicide Comrade Mayakovsky capped
his dying poem with a reproachful parody:

> ". . . in this life it is not hard to die,
>   To mold life is far more difficult."

But the new age had no patience with Mayakovsky's
own nonconformities, even when he insisted that they were
honest Communist nonconformities.[2] With his usual erratic

---

[2] One can hardly blame the emergent generation of Communist critics for losing patience with these early Russian

forthrightness, he screamed his defiance in some blistering, satirical poems, then surrendered. On April 14, 1930, he shot himself.

Peter Deriabin's Party idealism was only slightly blunted by his contact with such forbidden literature or unpleasant facts. Once, on his way to a meeting in his local settlement of Grishika, he fell in with a wandering shoemaker who had recently appeared in Ovsyanikovo. The man was very intelligent, and the mysterious manner of his appearance suggested that he was an exile or fugitive from European Russia. The shoemaker asked Deriabin what he thought of the current trials just ended in Moscow. It was 1938. Former Premier Rykov ("our dear Aleksey"), Nikolay Bukharin, Soviet Communism's greatest theoretician, and other officials had been sentenced to death for treason after a series of rigged trials. "I guess the Party was right in doing it," Deriabin said. "Bukharin, Kamenev, Rykov—they were all good men," said the other. "If they were all good men," Deriabin interrupted him, "Stalin would not have had to execute them." "You are young," the shoemaker answered, "and you don't know."

Throughout the rest of the purge period Deriabin kept his nose clean and as close as possible to the grindstone. He had enough of a sense of humor to twit the higher Komsomol or even Party bosses occasionally. He led the laughter after the Fominskoye town celebration of the October Revolution one year—at the height of Stalin's intra-party purges—when a grim-faced lady Party boss lectured the populace about behaving properly on the anniversary. "Never forget," she concluded in a fast monotone, "keeping-away-from-vodka-and-above-all-no-more-fighting-among-yourselves-long-live-Stalin." Because of his wit and gregariousness he had the added confidence and respect of most of the townspeople, who naturally looked up to him as a man of education. Many who were not his students came to him for advice—mindful also of his good official connections. Yet he kept a firm, safe grip on the Party line as

---

"beatniks." It was clearly difficult for official Moscow to take kindly, for example, to the antics of a poet like Igor Severyanin, who, on occasion, broke boards over his head in the course of recitation.

it was passed down to him. He never courted any kind of "deviation" in his work.

In 1939 Deriabin was given the supreme honor of a *Komsomolets*, an invitation to serve on the district committee. He declined, saying quite truthfully that added political work would interfere fatally with his studies at the Teacher's Institute. The Komsomol authorities were in the act of disregarding his nonacceptance when the matter was made academic by his conscription into the Soviet Army.

Shortly before he left the depot at Biysk for military training a few teacher friends gave him a two-volume set of Esenin's poetry. It was a bootlegged edition printed in Latvia, since publishing Esenin was by now proscribed throughout the Soviet Union. The orthodox Communist postulant accepted them with great pleasure and put them in his knapsack. By the time the war was over he had memorized everything in them.

CHAPTER III

Idiots In The Infantry

EVERYWHERE IN THE world, World War II acted as a catalyst on the lives of those who served in it, setting some in a totally new direction, confirming old resolutions, solving (or creating) unexpected problems. In the Soviet Union it was an irresistible whirlwind. Almost every citizen was swept up in its draughts. Nowhere was there a slighter distinction between civilian and military combatants.

A man's decision in wartime, as everywhere, was the matter of a sudden reflex to which he added what thoughts he was able to summon. In most countries the decisions were revocable, in the light of later events. In the Soviet Union one man's lightning battlefield decision could spell survival or ruin for whole families. To fight on, to accept capture, to desert, to run to the rear, all these choices of the battlefield occurred in what Russians call *Otechestvennaye Voyna*, The War for the Fatherland. They were made the more extreme by the totality of the Soviet war effort against the Germans. They were made irrevocable by the fact that each success or misstep was discovered and noted in triplicate by the judges of the State Security, who occupied the battlefields with their record books long after the participants had left them.

The very fact that Deriabin entered the Red Army in October 1939 was evidence of the grimness of the international situation as Moscow saw it. He had been called up twice previously for examination, in 1938 and 1939, but he was discharged both times since village teachers were still exempt from the draft. In September 1939, as Soviet troop units were preparing to cross the Polish border, a new directive from Moscow canceled all exemptions for teachers and other categories of government white-collar workers. On October 10, accordingly, Deriabin journeyed from Biysk to the headquarters of the Trans-Baikal Military District at Chita, where he was issued his uniform and mustered into the 204th Infantry Regiment of the 93d Division. With only a perfunctory examination of his papers and "characteristics" he was sent to the regimental school for noncommissioned officers.

Deriabin's rise in the Soviet Army would have been inexplicable in any other. Barely three weeks after putting on the uniform he was editor of the regimental news bulletin (in the Red Army a sensitive official job). Within a month he was a trusted subordinate of the political commissar attached to the noncommissioned officers' school. His impeccable political background was the explanation. In the sudden mobilization of so many millions any trusted Communist Party or Komsomol member was judged literally worth his weight. As surely as the political arm maintained control of the Red Army, Deriabin's rise was preordained. In November 1939, after barely a month and a half in the Army, he was made deputy political commissar for the regimental noncommissioned officers' school.

With this appointment began the village schoolteacher's awareness of the privileges given the "ins" in Soviet society. In return for delivering lectures about the course of international events selectively culled from the columns of *Pravda, Izvestia*, and *Red Star* and for his supervision of the school's social and athletic diversions, Deriabin was released from the normal duties of a soldier. When the commissar moved to Moscow he was put in his place. Militarily untried, he was nonetheless politically reliable, as the Party organizers believed. He was also young and cocky. When the officer in charge of the school tried to put him under strict military authority, compelling him to do the tasks and exercises which his low rank warranted, he complained to the regimental political officer about this unwonted interference with the political arm. The school officer was reprimanded. It was a signal lesson in Soviet tactics which Deriabin never forgot.

By the next year Deriabin was the secretary of the regimental Komsomol bureau, which established him in the Party hierarchy and, as it were, codified his temporary position. When the regiment went out on maneuvers Deriabin, along with the school commander, achieved the dignity of a man on horseback. He had an officer's uniform and good boots—an important factor in the Red Army; he attended the officers' mess and received a tremendous pay raise from 12 rubles 75 kopecks a month to 198 rubles 75 kopecks.

In the Army, as at home, Deriabin had the reputation of a sociable fellow, generally popular, anxious to help people almost as a part of his sociability. When the school cadres went on maneuvers he used to let friends put knapsacks on his horse, alternately, to ease the discomforts of the long route marches. It does not seem like much of a gesture by American standards, but in the Red Army it was quite a thing.

The long months of 1940 were a time of desperate waiting for the Soviet General Staff on the Asiatic front. In the tense days before the German invasion it seemed almost certain that the Japanese would plan an attack whenever Hitler did. The Red Army had fought already with the Japanese in 1938 at Lake Khasan and in the summer of 1939, when a serious clash had developed at Nomonhan on the Manchurian-Mongolian border, requiring tanks, masses of infantry, and heavy air support. When the war with Germany began, Deriabin's division, along with others, had been spending months of weary watch on the borders of Manchuria and Mongolia. Soldiers slept in the trenches, for the word had been issued to staff headquarters that war with Germany would mean a simultaneous attack by the Japanese. (Moscow did not completely trust the non-aggression pact with Japan finally signed in April 1941.) The divison was entrenched in a desert barren both of people and vegetation and swept by continual strong winds. Since the Japanese war was destined to be a completely defensive action most of the activity involved building trenches, bunkers, and earthworks.

In this atmosphere one of Deriabin's principal duties as a Communist morale officer for the troops was to fight the discontent that grew with hard work and boredom. The soldiers were vocally disturbed about staying in this desert, fighting against an invisible enemy. One soldier in a neighboring unit was overheard by his political commissar talking to a group of his friends about the futility of their efforts. "Who needs this damned desert?" he said. "Nobody lives here and nobody could want to live here. If the Japanese want it, why not let them have it?" He was accused of spreading counter-revolutionary propaganda and shot. Deriabin thought the penalty was extreme, but he admitted that such examples made the task of a political officer considerably easier than it might have been.

During this time he proceeded most successfully with his military education. He was graduated from the noncommissioned officers' school after nine months of training. At various times the higher political officers in the division offered to send him to the Army political school, but he declined. He told them that he had decided to dedicate his life to teaching—an answer which by Communist standards was almost irrefutable. In fact, he declined because of his dislike for what he had seen of the Army's cruel discipline. He had also a village egghead's distaste for the "low cultural standards" of so many Army officers. The recommendations for transfer proceeded upward, however, despite his disavowals, accumulating in his file as evidence of efficiency and Party fidelity.

In October 1940 he was transferred to the divison's engineer battalion as secretary of the Komsomol committee. This was a variety of political commissar's post, since most of the soldiers were in the 18–25 age bracket considered suitable for Komsomol membership. Here again he had a few brushes with senior battalion officers, and his insistence on the rights of political officers—which was invariably backed up at division headquarters—won him the local nickname of "the Komsomol god." But he stayed on good terms with both officers and men, useful to both since he had more freedom than the average junior officer to go off base and get needed supplies of vodka and other painchasers in nearby towns. By this time he had gained complete officer status. He was regarded by strictly military standards as fit to command troops.

In May 1941, while already serving as Komsomol secretary and a Party "candidate" in his battalion, Peter Deriabin made formal application for full membership in the Communist Party. He went through the same forms as do Party candidates today, for the ritual has long since been crystallized. First he presented the regimental Party committee with recommendations from two Party members and his boss in the Komsomol. He then stood before the entire Party group in the unit, gave a brief biography of himself, and prepared to answer some questions, as a means of proving his qualifications.

It was on the eve of the German invasion of Russia, which began June 22, 1941. In view of what happened six weeks later, some of the questions used seem anachronistic.

"Was it necessary to sign an agreement of non-aggression with the Germans?" Answer: "Yes, to insure the safety of Soviet frontiers."

"What do you think of Japanese international politics?" Answer: "Typically aggressive and imperialist, but incapable of standing up against the Soviet Army, as we demonstrated at Changkufeng and Nomonhan."

There was one more such political query: "Why did the U.S.S.R. need territory from Finland?" Answer: "For defense." Then the emphasis went back to basic ideology. When was the Communist Party organized? Who were its founders? What were the salient differences between Lenin and Martov?

The last question was a popular one on Communist Party membership tests, for it emphasized the apartness and the dedication of the true Communist activist.

"Martov," Deriabin said, repeating the approved answer, "said a person could be a Communist by merely paying dues and keeping up formal membership. One didn't need constant Party work and discipline. Lenin said every Party member must work for the Party and accept Party discipline."[1]

[1] As might be suspected the real controversy was a little different. Lenin wished to restrict Party membership to a "narrow" group of revolutionaries rigidly controlled by the leadership. Martov wanted a more democratic Party in which men would not "abdicate their right to think." Although he won in a free vote at the Brussels Congress in 1903, Lenin gave him an early lesson in Bolshevik tactics by brutally forcing a re-

The chairman then asked the members who voted for Deriabin. He was unanimously elected, since everyone knew that the committee had long since decided on his selection. A week later he went before the divisional Party committee and answered a few more stock political questions. Three months later he was given his Party card.

The delay was unusual but understandable, since the division had been put on the move by the sudden German invasion. When Deriabin finally got his Party card the Germans were already in Smolensk, pressing hard on the Soviet armies left to defend Moscow. In the chaos of the shifting fronts around Moscow, the card-printing and registering aspects of Communism, among others, had been thrown temporarily out of gear. But the chief of the political section found time, nonetheless, to present the card to Deriabin in person. He advised him to take good care of it, storing it preferably in his inside pocket under his tunic. (In some military clothing issues a special pocket was provided for Party cards.) The number was 4121243.

In September 1941 Deriabin's battalion was ordered to the front near Moscow. It was part of the desperate reinforcement that had already sent most of the Siberian divisions westward to stem the German invasion. He carried *War and Peace*, in several tattered volumes, with him on the tedious ride along the trans-Siberian railway. Like most of the Soviet Army, he was patriotically stirred by the German invasion. The task of a political officer became easier, as even the worst grumblers forgot their problems with the régime in the common danger from the common traditional enemy. The military situation, as he quickly found out, grew progressively more sticky. Scarcely one month after he arrived on the Moscow front Deriabin was wounded in the right leg by a mine fragment. He spent the next three months in military hospitals, where he resumed his duties as a political instructor after recuperating. He was finally certified as temporarily unfit for military service and granted three months' leave in his home town of Biysk.

In April 1942 Deriabin was found fit for service again

---

consideration. It was out of this dispute that the terms Bolshevik (for majority) and Menshevik (minority) arose.

and posted to the school for political officers at Novosibirsk. Again the urgencies of the military position sent him off instead to the front. He was sent to a reserve infantry division, the 284th, then stationed at Krasnoufimsk in the Urals, as a political officer assigned to a mortar company. The mortarmen were jokingly called the "culture" arm of the infantry. Their job was thought far better than that of the rifle or machine-gun squads. It was hard work lugging the mortars up a hill, but once you got there, ran the reasoning, you could stay—permanently, if German mortars or artillery found the range too quickly.

On September 16 the 284th Division arrived at Kamyshin, a farming town on the banks of the Volga, on the way to Stalingrad. The battle for Stalingrad had already been joined on the spearhead of Hitler's disastrously ordered advance by the German Sixth and Fourth Armored armies. New of the heavy fighting there had spread through the Soviet armies on other fronts, and it was the loudly expressed wish of almost every man in the 284th, as the division was finishing its training, that he be sent anywhere but Stalingrad. But the division, fresh and up to full strength, was earmarked as part of the uncommitted Siberian forces with which the Soviet staff hoped to turn the Stalingrad balance. (Sixty percent of its personnel, in fact, was Siberian—a concentration of men from one region which in normal times Soviet political-military planners avoided.)

Kamyshin was well known for its fine watermelon, and the Siberians stuffed themselves with this and every other bit of fresh food they could find in the area, anticipating that they would have little but canned rations for a long time to come. After four days there they were loaded into lend-lease Dodge and Studebaker trucks. They drove all day and all night, until they reached the east bank of the Volga opposite Stalingrad. By the time they arrived the Germans had advanced to within five kilometers of the city.

Deriabin's regiment established its headquarters at the village of Kalinin, in an apple orchard which soon turned into a desert through repeated German bombardments. German artillery fired constantly and low-level dive bombers flew almost around the clock, strafing the Soviet rear positions. So it was almost a relief when the troops were ordered out of this sitting-duck position to cross the river.

At 3 A.M. on a mild September morning Deriabin's company and several others were put aboard a river steamer for what most Stalingrad survivors remember as the world's worst ferry ride. The boat first pulled in at an island in the middle of the Volga, then went on to the Stalingrad side, where the troops debarked at the Red October factory. The entire city was then in flames. Smoke from rockets, artillery, and the fires of spent buildings mixed with the morning mists to give the first landing waves reasonably good cover. Thus the very intensity of the German bombardment kept their casualties down during the crossing and landing.

By midday the Siberians had established forward positions in a rubble-strewn gully called the Banny, to the east of the commanding German position on the Mamayev Hill. Deriabin's mortarmen set up their weapons in the basement and second floor of a new four-story high school; but for the first day they were unable to fire them, so intensely did the Focke-Wulfs and Stukas keep dive-bombing their positions.

Their casualties rose quickly. Twenty percent of the company was lost in the first thirty-six hours they were in action. Deriabin and eleven survivors of one platoon were cut off inside the school basement, sealed up by a sudden cave-in. The air was foul, mixed with the seepage from broken gas lines and every man there thought it was the last air he would ever breathe. As it happened, they were rescued by an almost miraculous freak. A direct hit on the building above them opened a path in the rubble and they staggered out.

The mortarmen joined the rest of the regiment in what threatened to be a literal last-ditch retreat back along the gully. But they managed to establish positions on three parallel streets close to the Volga. Deriabin's company set up the mortars in another ravine between the main rail line and the city street-car tracks. There they stayed for two and a half months, fighting a ceaseless seesaw of attack and counter-attack, but effectively stopping the Nazi advance.

At the beginning of October, Deriabin was formally certified in his rank of junior political commissar, the equiva-lent of a junior lieutenant, although he had long enjoyed a *de facto* officer's status, and he was made deputy com-mander of the mortar company. In their positional warfare his mortarmen fared not too badly. They dug themselves a capacious bomb shelter in the side of the railway embank-ment, protected by a heavy covering of steel plates and earthworks. This they used as living quarters and company headquarters. As is normal with this kind of unit, they kept shifting the actual firing position of their mortars to keep the enemy from pinpointing their positions.

In heavy bombardments they would retire to the compar-ative invulnerability of the company shelter, which they gradually furnished with a comfortable assortment of rugs, blankets, and other articles scavenged from the ruins of Stalingrad houses. From one house they even managed to recover an undamaged phonograph with a large supply of records.

Whenever they had to leave the dugout for food or am-munition, losses were heavy. Supplies were always short, depending on the precarious ferry across the river, and Deriabin customarily sent patrols down to the riverbank at night, hoping either to find new shipments of ammunition or to steal them from other companies—a practice which was reciprocated.[2] It was normal to send out three- or four-man details for this work and equally normal that one or two would be lost every time. At the beginning Deriabin called for volunteers for this duty. After a while he merely

[2] The extreme example of a unit's self-sufficiency was of-fered by the defiance of Senior Lieutenant Bezditko. His crack mortar company, in another regiment, became so widely publi-cized in the Soviet press that he was given special supplies of food, clothing, and liquor to keep morale high for the visiting photographers. One day late in the campaign Lieutenant Bez-ditko's vodka supply ran out, despite repeated and unavailing telephone calls to division supply officers asking for more. When nothing more was promised him Bezditko threatened to blow up his battalion supply dump and did so with two well-placed rounds. No one was killed, fortunately, and Bezditko was not punished. The regimental commander, with a knowing eye on Bezditko's publicity value, merely ordered the supply officer to make good the vodka deficiency.

detailed any four men available. The losses were inevitable, and everybody knew it.

Every foot of the no man's land in the Stalingrad streets was under the fire of both sides. Even night afforded little protection. Once a German officer was killed at night near the mortar position. Deriabin's first sergeant asked permission to go out and get his boots, apparently of excellent quality. "Go on, if you don't value your life," Deriabin told him. Crawling out toward the German, the sergeant was hit by a grenade and lost a leg. Two other men from the company were wounded bringing him in.

There was one area between the lines, however, that soldiers from both sides constantly braved heavy fire to visit. Some abandoned tank cars containing pure alcohol stood there on a siding. At intervals a soldier would run up to one of the cars, put a bullet into it, and fill his canteen at the improvised spigot. This practice continued until a previously untapped tank turned out to contain wood alcohol. After two men died from drinking this the divisional commander ordered all the cars blown up.

Almost incredibly some families, afraid of chancing the escape across the river, stayed in their homes in and around Stalingrad through the entire battle, coming out for food and water at night. It was common practice among the Soviet troops to hold their fire when these civilians went down to the Volga to fill their buckets. Then German soldiers began disguising themselves as women or old men for the same purpose, and the order went out to fire at anyone, regardless of age, sex, or nationality. It was perhaps the nastiest experience of the entire campaign to see civilians die this way.

There were other, less desperate, memories, like the first time Peter Deriabin ever tasted good German pumpernickel bread. After the trap closed around Von Paulus's Sixth Army the Germans relied on air-drops to keep up their food supply. They had special signals between air and ground to notify them of a food drop—three blue lights and a red, or similiar combinations. The Soviet troops, after watching this process for a time, discovered the code system and signaled the planes overhead themselves. As a result, through the courtesy of the *Luftwaffe*, the Russians were periodically treated to some excellent rations of German bread, cheese, and sausage. Since their own commissary was crude by comparison the German air-drops were always quite an occasion.

Through the privations of the siege the discipline of the division remained almost as tight as it had been in the months of garrison duty on the Manchurian border. The possibility of any malingering or desertion was kept minimal by a policy of cruel and widely publicized punishments. Their stringency bears much of the credit for the division's almost suicidal battle behavior.

Unit commanders, for example, took literally the Soviet Army regulation: "Death is preferable to capture." In February 1943 two private soldiers from Deriabin's regiment were recaptured from the Germans, after they had earlier been taken prisoner. They were shot after a summary trial, in front of the survivors of the regiment. There was no murmuring in the ranks about their execution. The survivors, including Deriabin, felt that anyone who had let himself be captured in such a bitter life-and-death battle had let his comrades down.

For it was not punishment or threats, severe as they were, which were responsible for holding the line at Stalingrad. The best explanation for the heroism of the Soviet troops lay in the very name: The War for the Fatherland. What saved Stalingrad, as with the other battles of that period, was the fact that every man was fighting as a Russian. For a terrible but in a way uncomplicated four years the distinctions between Party man and non-Party man, between deviationist, counter-revolutionary, and *Komsomolets* were pushed aside in the face of common danger.

Only one man in Deriabin's company was caught malingering: a Kazakh who purposefully shot himself through the foot. (He was sent to a penal battalion.) Only three or four others in the entire regiment attempted the same.

In the very act of mobolizing every ounce of this traditional patriotism for the war effort, the Party bureaucracy was doing its best to strengthen the cadres of trusted Communists, with a view to a new purge at the war's end. In the face of a bloodbath like Stalingrad the political officer's classic role was ludicrous, but it was insisted on. The Soviet armies, for example, had to fight almost to the end of the Stalingrad battle totally without air cover. Deriabin himself saw not a single Soviet plane. It fell to the political commissars to go among the troops, after a new German air bombardment, to explain why it was that the Red Air Force had not sent any planes to drive the Germans off. It was a hollow experience for a thinking man to pass through the dugouts the day after a punishing German air raid, carrying Moscow newspapers and communiqués telling of new air "victories" on that very front.

As the war effort grew successful the professional military officer assumed an importance he had not known since the early days of the Revolution. Field officers laughed at the political commissars bringing the troops reports of faked victories. ("WE know how they won.") One of the political officers in Deriabin's regiment, on his way around the platoons with his papers and propaganda exhortations, was sent to the rear by a battalion commander who told him curtly to "lay off and let them sleep." It was not an uncommon occurrence.

In December the regiment retook a few streets from the Germans and moved its positions forward. Shortly after this Deriabin was promoted to senior lieutenant and sent to regimental headquarters as assistant to the regimental executive officer. He became in effect the operations officer, the Soviet counterpart of an American S-3, with added political overtones. He worked directly for the regimental commander and his executive officer. He checked and coordinated the movements of the regiment's battalions. If a battalion was ordered up to the attack, for example, and reported its strength too low to take an assigned position, Deriabin would be sent to check the battalion commander's story. (Invariably, no matter what he reported, the order would be repeated from divisional headquarters: "Take it anyway.")

He was also responsible for keeping the division political officer informed about the morale and political condition of the troops. In the hand-to-mouth existence of the Stalingrad battle some of these reports to higher headquarters necessarily bordered on the ridiculous. If food had been undelivered for two days, as happened on at least one occasion, Deriabin would dutifully note that there was a "certain discontent among the troops."

The political aspect of the Red Army was still strong

enough to give Deriabin, by this time a senior lieutenant, an importance far beyond the three stars on his shoulder-boards. As the "elected" Party secretary of the regimental staff, also, he was in a position where no one other than the regimental commander felt comfortable about giving him an order, outside of pressing tactical commands. With the regimental executive officer, a lieutenant colonel, he had an informal but eminently workable understanding. From the purely military point of view it was in Deriabin's best interest to have the executive officer's authority on his side. The executive officer, for his part, was acutely aware of Deriabin's Party position, which included the privilege of direct access to the division political officer, a man second in rank only to the divisional commander.

Futhermore, Deriabin was privy to an embarassingly exposed salient of the executive officer's private life. The lieutenant colonel had taken a special interest in the regimental nurse. He pursued his courtship so violently that she complained to Deriabin, as the resident Communist Party functionary, that both her health and her disposition were suffering. On the face of things Deriabin had all the makings of a good Party disciplinary case against his superior, who was only too happy to have the matter forgotten.

In other regiments and other divisions this intra-service cooperation did not work so smoothly. On a northern front a divisional chief of staff, a non-Party man and a regular Army colonel, had rejoined his unit after he and a small group had been encircled for days by the Germans. The lieutenant colonel in charge of divisional counter-intelligence, a member of the State Security, automatically suspected the chief of staff of treasonable dealings with the enemy. To "expose" these dealings, if possible, he ordered an agent of his to make friends with the colonel and spy on him. The agent happened to be a nurse attached to division headquarters and attractive, so complications were foreseeable. The counter-intelligence officer cautioned her, therefore, to avoid any real intimacy with her subject.

The plan failed. On the colonel's birthday, after a long celebration of vodka and brandy, the nurse forgot her unofficial spying duties sufficiently to spend the night in the colonel's well-padded dugout. During these private festivities she confessed to the colonel that she had been ordered to do a horrible thing, to spy on him in the service of the State Security. Headquarters suspected him, she added, because of his encirclement by the Germans.

The next day the chief of staff ran into the counterintelligence officer in the mess. After exchanging greetings he told the man without ceremony: "I slept with your agent last night. Next time you send me one I'll sleep with *her*—and again and again, until you run out of them."[3]

Deriabin's regiment had begun the battle of Stalingrad with a force of some 2800 men. By the first of February, when the last fighting units of the German Sixth Army surrendered, there were only 151 men left alive and unwounded in the entire unit. Every battalion and company commander had been either killed in action or removed, wounded, to the rear.

The divisional commander had told his senior officers before the battle began that he had no wish to keep up his regiments' strength with replacements; they would "win or die." Accordingly, as units were repeatedly decimated in the battle, the areas they were responsible for were progressively narrowed by Army headquarters, and entire formations of fresh troops sent in to take up their old positions. By the end of January the 284th Division had virtually ceased to exist as a tactical unit. Most of its battalions were commanded by lieutenants. For his constancy in holding his positions the divisional commander, a Colonel Batyuk, was promoted to the grade of major general.

For several days after the surrender Deriabin and his men were on patrol duty, rooting surviving parties of Germans out of the city's ruins. Deriabin received the surrender of a German officer with some two hundred men who crawled wearily from the basement of a tractor factory, waving white flags. He took them to divisional headquarters for interrogation and sorting, a process which began with a mass plunder of the Germans' personal effects. Deriabin picked up five watches for himself and

---

[3] This incident was used very soberly in the counterintelligence school where the State Security officers were trained as an example of why a good State Security officer should never tell an agent anything more than necessary for the bare tactical fulfillment of the agent's mission.

charitably gave away four of them to others who had not come on the patrol. As an officer, he had to keep sharp watch on the Soviet soldiers guarding the prisoners. If not closely supervised, the guards used to strip all prisoners to get their clothes. Soviet officers objected to this practice on the very practical grounds that a stripped military man, even a stripped German military man, is difficult to identify.

It was shortly before the prisoner incident that Deriabin had his first contact with other non-Soviet foreigners. Along with other political officers, he was detailed to guide a group of foreign correspondents on a tour of the battlefront. He took them to the top of the Mamayev Hill, near where his unit had suffered its first heavy casualties, leading them along a rough path through the ruin of bodies and smashed buildings that comprised victorious Stalingrad. Aside from practical admonitions to avoid this or that obstacle he had no communication with them.[4]

Two days after the campaign for Stalingrad was officially over, training plans were announced for further action. Division headquarters were set up 20 miles from Slavyansk, on the North Donets River, and there a stream of replacements joined the cadre of survivors. The move towards Slavyansk (which was still in German hands) was doubly welcome, since it involved a trip through farming country relatively untouched by the war. The troops traded the German loot they had amassed at Stalingrad for fresh food to vary their drab Army diet. The commissary had functioned comparatively well during the campaign. But the moment the outcome was certain, in line with the Soviet régime's idea of a true economy of forces, the victors of Stalingrad were cut back to a bare subsistence ration of pea soup, black bread, and grits.

As the Germans retreated the re-formed division went into action again and fought its way southwestward to Odessa and into Bessarabia as far as the Dnestr River. In

[4] One of the correspondents on this tour was Godfrey Blunden, then reporting for the London *Evening Standard* and now a *Time* and *Life* correspondent in Europe. Blunden noted the incident in a passage from *The Time of the Assassins,* one of his two memorable novels about Soviet life in World War II.

the spring of 1943 Deriabin caught another bullet in the
right shoulder, during a sharp infantry fight over the town
of Apostolovo, in the Ukraine. He spent a month in the
division hospital and still moved creakily when he rejoined
the troops.

At the time the 62d Army, under General Vasiliy Chuikov, was sweeping on through the Ukraine, still rolling
hard with the momentum applied by the Stalingrad victory.
The advance was hardly a blitzkrieg; the retreating German army, ably led by Marshall Erich von Manstein,
fought hard and steadily, although the same could not have
been said of its Rumanian allies. So the Russian sweep was
actually a long succession of engagements and slow pursuit—"one day fighting, two days marching," as the soldiers called it.

By the late spring of 1944 the Soviet armies had
marched to within striking distance of the port city of
Odessa, the last heavily defended German strong point in
the area. Morale was high, and Chuikov called up the past
to reinforce it. One hundred and fifty years before, in
1790, the great General Aleksandr Suvorov had stormed
the Turkish fortress of Izmail, 120 miles southwest of
Odessa. "We have won at Stalingrad," Chuikov exhorted
his army, "and we are good enough to do what we did
before. Suvorov took Izmail, we shall take Odessa."

The Bug River was the last natural barrier the Russians
had to cross before they could sweep down along the flat
Black Sea coast to Odessa. But the swamps of the Bug
delta were themselves a formidable obstacle. In April 1944
Deriabin's division was forcing a crossing of the Bug at the
town of Novaya Odessa in the high tide of the Russian
advance. As operations officer Deriabin went up front
with the reconnaissance detachment to observe the German
positions. The platoon he accompanied was one of the first
Russian units across the river. As it happened, it was the
first to face the full force of an unexpected German
counter-attack which caught the Soviet troops before they
had been able to get adequate bridging equipment set up.

It was night fighting and treacherous. The regimental
commander, who was also up forward with Deriabin, was
killed by machine-gun fire. The forward elements of the

i
i
tl

fr
pe
had
but
ers,
the
the r

De
for a
when
at the
was w
back a
shoulde
Deriabi
taking a
that mor

men should be fighting on the line, and spe
that no fit men st
trolled rear areas to see
to help the wounded.
Almost enough consciousness to
retained enough attention in a hur
get medical attention a hur
stand up. He started walki
chance his new division o
was in an artillery ob
General saw the
barefooted and
field nurse in
to the div
Deri
and

                                        pockets,
                              Deriabin had just
                        a dead German.

When Deriabin came to, he was freezing cold and bleeding through the mouth. He tried to move his hands and could not. He had lost any feeling in his feet. But he could move his head slightly. He decided that he must be alive.

Some Soviet soldiers came along, part of the decisive wave which had been hurried up to secure the bridgehead after the first repulse. They tried to move him, but saw it was impossible without some sort of a stretcher. So they wrapped his feet in his uniform tunic, put him on a poncho, and carried him this way to the bank of the river, where they left him. It was about 11 P.M. on what was certainly the longest day in Deriabin's life. He lay there until dawn.

At six the next morning some rubber boats were sent across the river to pick up the wounded. (They had previously been unable to, because of the thick mud and the lack of light for finding solid ground on the bank.) Deriabin and other wounded men were deposited on the east shore, alone—an Army order specified that all able-bodied

cial details pa-
ayed behind even

by this time, Deriabin
realize that he had better
y. Amazingly he managed to
ng towards the rear. By merest
commander, Major General Vagin,
servation post not far from him. The
badly wounded officer stumbling along
recognized him. He immediately sent a
a jeep to pick Deriabin up and take him back
sion hospital.
abin spent the next two months in a field hospital
later in Odessa, after its recapture, before he was able
o rejoin his division at the front. When he reached headquarters he was invited to visit the chief of the divisional
political department, who asked him if he would like an
appointment to the Army counter-intelligence school in
Moscow. He had previously been recommended for the
military staff college, but his woundings and hospitaliza-
tion kept him from joining the proper class.

It would hardly be an exaggeration to say that by this
time Deriabin had seen enough of front-line warfare. Almost any temporary relief would have been worth considering. He had seen something of counter-intelligence work,
also, as a political officer, but his experience had involved
more front-line tactics than rear-area investigating. He did
know enough to appreciate the power wielded by the
counter-intelligence officers—all of them on detached duty
from the State Security.

On the other hand, the deviousness of their work did not
attract him, and he would have preferred a straight appointment to the military staff college. The initial reserve
he had felt in Siberia about entering the Army as a career
had vanished. It had become a business with him, if not a
career. Despite his narrow escapes at the front, he enjoyed
command responsibility.

He had understandable misgivings about staying in the
infantry. The infantry might be the "queen of the battlefields," as the saying went, but a man four times wounded

was more likely to remember the familiar Red Army slogan:

> "The sluggards in the artillery,
> Braggarts in the cavalry,
> Drunkards in the fleet,
> Idiots in the infantry."

If counter-intelligence had its drawbacks it was beyond dispute a safer branch of the service.

The division counter-intelligence officer, Major Bessonov, spoke persuasively on this theme: "Do you want to stay in the Army all your life?" he argued. "Aren't you tired of all this discipline? Look at our SMERSH[5] officers. Whether they have high rank or not, they are at home anywhere. Working in counter-intelligence is headquarters stuff. You need never go into the trenches again."

Deriabin conceded that the prospect was attractive, and back in his quarters he started to think of a few spy stories he had read, mostly by English authors, trying to imagine what real cloak-and-dagger work would be like. In a few days Bessonov told him that his clearance had come through. Long before being "asked" for his opinion about counter-intelligence work, Deriabin discovered, his documents had already been forwarded and processed. So the question of his own choice in the matter was, as he had suspected, academic. Whether he knew it or not, he was just the sort of man the State Security was looking for: young, wiry, intelligent, and possessed of a good Party record.

In June 1944 Peter Deriabin reported to the headquarters of the Third Ukrainian Front, where he took examinations for entry into the counter-intelligence school. He was one of eighteen successful "applicants" who passed, out of 150 initially chosen. The following month he said good-by to his friends at the division and prepared to hitchhike his way to Moscow, where the school was located. (The wartime Soviet Army made no transport arrangements for ju-

---

[5] The wartime name for military counter-intelligence. See page 67 for a complete explanation.

nior officers traveling to a new duty station.) The chief of the political department told him again how much the Party was depending on him for big things in the future. General Vagin brushed aside Deriabin's last offer to stay with the division notwithstanding. "You've been hit four times," he said, "and the next time you won't be lucky. Get out of here, and good luck."

With this the gates closed on Peter Sergeyevich Deriabin, the boy from Siberia who had at first resented the Army and wanted so badly to remain a schoolteacher with good Komsomol connections. He hardly imagined at the time how completely he was entering a new life which was gradually to sever all his old connections with relatives, friends, and neighbors—the bulk of the Soviet people, in fact—and tell him more than he ever wished to know about the men who ruled them.

CHAPTER IV

The Education Of A Chekist

ON DECEMBER 20, 1917, six weeks after the October Revolution, the new Soviet régime created an organization called the All-Russian Extraordinary Commission for the Fight Against Counter-Revolution, Sabotage, and Speculation. Its jawbreaking Russian title was speedily reduced to the abbreviation VCHK and the familiar, if most often whispered, word "Cheka." Lenin personally ordered it established. His purpose in doing so was more frankly stated by Feliks Dzerzhinsky, the maniacally industrious Polish nobleman who put the Cheka into operation, in his phrase "the avenging sword of the proletarian leadership." As Dzerzhinsky elaborated at the time:

> "The Cheka is not a court. The Cheka is *the defense of the Revolution* as the Red Army is; as in the civil war the Red Army cannot stop to ask whether it may harm particular individuals, but must take into account only one thing, the victory of the Revolution over the bourgeoisie, so the Cheka must defend the Revolution and conquer the enemy even if its sword falls occasionally on the heads of the innocent."

On December 20, 1957, the same secret police organization celebrated its fortieth anniversary, with a fanfare in Moscow that in itself belies the claims of the current Soviet leadership to have dissolved their police state. Nikita Khrushchev and his fellow members of the Central Com-

65

mittee of the Communist Party and the Council of Ministers of the U.S.S.R. joined in "warm" congratulations to
the Chekists on their "glorious jubilee." Ceremonial meetings of soviets and local Party activities were held everywhere in the Soviet Union. In the following year, at an
equally big celebration, a statue of Dzerzhinsky was cer-
emonially unveiled, and Dzerzhinsky's widow was brought
out of her retirement to preside over the occasion. As
loudly as it had the year before, the press bulged with ex-
travagant salutes: "the vigilant eye," "the strong arm of the
Chekist," "those watching over the interests of the fatherland," etc.

It is important to keep in mind this continuity of motive
and organization when reading the record of Peter Deriabin's experience as a "Chekist," for it is as much a record
of current fact as past history. The "naked sword" of the
leadership has not once been sheathed or even dulled by
the tremendous changes of four decades inside the Soviet
Union—merely polished. The State Security organization is
essential to a system which rules by compulsion. Its operations affect every level of Soviet society. Its air of constant
suspicion grew out of the days when Lenin and Trotsky
were changing the times and places of their conspiratorial
meetings for fear of spies or hidden informers. But it has
fastened its grip on the new generation of Soviet leaders,
who read the Western press with awareness and wear
Italian-tailored suits with aplomb, as surely as it dominated
the lives of the unwashed men in the rough uniforms of the
old Red Army.

In describing this organization we have used the words
State Security[1] throughout. But the State Security has gone
through so many changes in its title and protective coloration that it would be helpful to set them down at the beginning.

Almost from the moment of its founding the original
State Security had the power of both arrest and punishment,
given to it verbally by the Soviet leaders. It grew into a
monster swiftly, without benefit of formal authorization or

---

[1] A literal translation, incidentally, of the Nazi *Reichssicher-
heit Hauptamt*, the only organization comparable to it in modern history.

documents. Lenin and his associates used it from the first to crush rebellion and, after a few years, to suppress dissension within the Party itself.

Although it was later justified—and camouflaged—by statute and administrative order, it worked necessarily outside the law, its decisions ruthless and beyond appeal, as the most trustworthy and direct implement of Soviet rule. The leaders of world revolution never completely lost a slight bad conscience, however, about its necessity. Because of this, probably, the State Security went through periodic bureaucratic reorganizations, most of them founded on the theory that a thorn by any other name might look less prickly. In February 1922 the Cheka was reorganized into the State Political Administration (GPU). The next year, during the formation of the Union of Soviet Socialist Republics, it was reorganized and strengthened into the Combined State Political Directorate (OGPU). The success of the OGPU in terrorizing the Soviet people is too well known to need elaboration. The moment the Soviet leadership decided on rule by *mass* coercion, dating from the forced collectivization plan of the 1930s, the OGPU's function was magnified from that of a relatively secret terror organization into an instrument of mass action and thought control.

The OGPU was streamlined in 1934 to become the People's Commissariat of Internal Affairs (NKVD). In February 1941 the NKVD was divided into the original People's Commissariat of Internal Affairs and a new People's Commissariat of State Security (NKGB). Five months later the two were again merged as a reflex of the panic brought about by the German invasion. Two years later, in April 1943, they were again separated. At the same time, owing to war conditions, military counterintelligence was detached from the parent body and reorganized into Army and Navy branches of the Chief Directorate of Counter-Intelligence of the People's Commissariat of Defense of the U.S.S.R. It was this organization which was known familiarly as SMERSH, from a euphonious combination of its slogan: "*Smert'shpionam*—death to spies."

In March 1946 the NKVD became the Ministry of Internal Affairs (MVD). The NKGB became the Ministry of

State Security (MGB), and incorporated the Army and Navy SMERSH. After Stalin died these separated ministries were united again in the MVD, but on March 13, 1954, they were again separated into a Ministry of Internal Affairs (MVD), and Deriabin's alma mater, the Committee of State Security under the Council of Ministers of the U.S.S.R., known familiarly as the KGB.

The functions were then divided much as they remain today, although, owing to power shifts and bureaucratic reshuffling, an almost steady exchange of minor borderline bureaus goes on between them. The MVD (*Ministerstvo Vnutrennikh Del* or Ministry of Internal Affairs) was given control over the regular police of the Soviet Union (the "militia,") as well as the prison system and the 100,000-strong organization of special interior troops. It later took over temporary command of the 200,000 border troops, but ultimately lost them to the KGB. The KGB (*Komitet Gosudarstvennoi Bezopasnosti*) kept control of all counter-intelligence functions inside the Soviet Union, being as usual a punitive as well as an investigatory force; it also retained the primary responsibility for intelligence, counter-intelligence, and "terror" activities in foreign countries.

Through all this complicated window-dressing, the State Security officer has continued to be known by his old-fashioned name of Chekist. He is in a literal sense the arbiter and the orderer of Soviet society, and everyone knows it. The best description of the Chekist's relationship to the Soviet people remains the comment on the initials of the old OGPU which Deriabin first heard in the thirties. To most people they meant *O Gospodi, Pomogi Ubezhat'*—"O Lord, help me escape." The Chekist read the initials backwards: *Ubezhish', Poymayem, Golovu Otorvem*—"You escape, we will catch you and cut off your head."

Through the war years, even at the front, Deriabin had grown familiar with this distinction between the bulk of the population and the Chekists. For if he was not yet a full-fledged Chekist, his posts as a Party boss and a political officer had given him some insight into the primacy of "counter-intelligence." It was dramatized for him as he was en route to the Moscow counter-intelligence school in 1944 in an encounter with an officious fellow officer in charge of troop movements at a local railroad station. The officer held up Deriabin and a companion at the station, refused to recognize their rather informal Army passes and orders, and threatened them with arrest for desertion. Worried, Deriabin went looking for the local counter-intelligence officer, a lieutenant colonel. The colonel verified his orders, then without ceremony routed out the major general commanding from his quarters and ordered him to discipline his station officer. The general complied with such humility as to leave little doubt about the underlying command relationship. When Deriabin reached Moscow the relationship was badly stated in a short welcoming speech by the director of the school, a lieutenant general himself. "You are just the same as the leaders of the Communist Party," he told them, "except that you will work and carry out your functions in a different way. We shall now begin the study of these methods."

The Higher Army Counter-Intelligence School was the exact duplicate of the State Security School for the same purpose. Both of them were later combined into the Higher School of State Security. The curriculum concentrated on the techniques of controlling a subject population, i.e. the people of the Soviet Union. In Deriabin's day there was an added emphasis on Army counter-intelligence and the military, political, and economic study of the chief wartime enemy, Germany. Because of the war, the normal two-year course had also been accelerated to a compact twelve months.

The students in his division were all carefully selected officers, mostly captains, with a few majors and senior lieutenants, who had been similarly ticketed for State Security duty. They had a ten-hour working day divided into from six to eight hours of classroom instruction and at least two hours of individual study. Discipline was extremely strict. Unless an officer had a "B" average or higher he was not allowed to leave the building, a four-story red-brick edifice at 19 Stanislavskaya Street, facing the former German Embassy in Moscow (now used by the East German satellite). Even the ranking students permitted to go on a few hours' liberty in Moscow were required to notify school authorities where they could be reached at any time in case of emergency. Because of the intelligence nature of their work they were allowed to wear civilian clothes in their rare off-duty moments. (At that time civilian clothing was so scarce in Moscow that three or four suits—all they could find—were regularly exchanged among them.)

The course concentrated on regular counter-intelligence subjects: investigation, interrogation, and the detection of anti-régime elements in the Soviet population. There was considerable emphasis on the minutiae of filing reports and advising (or not advising) local or higher Party officials of arrests and interrogations. Investigation techniques ranked high in importance. Later classes were accustomed to practice their surveillance lessons by shadowing diplomats and other foreigners in the Moscow area. The internal politics of the U.S.S.R., Communist Party history, world politics, and geography were also given. There was a "humanities" course, consisting of intensive training in Russian language, history, and literature for those whose culture seemed to sag a bit at the seams. One "frill" course was added: a general instruction in etiquette, table manners, and elementary social niceties, including dancing lessons two evenings a week by accomplished young ladies from the Bolshoi Theater ballet.[2] Soviet intelligence likes its officers to be *kulturny*, as the Russians put it.

Besides the part of the curriculum dealing with foreign politics there was a class devoted to detailed study of the intelligence techniques of Britain, France, and the U.S., as well as Germany. The school directors made no equivocation about what this knowledge was to be used for. "Remember," they kept repeating, "that your allies today are your enemies tomorrow."

Behind all the formal teaching the officer-instructors at the school on Stanislavskaya Street strove to give a feeling of apartness to the students. An officer in the State Security, they reiterated, is more than a mere Party member or a government official. He is a Chekist, meaning that he is a Communist first, last, and always. Every act of his daily life must be bound to this premise: he eats, reads, falls in

---

[2] The extremely old-fashioned forms of dancing taught in such courses were responsible for the anachronistic prevalence at Soviet officers'-club dances of mazurkas, schottisches, and Viennese waltzes, as performed in pre-Revolutionary society.

love, thinks, visits, laughs—as a Chekist. In his work he must automatically divide the world into two classes of people: Communists and the others. All non-Communist parties, organizations, or activities are to him real or potential agents of the "class enemy." They are, whether they know it or not, "objectively counter-revolutionary."

To reinforce this principle and to justify it in the most concrete terms, the school began to furnish the students with a taste of their later perquisites. Despite the austerity of war conditions they received several new issues of uniforms and food, housing, and pay beyond that of their normal service rank. A long process of insulation had begun.

As they made the transition from officers of the Soviet Army to operatives of the State Security, without anyone ever enunciating the fact, the immediate objective of the organization was made clear to them. "In the *Yezhovshchina* [purges of the thirties]," the familiar saying runs, "the god of the State Security sat in the political section. During the period of collectivization god sat in the economic section. During the war god was in intelligence, after the war in counter-intelligence." The shifts in emphasis so suggested were, of course, reflections of the Soviet régime's major problem during each successive era.

When Deriabin left the counter-intelligence school in April 1945, the problem was the political control of the Soviet population.

In 1945 the Soviet Union, physically and spirtually, was swamped by the wreckage of the war. The sufferings of the people had been intense. The entire transportation system was in ruins. Trains could proceed no faster than 10–20 kilometers an hour, threading their way in and out of wrecked stations, past the ruins of untilled fields. The stinking, charred remains of Stalingrad were an unforgettable example of a city's degration.

When Deriabin traveled back from the front to Moscow in 1944 he had stopped overnight in a Ukrainian village near Poltava. His hosts were an old couple and their daughter-in-law who lived in the cellar ruins of their house. The upper stories had been shorn off by artillery fire, and the only ceiling left to the basement was the last of the unburned floor. The earth walls were lined with rough cloth. The people in the house did have a cow and a few pigs left to them and were able to produce a dinner of dumpling and potato stew garnished with homemade vodka. It is significant that Deriabin was very impressed by their living standard, which was far "higher" than that of the great majority of Soviet citizens, whether at home or at the front. Conditions had changed little in the year that followed.

Along with the physical damage there was a corresponding deterioration of the régime's authority. The death struggle of the war had forced Stalin to abandon all pretense of fighting for Communism alone, in an orgy of revived Russian nationalism. The pictures of Marx had gone into the dustbin. The national heroes of the war were the old great czars and generals of the Russian land: Suvorov, the brilliant tactician of the eighteenth century; Kutusov, the heavy-moving general who beat Napoleon in 1812 and lived on ever afterward in *War and Peace;* Aleksandr Nevsky, the medieval prince who conquered the Teutonic Knights. If the Soviet leadership retained any illusions about the popularity of Communism they were smashed by the desertions of Soviet troops through the early stages of the German advance and the smiles with which civilian populations at first greeted the Germans. The Germans, fortunately for the Communist leadership, were both too cruel and too nearsighted to glimpse their great opportunity, especially in areas like Byelorussia and the Ukraine. But it was not until the Nazi occupation showed itself in its true brutal colors that the propagandists were able fully to mobilize the appeal of Russian patriotism.

As long as the war lasted the Party and the State Security made their greatest efforts in the Army. The *politruks*[8] and the military counter-intelligence officers between them had kept the armed forces politically loyal to the state. Now the direction shifted. The weight of the State Security was to fall upon the home front.

The régime in Moscow was worried not only about the huge extent of wartime collaboration with the enemy. In a purely mechanical way the State Security's machinery had

---

[8] Short for *Politicheskii Rukovoditel,* "political instructor," the official designation for political officer.

been allowed to rust. Invasion and total war are no respecters of delicately interlocking security file systems and agent networks. The ablest officers of the State Security had been transferred to the armed forces. Many of them were now dead. The collective farms, those indispensable political devices for keeping the peasantry under police control, had been broken up by the thousands in the wartime dislocation, as had the neat Party organizations in the cities.

The first objective of the State Security was to reseal the political vacuum inside the Soviet Union. Throughout World War II, Stalin and the Soviet leaders had had to maintain lip service to their temporary unity with the Western Allies, in sharp contrast to the old attacks on "capitalist imperialists." Soviet troops at the front knew very well that a critically large amount of their supplies came from the Western Allies, notably the United States. The Army rode in American jeeps and trucks and ate specially prepared rations, tasting like indigenous Russian dishes but stamped prominently "Made in U.S.A." Soviet troops advancing into Germany and eastern Europe saw even among the ruins a standard of living which they had scarcely believed possible. They talked about what they saw. Indeed they looted whatever they could carry among these Western treasures to bring home to their destitute families. A German watch was quite an acquisition to a Soviet farm boy and demonstrably negotiable when he got home. Deriabin brought back three of them himself. He had little compunction about looting the people who had stripped off his boots while he was lying wounded in the Bug marshes.

The instructors at the Higher Counter-Intelligence School made no bones about the need for re-establishing Party discipline within the country. This would be done by the severest treatment of Soviet citizens, e.g. war prisoners and slave laborers, who had lived abroad during the war, and by reinstating the wartime Allies as the postwar enemy of the Soviet state. The process of political decontamination often went to absurd lengths. In August 1944 Deriabin and his fellow officers at the school were sent out on a two-week "furlough" to help farmers in the Ryazan Oblast near

Moscow[4] harvest their crops. Some of the "harvesters" were set to work in a warehouse unwrapping thousands of quarter-pound packages of butter marked "U.S.A." and putting the butter into wrapping with a Soviet trademark.

So the borders were sealed, the anti-Western slogans dusted off in *Pravda*, the return prisoners from Germany sent off for summary trials and the labor camps, while people who had actually fought against the Soviet Union, like members of the ill-fated Vlasov Army, were shot by the thousands. With this preliminary "prophylaxis" begun, the State Security got down to its second and major objective: to restore its control over every element of the Soviet population. In March 1946 there was a general reorganization of the Soviet governmental structure. It was at this time that the State Security, along with other commissariats, became a ministry of its own.

Deriabin had graduated from counter-intelligence school in the top ten of a 170-man class. He was first posted to Naval counter-intelligence headquarters in Moscow as aide to Lieutenant General Petr A. Gladkov,[5] the State Security officer in charge. This assignment turned out badly. Gladkov wanted an aid who did not smoke and could teach his children music (the personal element, as we shall see recurrently, plays a large part in Soviet staff assignment). Deriabin failed on both counts, although he and the General remained good friends. He ended up as a Komsomal secretary in Naval counter-intelligence headquarters, where he stayed for one year.

The capital city assignment was a witness to his good standing with the authorities. In the fall of 1945 he had been promoted to captain. He had been duly "elected" as

---

[4] The Ryazan Oblast, a Dogpatch-like region whose marshy soil permitted a level of bare-subsistence farming, was not thought of as a keen vacation ground. "God created heaven and earth," the folksy Russian saying had it, "and the devil created women and the Ryazan Oblast."

[5] It was General, not Admiral. The Soviet Navy, part of a completely unified service setup, in those days had its own intelligence organization, as did the Soviet Army. But the inner security, including counter-intelligence, has always been run by one separate corps, part of the State Security.

Komsomol secretary because of his trustworthiness and past Party experience. But his job was not yet an operational one. It involved the inspirational training, disciplining, and surveillance of the 126 young Komsomol members working in the headquarters staff. He was not overly happy with this kind of Party post, which combined various aspects of a drill sergeant, spy, instructor in Marxism, and part-time social director. He had also begun to worry about his family.

His father had died in 1936, his mother in September 1941. His brother, Vladimir, had been killed at the front. His nearest and dearest relative, his younger sister, Valya, was living with their uncle in Biysk. After the March 1946 reorganization merged Naval counter-intelligence with the new MGB, Deriabin asked for a transfer to the State Security office at Biysk or somewhere else in the Altai Kray.

His request was turned down. Refusal was probably due as much as anything to the fact that he had few friends on the personal staff of Colonel General Viktor Abakumov, who had taken over the Ministry of State Security. In fact, Deriabin's Navy superior, Lieutenant General Gladkov, was an old enemy of Abakumov's and had been removed from his office with the consolidation. This command byplay was Deriabin's first introduction to the personal power struggles of which he later saw so much in the Kremlin.

Uneasy about his family and worried now about his job, Deriabin used the connections he did have in Communist Party circles to obtain a discharge from military service. In April 1946 he took the slow train on the trans-Siberian railway out of Moscow to Novosibirsk. There he changed to the branch line and after a five-day journey arrived at Biysk.

He was tired of the war. The glamor of a cloak-and-dagger operative in the novels he read in school had worn off in the course of his indoctrination in the merciless routine of the State Security. Not only glamor had faded. What little he had seen of the inner workings of government disturbed even a good Communist like Peter Deriabin. He had seen how the State Security was shaping its own iron version of the better world the soldiers had talked about at the front, how the government was already preparing the population to fight another war, if need be, against its old allies. In the station at Altayskaya, waiting for a change of trains, he met an old friend who had gone to school with him. Sergey Lavrov had lost a leg on the front near Vilna. He was coming home, sick, wasted, and angry. "We won the war," he said to Deriabin, "and we received nothing."

Such bitterness was not unusual, but along with it, paradoxically, there went a certain vague hope for better things. In the closing passages of *Dr. Zhivago*, Boris Pasternak suggests this breath of hope as he describes two survivors of World War II and the mood with which they faced the future:

> "Although victory had not brought the relief and freedom that were expected at the end of the war, nevertheless the portents of freedom filled the air throughout the postwar period, and they alone defined its historical significance.
>
> To the two old friends, as they sat by the window, it seemed that this freedom of the soul was already there, as if that very evening the future had tangibly moved into the streets below them, that they themselves had entered it, and were now part of it. . . ."[6]

It had been given to Deriabin and his fellow students at the counter-intelligence school to realize—quite logically, long before the majority of their fellow citizens—that the rising hope was probably only illusion. But hope dies hard, and Moscow was a long way from home. It took a visit there to confirm his friend Sergey's angry words.

At home he found a chaos in its way worse than life either at the front or in the changing bureaucracies of Moscow. Both of his surviving cousins had been wounded: this average family, with one member killed, and three seriously wounded, exemplified the terrible totality of the war in Russia. One cousin hobbled about on crutches. The other could barely do light work. His widowed sister-in-law had kept her family going through the war by her job in a

[6] From *Dr. Zhivago* by Boris Pasternak. © 1957 by Giangiacomo Feltrinelli, Editore, Milano, Italy; © 1958 in the English edition by William Collins Sons & Co., Ltd.; © 1958 in the revised edition by Pantheon Books, Inc.

vodka distillery. Her salary was paid principally in kind, and she had supported her children by trading the vodka she received for money, food, and odd articles of clothing. Pensions and soldiers' living allowances were desperately low. "If I had not found this job," his sister-in-law told him, "we would all have starved." When she said this she was barely coherent. She had begun to drink heavily after such constant occupational exposure to temptation.

Deriabin had with him only about a thousand rubles saved from his military pay. (Postwar Moscow was not a cheap town to live in.) He gave his sister, Valya, then twelve, 800 to buy a dress, and he sold his own raincoat for 600 to get some food and rent a room for himself. He borrowed 300 rubles from a friend in the local State Security office at Biysk to go to Barnaul and look for a job.

It was seven years since he had been a teacher. He liked teaching and had planned to return to it. But the solid little life he had known was gone. There were new men in the school and at local Party headquarters. To go back there meant re-establishing himself once more almost from the bottom in an existence he now regarded as too routine to offer any kind of intellectual stimulation, though sufficiently disturbed by the shocks of war and the new peace-time order of Moscow to afford him the prospect of little real peace. He wanted to support his sister and also to marry. He visited an old girl-friend of his in Biysk, Tanya Zakharova, and started to see her regularly with reasonably serious intentions. Neither marriage nor any family support, however, would be possible on his prewar teacher's salary of 600 rubles a month.

As a captain in the State Security, by contrast, he would be getting 2000 rubles a month with a great many additional special favors: better clothes, good food, lodging and medical care. He had seen scant promise of any improvement in the life of the common people. His friends and relatives were bitter and incredulous that he had even wanted to return. "Why, you fool," they would say, "why did you come here? Everyone leaves here and goes to Moscow and other big cities—what did you want to come back for? We live in the middle of rich wheat country, and yet we have to queue up to get bread for ourselves."

After some half-hearted efforts at getting a position in

the school system and in the local Party offices, Deriabin overcame his quiet little burst of free enterprise and gave up. With a certain sense of the inevitable he applied for a job in the State Security.

The head of the office in Biysk was a friend of his, and he forwarded the application without delay—quite a concession by Soviet official standards. In June 1946 new orders came through from Moscow. Peter Sergeyevich Deriabin was reinstated in his rank of captain, assigned as a case officer in Barnaul.

CHAPTER V

The Case Officer

THE STATE SECURITY case officer is the cop-on-the-beat in the world's most ruthlessly efficient police force. To understand his functions and his powers one must go back to the premises on which the State Security operates. It is not merely an agency for investigation; it is aggressive and punitive. It does not wait for a "crime" to happen. It seeks "crime" out.

Each month every provincial and local branch of the State Security has the obligation of forwarding to higher authority a report, more or less detailed, on the "political and moral condition of the population." By Soviet legal standards the two adjectives in this heading are regarded as identical. The country which has made the greatest number of political prisoners in history does not acknowledge the existence of the term "political prisoner." Since no political differences are authorized or recognized within the U.S.S.R., an opponent of the régime, in whatever degree, can only be classed as an enemy of security. Thus, if one man steals and another man criticizes the government, their crimes are regarded by the Soviet courts as generally the same. Both "criminals" are simply being "anti-Soviet." In practice, of course, the man who criticizes the government is regarded as by far the greater danger. The basic goal of the State Security is to control the thoughts and curb the individual aspirations of the Soviet people, harnessing them to the régime's prescribed goals. It is not only departure from the imposed norm that each case officer is looking for. He is responsible for making the norm come true.

Like a safe-cracker who always wears a pin-striped suit on the job, the Soviet régime insists on justifying its unnatural supervision over its citizens with the forms and trappings of the law. The authority for the State Security's peculiar brand of justice has been, since 1927, Articles 58 and 59 of the criminal code in the Russian Soviet Federated Socialist Republic.[1] These define "counter-revolutionary crime" as a multitude of conceivable sins: treasonable activity; treasonable activity by one's relatives; the sabotage of government, industry, trade, communications, or credit systems; destroying or damaging any form of government property; or deliberately not performing one's duties if done with intent to weaken the government power. (The KGB naturally reserves the right to determine what an accused man was intending.) Activity can also be considered counter-revolutionary, and punishable by Soviet law, if directed against any other proletarian country outside the Soviet Union. This, incidentally, gives the State Security its "legalization" for imprisoning or executing foreign nationals who might have opposed a Communist régime inside their own countries.

The ways of the State Security can only be understood in terms of such gigantic "legalist" deception. The convention of unanimous public acceptance is as necessary to the Soviet régime as the convention of the fourth wall is to a man writing a play. This is the first lie that premises the State Security's operations. The second lie is the convention that the KGB, the State Security Committee of the U.S.S.R., is,

---

[1] There is technically no federal criminal code in the U.S.S.R., the enactment of criminal legislation being the responsibility of the individual Union republics. Since the republican criminal codes all adhere to basic principles laid down by federal statute, the RSFSR code—the earliest and the most widely administered—is taken here as a federal equivalent. The new criminal legislation enacted by the Supreme Soviet of the U.S.S.R. in December 1958 is again a statement of principles which will form the basis in due course of revised criminal codes in the various republics. For a detailed description of Soviet legal practices and their remarkable constancy about political crimes, see Appendix III.

as written in the Soviet constitution, subordinate to the Council of Ministers of the U.S.S.R., the official governing body. In fact, the KGB works directly for the Party and, in practice, by-passes the façade of formal "government." One of the ten secretaries of the Central Committee of the Communist Party is always assigned to direct State Security activities.

Every officer of the State Security is either a member of the Communist Party or a member of the Komsomol, which here as elsewhere functions as the Party feeder organization. All instructions or decisions about their activities must come from the Central Committee itself. In the provinces as well as in Moscow the State Security sends its reports not to Soviet government organizations but to the Party. The chief of the local KGB unit is invariably at the same time a member of one of the local committees of the Communist Party. He always operates in close co-operation with the local No. 1 man in the Party hierarchy. Indeed, one of his prime functions is to furnish No. 1 with detailed reports on the behavior and intentions of Nos. 2, 3, 4, and 5.

The average State Security case officer is a commissioned member of the force, with the rank of senior lieutenant, captain, or major, who has been trained either at a higher State Security school or like Deriabin, during the war, at the military counter-intelligence school. He operates either within the local offices of the State Security or on detached duty as, for instance, case officer in charge of security at a large factory, in a network of collective farms, or inside an Army division. In Moscow the case officer may find himself responsible for servicing a ministry or one of its branches. He may have to deal with a large railroad terminal, a theater, or an organization of writers, or several blocks in a city, several villages in the country. He may be the overseer of a tourist office dealing with foreigners or of a large hotel or restaurant. The deputy directors of most of the big hotels and restaurants in Moscow, notably those patronized by foreigners, are oftentimes members of the State Security.

When a new case officer reports for work he pays visits to the director of his assigned institution, the chief of the personnel office, the head of the paramilitary guard unit, to say nothing of appropriate Communist Party officals in charge of Party doings at that particular activity. (His welcome at all these offices may not be exactly heartfelt, but it is always polite.) Then he initiates a long and careful study of the personnel files of people in his jurisdiction, paying particularly close attention to Party members and both the extra good workers and Stakhanovites, and the conspicuously inefficient.

After this necessary orientation the case officer starts operations in earnest. He maps out a plan for achieving wateright "security" at the plant, theater, or the group of city blocks where he is officiating. The plans must be checked and approved by his superior, whose job it is, *inter alia,* to watch the case officer as closely as he himself watches others. Although he is stated to be concerned only with security matters and protection from "anti-Soviet" elements, in practice the State Security case officer is a kind of glorified management consultant.

His view of management problems, however, is not to be found in any economics textbook. To the Chekist inefficiency is the same as criminality, and criminality, by definition, is not an individual's deviation, but automatically a political crime against the state. To a mind trained in this pattern a faulty conveyor belt is sabotage unless conclusively proved otherwise. A fire in a factory suggests the existence of smouldering "anti-Sovietism" among the workers. A meeting of painters, or engineers, or residents in the same apartment house, if not organized under official auspices, is presumed to be evidence of some organized plot. An efficient factory, on the contrary, is primarily a place in which there is no "anti-Soviet" activity.

As individuals the State Security officers are often extremely intelligent, thinking people. But as servants and products of their system they can seldom afford to let their personal reasoning processes interfere with this basic premise of their job. And they seldom do. However knowledgeable a case officer may be about, say, the problems of a factory he supervises, inefficiency still spells treason—the work of "criminals," "enemies of the people," or "double-dealers" (*dvurushniki*). There is no shadow on the wall too vague or too small to bear investigation. It is easy to see how a strong-minded senior case officer could make himself the virtual operating director of almost any Soviet institution.

Most case officers maintain some form of operational "cover." The chief of the factory personnel section or his deputy, the head of the employment office, chief of the guards, or assistant directors *ad infinitum*—in almost any Soviet installation one of these people is bound to be a case officer of the KGB. As with a State Security official working in a foreign country ostensibly as a Soviet diplomat, the case officer keeps up the appearance of his "cover" and does the work involved. (His "cover" salary he generally pays back to the State Security. This is no great hardship since his normal pay as a KGB officer is invariably much higher.)

"The finer the net," one-time State Security Minister Vsevelod N. Merkulov used to say (before his own execution in 1953), "the more fish are caught." Operating on this principle, the case officer tightens his investigative mesh around anyone to whom the slightest suspicion attaches. Gossip is enough to start a complicated investigation. No specific crime or utterance need be alleged. If there is suspicion even of "counter-revolutionary" *tendencies* against a person, it is enough to start the wheels of the State Security turning.

The case officer must also probe the general mood of the people in his charge. He is, in fact, held responsible for it. Special reports must be made within a week or two about popular reception of any new directive. If Moscow, for example, abolishes the machine tractor stations, Moscow wants and receives a detailed account of the cheers, grumbling, or various half-submerged emotions with which the populace of the workers' paradise greeted this improvement. These reports are always frank and factual, very different from the propaganda that bases itself on them.

Besides his round-the-clock work in his own area the case officer has to handle the routine investigation checks which Moscow and his own provincial headquarters are constantly demanding for reasons which are seldom explained to him. The wife of Engineer Pavlov, for example, may be under investigation because her brother, at the other end of the country, has delivered himself of some unguarded régime criticism at a workers' bar. Technician

Mikhailov may be suspected of black-marketeering in another city. Writer Aleksandrov may have demonstrated "anti-Soviet" tendencies in a script he has written for a local play.

However varied the possible "crimes," they are all judged in the darkness of one great overriding suspicion. The régime prefers to deny the existence of individual misdeeds of a political nature. Everyone is presumed to be linked with someone else in a conspiracy. In Soviet security parlance one bad apple spoils the barrel, because the presence of one argues the existence of accomplices. The fact that an "anti-Soviet" person may indeed be a loner seldom disturbs the case officer. He knows from experience that the least he can do to satisfy both his local bosses and Moscow is to produce other "crimes" of a similiar nature, connect them in at least a vaguely related conspiracy, and deliver the completed package on Moscow's desk, ready for the appropriate punishment.

By Soviet logic there is no such thing as a simple "anti-Soviet" act. If a man has been saying things against the state, the State Security reasons, others have necessarily been listening to him. If another person hears any "anti-Soviet" propaganda and does not forthwith denounce it he is therefore automatically considered a "sympathizer" with the original culprit. There was a popular joke about this which made the rounds of the State Security offices in Moscow in Deriabin's time. Two men met in a prison exercise yard. "What are you here for?" asked the first. "I told an anti-Soviet joke," was the reply. "What are *you* here for?" "Ah," sighed the other, "when I heard this joke, I smiled."

Once the case officer decides to put Aleksandrov's deficiency or Mikhailov's misdemeanor on paper it is virtually impossible for him to turn back. Case officers are judged more on the quantity of cases under investigation than on the seriousness of the crime. So the average case officer inevitably finds himself acting out a sinister parallel to the storied American traffic cop who has to fill his ticket quota for the month, whether the cars in the block are illegally parked or not. The checks and counter-checks involved in the real investigation are formidable.[2] (An average report on one man's local activities can easily run to a hundred closely-typed pages.) But, barring rare cases, higher authority needs only decide what degree of guilt should be established and whether or not, at this particular time, formal prosecution would serve the best interests of the state. The question of guilt or innocence has long since been rendered academic.

In the Soviet Union today there are thousands of case officers who continue to work with the zeal of missionaries and the precision of bank clerks. They are the operators of this real-life Ministry of Fear[3] but not its immediate agents and suppliers. For, to control the people of the Soviet Union, the State Security relies, ironically but very naturally, on the people themselves.

Each case officer has between five and ten agents working for him, people who for a variety of reasons are dependent for their careers, if not their very lives, on the efficiency with which they spy on their fellow citizens. Roughly eight percent of the Soviet population has acted at one time or another as an agent or an informer. Agents, of course, represent a far lower form of fauna than the regular officers of the State Security, but their ubiquity and anonymity are the sinews of the police system. Every worker at a factory may know that the deputy director of personnel is an officer of the State Security. No worker, or anyone in Soviet society, has any assurance, ever, that the man next to him, the woman, or the child might not be the case officer's trusted confidential agent.

The Soviet Union is the only society in the world where the position of the informer is established by law and dignified by tradition. Every Soviet schoolboy is brought up on the story of "heroic" young Pavlik Morozov. In actual life he was a boy of ten who lived in the Urals during the famine of 1932. He overheard his father, uncle, and others discussing how to keep their grain from the government's

---

[2] See Appendix I for a sample case development.

[3] With apologies to Graham Greene for borrowing the title of his famous thriller, in which the Ministry happened to be Nazi in its coloration.

forced levies at a time when Moscow was exacting such heavy levies of grain as to force millions of families into destitution and famine. A good Young Pioneer, Pavlik reported his parent's crime to the local authorities. When the farmers found out about his spying his uncle killed him. The Soviet police, of course, killed his uncle and many others in retaliation, and Pavlik's name passed into the history books. Deriabin often recalled his example in the course of his own exhortations. It has been canonized in Communist youth groups as an example of the citizen's duty toward the state.

The obligation to "denounce" every instance of conceivable "anti-Soviet" activity is laid upon every citizen of the Soviet Union. Not to denounce is legally a crime. This theory is responsible for the continual propanda that "the whole nation is helping the organs of state security in their work." If the denunciations nowadays are not so strident or obvious as they were in earlier times, it is partly due to the greater efficiency of the machinery coordinating them.

The State Security, as befits its corporate sophistication, has long realized that the "inspiration" of Pavlik Morozov, even when backed by legal sanction, is hardly enough to warp natural human instincts by making a man an informer against the fancied crimes of his neighbors. A certain number of its agents *are* recruited on "ideological" grounds. All of the twenty-seven million members of the Communist Party and the Komsomol are presumed to be available for agent work and are often used in this capacity. Ordinary non-Party Soviet citizens, notably in the armed forces, are sometimes sucked into the State Security's vacuum cleaner by an appeal to their patriotism, particularly in cases where a man's proximity to a suspect makes him a valuable adjunct to KGB investigation. (In cases like this, as every Soviet citizen knows, it is not wise to decline the KGB's invitation.) But in general the most valuable agents are people who are compromised themselves. Few of them are very fond of their work.

This sort of recruitment is basically blackmail, and blackmail from which there is no appeal. The agent concerned may, and usually does, hate the régime; but he realizes that not only his own safety but the safety of his family depends on his doing the State Security's bidding. The

most valuable agents, as Deriabin encountered them, were
people hopelessly compromised either by their social origins, e.g. a woman's grandfather might have been a landowning *kulak* or a Czarist official, or by their past connections, e.g. a man's brother might have served against the
Soviet Union with the Vlasov Army in World War II. Here
the individual's choice narrows down to the KGB's favorite
set of alternatives: either the agent cooperates, or he goes
to jail.

Then there are the agents who knowingly or not compromise themselves. When Deriabin was in Moscow he ran
across the case of three students at the Moscow Institute of
Foreign Languages,[4] avid scholars in English. To further
their education they continually bought English-language
books and, when they could get them, copies of the U.S.
Russian-language magazine, *Amerika.* More seriously all
three of them had carried scholarly curiosity to the danger
point of trying to meet Englishmen and Americans in Moscow.

This was more than enough evidence to start any case
officer reaching for his preliminary investigation form.
But it was not yet good enough to make a real case. It is
one of the peculiarities of the Ministry of Fear, part of the
vestigial remnants of human responsibility in the Soviet
state, that the tissue of lies and half-truths must be woven
around a certain amount of valid testimony, or statements
from witnesses that at least appear valid, when the reports
are finally written. In the case of the three students the
case officer had nothing but a few surveillance reports that
they had been seen in the company of unidentified Americans. The three kept to themselves at the language school
and never talked about their meetings. So he badly needed
an informer.

He got his informer after looking over the investigation
reports on the three students themselves. Two of them had
unexceptionable records. The third, however, was vulnera-
ble, because he had used the desperate lie. On his school
entrance reports he had hidden the fact that his parents
were deported as *kulaks* to the Arkhangelsk Oblast in

---

[4] Not to be confused with the Leningrad institute of the
same name, which is a KGB institution.

1930. His brother, furthermore, had worked for the German police during the German occupation of eastern Russia in World War II; he was imprisoned and later died in a Soviet labor camp. It was understandable for the student to gloss over these "errors" in his Soviet background. To acknowledge either of them would have barred him from any university in the Soviet Union. But now he was trapped with them forever.

The chief of operations in the bureau concerned had the third student in for a visit. He asked him, in the usual friendly way, if he wanted to collaborate with the KGB. When the student refused—in itself a rare act of courage in a Soviet citizen—he was threatened with immediate exposure and denunciation of his false answers, to say nothing of arrest for his known contacts with foreigners. So he agreed. To save his career and what was left of his family, he began to spy regularly on the movements of his two friends, who would, in the fullness of time, be arrested. For the rest of his life he was doomed to be an agent of the State Security, his own safety dependent on some case officer's whims and a typewritten file of thirty closely-written pages.

A similiar squeeze play was used in 1950 on a fourteen-year-old girl, the daughter of a returned POW who lived at Dimitrov, near Moscow. She was approached by a State Security officer who suggested that she might like to tell the government about her father's conversations concerning his captivity in Germany, his thoughts on the West, the Soviet Union, etc. Such information, the agent explained, was only a part of the girl's simple duty toward the Soviet Union, already familiar to her through her membership in the Pioneer youth groups. The girl demurred for a time. She loved her father and wanted assurance that her reports would not be harmful to him. No one can be quite so reassuring as a State Security officer trying to pad his case file. "There is nothing to worry about," he told her. "By reporting what your father says, you will actually be helping him. He may have picked up confused notions when he was away from the Soviet Union. We want to straighten them out, to clear up any difficulties he may have getting adjusted to life back home." She began to inform on her father. The State Security people in Dimitrov thus acquired a reliable informer and a file on a new suspect, which grew heavier with the passage of time.

After he became a case officer, either in his own experience or through the files to which he had access, Peter Deriabin saw this little private scene of denunciation and recruitment played out thousands of times, on every conceivable kind of stage. A physician in Kiev had maintained a correspondence with relatives who were living in France, in which he had written some uncomplimentary things about the Soviet régime. Mail censorship picked up this lapse. He was confronted, accused of being an agent for a foreign "anti-Soviet" organization, and recruited as an alternative to going to prison. A soldier working in the library of a Soviet regiment was offered a chance at officer's school if he became an agent. When he refused he was faced with demotion and transfer to a rifle company. He joined the force.

Agent networks, thus formed, fester in every corner of Soviet society and in a huge variety of missions and responsibilities. Despite the casual approaches made to them, they are most carefully selected. The State Security recruits a simple informant with the flattering attention of a ballerina being selected for a role at the Bolshoi Theater. Certain classes of people, from the nature of their jobs, make better agents than others: bookkeepers, for example, personnel clerks, guards, and foremen. Some job categories, like those of janitor, house manager, passport clerk, or manager of a workers' dormitory imply by their nature a degree of State Security affiliation. But almost anyone is eligible for these fringe memberships in the world's most unpleasant club, as long as he is useful. Once a person is recruited his reliability is insisted on. Early in his days at counter-intelligence school Deriabin learned to stress one of the State Security's best-enforced working rules: "The agent answers with his neck."

When an agent is recruited and gives information he is paid. In Siberia, Deriabin paid his best agents an average of 150 rubles a month, depending on the information they gave him. A top-notch agent may receive as much as 1000 rubles monthly. The payment may be in money or in scarce goods, but some sort of payment is always made. The State Security is not content to rely solely on the bonds either of fear or ideology.

The money is distributed in a way that will avoid suspicion. Sometimes it comes in the form of presents on a person's birthday or special occasions, or a badly needed family vacation trip. But such gratuities are always accounted for. An agent signs for everything he receives, noting the date, the amount, and the type of payment. Another link in his chain. Even a token payment, suitably receipted, is enough to compromise him forever.

Agent security inside the Soviet Union is as strictly regulated as it is in foreign intelligence operations. Each agent receives a code name and a definite set of instructions. He meets the case officer only in situations where it might be normal for him to appear and at times of mutual convenience, generally after work. At their meetings the basic security precautions are always followed. The case officer will have a record player or a radio going to preclude any listening by the neighbors. He and the agent will always enter separately. The meetings are held as seldom as possible and as briefly. Generally they take place in the "safe houses" of the State Security, respectable apartments (if possible, fitted with two entrances) in neighborhoods that comport with the social and economic standing of the agent or, at least, of the case officer's cover.

Very little of this agent activity ever breaks surface. In the purge days of the thirties and the wartime forties the State Security worked with bloody hands in public. Few people could even visit the Soviet Union without some of the Ministry of Fear's operations rubbing off on their consciousness. But through the fifties, the operation has grown smoother and subtler. Arrests are still made, invariably at night, and the forced labor camps receive their cargoes of prisoners. But there are fewer arrests even since Deriabin was there, and some of the camps have been closed. A system that operates so well seldom needs any longer to flex its muscles in public, and it can afford to make concessions to the modestly expressed discontent of the Soviet populace with their restrictions. It is enough that the Soviet people know constantly that they are being watched, without ever being sure who is doing the watching.

There is a story long current in Moscow about two men, friends from childhood and near neighbors, who were talking alone one day. Almost without thinking they began to discuss politics. They were sitting on a park bench with no one anywhere near them. Suddenly the conversation ceased. "We'd better stop this political talk now," one said, "how do we know that someone among us is not an agent?"

CHAPTER VI

Surveillance In Siberia

IF THE DAILY round of a Soviet case officer is strewn with broken careers, wrecked lives, and the aborted hopes of his fellow citizens, it is no bed of roses for the case officer himself. In May 1946, Peter Deriabin married Tanya Zakharova, the girl whom he had begun courting the moment he returned to Siberia in 1946 from his first tour of duty as a State Security officer. She was a high-strung girl, spirited and contentious, whose normal questioning disposition was not improved by moving into a "safe house" in Barnaul. The safe-house existence, however, was by then an accepted convention in the State Security. What could be more secure than to have the place of rendezvous between agents and case officers established as the residence of a trusted case officer in the local State Security bureau and his family?

Tanya understandably chafed at the safe-house existence, although Deriabin did not mind it, and there were occasional scenes. Deriabin was highly enough regarded by the provincial State Security bosses, however, so that they chose to overlook this obvious gap in his conformity pattern. He was immediately appointed chief of the surveillance group in the Barnaul headquarters.

There were times when a State Security officer's position enabled him to act, if he chose, as a small-scale force for good and justice in Soviet society. Hungry relatives could be fed and helped to a decent job or a better education. Very few factory managers in the Soviet Union have been known to turn down the friendly request of a man who showed his State Security identity card. A local profiteer could be brought to justice and crooked dealings exposed without the need for complicated legal proof just by the fact of a State Security man interesting himself in a case. In a sense, the State Security officer is the Soviet family's counterpart of the rich uncle in capitalist society, although the riches he can hand out are less permanent, and his caution about helping either friends or relatives is immeasurably greater. It is very risky for a man to stick his neck out in Soviet society. Even a State Security officer is never really sure what hand might be holding the ax.

Barnaul, like Biysk, is one of those big little cities where everyone seems to know everyone else, and his brother. His very familiarity with the place more than negated the help that Deriabin, through his position, was able to give to his family and friends. Not long after he had returned to duty, his superior, Lieutenant Colonel Kalentyev, called him into his office for an admonitory chat. "Why are you going around with that fellow Pechenkin?" he asked. Pechenkin, as it turned out, was one of Deriabin's best friends. In the war they had served together in the same regiment. They kept up contact later in Barnaul after Pechenkin had been invalided home with an incapacitating nerve injury in his leg. Pechenkin was an interesting, well-educated man with a fondness for barroom controversy, and Deriabin enjoyed having an evening drink with him. Now, barely twelve hours after he had left his friend at a Barnaul tavern, he found himself looking at Pechenkin's file in the State Security office. The charge was plain: "anti-Soviet activity" in the form of public criticism of the government and government officials.

Deriabin thanked his boss for the warning, explained the association, and left. The next time he saw Pechenkin he gave him a warning in turn. "You shouldn't talk so much," he said. "I understand and I thank you," Pechenkin replied, "but I can't keep these thoughts to myself. Why do the leaders of the Soviet Union shut themselves up in the Kremlin and do nothing for us down here? Why can't we talk to them? What's so sacred about the Central Committee? I have heard that in the United States any man can go up and see the President if he wants to. Why don't these men listen to us?" Deriabin nodded in a vague gesture of sympathy. Occasionally similar thoughts occurred to him, but he entertained them very, very privately. He crossed Pechenkin off his social list.

Living for months on end in the same provincial town, a man can hardly avoid such incidents. Since the local office was a small one Deriabin's access to the files was extensive. He would see a familiar face on the street, perhaps exchange a greeting, and in the same split second recall that the face was connected to a file number in the State Security archives. Thanks to the office's efficiency, few people who were under investigation knew about it.

His wife's health was poor, and her doctor recommended that she do some part-time teaching in a "forest school" outside the city just to get some air and sunshine. The school was designed for sick or physically handicapped children, and Tanya grew very interested in rehabilitation work with them. She was particularly fond of one little boy, a very bright student who was handicapped by a case of tuberculosis long uncared for. She mentioned the boy to Deriabin one evening, telling him how much she felt he deserved a decent chance in the world. He thought the name sounded familiar, but could not just then identify it. The next morning he looked over his surveillance files in the office. The name was there. The bright child's father was a man whom Deriabin's men had been investigating for the past three weeks. He was not prominent, just a mechanic in an automobile factory whose misfortune was to have made a few slighting remarks about the régime while drunk. He was on his way to being classified "anti-Soviet," with predictable ugly consequences for every member of his family.

As chief of the surveillance group, Deriabin had charge of the primitive but vital activity known best to American detective story readers as "casing," "shadowing," or "tailing." The Russians have their own name for specialists in the surveillance business. Topol'shchiki, "the footsloggers," they were called.

The basic patterns of surveillance which he learned and applied in Barnaul remained the same as long as Deriabin was in the State Security. The Soviet State Security is in a technical way the most conservative of institutions. Established practices are as permanent and systematized as the floor etiquette in the New York Stock Exchange. There is an official bureau in charge of this activity, called the Directorate of Surveillance and Special Checking, which supervises major cases.

Surveillance personnel are organized in special ranks, whose translations would make Lord Baden-Powell turn over in his grave: Junior Scout, Scout Second Class, Scout First Class, Senior Scout Shiftleader, etc., up to the heads of sections and divisions. All of them are officers, and most are at present graduates of special surveillance schools, the courses at which last from three to six months.

The surveillance arm of the service seldom wastes any elbow grease on chance suspects. It is reserved for people against whom some specific evidence has accumulated, i.e. anything from participation in a suspected ring of foreign agents to a casual but established criticism of the government in public. It is generally used, also, when other means of detection have proved insufficient.

The "scouts" are equipped with all the conceivably useful tools of their trade. Each surveillance group headquarters contains wardrobes fully stocked with everything from generals' uniforms to workers' overalls. Disguises are constantly used, including special clothes with a double set of outside clothing, e.g. reversible overcoats and even reversible suits. A favorite item of scout equipment is the brief case or grocery bag that turns into a topcoat or umbrella through a judicious rearrangement of the snaps or buttons. There are also built-in cameras, concealed binoculars, and similar devices. Surveillance is one part of modern intelligence where the old E. Phillips Oppenheim props are still in service.

Deriabin took over the surveillance detachment in Barnaul without benefit of special training beyond what he had learned at the Higher Counter-Intelligence School, but he had little difficulty in mastering the state of the art. The "footsloggers" were organized loosely and, by comparison with other branches of the KGB, most covertly. All of the personnel lived in safe houses from which they made their rounds. They assumed various permanent cover positions, although they would rarely be found at them. (Deriabin's cover was a job in the city Communist Party.) The scouts never wore uniforms and made every effort to hide their connection with the State Security.

Each day the surveillance group would receive a fresh list of names and instructions from KGB headquarters. The amount of watching on a person would vary. One man might need attention from 7 A.M. until nightfall. Another would require watching around the clock. In any case, the officer doing the surveillance was responsible for the most minute kind of information about his subject's comings and goings. This demanded detailed observation of his habits: the places he went, his visitors, his exact route from home to the office and back, etc.

No mention was ever made of the reason for surveillance, the crimes for which a man was under suspicion, or his eventual disposition, although Deriabin himself was often privy to this information. The responsibility of the working surveillance officer began and ended with his watch over his subject's movements. Even the names of the subjects were codified for operational purposes. A worker at a factory, known for his dirty habits, for example, would be called for operational purposes *Gryazhniy;* literally, the Dirty One. The Dirty One would have his name affixed to the most minute record of his movements day after day, week after week, until the surveillance was declared finished, without the scouts knowing anything beyond their direct observations. Subjects were seldom put under surveillance for longer than a month. The periods ranged from a week to a month, depending on the importance and complexity of the case.

Every day in the Altai Kray, a province with a population of over two million, roughly one thousand people were being followed in this sort of investigation. There were about ten from each local *rayon* who were constantly objects of suspicion (naturally they changed as cases were added and disposed of). In a city like Barnaul, with a population of about two hundred thousand, there was a round figure of several hundred cases constantly receiving action at the State Security headquarters. The reason for this was very clear by Soviet standards. During the forced deportations within the Soviet Union before and after World War II, a number of suspect nationalities had been sent en

masse to Siberia. As a result, there were in Barnaul dispro-
portionate numbers of Poles, Volga Germans, Lithuanians,
Latvians, Estonians, or people otherwise foreign to the region. All this required redoubled vigilance on the part of
the security forces, since every non-Russian is considered a
potential threat to the state.

Only a few of these people were kept under surveillance
at any given time. Deriabin's staff comprised only six officers. For some, however, special treatment was accorded.
In the 1940s, before Deriabin arrived in Barnaul, the Polish official Oscar Lange, now head of the Polish Economic
Council and a veteran Communist fellow traveler, arrived,
as the representative of the Lublin government, on an official visit to the Poles who had been fraternally deported to
the region. The State Security gave Lange the full VIP
treatment, including a massive state banquet on his arrival.
At the banquet he obliged his hosts by getting gloriously
drunk. The security men saw to it that he remained in this
state for the two days of his stay. During his "inspection
tour" Lange was constantly escorted by a flock of State
Security officers. There is no doubt that he saw very little
of the true conditions among Poles in that area, privations
which he probably did not wish to investigate in the first
place.

The Altai Kray is a frontier region. Soviet officials,
given the chance to operate there with what amounted to a
clean slate, did their best to see that very few heritages
from former days were allowed to develop. Religion was a
case in point. The established Orthodox Church in the Soviet Union, generally speaking, is under the control of the
KGB. Most of the priests permitted in its parish churches
are put in unavoidably close contact with local State Security officers who, wherever possible, exploit their religious
prestige to get information about their parishioners. The
priest in Barnaul, for example, was a regularly-used agent
of the State Security's Religious Affairs officer there, one
Captain Gavrilov, who visited him every day at the beginning of his rounds. The religionists the State Security was
most concerned about were the nonconformist "fringe"
sects, like the Doukhobors, the Old Believers, or pious Orthodox folk of the so-called "underground" church, who

were not members of any of the official parishes but wanted to organize some. Whenever a person gathered a few fellow believers in his home it was *prima facie* grounds for State Security suspicion.

In December 1946, in Kamen, in the north of the Altai Kray, one Doukhobor was found to have helped his son evade military service. The State Security officials used this as an excuse in asking the Communist Party head of the area for permission to make a dragnet search of the particularly pious who showed a bent for organization. About thirty State Security officers converged on Kamen on a given day and made an extensive sweep-up of nonconformist believers. The operation was carried out, as are most such plans, in the dead of night. About thirteen souls were pulled in, most of them poor, shabby, but exceedingly fervent people who had been in their way the nucleus for possible groups of independent religious believers.

To a less thorough investigative organization a handful of religious people in a provincial town would hardly seem to pose a security threat. Yet the State Security saw any such development as a danger sign. A group of people talking about church would inevitably recall the old days when churches were more frequent and funerals and baptisms were commonplaces. The talk might then develop into protests about economic conditions, again with invidious comparisons between the present and the past. The only end of this kind of conversation, in the State Security's eyes, was "anti-Sovietism." After the religious operation in Kamen it was believed that any dangerous piety in the area was, for the time at least, securely curbed. Kamen, it must be remembered, was a town of only forty thousand people. When the number of such drives throughout the Soviet Union is totalled, the constant war on free religious thought shows up in perspective.

Deriabin took part in few such round-ups during his brief career as a provincial State Security officer, probably owing to his responsibilities as the local surveillance officer. But his cover as a member of the city Communist Party organization gave him the dubious fortune of assisting as a "juryman" at Soviet civil trials. The State Security trials themselves, those many-headed prosecutions under the all-embracing Article 58 of the old Soviet criminal code[1] are nominally conducted under the authority of the local public prosecutor; they are of course run off independent of any outside authority. (It would be a millennial occurrence in the Soviet Union if any prosecutor were to challenge a detail of a State Security "legal" proceeding.) Public trials of important criminal cases, however, generally warrant some representation from the State Security. Usually the State Security man, along with the representatives of the Party, Komsomol, or official trade unions, is seated with the judge in a trial board which still bears the name of "jury."

Since the Soviet legal system is part of a punitive rather than a judicial process, the concept of law in the traditional Western sense does not exist.[2] If a Soviet lawyer, for example, defends a client successfully or even too forcefully, he is immediately open to censure as an "enemy of the state." The censure may not come directly. But a critical article in the local Party newspaper or Party disciplinary action against the lawyer is as effective as any formal denunciation. With Soviet judges the situation is exactly the same. The accused must be regarded not as a man who has injured or offended another individual or group. By the very fact that he has disturbed public order or is declared to have disturbed public order, he is identified as a political enemy.

In December 1946, Deriabin was sitting as a "juryman" in a trial of three young factory workers (the oldest was eighteen) who had been caught absent without leave from their place of work in Barnaul. They had been gone only forty-eight hours when the militia, i.e. the civil police, caught up with them. The boys' only defense was need. At the factory they had not been adequately fed or housed. One did not have a pair of shoes. Another had literally not eaten for two days.

When the judge and jurymen retired to his chambers for

---

[1] For the Russian Soviet Federated Socialist Republic, that is. In the legislation of the other republics the article is given varying numbers—but it is always present. See note on p. 71.

[2] See Appendix III on current Soviet legal procedure.

discussion the judge estimated that five years would be an adequate sentence. Deriabin asked if the sentence could not be reduced to two or three years. It was not a very grave offense, he argued. Another official present suggested that the boys be set free. All of them agreed, he noted, that conditions at the factory were extremely poor. "Do you have your Party card with you?" the judge asked him. "Yes," he said. "Do you want to lose it by voting for a decision like this?" his honor added. There was no further argument.

When Deriabin again observed that the factory was at fault for bad housing conditions the judge explained the real necessity for giving the maximum sentence. He had talked the case over the day before with the director of the factory, and his summation was cold-blooded but to the point. "If you free them," Comrade Director had pointed out, "tomorrow I'll have nobody left working in the whole factory."

Factory conditions in most areas of the Soviet Union have improved since that time. But, as Deriabin found out time and time again in Moscow, the cold pragmatism behind the judge's stiff sentence remains the fundamental philosophy of Soviet "law."

Deriabin had not been a full year in his job at Barnaul when his wife Tanya died of pleurisy. Her death acted as a catalyst in confirming his decision to leave the Altai Kray. It had grown no pleasanter with the passage of time to operate as a ground-level State Security officer in his home province. Although he had seen enough of his organization's workings to sicken him occasionally, he knew now that there was little practical chance of leaving it. More precisely he knew that there was no chance of leaving the State Security and retaining any hope for a promising career in the Soviet Union and the money and prestige that go with it.

Every responsible Soviet official is aware to some extent of the lies he speaks and lives in the course of his daily work. Deriabin knew something of the lie even before the war, when he gave his rote lectures in Party history to students who knew no other. He was painfully conscious that a political officer had looked ridiculous trying to justify the glorious political and humanitarian goals of Communism to men fighting without air cover on the Stalingrad perimeter. He had watched the State Security files tell lies about their victims and helped judges give lying decisions about accused men. All of these things were affronts to his individual conscience. But what seems an outright lie to a historian or a detached observer can look little worse than an irritating discrepancy between future goals and immediate circumstances to a man living in the midst of a system that appears fixed, necessary, and inevitable. Needless to say, Deriabin saw no way to change the system by himself. And it is doubtful if at that time he even entertained the thought that life in the U.S.S.R. or elsewhere could be qualitatively cleaner.

The Marxist scriptures could still give him passing justification for a life of lying if it were lived in the service of the Soviet state. He knew no other. If the die were cast, he figured, it was far better to go on with the lie in Moscow, at the center of things, than remain in the provinces. He asked for a Moscow assignment through channels, but was refused. So, telling what by comparison to most of his State Security activities was barely a white lie, he next requested a few weeks' leave in the Caucasus. This was granted. The Caucasus rest hotels are not wildly popular in the month of January, so he was able to get his accommodations promised. On the way to the Caucasus he stopped over at Moscow.

Deriabin went directly from the Yaroslavsky railroad station to State Security headquarters at Dzerzhinsky Square. There he dropped in on an old wartime friend who was then an assistant to Major General Svinelupov, the Deputy Minister of the State Security. He explained his problem. His friend, the General's assistant, was sympathetic and pulled a few loose strings. Whereupon Moscow asked Barnaul for Deriabin's file and ordered him transferred to State Security headquarters.

He arranged to leave his little sister, Valya, with an aunt and uncle, who could give her a far more stable home than a widower brother. He left her most of his own household possessions, cleared up his remaining office details, and prepared to leave a second time for Moscow.

It took him five days to make the 2000-mile train trip between Barnaul and Moscow. The first leg and the simplest was the four-hour trip to Novosibirsk to make connections with the main line of the trans-Siberian. At Novosibirsk Deriabin ran into potential complications. He found a sight which is still occasionally encountered in the Soviet Union, but which in 1947 was an oppressive and inescapable fact of life: long queues of travelers camped on the station platform and inside the terminal, waiting hours and, in some cases, days for their tickets.

He hesitated around the queues just long enough to seek out the office of the railroad branch of the local State Security, where his pass and a few exchanged comments were enough to get him a place on the next Moscow train. He used his influence to get space also for a chance companion, an attractive blonde girl whom he had met at the station. He knew her from Barnaul, where she ran a sort of tea trolley at the State Security offices. She was on her way to Kaluga, south of Moscow, where her husband was serving a twelve-year prison sentence in a labor camp, for what she did not say. A wife visiting her husband in prison was a common enough occurrence, and he presumed from the very fact of her State Security employment that he was jailed on a criminal, not a political, charge. Politically safe and personable, she made a pleasant companion for the long hours rattling past the wooden villages and the wet winter countryside.

Other companions intruded from time to time to share Deriabin's large supply of vodka, ham, bread, and herrings bought at successive station platforms; but as the train went by the long-established way stations—Omsk and Sverdlovsk on the plain, then over the Urals to Molotov, Kirov, and Moscow—Deriabin could not help pondering on the odd linkage of events responsible for his trip. There were two things he was sure of. If the war had not come he would still be teaching happily at the high school in Fominskoye. The other was that, once uprooted, he now knew he could not possibly live this sort of life again. Except for an urgent home leave several years later, he never went back to Barnaul.

CHAPTER VII

The Shape Of Terror

PETER DERIABIN SPENT six years at State Security headquarters in Moscow. In that time, as an officer both in the Guard Directorate of the Kremlin and the operational branches of foreign intelligence, he had a unique opportunity to familiarize himself with the organization as well as the workings of the State Security. The nature and importance of his work, to say nothing of the function of the organization itself, would be hard to comprehend without some explanation of how this complicated mechanism is organized. For, if the beast has many faces and constantly changing shapes, the basic features of its corporate anatomy are well formed, hardened by precocious evolution.

The KGB, although far more powerful than any of the regularly constituted Soviet ministries, was publicly reduced to the status of a committee in 1954. This was intended to demonstrate that the Chekists were retracting their claws in the new atmosphere of post-Stalin democracy. The demonstration was a painless one from the régime's point of view, and it meant nothing more than a slight change of titles. The chief of the KGB has all the rights and prerogatives of a Minister: his committee is organized on a ministerial level, exactly like the formally named ministerial organizations.

The State Security is organized the way it operates: as a self-contained unit. It has its own supply corps and service personnel equipped to furnish everything from winter over-

coats to call girls, the bulk of these services concentrated in
the Moscow Guard Directorate. It can provide with equal
ease jails, troops, electronic technicians, translators, actors,
legal specialists, or medical services. It has been called a
state within a state.

This last statement is almost true, but not quite. The
Communist Party government of the Soviet Union, as it is
organized, depends too intimately on the State Security to
permit it a separate existence. The frightening power of
this police organ at the time of the *Yezhovshchina* forever
determined that its authority be split in the future between
two organizations. The present MVD—whose widely varied functions include the civil police power, the custody of
war prisoners and the government archives, map-making,
chemical-warfare defense, and control of the U.S.S.R.'s
hoard of precious metals—has just enough investigative and
punitive power of its own to preclude the State Security
(KGB) from operating as a complete law unto itself, capable of toppling Communist leaders as surely as the Prae-
torian Guard once overturned Roman emperors.[1]

The degree of the State Security's autonomy and comprehensiveness is nonetheless impressive. For it must parallel within itself all the functions and phases of the society it
watches.

The State Security has local directorates in every republic of the Soviet Union. These branches in turn control individual KGB networks down through *oblast, kray,* and
rayon compartments, ending with the local case officer in
his small dark kingdom of a town, a factory, or several
city blocks. It is part of the interlocking puzzle of Soviet
authority that all these provincial KGB organizations are
responsible to the provincial Party committees. (Occasionally they are disguised by incorporation within the Party
committee.) But since the KGB leader in every province
is, to put it mildly, a key member of the Party committee,
this setup is not so dualistic as it might seem. At the same
time, the chain of command from the local KGB organizations to Moscow is held more smoothly, tightly, and efficiently than anything else in the Soviet Union.

[1] See chart in Appendix IV for a list of the MVD and KGB
functions.

All of the officers in the KGB hold military officers' ranks, although they are in no way attached to the armed services, except those in the military counter-intelligence branch. Even enlisted personnel, like chauffeurs and typists, are all noncommissioned officers of the upper grades.

The organization breaks down in this way:

(1) THE FIRST MAIN DIRECTORATE:[2] Counter-intelligence within the Soviet Union. This is the keystone of the State Security. The First Directorate has the concern of fighting the real, fancied, or conveniently fabricated operations of foreign intelligence inside the Soviet Union. This includes a variety of activity: surveillance and shadowing of foreigners; operations against spies and "foreign parachutists"; protection and surveillance of all foreign embassy personnel; a school for teaching special surveillance methods.

One of the First Directorate's busiest divisions of late has been that in charge of Intourist operations and the allied Burobin *(Tsentralkoye Buro Po Obsulzhivaniyu Inostrantsev)*, the bureau of service to foreigners. Roughly seventy percent of the Intourist guides, organizers, interpreters, and service personnel are active KGB officers or agents. Many others are former active-duty State Security officers relegated to something like a working reserve.

(2) THE SECOND MAIN DIRECTORATE: The Foreign Intelligence Directorate. This Directorate, working through its scores of legal and illegal residencies throughout the world, conducts intelligence work, spying, sabotage, and terror outside the Soviet Union. It is also heavily involved in propaganda and large-scale penetration and subversion of foreign governments.

(3) THE THIRD MAIN DIRECTORATE (THE DI-

---

[2] For the sake of convenience in enumerating the directorates we have used the numbering system in currency several years ago. The specific numbers of the directorates, however, are constantly changing. What was the Fifth Directorate in 1952 may be part of the SPU or EKU in 1959. Such changes are only bureaucratic camouflage, almost endemic in the workings of the world's most concentrically-functioning bureaucracy. The basic divisions of authority, function, and responsibility remain constant.

RECTORATE OF SPECIAL DIVISIONS): Army, Navy, and Air Force counter-intelligence. Although the members of this group operate as counter-intelligence officers of the services, their job is not so much designed to work *for* the military as *on* them. This special branch of the KGB duplicates within the armed forces the exact amount and methods of surveillance which the parent body maintains on the Soviet people at large. If anything, it is more intense.

The ever-presence of the Third Directorate's men is one of the major reasons why the Soviet Army has been so little of a factor in internal politics. Its four divisions watch separately the Army, Navy, Air Force, and the combined General Staff. They spread their network down to company level. Each regiment and separate battalion has two or three officers of counter-intelligence assigned to it, each with his own network of agents and informers. Military intelligence, as distinct from counter-intelligence, is a separate service, restricted principally to the collection of strategic or tactical military intelligence in foreign countries (see Chapter XXI).

(4) THE MAIN DIRECTORATE OF BORDER TROOPS: This organization, picturesquely initialed as the GUPVO, has the official title of *Glavnoye Upravleniye Pogranichnykh Voisk.* It has been a part of the State Security since 1948, when it was transferred from the MVD. Its job, under whatever authority, is the physical sealing of the frontiers so that nothing can pierce the vacuum of Soviet society unless by express invitation of the rulers. GUPVO has its own intelligence and counter-intelligence organs. It works in neighboring foreign countries. It is responsible, also, for counter-intelligence in the areas just inside the Soviet frontiers.

GUPVO is not to be confused with the well-trained but tiny groups of border guards in democratic countries, e.g. the U.S. Border Patrol. To hold the keys to the locked Soviet borders securely requires a military force of at least 200,000. These troops are organized in "districts" and "detachments" equipped with tanks and artillery. They also include naval and air units. Yet no GUPVO detachment is in the slighest way considered to be under Army orders. This private army operates on the frontiers of the Iron Curtain as a law unto itself.

(5) THE SECRET POLITICAL DIRECTORATE (SPU):
By its charter this organization operates against a variety
of anti-Soviet elements—counter-revolutionists, terrorists,
etc.—who conduct "anti-Party" or "anti-Soviet" activities.
In recent practice the SPU's field is rather narrow, since
the formal opposition which it originally investigated has
long since been buried, literally. Currently it amounts to
the KGB's special police force in charge of eggheads. In
the Soviet scheme of things the intelligentsia—higher bureaucrats, artists, writers, painters, scientists and such—is
one of the most useful and at the same time the most suspect branches of society. The régime needs the intellectuals
desperately to run its newspapers, operate its propaganda
machine, educate the young, and get its sputniks into orbit.
But as Deriabin was later to find out in Moscow and Vienna, no intellectual is ever really trusted without a strong
harness and blinders.

This division of the State Security thus operates as a
small shadow Ministry of Education and Culture. It also
concerns itself with any other political stirrings against the
régime, whether intellectual or not. This includes, by Soviet
definition, religious activity and any nationalist movements, real or fancied, within the Soviet republics. Take
the hypothetical[8] case of a man who lived in Azerbaijan,
went regularly to the Orthodox church, read extensively in
the works of foreign writers, and was employed by a local
Party newspaper. He would be sure to have at least four
subdivisions of the SPU counter-filing him in their archives
and preparing his case for trial.

(6) THE ECONOMIC DIRECTORATE (EKU): This is
the State Security's eye on all the operations of the Soviet
economy. The EKU covers industry as well as agriculture.
Operating on the prescribed premise that inefficiency or
failure must mean subversion, the EKU's agents are constantly scanning the records of every collective farm, every
factory, every retail trading outlet in the Soviet Union. It is
the ultimate enforcing authority behind the past Five Year
plans, as well as the present Seven Year article.

(7) TRANSPORTATION DIRECTORATE: This outfit

[8] Highly hypothetical in view of the advances in Soviet security techniques.

interests itself in everything that moves in the Soviet Union, whether by air, sea, or land. The core of the Directorate supervises the Soviet railroad system, since the exposed systems of track offer the most fertile ground for sabotage. The Directorate's men watch over the trans-Siberian railroad and the Moscow subway with equal diligence. (The latter has its own special State Security section, directly responsible to the Chairman of the KGB.)

(8) DIRECTORATE OF SURVEILLANCE AND SPECIAL CHECKING: This Directorate, as its name suggests, is a service agency for all the others. When a KGB office requests secret surveillance of any Soviet citizen (as opposed to foreigners), it sends a written request to the Surveillance Directorate. This Directorate also makes arrests and conducts searches of people under investigation for political crimes. Until 1949 each of the other directorates did its own surveillance on what might be called a freelance basis. Now all of these are consolidated for better working efficiency, except for the First Directorate's private apparatus for shadowing foreigners and the special surveillance operations of the Guard Directorate.

(9) SPECIAL SERVICE DIRECTORATE: Communications. This office provides communication code security for all top-level government bureaus as well as the KGB. In addition one of its sections controls all coding and decoding operations within the Soviet Union. The Directorate is responsible for code security between the Soviet Union and all Soviet outposts and operatives in foreign countries.

Besides concerning themselves with Soviet diplomatic and intelligence liaison, the communications experts of the KGB devise codes for the use of all foreign Communist Party leaders. (The Russian language is used in all such codes.) For this reason this section traditionally operated as a part of the Central Committee of the Communist Party in Moscow. In 1954, at the same time that the world was being told of the KGB's "down-grading" to a mere committee, this office was significantly transferred to the KGB's direct jurisdiction.

As if the communications people did not have enough to handle, they have charge of radio intelligence, which involves them in the work of breaking or attempting to break foreign codes. They are also responsible for a large network of tracking stations designed to locate any illegal transmission activity within the U.S.S.R.

(10) SPECIAL INVESTIGATIONS OFFICE: This agency handles the investigation of especially important cases, notably those dealing with major espionage or "counter-revolutionary" plots against the government.

(11) DIRECTORATE IN CHARGE OF GOVERNMENT SECURITY: The Guard Directorate. This organization is responsible for the security of members and candidates of the Praesidium of the Central Committe of the Soviet Communist Party. It is heavily staffed. It is not uncommon for a high Party official to enjoy the services of from eighty to one hundred of its high-ranking employees. It supervises security at all government functions and handles important state visitors. As might be expected, the members of the Guard Directorate are more heavily checked and double-checked than any personnel in the Soviet Union.

(12) SECTION "K": Atomic Energy. This group has absolute security control of all nuclear and thermonuclear enterprises in the Soviet Union, military or civilian. It handles security screening of all atomic energy personnel.

Besides these twelve big compartments the KGB also has its administrative divisions, personnel office, schools divisions, including the regional State Security schools, the Higher School of Investigation, and the Higher State Security School of the U.S.S.R., an institution ironically but conveniently given the standing of a university law school.

There are six special support branches. The First Special Section is in charge of files, archives, and the essential card indexes without which the KGB would be more than half crippled. The other sections cover special technical, radio, and censorship departments, wire-tapping, and the manufacture of false documents. There are two separate divisions for communications between KGB installations and communications within the Kremlin.[4]

The sober compartmentation of the State Security, as orderly in arrangement as a bookkeeper's ledger, makes an odd contrast with its continuing principal functions of coer-

---

[4] There is also a prison section in charge of the few prisons under KGB control, which are used for current investigations.

cion and terror. its organization charts could look no weirder if George Orwell and Franz Kafka had planned them together when they were writing *1984* and *The Castle*. As a final demonstration, perhaps, of its own bureaucratic tidiness, the State Security fields its own footbal team. The Dynamo Sports Union of Moscow, which has periodically sent its teams touring Europe and Great Britain, is firmly sponsored by the KGB. One of its deputy chairmen is always the honorary head of the Dynamo club and all its members are officers or noncoms from either the KGB or the MVD.

The Dynamo team is composed principally of officers from the Guard Directorate and the Surveillance Directorate (the latter possibly selected for the ease with which they keep track of opponents on the field). They are free from regular duties as long as they play well. Good players, in fact, are often sought out to receive a bizarre kind of athletic scholarship in the organization. After a winning international tour their rewards are lavish. In the past they have included new cars, cash gifts, and new apartments.

On the day of a Dynamo match the KGB offices empty early, and a heavy percentage of their occupants head for the stadium. Rivalry among the Moscow fans is acute. The crowd's universal favorite is the Red Army team, and Dynamo, as can be imagined, is generally disliked. In moments of excitement hostile Moscow fans jeer, *"lyagavye, lyagavye . . .* (bird dogs)."* It is a consciously fitting epithet, and the crowds make the most of it at a football game. It is perhaps the only occasion in a Soviet citizen's life when he can talk back to the State Security and get away with it.

The effect of the State Security's close-grained organization is to produce something like a huge corporate microscope dedicated, like all good microscopes, to examining the successive secrets of thousands and thousands of cells. Its efficiency in so doing directly relates to the personal hatred which a Soviet football fan can put into the world *lyagavye* when he yells at the Dynamo players in Moscow. For the State Security exists in a state of undeclared war against every individual in the Soviet Union. When it is outwardly inactive, as during the later "Thaw" period after the deaths of Stalin and Beria, it is busy accumulating and sifting the questionnaires and cross-checks that furnish the starting ammunition whenever it is called on to declare its brand of war on any single person or group.

In the Soviet Union few skeletons ever stay long in the family closet. Over fifty percent of all families in the U.S.S.R. have some relative who was either jailed, sentenced, or put under investigation by the State Security. "The Soviet Union is divided into three parts," as the old saying used to go, "those who have been in prison, those who are in prison, and those awaiting their turn."

The 1958 revision of the criminal code makes some formal changes in the old law which implicated the family of a "counter-revolutionary" criminal in his guilt whether or not they assisted or even knew of his offense. But careful reading shows how little it has tampered with the hallowed State Security principle of guilt by association. However much a man may disapprove of his "anti-Soviet" uncle or sister or second cousin, a blood or marriage relationship constitutes grounds for the strongest suspicion. Nowhere in the world has guilt by association been institutionalized to such a degree.

Whenever a Soviet citizen gets a new job, enters a school, or begins military service, it is mandatory that he write a more or less detailed autobiography as well as fill out certain forms covering his family background, marital status, past employment, military service, etc. Along with such information, normal even in democratic countries for most people entering government service, there are four extra areas of interrogation: (1) a person's connection with the Communist Party or any of its allied activities; (2) his connections, or his family's connections, with any foreigners; (3) his activities, or his family's activities, during and before the October Revolution; and (4) his residence in any territory held even temporarily by enemies of the Soviet Union.

The first two areas are obvious enough. Communist Party membership is understandably a sensitive area of investigation. The slightest infraction of its regulations, down to non-attendance at high school Komsomol meetings, may cost a man and his family their livelihood if anyone in authority wishes to make a case against him.

But it is the two last which have been an abiding nightmare for huge numbers of Soviet citizens. There were, for instance, at least five million Soviet soldiers taken prisoner by the Germans during World War II. The survivors, on their return from captivity, were individually judged, tried, and—almost automatically—convicted of "anti-Soviet" activity.[5] They received sentences varying from immediate execution to imprisonment or deportation to Siberia. Although some classes of war prisoners were later amnestied, there is still little a former war prisoner can do to wipe out the stain on his record or on the records of every member of his family. The single fact that a man's brother was captured by the Germans is evidence enough for the KGB to begin a searching investigation of his position and "character."

The actual fate of the returned war prisoners was regulated by authority according to a rough sliding scale of their imagined complicity in "anti-Soviet activities." Almost twenty percent of them were either imprisoned for twenty-five years or shot. Another fifteen to twenty percent received jail sentences of from five to ten years. About ten percent were sent to frontier territories in Siberia for periods of not less than six years. Another fifteen percent went to industrial areas in need of work conscripts, like the Donbas or the Kuzbas. They could not return home after their assignment, although a few were allowed to bring their families with them. About another fifteen to twenty percent were free to go back home, although their offense at first made existence almost impossible as anything but an unregistered laborer. The few who got off scot-free were those obviously too wounded or incapacitated to have prevented capture when it occurred. "Better death," the wartime Army propaganda slogan ran, "than being a dishonorable prisoner." The State Security did its best to make this boast a postwar reality.

With the Revolution the law is equally strict. Hundreds of thousands of Soviet citizens have lost jobs, or worse, because their families were found to have an "elevated social status" before the Revolution. It goes without saying that

---

[5] There were some, of course, who were sentenced quite justly for collaboration in German atrocities, etc. These guilty ones represented only a minority of those "convicted."

anyone whose father or uncle fought on the side of the
Whites is doomed for any position of even modest salary
and responsibility once this *ex post facto* evidence of heresy
comes to light. Even residence in territory temporarily held
by White forces is enough to start a State Security investigation. Thousands more have had their careers and their
families imperiled by answering truthfully the deceptively
simple question on an official investigation form: "Did
you, or your relatives, live in any area occupied by White
Guards? If so, indicate where, when, for what period, how
long the occupation lasted, and your or their occupations at
that time."

There are other unspoken categories which invite State
Security investigation. The fact that a person's father was a
kulak, as the Soviets defined the word, is enough to mark
him as potentially "anti-Soviet." So is relationship to any
member of the clergy. When Deriabin was only fifteen he
received a warning from his local Komsomol boss that his
Party future would be jeopardized if he remained friendly
with a classmate, the daughter of the village priest. He
chose, with some trepidation, to defy the warning. Nothing
happened to him, as it turned out, but the girl was ultimately forced out of the school.

Since 1948 all Jews have been suspect. There is, again,
nothing set down in writing anywhere in the Soviet Union
saying that Jews are to be discriminated against. But every
officer of the State Security knows that the very fact of a
man being a Jew bars him from positions of higher responsibility and invites a detailed "criminal" investigation. Some
of the State Security's most competent officers, among
them Colonel Aleksandr Korotkov, the famous deputy
chief of foreign intelligence in the late forties and early
fifties, were forced to divorce their Jewish wives so as not
to jeopardize their careers in the service.

In some cases, especially in technical areas, Jews have
been allowed to remain in fairly high-ranking jobs because
of their individual indispensability. But even these people
live under constant threat of removal. The occasional opening of a Yiddish play in Moscow, for example, is merely a
sop to foreign opinion. Under Khrushchev, as under the
later days of Stalin, the Soviet régime is pledged to a peculiarly vicious form of anti-Semitism.

In Soviet "law," as it is practiced, there are no extenuating circumstances. An admission of compromising personal activity or the existence of "compromised" relatives is in itself direct evidence of guilt. It cannot be appealed. Since most Soviet citizens are well aware of the dangerous categories on the personnel forms, their only hope is to lie if they happen to fit one of them. They must lie on the questionnaires, in conversation, for the duration of their lives. In this way, as the product of constant necessity, untruth enters the marrow of every Soviet citizen.

It is one of the State Security's principal functions to find out these lies told by ordinary Soviet citizens. Sometimes they are uncovered quickly and used. More often exposure is deliberately postponed, the crippling facts held up for years in a person's file, awaiting the moment when the régime wishes to use them. Or the telltale lie may remain buried in the archives, unnoticed for years, until the person involved makes the one slight misstep that invites a detailed investigation. Then the evidence of his lie comes into Moscow from its burial places in the files and cross-files of provincial KGB offices throughout the country. Few careers survive such exposure.

During his own service in Moscow, Deriabin had occasion to watch all varieties of lie-and-exposure at work. Almost a copybook example was the case of a trusted Party member named Sivtsov, who was applying in 1952 for a responsible job with the Ministry of the Petroleum Industry. In the routine questionnaire about his relatives he noted that his brother, one Nikolay P. Sivtsov, had disappeared without a trace during the war, in 1942.

The resulting State Security investigation developed the fact that Nikolay was very much alive. He had been a prisoner of war in Germany between 1942 and 1945, when he was handed over to the Soviet Army by the Americans.

At this, Sivtsov was called up again before the Personnel Section of the Petroleum Ministry. (The personnel section of a Soviet office is far more important than its counterpart in other countries. In important ministries either the chiefs of personnel sections or their deputies are as a rule officers of the State Security, as was the case here.) He was again asked the whereabouts of his brother. He said he had received no information about him since 1942. Sivtsov stuck to his original story even after he was told that Nikolay was alive and living in the Soviet Union. He was requested to make a statement in writing that he knew nothing of his brother's whereabouts and had had no contact with him.

The State Security office in Astrakhan, where Nikolay lived, then made a full investigation. The case officer established that not only did Sivtsov know his brother's address but he had visited him that very year and helped him to build his house. To verify this statement the local office thoughtfully sent Moscow a picture of the two brothers fishing together.

Despite the evidence of Sivtsov's lie, nothing was said to him at that time. For his brother was not only under surveillance in the Astrakhan district, where he had been sent after returning from captivity, he was suspected of being an "American agent" and watched accordingly. In the face of this more important counter-intelligence goal nothing was done to Sivtsov. He was told by the Ministry simply that there was no vacancy and sent away to ponder the real reason for his rejection. His duly-attested lie about not having heard from his brother was filed away for use on a suitable occasion.

Sometimes the filed lie would not catch up with a man for an entire generation. This was the case with Colonel Anatoliy Gorsky, alias Gorin, until 1953 deputy chief of the American Section in the Foreign Intelligence Directorate of the State Security. Gorsky had spent most of his twenty-one years in the service abroad, which included three years as the "legal" resident in the United States. Through the same twenty-one years he had been a trusted Party member. In 1953, with years of official investigations and counterchecks behind him, he underwent a last formal security check by Moscow before receiving the post of head of the American Section.

In the process of this check one small discrepancy was noted in Gorsky's file. His questionnaires had all stated that his father was a country schoolteacher in the Krasnoyarskiy Kray. Some of the corroborating information confirmed this statement. There was, however, one nagging report, dated 1930, which established Gorsky's father as a former Czarist gendarme. In the 1953 investigation the deputy chief of the entire State Security, then Lieutenant General Sergey Ogoltsov, himself interrogated Gorsky about his "social background." When Gorsky returned the usual answer about his teacher father, Ogoltsov sent two officers to the Krasnoyarskiy Kray to investigate. Gorsky, as it happened, was half Jewish. "Find out about him," Ogoltsov ordered. "There is something wrong. And besides"—here again the mark of anti-Semitism—"I don't like his nose."

The investigators found that Gorsky was lying. His own father had indeed been a Czarist police officer. The man he claimed for a parent was a teacher from a neighboring village and no relation.

"Justice" operated quickly. Gorsky was discharged from the State Security and barely escaped losing his Party membership. He received a heavy reprimand. His service as a ranking Party member was forever over.

The files of the State Security are not infallible. They are sufficiently stern, given such constant checking, to warp human nature in the world's third most populous country, to produce an inner acceptance of treachery and double-dealing whenever it seems necessary and possible. But they have also developed a certain mental slackness which, for want of a better name, could be called "documentitis"; and Soviet "documentitis" has offered a fertile spawning ground for the sort of trickster that a healthier society would quickly expose. Constantly, in the course of the inevitable security checks, the State Security turns up cases of people who have twisted the supposed infallibility of documents to their own advantage. There was the famous story of a Sergeant Smirnov, a fun-loving soldier in the Leningrad Military District. While he was documents clerk in a staff office Smirnov had changed his name to Karpov in all his dossiers in order to avoid alimony payments due his three wives for three sets of children. He got away with the deception for four years before one of his wives managed to track him down.

There were many other soldiers in World War II who exchanged their documents with those of men killed on the battlefield. Then they went off to live a new life elsewhere in the Soviet Union, old ties neatly severed and a new life beckoning. It is impossible to estimate how many Soviet citizens, in and out of the army, are even now playing this documents game successfully. It is the end product of a society where the mark means more than the man.

CHAPTER VIII
Mr. Minister

A FEW MONTHS after Deriabin arrived in Moscow he ran into an old friend from Siberia on a street corner. The man took one look at Deriabin's comfortable clothing and the building he had just come out of—part of the two blocks of State Security headquarters at Dzerzhinsky Square—and extended his hand with a smile of congratulations. "Hello, Mr. Minister," he said.

Moscow in 1947 was hardly a comfortable city by Western standards. The critical conditions of food and housing showed themselves in the huge incidence of crime. Muggings, robberies, and murders were commonplace. It was dangerous to walk after dark in most quarters of the city. State Security officers, who counted a great deal of night work among their duties, were issued small automatics on being assigned there and were ordered to carry them at all times in the pockets of their civilian suits. Yet the prize of working in Moscow outweighed any amount of inconvenience or discomfort. There was justification in the Siberian friend's cheery "Mr. Minister." A senior case officer in Moscow, as Deriabin was, might never see the inside of a ministerial office suite, but he was definitely on his way up in the Soviet world.

The advantages of a Moscow job were formalized in differences of salary and allowance. Captain Deriabin's salary had been 2700 rubles a month, at the time he left Barnaul. His Moscow salary was 4200. The ranks involved were the-

121

oretically the same.[1] But a Moscow assignment was worth several stages of formal promotion in any provincial headquarters. A senior case officer in Moscow, if he wished, could easily get himself transferred to a post as a chief of section in the provinces or even a deputy minister in the State Security apparatus of an out-of-the-way Soviet republic like Uzbekistan. Such transfers were rarely requested.

Within the organization officers spent years alternately scheming, flattering, and undermining superiors or influential associates for the chance of a Moscow assignment. Not only was a Moscow job the surest kind of status symbol in Soviet society, it was also the best way to protect oneself from the ill effects of seismic changes in higher authority. The officer on duty in Moscow could sense a shift in power, say, from the Beria faction to the Malenkov faction and build his own kind of bureaucratic earthquake cellar to withstand them. Pity the poor chief of section in Omsk, Arkhangelsk, or Tashkent who had to work out his own plans and counter-plans without the benefit of Moscow information.

None of the succeeding Soviet régimes has done anything serious to alter the tremendous centripetal urge of all Soviet officials; a Moscow job is as important under Nikita Khrushchev as it was under Stalin or Malenkov. Now as then, the differences in status are explicitly outlined and clarified by influential assistants to ministers and chiefs of personnel sections. In Deriabin's time it was a common-

---

[1] Military ranks apply as far as status is concerned: junior lieutenant, lieutenant, senior lieutenant, captain, major, and so on. Special State Security titles indicate operational ranks:
Pom Operupolnomochennyy—junior case officer
Operupolnomochennyy—case officer
Starshy Operupolnomochennyy—senior case officer
Nachalnik Otdelenia—chief of subsection
Nachalnik Sektora—chief of sector
Nachalnik Otdela—chief of section
Nachalnik Upravlenia—chief of directorate
Nachalnik Glavnoyo Upravlenia—chief of main directorate
Predsedatel' KGB—Chairman of KGB
All these "chief" ranks have both assistants and deputies: deputies may stand in for their chiefs, but assistants are strictly adjuncts to them.

place for a man to be fired from his Moscow post but allowed to take a job in the provinces. Such transfers were generally accompanied by a rough reminder "not to come back."

The difference between Moscow and the provinces was measured for Deriabin by his own relationship with Colonel Vladimir Ruzin, who had been his boss in Barnaul. Ruzin was an efficient officer, good-humored and personally likable, whose career had taken some unexpected twists and turns because of his attractive wife, Valya. Valya enjoyed the good things of life to a fault. In the course of a year's service at Barnaul, for instance, she bought herself seventy pair of shoes. She demanded and got the constant services of a State Security car and chauffeur and, apparently, was not above requisitioning a junior officer, now and then, for various services. As word of her behavior filtered up to Moscow, Ruzin's position at Dzerzhinsky Square deteriorated accordingly. In the State Security conspicuousness is not exactly regarded as a virtue.

Deriabin had manipulated his own transfer to Moscow without Ruzin's help, and the senior officer was quite angry when he heard about it. As soon as the definite Moscow orders arrived, however, Ruzin gave up his opposition. He frankly asked Deriabin to "see what you can do for me up there." Ruzin had been optimist enough to keep a two-room Moscow apartment after his transfer to Barnaul, against the day when he could wangle a new job in the capital. He gave Deriabin the key before he left Barnaul, and for two months Peter lived alone there.

Unfortunately for Ruzin he was already under Moscow investigation. A visiting three-man investigating commission turned in an unfavorable report on him, despite the efforts of the Barnaul office to propitiate them by more than usually lavish entertainment, and he was removed from his State Security job altogether. He returned to Moscow in panic, only to make the fortuitous discovery that a friend of his, a general in the State Security, had been recently kicked upstairs to the soft job of deputy director of the crucial currency reform then going on in the U.S.S.R.[2]

___

[2] Because of wartime speculation and the quantities of forged notes the Germans had put into circulation, currency

Ruzin saw the general and was taken on as his special assistant. It was a year's work and in Moscow.

At the end of the year the best Ruzin could find for himself was the cold comfort of a job as deputy chief of the transportation directorate of the State Security in Kazakhstan. To work in Alma-Ata, the capital of Kazakhstan, would not have been such bad duty. But the transportation directorate's headquarters were located near the dirty railroad yards of Karaganda—about as far away from a Moscow assignment, spiritually speaking, as one could get. In desperation he sent Valya back to Moscow to do some personal lobbying for him. Assisted by this persuasive ally, Deriabin was able to use his contacts in getting Ruzin a transfer to the former Polish city of Lvov, which had been annexed by the Soviet Union during World War II.

Lvov was several steps forward on the come-back trail for Ruzin, and the year following Stalin's death he managed to return to Moscow as a chief of a subsection inside State Security headquarters. After the arrest of Beria, however, he was again sent out to the provinces with one of the Personnel Section's "don't come back" admonitions. He didn't.

The contrast between his own rise and Ruzin's decline was enough to impress Peter Deriabin with the value of on-the-spot personal contact in arranging one's career. As

---

reform was essential. It worked in this way. People who had kept their money in the bank were reimbursed note for note through the first 3000 rubles, then given ten percent of the amount thereafter. A flat ten percent of whatever money they exchanged was returned to those lacking bank deposits (this category included all dubious "speculators," i.e. everyone with an overlarge nest egg who was afraid to hatch it in public). This process did not produce so many hardships as one might anticipate, since few Soviet citizens were good for 3000 rubles in the bank in the first place. But it did strike heavily at those whose entire savings were kept in their own pockets.

Deriabin had sixty rubles at the time of the reform. He thus emerged from the bank with six, the price of a visit to the barber and two bottles of aftershave lotion.

Government officials in the know were of course able to "persuade" local bank officials to antedate their bank deposits. But it took a rarely ingenious operator, nonetheless, to save more than the statutory 3000 rubles in the process.

he later had ample chance to reflect, the Soviet Union's bureaucracy, unchecked by any democratic restraints, displayed dangerous and often contradictory extremes of two normal bureaucratic tendencies in its workings: the inflexibility of official orders and the immense power of unofficial personal influences. His own rapid rise in status had been partly the result of connected chance. If there had not been a shortage of history teachers in Siberia he would not have been teaching Party history at such an early age; if he had not taught Party history he would not have been so readily given an assistant political officer's appointment in the Army; if the political officer had not been ill he would not so soon have received his promotion. . . . Once he was injected into the Army political mechanism there was even less Peter Deriabin could do about the course of his own career. He was a prisoner of official instructions. Essentially he was in the State Security, after all his training and indoctrination, because "Moscow" wanted him there and that was that.

Yet once in Moscow, he was quick to discover that "Moscow" itself, with all its moods and switches, was often but the merged result of thousands of individual influence-peddlers, bureaucrats of classic mold who could run wild behind the shelter of their ministries as long as they hewed to the régime's current basic policy. Deriabin's alacrity in arranging his own transfer showed that his precocious experience shuffling people and papers in the Komsomol and the Army had not been wasted. (The fact that he managed to leave the service in 1946 was due largely to the general postwar confusion.) But in the face of his friend Pavel Zuikov's activities Deriabin's own concept of "dealing showed up as comparatively restricted.

Pavel was a born "fixer," the sort of man the Russians call an *Arap*. He ran into Deriabin for the first time at the counter-intelligence school, where they became friends. Shortly after Pavel was posted far to the north in Murmansk, since his academic record had not been such as to give him an immediate Moscow appointment. Likable as well as quick-witted, Pavel grew popular with the other officers at his station and got himself the Soviet equivalent of good "fitness reports" thereby. He was apparently contented. But when the head of their branch came out from

Moscow on an inspection tour it was Pavel who managed to corner him for a long private conversation in the course of which he convinced him that he needed another bright young man to help run the Moscow office.

It took only a few months of maneuvering inside State Security headquarters for Pavel to get his highly strategic post as personnel assistant to the Deputy Minister. The Deputy, Major General Svinelupov, was disliked by the Minister, Colonel General Viktor Abakumov; Abakumov was not strong enough to remove him, but he was able to hinder his operations, and there was little communication between them. Svinelupov himself, not a forceful man, was happy to delegate authority. Pavel moved smartly into the breach, signing transfer orders with abandon, transferring generals, dismissing colonels, or staffing the Moscow office with trusted friends of his own, like Deriabin. If a high State Security official did not like Pavel's tactics he had always the right to appeal to Abakumov. But this maneuver could easily backfire. Although the Minister could reverse any of his deputy's decisions, there was always the chance that he might enforce them and with greater severity. This was a chance which few experienced State Security officers were willing to take.

There was no doubt but that Pavel was a powerful aid to efficiency at State Security headquarters, but he was also fond of breaking up his paper work with long informal conversations with his friends. Deriabin got into the habit of visiting him often after he came to Moscow. It was a confessedly pleasant situation for a recently obscure case officer from Barnaul to find instant access to the key man's office, past a waiting room full of nervous colonels, deputy ministers from provinces and republics, or Moscow section chiefs. In the course of their talks, also, Deriabin learned a lot more than he knew about the goals of the good Soviet bureaucrat and the footwork necessary for reaching them. "When I first started," said Pavel, "I believed in everything, just like you do now. By the time I worked my way higher up I realized that the one important thing in this place is to make yourself comfortable."

For a short time Deriabin worked in his friend's office as a supernumerary assistant. He asked for a transfer from this work himself, feeling that it smacked too obviously of favoritism. So it was arranged that he spend a few months screening soldiers from the military units assigned to the Kremlin to see how many were eligible for further training at the State Security school for members of the Guard Directorate.

Deriabin began to enjoy life in Moscow, even after he was forced to give up Ruzin's commodious two-room apartment. His first marriage had been a brief and rather stormy chapter in his personal life, heavily marred by his wife's hostility to his little sister, Valya, toward whom he felt extremely protective. Tragic as Tanya's death was, he could not help feeling a certain sense of relief that it was all over. He felt a new importance, working in Moscow again. And he surely had no complaints about living the life of a postwar bachelor in a postwar city where a good man was hard to find.

Finally, although he only half admitted it, he was relieved at no longer having the job of spying on his fellow citizens. His first few months back in Moscow involved him almost exclusively in the adminstrative work of a large headquarters. Wherever the State Security's business might lead on its periphery, it was gratifyingly impersonal to be approving requisitions and shuffling records in the headquarters building on Dzerzhinsky Square.

In the late spring of 1947 his temporary screening work was ended. Pavel arranged for his assignment on the staff of Colonel Serafim Goryshev, who was slated to take over the Personnel Section in State Security headquarters. This had barely been arranged, when Goryshev was suddenly switched to the post of assistant to Lieutenant General Vlasik, the boss of the Kremlin's Guard Directorate. He took Deriabin's file and his destiny with him.

Deriabin therefore found himself reporting to the Guard Directorate. "I didn't think you'd mind," Goryshev said. "It is a better job and more restful." Peter checked with his friend Pavel at headquarters for a further rundown. "Well," he answered cautiously, "you'll have good food and good clothes . . . and Goryshev will take care of you. Otherwise I wouldn't let you go over there. The Guard Directorate can be pretty sticky. It's awfully close to the top."

CHAPTER IX

The Guard

ON A WINTER afternoon in the tense war year of 1942 a lone Soviet soldier, rifle slung over his shoulder, marched into Red Square. He made for a small fenced-off enclosure above a slight rise of ground, called *Lobnoye Mesto* (the place of skulls) from its historic use as the execution place of the Moscow Czars. He sat down on a bench there, unhooked his cartridge belt, and raised the rifle to his shoulder, the while looking at the almost deserted space around him. In the war years the entirety of Red Square was under the strictest watch, and few were foolish enough to loiter there. He was 150 yards away from the Spassky Gate of the Kremlin, which is where he pointed the rifle.

There were at the time some forty members of the State Security on duty in Red Square, well armed and watchful. But by curious common consent they approached the single soldier cautiously. When the man told them to keep their distance "or I will shoot," their caution turned into a kind of half-paralyzed confusion. Some guards continued to surround him, others were busy at the telephones to higher authority, demanding orders. No one knew who the strange soldier was.

When the telephoning finally brought out the major on O.D. duty, who had been taking a shower, he screamed at the guards to shoot the man. Before they could execute the order a black Packard limousine had edged out of the Kremlin gates with no less than Anastas Mikoyan, then as now one of the ranking personalities in the Soviet Union,

129

inside. The soldier dropped to one knee and quickly and accurately pumped three shots into the car. If the Packard had not been gifted with regulation Soviet bullet-proofing Mikoyan would have been a dead man.

Seconds after the soldier fired he was dead. His name, like his bullet-riddled body, has long since gone to ashes, known only to a few archivists in State Security headquarters. His assassination attempt, like all except a few studiously publicized efforts in this line, is unknown to the Soviet public. His own family never learned what happened to him. But the odd nature of his effort, the hesitation in his informal execution and its consequences, taken together, make a most accurate comment on the workings of the Soviet police state, unchanged in its substance, whether in 1942, 1932, or 1959.

The actual story of the soldier's assassination attempt is the simplest thing in the world. He was a peasant conscript from an infantry division stationed at that time in the Moscow vicinity. Recently he had heard from his mother that she and his family were almost starving because of the hardships of the war and desperately needed his help at home. He had shown the letter to his company commander, asked for a brief furlough, and been refused. (Hardship furloughs were never a strong point in the Soviet Army.) Enraged at this, he had deserted, walked past his unit's checkpoints in the dark, and headed for Moscow in a frame of mind to "get one of those bastards" in the Kremlin. That he had walked armed into Red Square at all, without a prior challenge, was an accident attributable to wartime confusion and the half-noticed presence of hundreds of thousands of armed individuals in the Moscow area.

Why had the soldier not been challenged or shot directly? The answer to this question, incomprehensible to a guard or secret service officer in most other countries, would seem logical to anyone in the State Security: no one could be sure that someone in higher authority had not sent him—someone, presumably, who did not like Mikoyan. Being thus momentarily uncertain, none of the guards was willing even to take a shot at an obvious assassin until he was reassured by direct command of higher authority.

These cautious professional estimates of the situation turned out to be wrong. There was no secret conspiracy, but it took almost a year of detailed investigation to prove it so. The course of this investigation, run by the highest authorities of the Soviet intelligence system, nicely demonstrated the penalties which the Soviet Union attaches to failure. The entire company of the Kremlin Guard Directorate on duty that day in Red Square was transferred to duty in the provinces. Its officers and key N.C.O.s were imprisoned. Six of them received terms ranging from five to ten years. (The company commander, who had some influential friends, got off lightly with only one year.) Punishment visited on the Army was far worse. The would-be assassin's platoon commander and company commander were stripped of their rank and sent to fight in penal battalions at the front. So were the battalion commander, the regimental commander, and the general of division. Only one or two survived.

No head was left untouched in the investigation. One of the Guard Directorate's security officers, Captain Shestakov, from whom Deriabin learned the story, spent a year in jail simply because he had once approved the security clearances for most officers of the Guard company involved.

Peter Deriabin heard the full account of this in 1947, shortly after he had moved over to serve in the Guard Directorate himself. He never forgot it. For the little life drama played out on the *Lobnoye Mesto* set in focus the extreme levels of suspicion at which the Guard Directorate operated and the penalties and inefficiencies which were suspicion's products. The Soviet system exacts its human toll for failure precisely because the cornerstone of the modern Marxist system, as its Moscow interpreters have to preach it, is its own infallibility.

The State Security as a whole finds the binding justification for its investigative processes in the resulting Soviet convention: that every slip or accident must be blamed on *somebody*. The Guard Directorate at the heart of the security mechanism is charged with safeguarding the ruling Party leadership. Here at the top the penalties for a misstep are the heaviest in Soviet society.

It did not take Deriabin long to discover that the perquisites of the Guard were a thin camouflage for the knife-edge margin of safety enjoyed by its officers. Coming in with the best of recommendations, he was nonetheless quick to acquire the protective coating of caution necessary for survival. For if a sure-footed bureaucrat at the center could enjoy prestige and freedom of action in the Moscow spotlight, there was no dark corner to hide in if he slipped. In the Guard Directorate the possibilities of slippage were almost infinite and the chances for escaping penalties almost nil. Spatially as well as spiritually the Guard worked in a closed secret world of its own, sealed even from most contact with other organs of the State Security.

There are two cities in Moscow, in the literal sense of the word. The first is the visible metropolis of some five million people, familiar to travelers and most newspaper readers as the home of the Moscow subway, the Bolshoi Theater, Intourist, and the outside of the Kremlin. One might assume that the second city, the half-visible center of Soviet authority, begins and ends inside the Kremlin walls. As Peter Deriabin, a new officer in the Personnel Section, grew familiar with the Guard Directorate's installations, he discovered this second city to be far larger and far more tightly organized than he had ever imagined, the most alert, suspicious, and intricate system ever devised for the insulation of a ruling caste from the life around it.

Take a map of Moscow and spread it on the table. Look at the complex of streets within the Sadovaya Ring, centering on Red Square and the Kremlin. Not far from the Kremlin itself is the hive of State Security buildings on Dzerzhinsky Square, Dzerzhinsky Street, Malaya Lubianka Street, Kuznetsky Most Street, with the MVD headquarters further off in Ogareva Street, barely a few pirouettes away from the Bolshoi Conservatory. Then trace the streets leading outward from the Kremlin, like the spokes of a large wheel, along Gorky Street, past the special KGB living quarters along Mozhayskoye Chaussée, First Meshchanskaya Street, Arbat Street. Continue them out to the open spaces in the suburbs, along Rublevskoye Chaussée, Dimitrovskoye Chaussée, Yaroslavskoye Chaussée, where Krushchev now lives.[1] Pencil in a few heavy dots elsewhere: a house on Bolotnaya Street, a house at the corner of Staropansky Street, 3 Yeropkinsky Street, 11 Sirotsky

[1] See map inside back cover.

Street, the complex of buildings at Kaluzhskoye Chaussée, where a special department of the Guard watches the Academy of Science. Extend another line to Pokrovsky Boulevard and the barracks of the two divisions of MVD and KGB troops kept in constant readiness for possible work in Moscow.

This is the secret city of the Guard Directorate, the *Okhrana*[2] of the State Security forces which guard the Soviet leadership. It has more than troops living in it. For the Kremlin and its allied buidlings there is a separate power plant and a separate communications system. On the outskirts of Moscow the secret city has its own farms and slaughterhouses, whose produce comes daily into the Kremlin along well-defined routes. (Depending on current official whim, they are sometimes put under the nominal authority of the Ministry of Agriculture.) The farms serve the Kremlin buildings and the thirty-odd private houses and apartment buildings also within the secret city: the residences of the Praesidium of the Central Committee of the CPSU, guest houses for foreign Communist visitors, and homes for a few families of departed Communist heroes.

Serving these buildings, also, is a small army of plumbers, electricians, doctors, cooks, valets, handymen, and almost every other variety of professional and service help. (Only lawyers are not needed.) Their age and type of service has no end; charwomen and specially paid prostitutes are included. All of them have in common a small State Security identity card.

The most the visitor to the Kremlin sees of the Guard Directorate is a few members of the spotlessly behaviored special Guard battalion who are posted at virtually every door and hallway in the official buildings. The battalion is composed entirely of officers and has the strictest standards for entrance of any military organization in the Soviet Union.

Over and above the few obvious and public sections of

[2] *Okhrana* is simply the Russian word for "guard," and it is used familiarly to describe the Directorate among KGB people. In pre-Revolution days the word *Okhrana,* or more properly *Okhranka,* was used to designate the Czarist secret police. So Russian tradition has by now attached definite connotations to the word.

the Directorate, like the Guard battalion, a total of some 15,000[3] State Security officers keep a twenty-four-hour watch over the heavy dots on the map and the roads connecting them. Each man has his block to watch. He knows that in the course of his daily duties other eyes are watching him and reporting back to headquarters. Suspect lists and investigative checks run in an unending stream into the Guard headquarters over the old Lubianka Prison, on Dzerzhinsky Square. If a passer-by spends more than thirty minutes in any area of the secret city an investigation is begun on his movements. Depending on the immediate findings, it may very well encompass family, friends, and relatives thousands of miles away from Moscow.

Like all organs of the State Security, the Guard Directorate prefers to work silently, showing its presence to as few people as possible. Only in an emergency do the constant watchers act, and then their work is sudden and ruthless. One day in 1949, while Deriabin was working in the Guard Directorate, a jeep with four Soviet Army officers in it was jogging at a leisurely pace toward the intersection of Mokhavaya Street and Kalinin Street. The officers were either lost in meditation or, more probably, slightly drunk after a party. In any case, they ignored the amber warning light flashing at the corner, which signified that some vehicles of Praesidium members were passing en route to or from the Kremlin.

As the jeep started across it was sprayed with machine-gun bullets from a passing Guard car in the official entourage. All four officers were killed. In five minutes the jeep and their bodies had been removed from the spot. The incident was a rare one, since most residents of Moscow from long experience have learned never to trespass on the area of the secret city, or as much of it as they know. But it is typical of the Guard Directorate's reflexes.

[3] This number is a current estimate. As will be explained further, the Guard Directorate has been alternately reduced and expanded with the shiftings in Soviet leadership policy. As with other sections of the State Security, its bureaucratic shape and command structure are subject to unending change. But the functions, as here set forth, remain.

At Party congresses or meetings of the Supreme Soviet, to guard against any sudden subversive tendencies on the part of the handpicked delegates, an armed Guard officer sits at every table of fifteen or twenty delegates. There is an armed Guard officer, also, for every twelve persons in the gallery.

Few Soviet citizens, including Party members, realize the meticulous care which the Guard Directorate lavishes on the Red Square parades or other Moscow official functions. Lists of suspects are posted in State Security offices before the event, and these people are kept under close watch for its duration.

At all these Moscow parades or demonstrations in Red Square, whatever their nature, every third person on the reviewing stands is a member of the State Security, heavily armed with concealed weapons. To keep the "loyal troops of the Soviet Army" or the "spontaneous demonstrators of the grateful working masses" from too close contact with the Soviet leaders in the reviewing stand, the right files in every column are composed of State Security officers or agents or, at the least, trusted Party members appointed by their local committees and given special clearance for their duties. There are times when as many as ten columns of eighteen files apiece will march through Red Square. The far right file of each column belongs to the KGB.

One of the Guard's principal responsibilities during military parades is to see that none of the troops involved is carrying any live ammunition. The penalty for an omission in this case is twenty-five years at hard labor for the soldier carrying the ammunition, his officers, and all State Security officers involved in his clearance. As further insurance against excessive demonstrations of popular zeal the State Security unfailingly stations a full battalion of its own troops, armed with automatic weapons, in the basement of the Lenin-Stalin mausoleum, with reserves of more militia and KGB troops standing nearby, generally in other basements along Vetoshny Lane. Machine-gun posts are set up on the wall of the Kremlin and armed guards posted in the attics of the Kremlin and on the roofs of some of the nearby buildings: St. Basil's cathedral, the GUM department store, and the Museum of History.[4]

On these occasions every available man is mobilized to supplement the regular Guard Directorate officers. It was as part of the reserve State Security forces, in fact, that Deriabin had his first taste of this kind of guard duty—during the World War II victory sports parade in Red Square, which was held on August 13, 1945. All foreigners are closely watched on such occasions, no matter who they are, for the dual purpose of their own protection and the Praesidium's. Equipped with a pistol, Deriabin was posted on the mausoleum reviewing stand, three feet away from a not-too-dangerous American guest at the celebration named Dwight D. Eisenhower.

The organization of the Guard Directorate is as closely woven as a suit of chain mail. It serves, even within the State Security, as a self-contained unit equipped to run itself independent of any other Soviet organization. It includes the Guard battalion, a special service regiment in the Kremlin, a service company, pass control and communications sections for the Kremlin, a large section of personal guards for members of the Party Praesidium, and sections for the geographical surveillance of every inch of the secret city. These are meticulously organized. For example, the subsection of the Second Section in charge of street surveillance is assigned the inspection of attics, basements, water mains, telephone wires, etc. in the guarded areas. In Deriabin's time it was called, appositely, the Subsection of Above-and-Below-Ground Maintenance.

Training, construction, transportation, and living quarters are under the governance of special sections, some of them pocket-size replicas of larger organizations in the main KGB. There are also separate detachments for the Guard Directorate enclaves outside Moscow: the suburban summer *dachas* of the régime leaders outside Moscow, along the Mozhayskoye and Rublevskoye Chaussées, and

---

[4] Despite such precautions, one post-parade check-up in the late Stalin era revealed a single spent bullet lodged in the wall of the mausoleum, just below the reviewing stand. No one was ever able to trace its origin, despite a prodigious investigation.

the official summer colonies for Soviet higher-ups at Sochi on the Black Sea coast and Kislovodsk in the Caucasus.

The officials who are privileged by or, often more aptly, subject to Guard protection vary in number and identity. Generally, however, in addition to the Party officials of the Praesidium, the former Politburo,[5] certain leaders of the government apparatus are given this escort: the Chairman of the Councils of Ministers of the U.S.S.R. and his deputies, the Chairmen of the Councils of Ministers of the component Union republics, etc. Officials heading the Party committees in the republics as well as on the *oblast* and *kray* level are under the Guard's protection. So are the Party leaders in satellite countries, through the agency of Guard-controlled local organizations. Guests of the régime visiting the U.S.S.R. are accorded special attention; a Guard chauffeur was once dismissed from the service after his car carrying Liu Shao Chi, currently Premier of Communist China, *almost* collided with a truck. (The truck driver drew a year's jail sentence.)

The Foreign Ministry of the U.S.S.R. is under the Guard's protection, as are certain scientific installations and some leading scientists and technicians, men like the atomic physicist Petr Kapitsa, Aleksandr Nesmyanov, head of the Soviet Academy of Sciences, Aleksandr Topchiev, the Secretary of the Academy. Certain military leaders are also the object of the Guard's attentions.

This organized scheme of protection grew up gradually. Until 1943 the Guard was only one section of a directorate inside the State Security. It became an independent directorate in that year, steadily increasing in power and scope until its consolidation with the separate Kremlin directorate in 1947. Since then, allowing for the usual changes in title, its structure has remained the same.

While Stalin was alive he had a personal guard of 406 men, who traveled with him constantly. It is no small tribute to their vigilance to record that only two definite assassination attempt were made in the space of twenty-five

[5] The old Politburo was reorganized by Stalin into a bigger Praesidium of the Central Committee of the CPSU in 1952. Its function remained the same, however.

years. The first was a shooting by a would-be assassin near Adler, in the Caucasus, in 1930. The second was an ambitious assassination plan hatched by German military intelligence, the *Abwehr*, in 1942. A Soviet officer, taken prisoner by the Germans and later working for them, volunteered to re-enter Moscow for the express purpose of killing Stalin. He was to drive a motorcycle down Arbat Street, the route Stalin took between his *dacha* and the Kremlin, and hurl a bomb into Stalin's car while passing it. The plan was carefully conceived, but it was exposed by a Soviet agent who had penetrated German intelligence. The would-be assassin parachuted into the woods near Moscow, but he was caught shortly after and shot.

There was one other anti-Soviet assassination plot among members of the militia in Moscow in 1947. Directed not against Stalin but all the Politburo members, it was one of the few "plots" exposed by the State Security in recent times which actually was a plot and was directed against the régime. After the militiamen were detected and exposed by the State Security there was a gigantic purge of the entire Moscow militia, i.e. the normal civilian police department, in which some 1200 men were dismissed, if not imprisoned. As a result, the Section on Street Traffic Regulation was made directly subordinate to the State Security.

There was nothing subtle or self-effacing about Stalin's guard details. When the old dictator traveled he was screened by a covery of bullet-proof Packards or, later, Zises packed with State Security men from the Guard Directorate's First Section. When he traveled to Sochi for periodic vacations all the railway switches on the way were closed and sealed, and each switchman was accompanied on his work by a member of the State Security.

No one was ever told anything of Stalin's movements in advance. The only warning of his approach, in Moscow or elsewhere, would be the amber lights blinking at the street corners and the sudden screaming cavalcade with Colonel Kirilin of the Guard shrieking obscenities and frequently spitting in the faces of passers-by who seemed to be too close to the cavalcade for comfort. The spat-upon were at least fortunate enough to be warned, for the Zises stopped for no one. In 1949 a pedestrian was run down when he got in the way of the entourage on Borodinsky Bridge. His body was sent off to the morgue by the State Security people guarding the route. No enquiries were ever made about his residence or the whereabouts of his family.

The privileged position of Stalin's bodyguard protected them from the rigid standards of public conduct set for regular State Security officers. Street fighting and drunkenness were common among them when they were off duty, and their relatively high rank (Stalin's private chauffeur was a major) helped keep them almost immune from outside discipline. In the summer of 1950 some of the Guard members were "relaxing" in Sochi. Strolling down to the town market place after a heavy drinking bout, they started to annoy the women selling fruit and vegetables there. When a local man tried to help the women, one of the guards, Kolbasin by name, struck and killed him instantly with a blow to his neck. Kolbasin was 6'6" tall, a brute of a man with heavy bearlike hands. The chief of the entire Guard Directorate, Lieutenant General Nikolay S. Vlasik, called him in to account for his action. After hearing the story he said: "According to the law you should be arrested and severely punished for killing a man. But you did kill him with a single blow. We need men who are that good with their fists. Allow me to express my appreciation."

This rampant viciousness was part of the "monstrous" network of crimes "exposed" and attacked by Nikita Khrushchev at the Twentieth Party Congress in 1956. "Arbitrary behavior by one person"—as Krushchev told the Party delegates—"encouraged and permitted arbitrariness in others." In the purges of the security organs following Stalin's death every ranking member of his personal guard was either imprisoned, sent to Siberia, or, in the case of a few lucky ones, transferred to obscure positions somewhere in the provinces.

Even before Stalin's death a special board composed of Malenkov, Beria, and Bulganin had investigated the Guard Directorate's operation at the request of the Finance Minister, in a rough Soviet equivalent of a budget-cutting drive. In the resultant purge, which took place in April 1952, colonels and generals were imprisoned or transferred wholesale, and about 7000 people were taken off the Guard's rolls. Most of them were sent to other State Security organizations. The Street Traffic Section was restored to the control of the local Moscow militia, the special Provisions Section, which controlled the farms and slaughterhouses for the use of Praesidium members, was turned back to the Ministry of Trade, the Supply and Construction Sections put back in the State Security's main Supply Directorate.

In view of Krushchev's later emphasis on a tightened State Security apparatus, such reorganizations, although they had temporary effect, amounted not so much to a real cleanup as a mere device for sweeping the viciousness under the rug. The Guard Directorate, like other organs of the State Security, continued to perform the same functions under different names. The guard personnel who had been taken away from Stalin were replaced through the years by a steady build-up in Khrushchev's entourage. If a daily plane was no longer needed to fly two freshly-slaughtered baby lambs from the State Security farm near Moscow to Stalin's vacation place (he liked *shashlik*), similar services are now being done for Khrushchev.

But Khrushchev did make the Twentieth Party Congress speech denouncing the "cult of personality." So he has, unlike Stalin, made strenuous efforts to play down the extent to which the State Security serves him. A 1958 American visitor to Khrushchev's villa in Sochi faithfully recorded in print that only one sentry stands outside the grounds. He was understandably unaware of the officers in civilian clothes, each picturesquely armed with two pistols and dagger, who day and night patrol the approaches to these *dachas* as well as the buildings themselves. Similar misconceptions would seem to operate in the case of U.S. correspondents favorably contrasting Khrushchev's recognizable security guard in Moscow—designedly few in number—with the apparently heavy Secret Service guard attending President Eisenhower.

At present Khrushchev has a personal bodyguard of more than forty men, headed by Colonel Ivan M. Stolyarov, and the number is on the increase. That this is only one tenth of Stalin's suite is less an indication of a reform in Soviet tactics than a contrast between Stalin's pathological suspiciousness and Khrushchev's advanced sense of public relations. Foreign journalists could hardly be more wrong with stories like the homey account of Khrushchev's

activities in a U.S. magazine, which suggested that most of
the cooking in the household of the First Secretary is done
by his wife. It is doubtful if Mrs. Khrushchev has seen the
working end of a kitchen for a good many years. Even
before he consolidated his personal dictatorship Khrushchev maintained the following household in Moscow:

Two cooks
Four waiters
One housekeeper
One lady's maid
One barber
Two caretakers
Three charwomen
One gardener
Three chauffeurs for his personal use
Two chauffeurs for his wife

All such personnel must be registered by the State Security,
if not actually enrolled as noncommissioned officers.

In 1952 the total strength of the Guard Directorate was
16,170, despite the pruning efforts of the Finance Ministry. In succeeding years its numbers were cut in accord
with the post-Stalin liberalization policies. Now the tendency is to expand again as the reins of the dictatorship
gather in Khrushchev's chubby fist. Until the latest shake-
up in Moscow the head of the Guard has been General
Lenev, a friend of Khrushchev's—understandably. He can
count on immediate replacement if the régime changes or
even shakes a little, as others have before him. When Molotov fell out of favor in 1952, for example, Deriabin found
himself conferring with his boss, Colonel Goryshev, about
the fate of Molotov's bodyguard, a Colonel Aleksandrov.
"Well," said Goryshev, "if they fire Molotov, we'll fire
Aleksandrov." After a thorough search of Aleksandrov's
documents investigators were able to unearth enough ten-
ous evidences of "Trotskyism" to justify his dismissal, in
case it was needed.

A year later, as events turned out, it was Goryshev himself who was put on the toboggan and transferred. Goryshev, at the time a deputy chief of the Guard Directorate,
was at that luckier than some of the Guard Directorate's
former heads, e.g. General Vlasik, who ultimately died in
prison, or Lieutenant General Spiridonov, relieved "due to

illness" in 1953. Major General Kuznetsov, fired in 1947, died a year later. Major General Kuzmichev, who was imprisoned by Stalin in 1952, freed and given the Directorate by Beria in 1953, was shot later that same year, along with his master, for installing "illegal" listening devices.

CHAPTER X

"Shall We Make A Quick Check?"

PETER DERIABIN'S IMMEDIATE business in the Guard Directorate was counter-intelligence. It was the job of his and allied sections, by their investigative effort, to cement the Guard's peculiar combination of individual uncertainty and corporate efficiency. In the Soviet scheme of things they answered the old Latin question: *"Quis custodiet ipsos custodes?"* He belonged to the group of specialists and section heads who were specifically exempted from the eight-year education limit that prevailed among the rank-and-file Guard officers and men.

Deriabin's command was a subsection, the fifth of thirteen such subsections in the Guard Directorate's Personnel Section. Each of them handled the constant investigation and rechecking of certain parts of the Guard. Deriabin and the eleven officers under him were responsible for the behavior of some 2350 uniformed and plainclothes Guard officers working in and around the Kremlin. Although they were assisted by the inevitable agents and file systems, they did a round-the-clock business. If the work was not so mentally taxing as in other sections of the State Security it offered no slack periods.

His working day began at 11 A.M. and continued to 5:30, when he took a three-hour break for supper and whatever social activity he could squeeze in. On the next half of his shift he worked from 8:30 P.M. to 1 A.M., sometimes later, for the job of unending check and recheck was physically formidable.

Most of the daily investigative reports posed questions that no one but a professionally suspicious system of government would think worthy of attention. Why was Senior Lieutenant X drinking at one particular bar off duty? Why had the brother of Captain Y made a trip from Kharkov to Moscow? Did the wife of Junior Lieutenant Z have a brother-in-law with relatives abroad? Deriabin would decide what action was necessary in every case, conduct cross-referencing in the files, and order special investigations, if need be, by the State Security apparatus in the provinces.

He had access to the files of every man in the Guard, irrespective of his position or duties. He also knew that there was someone in either the Personnel or Special Inspection Sections who would soon be working on his own. (Since Deriabin, however, by virtue of his position was a member of the innermost "in" group, the man working on his file was usually a good friend who would not be averse to comparing notes with him.)

The Guards, as indeed the other officers of the State Security, were obliged to report any and all changes in their private lives to the Personnel Section: marriages, births, illnesses, and the moral and legal troubles of their relatives, if any. A full-dress security check was made on every man at least once every year[1] to supplement the constant sifting of rumors, observations, and surveillance. If a check turned up some damaging but minor irregularity, e.g. excessive social drinking, obtrusive family quarrels, or relatives in minor trouble with the police, a man would be punished only with transfer to some less sensitive post in the State Security. But a major slip-up, in the eyes of the State Security, meant instant dismissal and, generally, personal tragedy.

Drinking was the most common non-political offense against the Guard's discipline. To show up on the job smelling of vodka could mean dismissal, at least in the lower echelons. (Since lower-grade vodka gave off an almost ineradicable odor, the solution to this problem for a man who liked a cocktail hour before returning to duty was to drink only the expensive odorless *Stolichnaya* variety.)

---

[1] And on Stalin's guards, twice a year.

Deriabin slipped up in this department only once and in a minor way. After leaving his borrowed two-room flat he lodged for a time with an actress friend and her mother in a small apartment on Maly Komsomolsky Street, only three blocks from his office. Once during his evening break he drank a few glasses of very strong honey beer (something like the old English mead) with them and reported to work slightly tipsy. The Party boss in the Personnel Section launched an investigation, but concluded it after a few preliminary questionings. It was decided not to let a little matter of an evening's drink come between the Guard officialdom and an officer who was not only efficient but had demonstrably good connections elsewhere in the State Security. So, unchastened even by a formal reprimand but considerably more cautious, Deriabin returned to the rather monotonous business of checking others.

A principal reason for the job's monotony was that the officers had all been thoroughly double-checked to begin with. If nothing else, Deriabin's job there taught him volumes about the methodical sifting processes of which the State Security is capable.

It underlines the importance of the tie between the State Security and the Party leadership to note that almost all recruits to the Guard Directorate are picked by the Party. Since the war the Central Committee has sent out specific requests to Party organizations throughout the Soviet Union, asking them to recommend candidates. No man can be enlisted in the Guard without the specific approval of his local *rayon* Party committee, backed by a heavy file of comments on his personal and official life to that moment. Some members are taken into the Guard directly from the Soviet Army or from the State Security or MVD troops on duty in and around the Kremlin. In all cases, except for a few strictly service personnel, they must be Party members or members of the Komsomol.

The security check required for a new Guard member is a tough case officer's dream. A man with relatives in prison is automatically rejected, to say nothing of someone who has ever run afoul of the law himself. So is anyone whose relatives include former *kulaks*, prisoners of war, or even persons who may have been abroad on Soviet govern-

ment business. No member or past member of the Guard
Directorate is ever allowed abroad, unless in the course of
a special mission guarding a Soviet Foreign Minister or
a high-ranking delegate to an international conference.
(Deriabin himself was posted abroad only because of a
bureaucratic oversight in the administrative disorganization
of the immediate post-Stalin period.)

The Guard was and is virtually an all-Russian organization. It is an interesting comment on the Soviet régime's
tolerance of minorities that only three national groups are
represented in it, out of the Soviet Union's total of more
than one hundred peoples. There are Russians, along with
some Ukrainians and Byelorussians. There are also a few
Armenians in the entourage of their compatriot Anastas
Mikoyan, and in Beria's salad days there were some Georgians; but since Beria's execution most Georgians in Moscow
are found on shoeshine stands.[2] Until 1949 there were almost 150 Jews in the Guard. Almost overnight, after a
secret directive from the Central Committee, they were all
released from their jobs and sent away on various pretexts.
It was part of the aftermath of the notorious "Doctors'
Plot" allegedly made on the life of Stalin, which was later
exposed by Khrushchev as a forgery. Several of the doctors
involved were Jewish, a fact which gave the régime an
excuse for showing off its always latent anti-Semitism.

There is one great peculiarity in this rigid selective process: the educational standard. Except for its own counter-
intelligence personnel and operational staff sections, the
Guard Directorate normally does not enlist anyone who has
received more than eight years of schooling. The State
Security wants its elite corps to be patient, mechanically
alert, and trustworthy. The last requirement, by its own
admission, clearly conflicts with high educational levels.
The late General Vlasik, when he bossed the Directorate,
summed up the official view admirably: "We don't need

[2] Traditionally Georgians and Armenians have operated
shoeshine stands on Moscow street corners. There is an old
story from the Stalin era about a visitor to Moscow who was
looking for two well-known streets there: Big Georgian Street
and Little Georgian Street. "The Big Georgian," he was told,
"is in the Kremlin, and the Little Georgians are on the street
corners."

the rotten intelligentsia." Vlasik himself was a case in point. He had received only three years of education in a village school before the Revolution, and he could barely sign his name.

In 1947 Vlasik lost his job for this very reason; even the Central Committee felt that the chief of the Guard was a somewhat over-spectacular example of Soviet anti-eggheadism. (He got the job back temporarily after forcing his way into Stalin's *dacha* for a personal appeal to his old boss.)

When a recruit comes to the Guard he is given a certain amount of security schooling: three months to a year, depending on his abilities. He studies methods and techniques of the State Security, notably surveillance; the expert handling of all types of small arms and machine guns; and the inevitable history of the Communist Party and its leaders. There is also a heavy emphasis on physical training and unarmed combat. Each year upward of four hundred candidates are accepted into the Guard's special school, graduating as junior lieutenants in the State Security.

The ideal Guard officer is a man who finishes this training satisfactorily, his reflexes sharpened and unclouded by any instinct for intellectual speculation. By way of example, instructors sometimes cited the fast action of a subordinate officer guarding Lazar Kaganovich in the years before Kaganovich went into disgrace as a member of what Khrushchev calls the "anti-Party group." Kaganovich and his bodyguard were walking down a corridor of the Kremlin late one evening when they ran into one of the cleaning women. The woman, startled by coming face to face with a life-size Politburo member, dropped her handbag in surprise. Without a second's hesitation the guard threw himself across the corridor and fell on the handbag. Suspecting it to be a bomb, he was trying to blunt the force of the explosion with his own body. Kaganovich made a coarse joke about the guard's fright, then peeled off his wristwatch and gave it to him.

No man was ever forced into service with the Guard, but to join it is like entering a long one-way street. If a man shows his discontent and repeatedly asks for his release, he can "resign." But his resignation is followed by expulsion from the Party or Komsomol and a bad reference from the State Security, to say nothing of his establishment in the State Security files as an "anti-Soviet" type who would require constant surveillance. It is impossible for a person who has thus "resigned" to get a decent job anywhere in Soviet society. No one will hire a man whose name is so obviously under a cloud with the KGB. This kind of release is called, in State Security circles, a "wolf ticket." In a significant number of cases people who got their release from the service in this way committed suicide shortly afterward.

If, on the other hand, a Guard officer minded his business, kept his eight-hour watches along the darkened streets of Moscow or along the lonely approaches to the *dachas* of the Soviet hierarchy, waited for the "triumphant masses" to trudge through Red Square year after year at his machine-gun post underneath the mausoleum, stayed away from liquor on the job, and never talked about what he did, he would be allowed in time to retire gracefully from the service. After twenty-five years of service he might receive a pension amounting to as much as eighty percent of his old salary.[3] It was more probable, however, that he would be given a faked medical discharge instead (the Soviet government dislikes handing out too many pensions) and a sinecure checking hunting rifles or caviar or TV sets in the branch of the Supply Section which serviced the Praesidium members and their families. He would reach retirement without noticeably increasing his rank. Guards seldom attain the grade of major, and few go that high.

If a Guard officer, however, got himself into any trouble before pension time and was dismissed for it, he had no hope of appeal. The man who tried an appeal merely complicated his own case. Not long after Deriabin came to the Directorate the wife of one Lieutenant Matveyev was discovered to be in correspondence with her aunt, who lived in Belgium. This was considered automatic grounds for dismissal, and Matveyev was so informed. For two months

[3] In the Guard Directorate one year of service was reckoned as two, for pension purposes. It was not a place of employment where long tenure was much of a probability. At that, it would take twelve and a half years of service before a man could get full pension.

poor Matveyev pounded the streets, looking unsuccessfully for other employment, the while continuing to protest to both the State Security and the Communist Party that the fact of his wife's corresponding with an aunt was no concern of *his*.

When all these appeals were ignored Matveyev, who was by then starving, walked into the U.S. Embassy in a vain effort to get some kind of assistance, if not asylum. No one there was able to do anything for him. The minute he left he was picked up by State Security agents who had followed him, and given a five-year jail sentence.

Another officer withheld information that his brother-in-law had been a prisoner of the Germans in World War II. Despite the fact that he had an excellent war record himself, he was fired straight-away on the charge of withholding information. (He would also have been fired if he had disclosed it.) He too argued his case up to the then Minister of the State Security and the Central Committee of the CPSU, but he got no satisfaction. His wife was pregnant, and he had spent all his savings. In desperation he walked into the Moscow Party committee and threw his Party card down on an official's desk. "Take it!" he shouted. "What good is it? What does the Party do for me?"

Unperturbed, the head of the local Party's Special Control Sector telephoned Deriabin, who had been the officer's superior, and asked him rather sharply what kind of people the State Security had been employing lately. "A man like this," he added soberly, "can be of no use to the Party." Deriabin reported the conversation to Colonel Goryshev, then in command of the Personnel Section. Goryshev ordered the officer put under special surveillance.

The State Security shadows reported that the officer continued to talk about the injustice of his treatment; and he had told friends about throwing away his Party card. While under surveillance he stole a woman's handbag at a railroad station, which contained 2000 rubles. "Ah, a good way to get rid of him," the Colonel said when this theft was reported. The officer was quickly arrested and given the standard penalty for purse snatching and similar crimes: three years.

At that, the purse-snatching officer was better off than a member of the plain-clothes detail working the streets in

Moscow, who committed suicide while awaiting a decision on a major dereliction of duty. A passer-by had crossed the street one afternoon in the middle of a cavalcade of Politburo cars with State Security escort. The man had been run over and killed by one of the security cars. The death had taken place in the officer's district. He was held responsible not for a dead pedestrian, but for having let an unauthorized person cross a street at an unauthorized time.

The job of investigating the derelictions of one's fellows poses a heavy strain on a man's own habits. A Chekist must keep his nose clean off duty as well as on the job, at least until he reaches the high level of the "New Class" Soviet society, where debauchery is organized and beyond criticism. Aside from his honey-beer drinking episode Deriabin had only one close call in his own personal life while he was with the Guard Directorate. It involved a casual female acquaintance, a woman from Barnaul, who had met him while on a visit to Moscow.

He took the woman out a few times, and then she went back to Siberia to wait for her husband, an Army major who was finishing a jail sentence for misappropriating military supplies. (In the Soviet system people jailed for such non-political crimes are sometimes able to return to their old jobs after the prison term is over.) A month after she had returned home she sent Deriabin a letter announcing that she was to bear his child. She demanded a large sum of money, threatening to denounce him to the State Security for immoral conduct if he refused to pay.

Deriabin knew there was no truth in the charge, but he also realized that the woman, a Party member, was no fool. She knew very well that *any* denunciation, no matter how false or frivolous, is subject to investigation. The very fact of an investigation would be damaging to anyone in Deriabin's position. So, since she needed money . . .

He took the letter in to the Party secretary of the State Security, General Rogov, and asked his advice in dealing with the problem. The General's answer was characteristic of a service with a horror of personal entanglements. "You fix it yourself," he said, "I don't care how you do it. Take some leave time and go back to Barnaul. But see that she doesn't bother you again. We can't afford to have this sort of thing happening."

With this advice Deriabin took the train back home again to confront his accuser. As luck had it, her husband, the errant major, had been released from prison a few days before and was home. He met Deriabin at the door and heard the whole story. His reaction was forceful and direct. Screaming, "Whore! Bitch! Cheat!" he started to beat the woman and did this so strenuously that Deriabin advised him to stop, unless he wanted to pick up another jail term for manslaughter. Then Deriabin wrote a paper for the wife to sign, acknowledging that her "pregnancy" letter had been nothing but blackmail. She refused. Whereupon he played his best card. "You sign this now," he said, "or I go down the street to see my friend in charge of the State Security investigation section and have him start an investigation on you tomorrow. Before they are through with you, you will be sorry you were born." The woman signed. As Deriabin left, the major started to beat her again.

Not long after this episode Peter Deriabin married for the second time. By instinct a family man, he disliked living a bachelor's life in borrowed lodgings; the dubious pleasures of social life in Moscow of the late forties were hardly a compensation. His new wife, Marina Makeyeva, whom he met in the Kremlin, was herself a trusted Soviet employee. At the time, she worked in the Politburo as a stenographer in the office of Lazar Kaganovich. Some six months after their marriage in June 1948, they were given an apartment in the ten-story State Security apartment house at 48a Chkalova Street. They had one big room and shared a kitchen with two other families, a luxurious arrangement by general Soviet standards. As a chief of a subsection, Deriabin rated a car and a chauffeur, and his salary enabled him to rent a small *dacha* in the pine woods at Mamontovka, twenty miles from Moscow. In line with normal Soviet official behavior he used his official car for domestic travel as well. When the Deriabins went to the *dacha* the chauffeur went with them.

His 4200 rubles a month was an excellent Soviet salary, well above the 2000 rubles of a factory superintendent or the 1000 given the highest type of worker. An officer in the State Security, especially in the Guard Directorate, received, in addition, scores of little perquisites which would have meant thousands of rubles expense to an ordinary So-

viet citizen. Every two years officers of the Guard received
two complete sets of clothing (uniforms and clothes).
Everything they received was of far better quality than
normal Army uniforms or the civilian clothes available at
all but the most expensive stores. And the high salaries enabled them to get extras not within the grasp of ninety-five
percent of the Soviet people: the Hungarian suit, the
fleece-lined lady's coat, the bottle of good *Stolichnaya*, butter. When their child was born, in 1949, Deriabin's wife
went to the Kremlin hospital, where she received the same
attention given a semi-private patient in an American hospital. This would have represented unheard-of luxury to
most Soviet mothers.

For all these privileges Deriabin worked hard. Through
almost five years in the Guard Directorate he struggled
with the same basic monotony of his job, a thatch-weave of
routine checking and probing which was as uninspiring on
its level as were the dreary eight-hour watches of the plain-
clothes[4] details in the streets. It was not only disastrous to
let himself get rusty at this kind of work; on the other side
of the medal, it was of the utmost importance to a man's career that he do it well—in every detail. Intelligent and loyal
service at the center of things was the perfect foundation
for a career in the New Class hierarchy of the Soviet Union.

In 1949 Deriabin took advantage of a change in his duty
hours to begin classes at the Institute of Marxism-
Leninism, the well-known ideological command and general staff school whose diploma was almost essential to a
good Party man on his way up. His decision to attend
school again was hardly the result of idealism. A year's
service in Moscow, on top of his previous experiences, had
rubbed most of the paint off his Komsomol enthusiasm
about world revolution. But he wished to get his final
Communist instruction over with as soon as possible before
his office and family responsibilities multiplied.

[4] The word "plain-clothes" is not meant to distinguish the
street details from the rest of the Directorate. Except for the
actual guard units on sentry and patrol duty, most of the officers like Deriabin rarely wore uniforms during their Moscow
assignment.

He spent two full years at the school. Classes were held three times a week at night, and the sessions lasted four hours each. The instruction was not inspiring, consisting principally of windy lectures and rote exercises in "dialectic"—low-level Party history courses carried to the nth power. But Deriabin's attendance at the Institute of Marxism-Leninism did give him an excuse to visit lectures at the nearby Academy of Political Science. Using his State Security card as his ticket of admission, he often slipped into the crowded lecture halls where Soviet scholars were explaining their version of non-Soviet philosophies or political beliefs. Petr N. Pospelov, veteran Party member and editor of *Pravda*, who had been put in charge of propaganda by the Central Committee, was one of these; so were Andrey Vyshinsky, who lectured on justice and foreign policy, Sergey Krylov, the authority on international law, who gave a course on the Nuremberg Trials, and Pavel Yudin, the Communist theoretician, now Ambassador to Communist China.

Deriabin had grown cynical about all forms of politics, but some of what he heard about this other world made an impression on him. He was careful to keep it to himself, even inside the groups with whom he associated.

Almost all his associates, the friends he made, and the parties he went to were within the orbit of the State Security. It was more comfortable, and safer, to avoid most other associations. Inside and outside the office the secret world of the State Security had interests and even a private language of its own. Even when Deriabin and some of his fellow officers were stopping at a bar, one of the brassy and expensive American imitations that had sprung up in Moscow, someone would suggest a drink with the customary slang salutation used in their work: "*Otmetit'sya?* Shall we make a quick check?"

This was not the tightly closed society which he was to meet later, when he worked with the elite and comparatively sophisticated group in foreign intelligence. But it had already grown uncomfortable to keep up too much contact with old friends. It was embarrassing enough to note the contrast between his friends' and relatives' shabbiness and his own comparative opulence. It was more embarrassing, and potentially dangerous, when friendship touched on

State Security business. In the provinces the State Security man might help his civilian friends; in the Guard Directorate it was different.

Peter Deriabin tried only once to help out someone he had known. He received a letter from a man he had known in Novosibirsk who had been sentenced to ten years at hard labor for stealing bread from the collective farm where he worked. Deriabin took the letter immediately to Goryshev, since the very possession of a letter from an accused was potential incrimination, and asked him if he could do anything to help. The Colonel told him what to do with the letter in rough but explicit terms.

The few old friends and relatives Deriabin and his wife did see were polite to the point of embarrassment. When Deriabin said he worked for "the Kremlin" everyone knew exactly what he meant. Host and hostess would drop whatever else they were doing to refill his glass or give him the best of the food.

Only occasionally did the fear and the hate behind the solicitude break surface—mostly under the stimulus of very strong drink. In the summer of 1952 Deriabin and his family went to a party at a *dacha* near his own, at which a well-known literary man was present, a poet. The poet had been told by whispers from his relatives there that Deriabin was an officer of the State Security, but he disregarded the warnings and lurched over for a brief political discussion. He wrote very little any more, he said, and he wanted to explain why. "They closed my mouth, and I don't have enough air to breathe. I can't write by order about dirty peasants and Stakhanovites. I know you are part of 'them,' but I am not afraid of you. I know you know everything about me—you may have read my poems. I wrote many poems in the Patriotic War, because I love my country, but not now—— If you haven't read my poems, well, here I am—you can read me now. . . ."

Even when dealing with actual or suspected "enemies of the people" Deriabin liked to avoid scenes. He belonged to a quiet-spoken school of political law enforcement, now less of a rarity in Soviet police circles than formerly. So he turned away the poet's challenges with what he hoped would be construed as a friendly warning, at least when the poet woke up the next morning. "If you talk more quietly," he said, "it might be better for you."

When they heard about this exchange the poet's relatives were in a state of near panic. Deriabin tried to smooth over their fears. He secretly admired the poet for speaking his mind—he had come to know how precious this faculty really was—and he finally said so. He ventured to add that the time was probably not yet ripe for the state publishing houses to produce any new editions of the man's books.

Deriabin was more sensitive to such encounters than most of his fellow officers, although it would hardly have been politic to show it. In almost five years at the Guard Directorate he had done well, with a good reputation both in State Security and in Party circles. He liked his car and his *dacha* and the drinks he could afford to buy at the reasonably expensive restaurants. He did not like his work much nor the human trouble that formed its principal subject, and he worried about the future. He read a lot. He used to smile tartly at a little verse in Pushkin, describing a Count Vorontsev, one of the poet's superiors in the official society of an earlier day:

> "Half hero, half ignoramus,
> What's more, half scoundrel,
> Don't forget.
>
> On this last score,
> The man gives promise
> That he'll make a full one yet."

CHAPTER XI

The Interrogators

THE OFFICE WHERE Deriabin worked in the Guard Directorate was a large room on the second floor of the State Security building at 2 Dzerzhinsky Square, better known internationally by its more familiar name of Lubianka Prison. The jail capacity of the Lubianka had been reduced since Feliks Dzerzhinsky started putting the OGPU's captives there in the early 1920s, owing to the construction of so many similar facilities throughout the Soviet Union. There are two other State Security prisons in Moscow, Lefortovo (where Beria was confined before his execution) and Butyrskaya, to share the few key prisoners which the State Security kept outside the regular jail network of its sister service, the MVD. No more than two hundred can be accommodated in the Lubianka. But the Lubianka has remained the symbolic fountainhead of Soviet justice. Investigations are begun in the offices overlooking the inner prison yard, and they end in the solitary detention cells below them. From where he sat Deriabin could see the prisoners in the courtyard when they were led out for exercise. They made a disturbing reminder of his purpose in life as a State Security officer, particularly since so many of his bosses were, from time to time, to be found among them.

There is a quote of Lenin's which bobs up somewhere in every State Security instruction course: "The judicial processes should not do away with terror. To do this would be self-deception. Instead the process should be based on ter-

157

ror and should legalize it as a matter of principle, clearly, without any shamming or attempts to make it look better." The application of terror in some form to its prisoners is an ever-present technical problem for the State Security.

Soviet methods of interrogation are the world's most dramatized and discussed question-and-answer system. The device of the forced voluntary confession, that awesome combination of the revival meeting, the Inquisition, and the third degree, is original with Soviet Communism, and it will stand as one of the basest inventions in human history. To people who live outside the Soviet system the State Security interrogator's success in producing such confessions has the look of black magic, or at least a devilish application of new scientific discoveries. It is most difficult for a Soviet citizen to explain this process. Although he knows that any prisoner, whatever his background, has his breaking point, his own upbringing has conditioned him to expect the forced voluntary confession as a normal outcome of arrest. It has been, after all, the rule in his own society for over forty years.

Deriabin was not an interrogator, but he swam so deep in the blood stream of the State Security system that interrogation techniques were familiar to him. Many of his friends specialized in this art. The interrogator's slang term for beating—"I gave him a few hot ones"—was part of the State Security vocabulary when he came to Moscow, and it has remained so. Like other experienced officers of the State Security, he came to take the "confession" for granted in any really serious case, from Lavrentiy Beria to a teen-ager caught trying to cross the Soviet border.

A good starting point for studying this interrogation technique is the motive of the interrogator. The case officer, as we have seen, is virtually committed to a conviction the moment he opens a formal case file. The KGB, as the saying goes, "never arrests anyone who is not guilty." The need for a confession of guilt, however, comes not only from the interrogator's desire for promotion and survival. There is also the practical need to protect the State Security's own agents and informers who were responsible for opening the case in the first place. If the investigating officer has to rely on his agents for witnesses he automatically destroys a good intelligence network by bringing it out in court. The accused may recoil in surprised horror when he hears the testimony accumlated against him and learns or suspects the identity of the informers. But the interrogator sees to it that no one on the outside shares this knowledge.

The interrogator conducts his investigation as the representative of the Soviet state, and the Soviet state never makes mistakes. It is only individuals who make mistakes, in the Soviet context, by wilfully "distorting" or "falsifying" the clear precepts of Communism. Any State Security investigator has had this principle drilled into him long before he reaches the prison cell or the interrogation room. But in his zeal to prove its truth—and get himself a raise to senior case officer or deputy section chief in the bargain—he ends by brain-washing himself as well as the prisoner.

These starting premises in the Soviet interrogation technique have been changed not a jot or a tittle by the various political "relaxations" since the death of Stalin. The degree of violence in the interrogation process, however, has been cut down sharply. In the *Yezhovshchina*, the title by which the purges of the thirties are best remembered, no holds were barred. Records disappeared along with prisoners, or they were never made. Torture, or at least heavy beatings, was almost inevitable in the smallest of cases. Psychological pressures too were so intense that they frequently exhausted interrogators as well as the prisoners involved.

As late as 1953 the interrogators were backed by terror devices which would have done credit to the worst of the Gestapo professionals. From 1946 until that year, the State Security maintained at its Moscow headquarters a quietly notorious laboratory called "The Chamber" (*Kamera*). Its staff consisted of a medical director and several assistants, who performed experiments on living people—prisoners and persons about to be executed—to determine the effectiveness of various poisons and injections as well as the use of hypnotism and drugs in interrogation techniques. Only the Minister of the State Security and four other high officers were allowed to enter.

The laboratory prospered. The "doctor" in charge was given a special degree of Doctor in Medical Science by Moscow University and nominated for a Stalin Prize for his "researches." The Soviet régime announced The Chamber's closing to a select group of State Security officials in October 1953, after blaming its existence on the Beria excesses. It has probably not been reactivated; but its researches continue to be exploited by selected personnel of the State Security.

The Chamber, while it lasted, had been under the Commandant's Section in the administrative directorate of the State Security apparatus. It was this section which supervised all executions of political prisoners condemned to death, in addition to its normal physical security duties. This aspect of its work was carefully hidden even from most officers inside the Moscow headquarters. The bodies of those executed were carted off at night from the place of execution in the Lubianka. They were driven to the crematorium opposite the Voroshilov Army General Staff Academy, in trucks painted to look like normal commercial delivery trucks. The trucks were appropriately lettered with "Milk," "Meat," etc. on their panels.

For his work in supervising the executions—"for separate special assignments of the Minister," as the orders read—the Commandant, Major General Blokhin, received an additional stipend of 4000–5000 rubles in addition to his monthly 7000-ruble salary.

His assistant, Colonel Orkunev, was similarly well favored. But when Deriabin made his acquaintance, Orkunev, a fifteen-year veteran of the execution detail, was showing signs of strain. He was officially the chief of an operational subsection in the Guard Directorate, but he drank too much to be fit for office duty. By 1951 he had taken to copious drinking during working hours. (Because of his close friendship with the current State Security Minister, Abakumov, no one dared reprimand him for this.) Ultimately he lapsed into a state of complete alcoholism. He developed a speech defect. The more fastidious officers shunned him as he lurched down the halls of the Dzerzhinsky Square headquarters, saliva and *Stolichnaya* dripping from his mouth. He was removed during the purges of the early fifties.

Such crudities are now in disfavor. No one is beaten to death. Tortures are largely psychological and, even then, less intense and far less frequent than they were in 1939 or 1949. But the devices of beating, torture, and privation remain within the interrogator's grasp, to be used in case of necessity.

The interrogation terror first slackened sharply in 1953 in line with the general easing of pressures inside the Soviet Union at the end of Stalin's rule. The relative weakness of the succeeding oligarchy, in comparison to the absolute rule of Stalin, forced obvious concessions to public opinion in their country, as faithfully reported to Moscow by the provincial outposts of the KGB. The public easement of prison life was part of the same directive that downgraded the State Security to the status of a "committee."

These concessions have been sharply braked as a result of Khrushchev's consolidation of power. Yet the very fact that Khrushchev denounced repressive measures in his Twentieth Congress speech to Party leaders makes it very hard for him to restore the old severities in full. His kind of personal dictatorship works on a more complex set of premises than Stalin's, and it is not nearly so total. Khrushchev's régime has proved itself fully capable of repressive acts as ruthless as Stalin's, e.g. the Hungarian atrocities. But it prefers for its own sake to avoid open severity, if possible: a political enemy in prison or the equivalent looks better and stronger for a modern Soviet régime than the political enemy's hasty execution.

On the interrogator's level the *relative* relaxation of the post-Stalin and the early-Khrushchev eras means a general tacit order to go easy on a prisoner as long as he co-operates and avoid unnecessary violence. Mere suspects are not to be physically harmed. The régime does not want to have them spreading stories of a new terror. Neither are short-term minor "criminals." They will be released too soon. But if the interrogator needs violence or more than the usual psychological pressure to get his "confession," he will use it, especially on a person charged with a serious crime who will not be able to tell his story on the outside for another fifteen years, if ever.

There is no fixed system of interrogation. It depends on the current Party directives, the conditions of the State Security investigation apparatus, and the relative peace or restlessness of the locality. A man who gets off with a warning in Vladivostok might have been thrown into solitary in Tashkent. But certain general rules are observed.

When the accused is brought into the prison he is stripped and searched thoroughly. Any contact with the outside is forbidden. Food parcels are not allowed.

The accused are put into two-man or four-man cells. Solitary confinement, especially in important cases, is also very usual. The lights are left on day and night. Guards constantly watch the prisoners through a small hole in the door, known familiarly as the "wolf's eye." There are certain routine devices of psychological torture by now familiar to most readers of political literature. Interrogations usually take place at night. They are lengthy and repetitive, their effect furthered by physical discomforts like long periods of forced standing. Isolation is almost water-tight. Guards take the prisoner to the interrogation room in such a way that he never sees another living soul on the way.

There are two things which the interrogator sets out to establish in any prisoner: a sense of guilt and a sense of doom. The sense of guilt is fostered by every means at the State Security's disposal. The interrogator is often the same case officer who has built up the case against the accused, so his convictions about guilt are particularly strong. The accused is faced with a bewildering mass of documentation and often confronted by witnesses against him. Forgeries, faked documents, faked witnesses are commonplace in this process. Even his own initial statements are sometimes forged or distorted.

In Moscow the more important prisoners are subject to processing by psychologists and, in some cases, hypnotic treatment. Drugs are used sparingly, certainly not to the extent that is popularly supposed. Most prisoners produce their "confession" without the need of artificial stimulants. The regular process is enough: documentation and confrontations, threats against a person's family, nightly interrogations, solitary confinement, etc. The investigator begins by "reasoning" with the prisoner. Next comes the stage of threats and violent accusations. If the man still resists he may then be beaten or subjected to various other types of pressure: sudden changes in the prison routine, exhausting interrogations, cramped cells, sub-freezing temperatures, etc. The primary object is to take away his will.

One of the most powerful weapons against the prisoner all through this process is the maddening assurance of all his interrogators that he is guilty. No doubt is considered even a possibility. This simple human pressure is very difficult for most people to stand against, especially when they are themselves products of the system that uses it.

The second goal of the interrogator, the feeling of doom, is the natural follow-up to the implanting of guilt. Regardless of how the accused feels at the time of his arrest, he is made to know that there is no escape for him. "You will never get out of here," the interrogators tell him, "and don't expect help from any of your friends." And there is that most powerful of arguments: "Everyone here always confesses." If a prisoner refuses to confess he is pictured as a positive stumbling block to national progress.

Here the interrogator injects the third and final thought of a Soviet interrogation: that the only path to freedom lies through work in a labor camp or some similar institution for the benefit of "our great country," that the only service to humanity the prisoner can render is a full confession to warn others away from his own "crime."

This is brain-washing as practiced by its originators. It is simple, effective, and unbelievably cruel. Therein lies its mystery. The reason so many Americans deduce awesome mechanical or medical apparatus at the service of Soviet interrogators is their inability to comprehend a system so devoid at its roots of mercy or human decency. Soviet interrogation methods, like Soviet trials, judges, and "juries," are completely outside American experience. They operate on the analogy of a traffic accident in a nightmare. A man who runs afoul of the Soviet state is like a pedestrian just run down by a truck. The truck driver also turns out to be the policeman investigating the accident and the judge who decides on the fault involved. This multiple personality is not interested in which party was at fault in the crossing accident: the truck or the pedestrian. Because the pedestrian has collided with the truck he is automatically at fault, since the truck, because it was moving, was obviously going in the right direction and at the correct speed. Therefore the only problems at issue are how quickly the pedestrian will sign a paper admitting his guilt, what penalty should be assessed against him, and how his example may best prevent future pedestrians from scratching the truck's fenders.

Soviet citizens learn to accept this statist logic. They realize that every person accused and arrested by the State
Security is considered guilty.[1] There is a bitter joke, told
during the Stalinist period, that exemplifies this attitude.
Stalin has lost his pipe. He telephones the State Security
and demands that they find it immediately. Two hours later he finds the pipe, which had merely fallen into one of
his boots. He telephones the State Security again and asks
them what progress they have made. "We have arrested
ten men already," the Minister reports, "and the investigation is continuing." "As it happens," says Stalin, "I have
found my pipe. So free them instantly." "But, Comrade
Stalin, seven of them have already confessed."

The confessions, like the investigations of the case officer, must always implicate accomplices. One of Deriabin's
friends, an officer on the Special Investigation Board of
the State Security—to which most interrogation specialists
are attached—told him about a Jewish man of middle age
caught while trying to escape to Poland and thence, as it
seemed, to Israel. After some rough handling he admitted
that he was indeed trying to escape. "There is no hope for
a Jew in the Soviet Union," he said. The interrogator
suavely agreed with him, realizing that it was in all probability a purely individual escape attempt, but kept up his
threats and pressure until the names of some "accomplices"
had been put into the file. Then the State Security was
ready for the sentencing.

Even more frustrated than the Jewish prisoner, and
equally badly handled, were two Russians who had sealed
themselves up inside a huge crate containing agricultural
machinery being readied for shipment in the port area of
Rostov. They stayed patiently inside the crate after it was
put aboard a ship and during the course of a journey that
completely exhausted their food supply. It was their mis-

---

[1] The State Security's convictions are sometimes reversed by
higher authority, but only for political reasons. Some Old Bolsheviks were released from prison by Khrushchev following his
denunciation of Stalin, and their sentences declared unjust. But
this was done as a political gesture, in an attempt to establish
Khrushchev as a direct link with the tradition of Lenin and the
early Bolsheviks, miraculously reforged.

fortune that the crates were unloaded on the dock the moment the ship arrived in Durazzo, Albania (not that an Albanian landfall would have done them much good, anyway). Soviet experts, eager to give immediate demonstrations of their new agricultural machinery, were surprised to find two fugitive countrymen wrapped along with it, hardly testimony to Soviet progress in other fields of human endeavor. But they lost no time in sending the two men back to Rostov. There the local State Security office was able to produce a most satisfying list of accomplices, virtually a conspiratorial network, in fact, although in reality only one man had helped them.

The subjects, time, and circumstances of such stories may change, but the stories go on. The tactics of interrogation may have grown softer, but the principle of this Soviet art and its goal are unchanged. Twenty years ago, in the days when the State Security still went by the name of NKVD, another of those ubiquitous Russian wordplays was made from its initials: *Neizvestino Kogda Vernesh'sia Domoi*—"You never know when you will get home." With the present KGB an accused enjoys the same uncertainty.

CHAPTER XII

Double Life Of A Party Man

FOR THIRTEEN YEARS the most important factor in Peter Deriabin's life was the care and feeding of a number. No. 4121243 was the serial stamped on his Party card and the number on the face of his file, both in the central Party headquarters in Moscow and the various local committees with which he served. Almost until the moment of his flight from Vienna, File No. 4121243 was a fat and impressive collection of documents, full of testimony to Deriabin's efficiency and loyalty to the Communist Party.

One cannot begin to explain Deriabin's rise in the New Class hierarchy of the U.S.S.R. without reference to this Party number and how it was used. His quick promotions, his transfer to Moscow, his successful entrance and exit sequence in the Guard Directorate—all these happy coincidences could hardly be the result merely of efficient work and occasional good "contacts" during office hours at the State Security. They make sense only in the weird perspective of two careers lived jointly by the same man, his performance in each constantly affecting his record in the other: his official career and his career in the Party. The same double life is lived by any Soviet official who is a Party member of standing (and almost all are). It says much for the essential role played by this double government in preserving the Soviet system that it was thought necessary to maintain it in the State Security, which is itself the principal executive arm of the Communist Party.

The manner in which the Communist Party controls Soviet institutions is hardly a secret. It is comparable to the standard apparatus used to domesticate American corporations in the days before the anti-trust laws: a giant holding company managing scores of subsidiaries through interlocking directorates staffed with its own appointees. The holding company may originally have been a productive economic organization in its own right, but as it extends its sway over more and more aspects of business life its own original organic functions atrophy. It ends as a device for power and profit, dedicated solely to the maintenance of its own rule over the subsidiaries.

Translated into political terms, this is the story of the Communist Party of the Soviet Union. Naturally the Party's devices for keeping control of the entire life of a country are far more complicated and inclusive than the old-fashioned holding company's method of exploiting its business subsidiaries. But the principle is the same. Similarly, also, the Party's original ideological dedication and revolutionary impulses—the factors which enabled the Old Bolsheviks to make of it a valid if repulsive political organization—have gradually given way to a single-minded pursuit of power and profit. The profit and the power both are restricted as far as possible to the small circle of Communist leaders and their faithful servants inside the Party.

To insure its continued control the Party must penetrate into every section of society in the Soviet Union. The penetration interlocks. Take any town in the Soviet Union. The highest authority in the town is the Party committee. The committee has special sections or at least individual "instructors" to cover every aspect of life inside the town, from factory management to athletic teams. There is an over-all authority for propaganda. There are sections for watching the family and social life of Party members, a section for education and science, and an office which controls the Party's subsidiary organizations like the Komsomol, the puppet trade unions, etc.

Beneath the local Party committee are smaller committees running the affairs of Party members in individual factories, schools, etc. Each smaller committee is a duplicate of the larger one, on its own scale. Above the town committee, in turn, are committees for *rayon, oblast, kray* and republic, in which the town committee's functions are duplicated but greatly expanded. At their apex are the members and candidates of the Central Committee in Moscow, the 255 men who run the Soviet Union, or, more exactly, the men who are immediately responsible to whatever dictator happens to be running the Soviet Union.

The Party does not rule directly. It has no formal apparatus for controlling the decisions in a factory or a collective farm. In front of it stand the legally constituted organs of government and business and social activity in the U.S.S.R. The highest authority in a town, formally speaking, is the chairman of the town soviet, and so on, up to the Chairman of the Council of Ministers of the U.S.S.R. There are independent artists' groups, and steelworkers' unions, and hospital directorates, each with its own well-linked chain of command, with nothing said in its charter about Party membership. Yet the leaders of each group are Party members, each of them responsible to his local committee, if, indeed, he does not run it. So it is the Party members who control the decisions on the official level. They account for them on the Party level.

Every activity in the Soviet Union has its weekly Party meeting which discusses and criticizes the professional and personal problems of its members. The purpose of the meeting is direction and discipline. The members are told the goals to which they must aspire. They are admonished when they slip. If a man does sloppy work, drinks heavily, or divorces his wife, he comes up for Party censure as surely as if he had criticized Khrushchev's agricultural policy or falsified the fact that his brother was in prison. The censure is not moral. It is irregularity of any sort that the Party fears. Its ideal is the intelligent norm, with as little capacity as possible for free-will.

The Communist is not supposed to have a private life outside his organization. Everything he has and does—family, profession, hobbies, friends—is subordinated to the fact of his Communism. He is a Communist not only when he is at Party meetings. He is a Communist everywhere and at all times. As such he is "responsible" for non-Party people; that is to say, he has an obligation to insure their loyalty and, if necessary, inform on them.

Discipline in the Party is severe, but it is obeyed. All the Party organization need do to a man is take away his Party card, and he is through. He can get no responsible job in the Soviet Union, nor in all probability can members of his family. His living standard plummets. He loses his apartment. He can get no vacations. All these things the Party controls. And even if the Party does not directly control an activity it will give no favors to a man with a bad Party record against him.

Conversely a Party card and a good record constitute an irreplaceable passport to preferment. They stand for political loyalty in a world where politics constantly take precedence over efficiency. Deriabin's card No. 4121243 not only had no derogatory information registered against it; it belonged to a man who had the fortune to do jobs well in a crucial area at a time when competence was scarce. His competence at his work, both Army and State Security, in turn gave added purpose to his Party superiors' desire to promote him—thanks to past experiences, the Soviet Party is extremely sensitive about good Communists who fail at their everyday work. As a result, Deriabin's very success makes a revealing introduction to the mechanics of Communist rule in the Soviet Union. Behind almost every step he took on the ladder upward, in both the Army and the State Security, was a corresponding rise in his Party status.

Accident and scarcity, as previously noted, played their part in his success as a Communist. On entering the Soviet Army the youngest high school teacher in the Altai Kray found political officers and instructors at a premium. His record as a leading *Komsomolets* qualified to teach Party history marked him for rapid promotion. After only three weeks of preliminary training he never more had to stand guard duty, perform kitchen police, arise with early morning reveille, or perform any other functions of the private soldier. He was too well employed on th regimental newspaper, on his way to a career as a politically reliable member of the Soviet armed forces. Each Komsomol and Party post led to another, Deriabin discovered. Like membership in the ascending grades of some fraternal order in the United States, the upward transition went on almost independent of the man involved, with significant difference that no promotion or new responsibility could be safely refused if high authority wanted it. So his career in the Party became a replica of the hard-working days in the local

Komsomols in Siberia. In 1942 he became Party secretary at his regimental headquarters. In 1945, after leaving counter-intelligence school, he was "elected" Komsomol secretary for Naval Counter-Intelligence headquarters in Moscow. He was a deputy Party secretary for the Personnel Section while working in the Guard Directorate and later Party secretary for the Austro-German Section in the State Security's Foreign Intelligence Directorate.

In each of these jobs Deriabin gained some insight into the functioning government of the Soviet Union. It is a government in which very few of his fellow countrymen share, Communists included, but to which *only* Communists can claim admission. Most of the seven million Party members in the Soviet Union are recruited young, as Deriabin was, from among the twenty million members of the Komsomol. Until a person is twenty-six entrance into the Party is virtually impossible, except through the Komsomol. And it is the youth, entering in this manner, who make the best Party candidates.

A true Communist is a man who feels certitude, at least in the beginning of his Party career. Deriabin and his companions in Siberia had found in Communism the only hope for talent to escape poverty and its drab surroundings. Having thus provided a viewable horizon for the very young, the Communist faith first gained authority over them, then absorbed them. In the minds of Deriabin's generation and those who followed it, the word "Communist" became associated with maturity and wisdom. It was easy, therefore, given the trusting propensities of human nature, to persuade young Communists to defy the evidence of their senses and their own logic if the Party so ordained. If the Party is so great and wise, their thinking ran, it must have a reason for doing as it does.

Such blind trust is not unknown elsewhere. The veteran reader of the New York or the London *Times*, for example, has been known to doubt his own eyesight if the newspaper's account of a happening, backed by its reputation for wisdom, contradicts his personal observation. A theatergoer or a book reader may revise his own judgment of an offering, on the basis of what his favorite critic has to say. A person given to psychiatric consultation may repudiate his own logic and judgment if the psychiatrist seems to disagree. Back of all these relatively familiar phenomena in free societies is the simple suspicion: "They must know more about it than I do." The success of Communism in ruling a country rests on its implanting these simple suspicions, many times magnified, in the minds of its Party workers, in producing a gross, frightening extension of the omniscient "They." When a person finally gets to be one of "Them" he is generally too implicated in the technical work of creating this omniscience to waste time or risk security by even half-publicly doubting it.

In this way, up from the Komsomol through the State Security, Peter Deriabin came to share in the Soviet Union's real government. He was first of all a Party activist, one of the million-odd Party members who spend a considerable part of their working time on Party business. Included in this group are the members of the all-powerful committees governing Party organizations in cities, districts, regiments, and ministries throughout the Soviet Union. They number about 250,000. Inside this 250,000, like the holder of higher degrees in a Masonic order, stand the top leaders of the Party, who number about 20,000. They are the members of the provincial and area committees and the Central Committees of the Communist Party in the Union republics and, finally, of the Central Committee of the CPSU in Moscow.

Among this 20,000 and in the echelons of activists below it, power is wielded effectively and almost always decisively by the Party secretaries. Their job is the same on whatever level, and Deriabin learned it well.

The Party secretary in the U.S.S.R. is an extraordinary combination of bureaucrat, ward heeler, and professional fixer. On occasion he also fills the roles of social director, recruiting sergeant, and sentencing judge. He is the essential element in the entire Communist structure. Without him it would collapse.

In any Party organization it is the secretary who controls the personnel lists. He has to preside over the induction of new members and must recommend them if they are to be admitted. A secretary's recommendation is what counts in the official making of a Communist. All the ambitious questions are so much window-dressing.

It is the secretary also who determines the agenda of the

Party meetings and thus shapes their course. If Comrade X has been notably slack in fulfilling the production quota at his factory, all the secretary need do to give X a reprimand or worse is steer the conversation to the subject of factory quotas. Human nature and man's propensity for discussion will take care of the rest. X will emerge with some sort of censure or exhortation rendered in the most "democratic" manner.

If Comrade Y has been consorting with suspected "anti-Soviet" persons the secretary has only to put the assessment of "anti-Party elements" first on the agenda; gossip and every Party member's sworn duty to inform against his fellow will round out the picture of Y's danger or disgrace. If Comrade Z needs to be read out of the Party or his neighbor seems good Party material, it is the secretary who determines what should be done, how fast, and to what purpose.

The Communist Party makes a great point of its inner democracy. In actual fact, although Party members may exercise a certain right of election in the lowest echelons, their free choice is always circumscribed by the secretary's presence. He is the man in charge of accepting nominations, hearing petitions from the floor, recognizing speakers, and approving committees. He is thus able to maintain a Party dictatorship within the outward trappings of democracy, at the best, by a judicious use of parliamentary procedure and, at the worst, by a combination of threat and exhortation.

Party secretaries are nominally "elected" by the rank-and-file. Actually they appoint each other, down the line from the Central Committee of the CPSU in Moscow, whose First Secretary is the dictator of the country, as far as the smallest provincial Party committee. All Party secretaries, the regulations explicitly say, must be confirmed by the Central Committee in Moscow, from the *rayon* secretaries on up. If a secretary is not confirmed he must be immediately replaced. Below the level of the *rayon* it would be a rare and suicidal Party committee which would nominate a man not approved by the district secretary beforehand. For the provision of confirmation has been so construed that the appointment of Party secretaries is in fact the province of the secretary next highest up the line, like the laying-on of hands by a bishop.

This episcopal succession of Party secretaries, in turn, supports their authority with the rank-and-file. When a man is in known possession of a potent whip he seldom has to display it. So the meetings of the committees go on with the trappings of democratic discussion, all arranged by the thoughtful Party secretary. He has charge of the Party rolls. He submits the reports to Moscow through the echelons intervening. He receives the praise or censure of Moscow for the committee's work. In the local edition of the Communist holding corporation he is the one who keeps the books and chairs the board meetings. To challenge his authority successfully would take a supreme effort of unity and circumspection among the committee members, plus some very well-placed friends on higher levels. It is one function of the State Security to discover such efforts and root them out before they come to fruition.

The secretary's job is no sinecure. Like the case officer in the State Security, he is a man with a quota. It is his job to enroll good Party members as they appear in his jurisdiction. This is especially true for gifted technical personnel who for various reasons have held off from joining the Party heretofore. If a man is a competent physicist and shrinks from joining the Party out of unexpressed conviction, the Soviet Union is not now so rich in talent that it can afford to dismiss him or send him off to penal servitude for the modern form of *lèse-majesté*. On the contrary, it mobilizes every resource to "persuade" the man to join.

Like a small-town Mephistopheles, the Party secretary will come around frequently to visit such valuable workers; affiable, chatty, asking nothing at first. Instead, he makes it his business to find out what the indivdual needs either in his job or his personal life. It may be that his wife is ill and desperately wants a vacation. Presto changeo, something can be arranged, through the Party, for a two-week trip to some Black Sea resort. Alternatively the non-Party chief engineer may be desperately in need of some vital parts to fill a factory's production quota. The proper ministries have been written, but delays seem inevitable. Along comes the Party secretary with a friendly offer to get some help through his channels. Working up through the Party hierarchy, he can get a directive to unfreeze the wanted machinery far more quickly.[1] The engineer is inevitably impressed. The Party, he reasons, does get things done. And he is in the secretary's debt.

Thus, when the secretary drops the heavy hint that he might enjoy Party membership, he accepts. Now the Party can point to Engineer Chistyakov, for example, a fine specimen of Soviet industrial man who has joined the Party at the advanced age of fifty because he recognizes that the Party members are leading the fight toward the better life. Hardly idealism, but it is a telling example to the rest of the citizenry.

Recruitment is the pleasant side of the Party secretary's duties. The other side of the coin is exercise of his disciplinary functions. The Soviet Union has a sanitized constitution guaranteeing every variety of freedom and embodying every kind of protection for liberties. How can people be disciplined, therefore, for offending the Party line, when nothing they do is contrary to the constitution's provisions? The answer is the Party meeting, the kangaroo court of the Soviet Union. Organized formally to canonize popular sentiment against an offender, it acts in practice as an instrument of the dictatorship's discipline.

A Party member, like a European national in a nineteenth-century African colony, is rarely disciplined through the formal organs of justice. His court is the Party meeting. It is organized (by the secretary) to consider various deviations from the approved Party conduct (as the secretary sees it), with a penalty to be decided by the Party members assembled (on the secretary's motion) and to be ratified by higher Party authority (after the secretary's recommendation). No ward heeler in non-Communist countries ever held such power in his hand.

As a result of his powers and the way he uses them, the Party secretary is very apt to be unpopular among the rank-and-file. Occasionally his overexploited comrades can use the secretary's own position to trip him up, without

---

[1] Considerations of this sort led Khrushchev to abolish the old system of industrial ministries entirely in 1957, thus giving far greater authority to local Party leaders for supervising industrial enterprises.

risking the dangerous expedient of informing on him to the State Security, which may backfire on the informer. Some of Deriabin's friends in the Army organized one such effort very successfully. It hinged on money matters: the Soviet Union's constant need for more collections from its people and the secretary's constant habit of gambling away his own funds.

Each month most Soviet working citizens contribute a certain proportion of their salary to government loan subscriptions at established rates.[2] The subscriptions are "voluntary," indications of the "spontaneous love of the working masses for their government," as the Soviet press is wont to put it. Translated from "double-think," this means that they are compulsory. No one ever wants to participate in the subscription campaign. Since the loans are never repaid and are specifically not redeemable, a person's contribution is actually an extra tax levied by the State. But if an employee does not "volunteer" his contribution as part of his factory's or *kolkhoz's* loan drive, he can speedily find himself demoted or out of a job altogether. Naturally the firing always takes place for another reason.

Party members, as the exemplars of Soviet society, are heavily involved in all the subscription drives, which generally siphon off from one to three months' worth of a person's annual salary. And in whipping up enthusiasm, it is the Party secretary who leads the pack, like the summer-camp social director who is duty-bound to be last off the dance floor and first in the pool.

A certain Party secretary for a Soviet Army departmental office in Moscow had distinguished himself for arrogance in office, informed on several innocent persons, and used his authority for personal graft, as so many secretaries do. He gambled extensively with these ill-gotten gains. At the beginning of this particular subscription drive he was known to be in very poor shape financially, because of his gambling losses. He was correspondingly unenthusiastic

---

[2] This was once actually a lottery, with a drawing twice a year and a small number of winners. (Deriabin once won 600 rubles on it.) Khrushchev, seeing no reason why the house's profit margin should not be a round one hundred percent, later froze all winnings "at the people's request."

about the drive. Yet as Party secretary he was duty-bound to give an "example" to his committee by pledging a larger amount than anyone else.

Just before the meeting the officers in his unit persuaded one of the lowest-paid employees there, a stenographer, to make an outrageously large pledge. They pooled their own resources to reimburse her for her trouble. When the secretary, with a show of cheerfulness, called for pledges the stenographer stood up and offered fifty percent of her next six months' salary for "our glorious Soviet fatherland." Ashen-faced, the secretary congratulated her. Then, as was necessary to keep up his own "leading" position, he announced that he was contributing sixty percent of *his* salary, inspired by her example. A wave of heartfelt applause went up from the assembled Party members. Not long thereafter the secretary had to leave the area, having been rendered hopelessly insolvent by his combination of gambling losses and "voluntary" contribution. His loyal Party members congratulated the stenographer and themselves on a successful and by no means atypical piece of Communist in-fighting.

When Deriabin was in the Army he got his Party secretaryship by the numbers. The need for military discipline eliminated some of the window-dressing that accompanies the choice of Party secretaries in civilian life. He was summoned to the office of the division political officer and informed that he was to be the Party secretary in his regiment. The choice was confirmed as soon as the tactical situation permitted a mass meeting of Party members in the regiment.

After he had joined the State Security he was again "summoned" to Party office, as we have seen, as a Komsomol secretary in Naval counter-intelligence headquarters, as a deputy secretary of his section in the Guard Directorate, finally as Party secretary of the Austro-German Section in the Foreign Intelligence Directorate. In all these cases his selection was foreordained, since his good Party record automatically made him a member of the club. But the maneuvers involved with his last appointment, as Party secretary of the Austro-German Section, in themselves illustrate the pitiful limits of democracy in the Soviet Union.

When Deriabin arrived in the Austro-German Section he

was greeted effusively by one Major Afanasiy Zagorsky, an ambitious young veteran of the American Section who was then serving as acting Party secretary. Deriabin suspected the warmth of Zagorsky's greetings and had his suspicions confirmed when the Section chief called him in for a conference several weeks later. Using the acting secretary as his authority, Deriabin's boss asked him why he had been criticizing the deputy head of the Section. He had, it seems, mentioned in Zagorsky's presence that the deputy seemed ill-suited for his job. Zagorsky had promptly tattled. Under pressure Deriabin admitted his criticism, added that it represented merely casual opinion, and suggested that a Party boss should be better equipped to sift the seriousness of charges before presenting them. The Section chief tended to agree.

Not long afterward the elections were announced for the Section's Party committee. At this, the lowest level of Party authority, a certain amount of democracy is permitted. At least Party members can choose to some extent among "candidates," all of whom have been certified as sound by general Party opinion and not vetoed outright by the next-higher committee or the office or factory section chief.

Zagorsky had informed on others besides Deriabin. He was pompous, oily, and in the view of the rank-and-file members, completely untrustworthy. So virtually all the members of the unit agreed to cross his name off the ballot. (Some seven or eight names were allowed on the ballot, of whom five were to be selected as committeemen.) To preserve the appearance of solidarity, however, several officers arose to make perfunctory speeches nominating Zagorsky for the committee. This requirement satisfied, the candidate stood up for any possible questions about his qualifications. A lieutenant colonel asked him with some sharpness: "You say you are forty-two years old. I'd like to ask you why you did not become a Party member until 1944, during the war. Why did you wait so long to join the Party?" While Zagorsky stammered on the platform a voice hollered from the back of the room: "He was afraid the Germans would win and he'd be caught and executed as a Party member." There was general hilarity. In the election Zagorsky received only two votes. Deriabin, who was already popular among the Section officers, was elected in his place.

So much for democracy and popularity in the Communist Party. A man cannot go beyond this primary level of authority without the specific approval, if not the invitation, of the Party higher-ups. When Deriabin was elected to the five-man committee he found out that an invitation has the force of a command. His Section chief asked him to be Party secretary for the unit. He declined on the grounds that he needed all his time to learn his new job. He was asked to "think it over" for two days. During this time he was summoned before the next-higher Party secretary, who stressed the "importance" of accepting. He could not refuse. Thus, after exhibiting briefly their independence, the members of the unit, to say nothing of Deriabin himself, were again impressed with the fact that no key position in the Communist Party of the Soviet Union can ever be filled in a democratic manner.

Being a Party leader in the sophisticated circles of the State Security imposed few demands on Deriabin's faculty for discipline and exhortation. Not only were all of the officers *ipso facto* Party members of some standing, but they knew enough about the world outside Communism that the explanations of the Party line need be only perfunctory. Everyone there, in fact, knew more than was good for him. The clerical personnel, however, had to be exhorted and checked on. Deriabin found himself giving the same kind of speeches and leading the same kind of discussion groups he had been used to in his days as a Komsomol secretary.

A Party secretary's lectures must try to ride every wavelet of the Party line. Accordingly, at the time of Communist agitation in Western Europe, in the late forties, Party members would be carefully briefed on developments like the Marshall Plan. Deriabin would remind his groups that France and Italy, for instance, were not intended to go Communist, since the Soviet Union would be unable to support them. The United States could very well continue shouldering the burdens of Western Europe, and Communist activity there was merely diversionary for the time being. So ran the explanation.

In the early fifties, when consumer agitation for better goods began to develop, the argument shifted back to the economy. "Why can't we get lipsticks?" women clerks would ask Deriabin after one of his economic explanations. "Socialism can be built without lipsticks," the answer followed; that was an easy one. Then Deriabin would go into the ancient appeal for bigger and better capital goods production. "The quicker we build our heavy industry," he urged, "the quicker you can get your lipsticks."

Toward the end of the Stalin period and after, this rigid insistence on capital over consumer goods was eased, as Malenkov and Khrushchev successively responded to the popular pressure for a better life. Yet anyone who argued too hard for luxury goods, even in these times, ran the automatic risk of being denounced as a profiteer or a person who did not take the goals of Communism seriously. It was always safer, when discussing a purchase in public, to say "I had to get it" rather than "I bought it." As a Party veteran, Deriabin knew such tricks well, and they became second nature in his dealings with people around him.

What might with irony be called the "pastoral" side of his job as Party secretary irritated him the most, for it involved a constant prying into the private lives of others. At every Party ceremony or at the celebrations at the State Security officers' clubs, Deriabin was on hand to see that nobody got drunk or disorderly. More exactly, he was to record who did and act on the matter, as he thought fit, at the next Party meeting. At least once a year a Party secretary is supposed to pay a social call on every Party member in his jurisdiction for a first-hand glance at his manner of living. "Did the apartment seem beyond the member's means?" Deriabin's check list ran, "Was it disorderly, indicating an unpleasant home life? Drinking going on . . . ?" These social calls were awaited with understandable concern by the inspectees. Their success generally depended not so much on the condition of the household as the relationship the householder enjoyed with the Party secretary. Naturally every effort was made to entertain him properly. If the refreshment offered was accepted the hosts could breathe easily. "When the vodka bottle comes out," as the Party saying ran, "inspection is over."

The most inflexible items on any secretary's mental check list are the libraries and the wall decorations. Few Party members would be caught with any dubious or condemned books on their shelves. In Deriabin's time it was advisable to have, as positive evidence of Party interest, the works of Lenin and, in the earlier dispensation, of Stalin in plain sight. (More recently Khrushchev has been propagating a five-foot shelf of his own.) Most Soviet families have at least one picture of a Party leader in their residences. With Party members, the more the merrier. Deriabin, who was anxious to save space in his Moscow apartment, solved the problem by having one picture of Lenin and Stalin together hung in the center of his wall. He was thus able to devote the rest of the wall to landscapes, which he liked.

In each of the questionnaires he conducted for Party members or Komsomols about to enter both the Party and the State Security apparatus, Deriabin had to continue this encouragement of the unvarying norm. The questions changed only slightly from those he had to answer at his own reception into the Party: "What do you know about Lenin?" "Why are there no strikes in the Soviet Union?" "Why did we win the victory in World War II?" They grew more complex with a candidate's education level. A university student or graduate, for instance, would be asked less about the life of Lenin and more about the precise differences between utopian and scientific socialism.

In no case are the Party examiners interested in how much a man knows. They ask their questions to find out as much about him as possible. A clerical worker will be asked, "What kind of note did the Soviet Union send to the United States three days ago?" not to test his political aptitude. It is to make sure he has been reading official accounts in the daily press. If the secretary asks a man, "What do you know about the agricultural policy of the Soviet Union?" he wants neither knowledge nor opinion, but a faithful repetition of what the Party has said about agricultural policy. That is what makes a good Communist, at least on the lower echelons of the Party "struggle."

If the problems of a Party secretary in the State Security were lessened in one direction by his officers' solid Party

background,[3] they were intensified in another. A Party job
in the State Security was a tricky proposition for the very
reason that the entire organization was so intimately involved with the Party. With its files and inner organization
the State Security is the one group in the U.S.S.R. capable
of wresting control of the leadership from the Central
Committee of the Party. Fully appreciating this, the Party
bosses insist on the most rigorous system of checks and balances within the State Security. There is a corresponding
Party committee inside every level of State Security activity. There is constant communication, not to say mutual
interference, between State Security units and local area
Party committees, on which, however, the local State Security boss is always represented. Precisely because Party and
official organization come so close to merging in a State
Security unit, the régime tries its hardest to keep them se-
perate, so that two lines of communication, not one, go up
from them to the Central Committee of the CPSU.

A few years of participation in the resultant in-fighting
gave Deriabin a frighteningly clear picture of the Party's
actual "struggle," true mission, and capacity for truth-
telling. His job as a Party secretary was to paint the line
convincingly. Whether the line involved lies or the truth
was of no consequence, as he well knew. Lying thus became part of his livelihood. It brought with it an inner disgust, which deepened as he knew more about the leaders
on whose behalf the lying had to be done.

It should be emphasized that by 1952 Deriabin's knowledge of the lies he defended was explicit and well docu-
mented. Not only did he have access to Western newspapers, uncensored news reports, and press summaries in the

---

[3] He had none of the individual recruitment problems of the
normal Party secretary or the tension between a cadre of Party
members and a non-Party majority. Some recruitment he did
deal with, but on a more basic level. Each year, or more frequently as needed, the Central Committee would send out a
directive titled *The Recruitment of Communists and Komsomols into the Organs of State Security*. This required, for instance, that the Moscow city committee pick and assign for
work in the State Security a definite number of Communists,
550 in 1951, 450 in 1952, etc. It was the same in other cities
and districts throughout the Soviet Union.

course of his work, but he continued to read very widely in the Russian classics and certain permitted translations of foreign works—Shakespeare, Hugo, Zola, Poe. They refreshed his dim childhood memories of a world which had not yet been swallowed up by the Soviet system.

He also had the chance to explore the work of Communist heretics who are known to the bulk of Soviet society only by the epithets used in the régime's periodic denunciations. In 1951 he completed his night courses at the Institute of Marxism-Leninism in Moscow. This work, added to the credits acquired at the Higher Counter-Intelligence School, gave him, at last, the higher university standing he had for a long time coveted. In the courses there, as well as at the Political Science Academy lectures, he had read the works of disgraced Soviet leaders like Nikolay Bukharin and philosophers like Mikhail Bakunin, the anarchist foe of Marx. Naturally he read them only in the official context of heresies to be refuted; but he *was* able to read them, and their ideas survived in his mind. They were enough to demonstrate with finality the crookedness of the current Soviet ideology even when judged by Marx's own premises. He noted in particular a short statement of Bakunin's, commenting on statist trends in Russian society: "The Russians are getting bigger and bigger, but they are gaining no friends."

CHAPTER XIII

Who Votes

SINCE THE SOVIET Union officially classes itself as a democracy, it may be instructive to add a word about the matter of voting as it is understood by Soviet citizens. Peter Deriabin was involved in the Soviet electoral process on two counts, as an officer of the State Security and an officer of the Communist Party. In both these capacities his job was to eliminate any element of chance or choice from the polling, whether in the elections for the Supreme Soviets, or the even more closely watched elections for delegates to the Party Congresses.

The Soviet theory of elections has been too well demonstrated to need detailed explanation here. Briefly, the people are asked to vote their approval of single slates of candidates who have been selected beforehand by Party nominating committees. The only way to demonstrate opposition to the candidate is to cross off his name from the ballot or to substitute another one. Every official at the polls is alert to see that this does not happen. Soviet voters know by real or inherited experience what awaits them if they are caught in the act of making a protest vote. Compared to the Soviet voter, even a black voter in Mississippi could be said to enjoy a thoroughly democratic franchise.

When the new Soviet constitution was announced in 1936 a great many people believed that an era of free elections was in the making. Deriabin and his Komsomol friends, as they went about the villages explaining the wonders of the new freedom, sincerely believed that some mea-

185

sure of choice would be allowed. Many voters went to the polls prepared to cross out official Party candidates. They sometimes did so. There were slip-ups in the machinery for making nominations.

In Biysk, for instance, a young woman named Kostramikina, a weaver in the Biysk textile factory, was nominated as a candidate for deputy by her fellow workers. They hung her pictures throughout the city, organized rallies, and called loudly for the election of a real workers' candidate. But she had not received Party clearance beforehand. The State Security investigated her two days after her nomination and unearthed the evidence, with suspicious ease, that her parents had actually been well-to-do property owners and hence "anti-Soviet." That night her pictures were torn down by agents of the State Security. The next day the local Party committee substituted in her place a "safe" worker, hand-picked by the secretary. Poor Miss Kostramikina, shattered by this sudden change of fortune, hung herself some days before the election.

When the voters finally went to the polls they were disillusioned to find that virtually all insurgent candidates like the Biysk textile worker had been stricken from the lists. There was, moreover, only one name on the ballot for each position, despite the propaganda that the voters could make their choice by crossing out the names of candidates they did not want.

A few bold spirits made their protest by crossing out the single name offered them or writing in another. But the State Security set out to hunt them down, and they paid heavily for their independence. The voters learned their lesson and huge majorities have been rolled up for the government slate ever since. For everyone knows the danger in any deviation from the norm. The trained Soviet citizen now takes his ballot and publicly drops it into the ballot box. Although a polling booth is provided in case a person wants to cross out or otherwise qualify his choice, a person invites an investigation by entering it.

In spite of such control some dissent occasionally tries to register itself. That is why the State Security mans the polling places at every election district. Officers are there to see that every voter drops his worthless vote into the public ballot box. If a man enters a booth his name is automatically registered on a "suspect" list. The official poll watchers go to incredibly petty lengths to examine the exact nature of his heresy. If two voters enter a booth consecutively a member of the voting commission follows the second man inside, ostensibly to see whether everything is in order for him. Actually he goes in to check the pencil point used by the preceding man, to see if he has used the pencil to cross off the Party candidate's name. (The pencil points are kept constantly sharp to facilitate this means of checking.)

This extreme of snooping is accepted State Security procedure. Following the balloting, all ballots bearing crossed-out names are forwarded to local State Security headquarters for detailed analysis along with the reports of the poll watchers. Scarcely five percent of the voters ever bother to risk displeasure by entering the polling booth. But it is among this five percent that the régime sees its potential enemies.

The investigations that follow are almost ludicrous in their intensity. A year before Stalin's death, Deriabin served on the commission regulating the voting for members of the Guard Directorate. In his district four persons had the temerity to cross the names of Molotov and Bulganin from the ballot. It was five years too early for them to benefit from the denunciation of these two gentlemen by Khrushchev as "anti-Party," and there was a terrible fuss inside the Party secretariat. The next day, at a closed meeting of Party secretaries from the Guard Directorate, the secretary of the Directorate's Party committee, Colonel Shatalov, lectured them: "Comrades, we are in disgrace. In our midst there are enemies who crossed off the ballot our leaders, the men whom we protect, Comrades Bulganin and Molotov. What are we to do?"

One of the secretaries present came up with a foolproof Communist solution. He advised removing all the pencils from the ballot booths. If anyone entered a booth a Party worker could then give him a colored pencil, thus handily identifying the culprit and the manner of his rebellion. This was too bare-faced even for the Guard Directorate, however, not because it was "undemocratic," but because it showed such patent lack of confidence in the officers'

Party solidarity. An investigation was ordered instead. It went on for ten months, but the guilty men were never found.

Earlier, during the course of a Party election at the Guard Directorate in 1949, one of the officers present, looking through a souvenir photograph album, spotted a black X drawn through Stalin's picture. The reverberations following this discovery were heavy. The entire section was broken up and the officials of the Party organization dismissed. But here, too, the culprit escaped.

It goes without saying that every official candidate to the Supreme Soviet is first given a detailed political fingernail inspection by the State Security. It is only after this that his candidacy may be discussed by the various Party organs. The candidates are apportioned on a quota basis after the Central Committee in Moscow has determined in advance how many Party members, how many non-Party people, how many soldiers, workers, *kolkhozniks*, teachers, etc. are to be represented.

All this security inspection for the Supreme Soviet elections is intensified when the rank-and-file makes its choices for the delegates to the Party Congress. Deriabin had the dubious good fortune to work directly in the elections for the Nineteenth Party Congress in 1952. He followed the Congress through three months of careful preparation and attended it as part of a special surveillance and security detail. If anything was needed to seal his rising contempt for the "free" workings of the Soviet Party, the Congress was it.

The Party Congress took place in October 1952. Three months before that time, all Party organizations received a brief announcement of the time and agenda, as decided on by the Central Committee. The announcing circular ordered Party secretaries to hold electoral meetings on every level of the Party organization. The theoretical purpose of these meetings, as outlined, worked in the finest traditions of "democratic centralism." Primary Party organizations were to elect delegates to attend the *rayon* conferences. These in turn would elect representatives to the *oblast* conferences, who would, in turn, select the delegates to attend the All-Union Party Congress, so many from each of the fifteen Union republics.

The practice worked differently. Deriabin and the other Party secretaries in the State Security headquarters, as part of a district committee, were secretly notified beforehand of the Congress date and told to start preparing their lists of candidates. In a series of meetings conducted by the Party secretary next in rank they were told what kind of delegates were wanted and how many and, finally, given a list of selected nominees from their districts.

The signal given, the Party secretaries set out to "push" the nominations of the approved official slate. They did not have to work very hard. For a matter like a Party Congress the rank-and-file knew very well that the secretary's nominees had authority behind them. So there was little initiative from the floor of the meetings, other than a certain spirit of selectivity among the approved candidates. This much is permitted, if only at the local levels of Party comity.

After the delegates went beyond the primary committee level all freedom of choice went out the window. Even in the primary Party elections representatives from the *rayon* committee had circulated among the members to see that conformity was enforced. Before the meeting of the *rayon* committee took place every candidate had received a thorough personal scrutiny from both Party and State Security agencies.

In the case of the State Security headquarters itself the Party meetings in the various Directorates corresponded to those of districts where the Party was organized on a regional basis. Long before the chairs were put into place every conceivable detail had been arranged in advance. The Party secretary of the Directorate distributed rough notes of his speech to the lower Party secretaries. About fifteen persons, Party secretaries and trusted Party members, were scheduled to make "spontaneous" nominating speeches for prescribed candidates. The Party secretary of the Directorate, who chaired the meeting, had a complete list of his spontaneous speakers. He refused to recognize anyone else from the floor—not that a State Security Directorate would contain any foolhardy volunteers.

At this meeting Deriabin, along with other official candidates, was chosen as a delegate to the Party conference of the Ministry, corresponding to the *oblast* congresses of

the area Party organizations. There was no doubt about his
election. In Party elections even the cheap concession of
the separate balloting booth is lacking. Every man present
must vote by handing his ballot to the presiding officer. A
special checking committee is present to scan the vote in
case any attempt is made at a really spontaneous nomination.

The next step was the Party conference of the Ministry
which was to elect delegates to the Moscow city Party conference. At this democratic gathering Deriabin's duties were
well defined. He was designated third speaker, charged
with the nomination of one of the approved candidates.
His speech lasted only a few minutes, long enough to
laud the virtues of the candidate as a good Party man and
a capable member of the State Security. His nominee, like
the other members of the official slate, was of course immediately approved by the assemblage.

In addition to this local selection process and the investigative checks by the State Security, every representative to
the Party Congress, from the provincial level upward, had
to have the express approval of the Central Committee in
Moscow. (The Central Committee, like a housewife ordering a market list, had already notified every provincial
Party committee of the types of delegates wanted, e.g.
twenty-five workers, seven teachers, sixteen Party officials,
nine Komsomols, ten journalists, etc.) By the time those
designated reached Moscow they were already allotted to
various working committees as smoothly and as irrevocably
as they were boarded in hotels. It was all, essentially, a
matter of logistics.

This group of 1359 delegates was acclaimed by the Soviet press as a great working example of how the Communist Party practices democratic centralism. The same editors
who wrote the panegyrics had already received confidential
instructions on editorials which would comment on the various measures the delegates would shortly spontaneously
adopt.

The method of selection at the Nineteenth Party Congress did not disappear, it might be added, with the end of
"Stalinism." In fact, Stalin's grip on the Party tactics had
weakened by that time; after the opening day he spent only
fifteen minutes at the Congress during its week of meet-

ings. The Twentieth Congress was organized in exactly the same way, as was the Twenty-first. Not since the thirties has the Party rank-and-file been able to raise the smallest voice at such a gathering without the sanction of the leadership.

Soviet Communism has long since passed the point where its products protest at this kind of rubber stamp. The rule of the Party secretaries is taken for granted. If force originally established their rule, long habit has canonized it. An ordinary Party member questioning this routinized electoral process would look as unseemly as a lemming suddenly breaking ranks at migration time and demanding to know whether the trip to the Arctic Circle was really necessary.

CHAPTER XIV

The Stalin Succession

IN THIS SACRED grove there grew a certain tree round which at any time of the day, and probably far into the night, a grim figure might be seen to prowl. In his hand he carried a drawn sword, and he kept peering warily about him as if at every instant he expected to be set upon by an enemy. He was a priest and a murderer; and the man for whom he looked was sooner or later to murder him and hold the priesthood in his stead. Such was the rule of the sanctuary. A candidate for the priesthood could only succeed to office by slaying the priest, and having slain him, he retained office till he was himself slain by a stronger or a craftier.

. . . year in, year out, in summer and winter, in fair weather and in foul, he had to keep his lonely watch, and whenever he snatched a troubled slumber it was at the peril of his life. The least relaxation of his vigilance, the smallest abatement of his strength of limb or skill of fence, put him in jeopardy; grey hairs might seal his death-warrant. His eyes probably acquired that restless, watchful look which, among the Esquimaux of the Bering Strait, is said to betray infallibly the shedder of blood. . . .[1]

---

[1] From *The Golden Bough* by Sir James Frazer. © 1922 by the Macmillan Co.; © 1950, Barclay's Bank Ltd.

Although Sir James Frazer wrote these words in *The Golden Bough* to describe the ancient sacrificial priesthood of Nemi in the Alban Hills near Rome, they fit almost perfectly the principle of power succession in the Soviet leadership. At the very top of the Praesidium the actual execution of the deposed member of the priesthood is often postponed because of political considerations. It may be temporarily commuted to imprisonment or exile. Stalin himself did not order a single execution of a major figure until six years after he had assumed actual power. But in the long run the deposed priest must be slain.

Just as the State Security is the principal executor of these changes, its own leaders are the first to suffer from them. Their removal is the warning symptom of a bigger power struggle or, at the least, of a change of policy among their employers. Within the State Security the drama of the priesthood of Nemi has repeated itself through the years like blood-spattered clockwork. Which explains why senior State Security colonels view with mixed feelings a promotion to general or Deputy Minister.

The founder of the State Security, Feliks Dzerzhinsky, was the only operating leader of this body who is definitely known to have died a natural death. He expired of a heart attack, brought on by overwork, on July 20, 1926. His working successor was Genrikh Yagoda, who quickly brushed away the nominal leadership of Dzerzhinsky's fellow Pole Menzhinsky.[2] Yagoda became Stalin's instrument of terror through the twenties and early thirties. He broke with Stalin over the forced collectivization policy in 1929; but he was not removed from office until September 1936, probably because he had been too powerful to challenge.

Yagoda's successor was Nikolay I. Yezhov. He enjoys the debatable honor of titling an entire period of Soviet history, the *Yezhovshchina*, because of his almost total purging of the Old Bolsheviks. In March 1938 Yagoda was put on trial, along with Bukharin and Rykov, in the Moscow purge. It was Yezhov who presided over his execution shortly afterward.

---

[2] Menzhinsky may in fact have been the first victim of the priesthood struggle; but there is no accurate information on the manner of his death.

Yezhov's deputy was an up-and-coming Georgian named Lavrentiy Beria. Beria pushed Yezhov aside in December 1938, after Yezhov had held office for only two years. After Beria was securely installed Yezhov disappeared. There was no trial or other notice of his fate. It was the general conclusion that Stalin ordered his disposal because he knew too much about the purges and Stalin's direct involvement in them.

During World War II Beria assumed higher duties and divided operational control of the State Security and military counter-intelligence organs between two deputies, Vsevolod Merkulov and Viktor Abakumov. In 1951 Abakumov was removed from office after intrigue among anti-Beria forces on the Central Committee. He was executed in 1954. (Merkulov was killed earlier.)

Vasily S. Ryumin was the man who displaced Abakumov as operating head of the State Security in 1951, although he was ranked only as Deputy Minister. (The nominal Minister, Ignat'ev, was a weak Party functionary.) In 1953, during Beria's return to control of the State Security, Ryumin himself was arrested. He was executed the following year after a brief period of freedom.

When Beria was arrested and prepared for execution, another deputy of his, Sergey N. Kruglov, was installed as head of the State Security forces, with a veteran Chekist general named Ivan A. Serov as *his* deputy. In 1954 Serov took over the State Security, reorganized as the KGB, and Kruglov was shunted over to command the less important MVD. Kruglov was separated from this job in January 1956 and replaced by another henchman of Khrushchev's, one Nikolay P. Dudorov. Kruglov's present address is unknown.

In January 1959 Serov was abruptly removed as chief of the State Security and transferred to another post in the government. His replacement, Aleksandr N. Shelepin, was a Komsomol organization leader with no previous State Security experience. After a look at the preceding history it can be deduced that the senior State Security generals were notably undismayed at being passed over for the top job.

Peter Deriabin lived through the most confused of these retributive cycles within the State Security. It was in some ways the worst, since it included the prelude to Stalin's

death and its aftermath. But its pattern of arrest and
counter-arrest was only the partial reflection of convulsions
inside the Soviet leadership. The classic period of turmoil
in Russian history was the so-called Time of Troubles, the
interregnum between the death of Ivan the Terrible, in
1584, and the crowning of the first Romanov, in 1613. The
Time of Troubles lasted almost three decades. It is a backhanded tribute to the Soviet leaders' infinite capacity for
in-fighting that they managed to pack an equivalent
amount of danger and tension into the period 1949–57, but
without disturbing either the outward peace of the realm or
the apparent continuity of government administration.

When Deriabin came to work at the Guard Directorate
the Soviet government was still a monolith. Stalin ruled,
and Beria, through his subordinates and deputies, demonstrated some consistency in managing the State Security.
Job security, in other words, was good, comparatively
speaking. For instance, the Commandant of the Kremlin,
an old Chekist lieutenant general named Nikolay K. Spiridonov, had held his post since 1938. "Kolya," as he was
unpopularly known, was an unappetizing physical specimen, short and paunchy, with a round, shaved head, and
not very attractive socially. He was generally feared and
disliked by those serving under him. But at least his long
term in office was warrant that the Beria régime in the
State Security was by and large stable.

The growing suspiciousness of Stalin in his declining
years, however, was lending boldness to the factional fighting inside the leadership. The dictator himself ordered the
liquidation of some promising subordinates. Nikolay A.
Voznesensky, whom Deriabin thought much the ablest man
on the Politburo, was executed along with the powerful
boss of the Leningrad Party organization, A.A. Kuznetsov,
in the "Leningrad Plot" of 1949. The "plot" was fabricated
by the State Security Minister, Abakumov, at the express
wish of Stalin. This happened only a few months after the
fortuitous death of Andrey Zhdanov, Kuznetsov's predeces-
sor as Party secretary in Leningrad, who had been the most
powerful of Stalin's underlings.

In the early part of 1951 there was gossip among the
Guard Directorate officers about the possible fall of Abakumov. The Minister was repeatedly summoned to report to

the Central Committee of the CPSU. On one occasion he was called there four times in the course of a single day. In July 1951 the ax fell. An order was published, signed by Stalin, announcing the appointment of Lieutenant General Ogoltsov as Acting Minister. Nothing was said about Abakumov, who was then beginning his protracted journey to the firing squad. The word came down, also, that the Central Committee was dissatisfied with the work of the State Security. Translated in terms of the Kremlin power struggle, this meant that Malenkov, Bulganin, Khrushchev, and others were attempting to infiltrate Beria's control of the State Security apparatus.

By the summer of 1951 there were arrests throughout the upper echelons of the State Security. The atmosphere became progressively more nervous, especially within the Guard Directorate, as officers began to anticipate another convulsion similar to the last turn-over, in 1938, when Beria followed Yezhov and considerable numbers of State Security men got themselves caught in the turnstile. In May 1952 a three-man commission—Malenkov, Beria, and Bulganin—took over the investigation of State Security activities, ostensibly with a view to restoring budgetary efficiency and eliminating waste. Along with the waste, as previously noted, they eliminated several important State Security department heads.

Lieutenant General Vlasik was dismissed from the Party and sent to Sverdlovsk as deputy chief of a labor camp. Several other high-ranking colonels, including Deriabin's former boss, Colonel Goryshev, were similarly transferred. Goryshev's labor camp was at the city of Molotov, in the Urals. A job bossing a labor camp, it can be deduced, was not exactly regarded as a plum in State Security circles. Considering the distances involved and the amount of surveillance in practice, the commandants were almost as securely on the ice as the inmates.

A new chief of the Guard Directorate was installed to replace Vlasik, a Colonel Martynov. Martynov was a younger man, known to be personally acquainted with Khrushchev, Malenkov, and other members of the Praesidium. Before his elevation he had held the relatively humble post of chief of guards on the Central Committee building. In former times the substitution of a Martynov for a

Vlasik would have been out of the question. Vlasik was a trusted retainer who had guarded Stalin for twenty years. But a suspicion implanted in Stalin's mind about a man's loyalty was enough, in those late days, to dismiss him summarily.

The Kremlin doctors were arrested in the fall of 1952, after the State Security had spent a year working up a case against them. The Doctors' Plot was one of the most enigmatic happenings of the modern Time of Troubles. It was announced in January 1953 as the conspiracy of some highly-placed physicians to assassinate prominent members of the Party and the Army. Most of the physicians were Jewish, a fact which was no coincidence. It was undoubtedly an effort by elements in the régime to release some of the growing popular unrest of the last Stalin days through the traditional escape valve of anti-Semitism.

Although the new Deputy Minister, Ryumin, and his aides had spent a year fabricating the "plot," they had acted with great secrecy. As close as Deriabin was to the inner circles of the State Security, he did not hear of this until Dr. Egorov, the chief of the Kremlin Medical Directorate, was removed from his post. The Doctors' Plot spelled more trouble for the State Security, or at least the surviving Beria men at its head. As nearly as can be learned, it was an attempt to undermine Beria's position by impugning the vigilance of the State Security. For its "disclosure" was followed by a heavily stimulated press campaign demanding to know why the doctors had been "allowed" to pursue their nefarious ends, etc. It was probably instigated by A. N. Poskrebyshev, the head of Stalin's personal secretariat, who grew increasingly powerful as the dictator weakened. But it backfired on its instigators, since it was so palpably untrue. Beria and his henchmen counter-attacked, so to speak, inside the Central Committee, and the decision was made to release the surviving doctors even before the death of Stalin.

On March 6, 1953, the death of Stalin was announced to the people of the Soviet Union. No one knows to this day to what extent his associates helped along the course of his final illness. It is a fact that the Deputy Commandant of the Kremlin, Major General Kosynkin, in charge of operational arrangements for guarding Stalin, died of a heart attack two weeks before Stalin. Or so the announcement said. Poskrebyshev, the head of the secretariat, disappeared the night of Stalin's death. He has never been heard of since. "Kolya" Spiridonov, Kosynkin's boss, speedily put in for retirement on grounds of illness. He was allowed to leave the Kremlin and Moscow in May.

While the members of the Praesidium began preparations for the fight for succession the death of Stalin was the signal for a significant number of State Security officers to come out of the obscure positions where they had been hiding. Lieutenant General Rumyantsev, for example, had been relieved of his post as head of Stalin's bodyguard in 1944, after a mistake in railroad routing arrangements. He became once more a man to be reckoned with inside the Kremlin. Major General Kuzmichev, Beria's faithful henchman, was released from his 1952 imprisonment and put in charge of the entire Guard Directorate. Beria himself openly took over as Minister of State Security.

The worried professionals inside the State Security breathed a sigh of relief on the news of Beria's appointment. They trusted him as a man who knew their problems and as an excellent administrator. They were quickly deceived. In the struggle for power inside the Kremlin, Beria put all his hopes in his ability to use the State Security mechanism in his own interests. His only immediate interest in the State Security, therefore, was to insure its corporate loyalty.

The resulting upheaval was worse than anything inside the State Security since the late thirties. Officers were removed wholesale at all levels. The transfers in Berlin, although an admittedly critical area of the State Security's operations, give a fair idea of the magnitude of the changes; out of 2800 officers and other employees there, 1700 were transferred, recalled from Germany, or dismissed from the service.

Obscure lieutenant generals whom everyone had forgotten, men dismissed for drunkenness, graft, or worse, were pulled out of the woodwork by Beria and put into positions of authority. The only criterion of choice was their personal loyalty to him. Members of minority racial groups—Letts, Byelorussians, Caucasians, and Central Asians—were put in charge of State Security installations in their respective republics, a step which did not endear Beria to the great majority of Russians inside the Moscow headquarters. Most ominously Beria ordered Colonel Karasev, the chief of the Second Technical Support Section, as the wire-tappers were euphemized, to wire the offices of all other Praesidium members, conspicuously including Malenkov, then the Party leader. He set about removing and appointing State Security leaders without the normal process of checking with the Central Committee. He attempted to interfere in Communist Party appointments, with varying success, and gave area State Security officers orders to keep close watch on all Party officials in their areas. One of these was the head of the Kamenets-Podolsk Oblast Directorate in the Ukraine, Major General Strokach, who happened to be friendly with his local Party secretary. "I can't understand it," he told his Party friend; "I received an order by telephone today from Beria, telling me to keep a check running on you." When the Party secretary called Moscow the cat was out of Beria's bag.

This was the last obvious tip-off that Beria was playing a dangerous lone game for power. He was the front-runner and the other members of the Praesidium set out to bring him down. Their trusted ally in this process was Beria's principal deputy, Sergey Kruglov, who was assigned to report on his boss's movements. Kruglov wired Beria's office as efficiently as Beria had wired the others, using trusted technicians from the MVD, where he had formerly commanded.

On the night of June 26, 1953, Deriabin was leaving the State Security offices when he noticed some Army tanks cruising through Mayakovsky Square. It was an unusual sight, there being no parade on the next day to justify their appearance. He decided that there must have been some transfer of armored units in the forces around Moscow.

The next morning he found out what the tanks had been up to. He ran into a friend of his named Igoshin, who supervised, among other things, recruiting for Beria's personal bodyguard in the Guard Directorate. "Have you heard the news?" Igoshin asked. "Our boss was arrested last night."

By evening on the 27th the information was current among high-placed State Security officers in Moscow.

Beria had been called to the Praesidium offices on the morning of the 26th to answer some questions. When he entered the conference room in the Kremlin, Marshal Klimentiy Voroshilov walked in directly behind him, bearing a warrant for his arrest. "In the name of the Union of Soviet Socialist Republics," he said, "Lavrentiy Pavlovich Beria is hereby placed under arrest." The other members of the Praesidium questioned Beria throughout the day about his plans for seizing power, then sent him off to Lefortovo Prison. His most trusted deputy, Colonel General Bogdan Z. Kabulov, was arrested at 6 P.M. the same day by the disloyal deputy, Kruglov.

It developed that Beria had planned a coup of his own for the 27th. He had won over Colonel General Artem'ev, Commander of the Moscow Military District, or at least neutralized him. By the 26th Artem'ev had sent almost the entire Moscow garrison off to Byelorussia on maneuvers. This left Beria's MVD and State Security troops theoretically in command of the city.

Unknown to Beria, however, and thanks to Kruglov's efficient wire-tappers, Bulganin, acting for the rest of the Praesidium, had called in the Kantemirovskaya Division to Moscow. This was an armored command not subordinate to Artem'ev. It was this division's tanks which Deriabin saw late on the night of the 26th. To support their armor Bulganin summoned some of Marshal Semen Timoshenko's troops from the Byelorussian Military District. Beria's *putsch* was licked before he moved.

The arrest of Beria was not made known to the Soviet public until July 10. By this time a two-month purge of the State Security was in full swing. All chiefs of directorates and their deputies and chiefs of sections were removed; but the purge did not reach into the lower or middle ranks. Five high-ranking officers, including the former Mininster, Merkulov, were arrested along with Beria and Kabulov. They were all shot together in December 1953.

Before the execution Beria was interrogated repeatedly by General Roman A. Rudenko, the Chief Prosecutor of the U.S.S.R., assisted by various technical interrogation specialists from the State Security. (Beria's own principal qualification as an interrogator was his proficient use of blackjacks, *dubinki*, several of which were found in his

desk on his arrest.) He gave his interrogators little satisfaction. At one point he went on a hunger strike. Rarely did
he answer a question in more than monosyllables, although
in the course of time admissions to some of the charges were
coaxed from him. They were incorporated in a seventy-five-
page report which accused Beria specifically of trying to
put himself above the Party and seize power; and, incidentally, of immorality, torture, inefficiency, and espionage
work for the British in the Caucasus in 1918, along with
various other things.

Few tears were shed for Beria in the decimated ranks of
the State Security. Not only had he proved capricious and
disastrously given to favoritism. He was a Georgian, and
his favoring of minority groups mobilized a great many latent Russian prejudices against him. Georgians had done
very well under Stalin, e.g. taxes were lower in that republic than anywhere else in the Union, and they were constantly suspected of plotting against their former Russian
masters.

There was little doubt about strong Georgian support for
Beria's conspiracy. Several days after the arrest, but before
it became known, Deriabin's wife telephoned him in great
excitement from Sukhumi. She had been staying at the
house of the vice-chairman of the local Party committee, a
Georgian. This man's wife had told her that the Georgians
would soon carry out a St. Bartholomew's Night of their
own throughout the Soviet Union, "slaughtering all of
you." She wanted to leave Sukhumi immediately and warn
someone in authority. Deriabin laughed and told her to
watch the newspapers, for she had no longer anything to
fear.

Yet the death of Beria promised little relief, especially
for the officers of the State Security. Alarmed by the near-
ness of Beria's success, the Central Committee instituted a
new system of checks and balances for the security forces.
Trusted bureaucrats from the Central Committee organization in Moscow were posted as deputies to State Security
men running Moscow directorates or provincial offices.
But these deputies had to tread lightly, in view of the uncertainty about the relative strength of Malenkov, Molotov,
Bulganin, Khrushchev, and others. Even the traditional

rules of the Soviet priesthood of Nemi were confused and obscured in the new polygonal fight for the succession.

As the position of the leading contenders bettered or worsened, denunications and retracted denunciations multiplied. The more prominent a person was, the more fearful of the outcome. There was the case of Olga Lepeshinskaya, the second-ranking Soviet ballerina—at least until her arrest for shop-lifting in Brussels in 1958. Lepeshinskaya was married to one Raikhman, a lieutenant general in the State Security and a known adherent of Beria. In August 1951, during the major purge of Beria supporters, Raikhman was carted off to jail. Lepeshinskaya hastily divorced him. "He is not my husband any longer," she said, presumably with a tremor in her voice, "if he is an enemy of the people."

Then the pendulum swung back. Raikhman was released and restored to power as Beria moved back into the State Security in force in 1953, peopling its offices with his supporters. Lepeshinskaya remarried him, having discovered that he was not an enemy of the people after all. After Beria's execution Raikhman was sent off to the labor camps once more, probably permanently. Nothing loath, Lepeshinskaya divorced him and went back to the theater.

Shortly before this, Deriabin had a narrow escape himself which evolved from a simple disciplinary problem in his office. One of the secretaries there, a reasonably attractive but lazy girl, was doing slack work in the office, preferring to conserve her energies for social life. He reprimanded her severely both in the office and at Party meetings, but there was no improvement. So he had her transferred to a less desirable job.

A month later the head of the Special Inspection Section called him in about a letter, written anonymously, accusing him of spreading rumors; specifically of talking about the misdeeds of Stalin's family. The Colonel told Deriabin he would have to face a Party committee to answer for it. "What exactly did you say?" he asked. Deriabin acknowledged that he had cracked a single joke one day in the presence of office employees about the debauches of Stalin's son, Vasiliy. "You shouldn't have," the Colonel said. "But it's true, isn't it?" replied Deriabin, who knew the Colonel rather well. He then explained that the letter must have come from the girl he had fired.

A denunciation for "talking," even one that comes in an anonymous letter, is a far more serious thing in the State Security headquarters than any amount of moral censure. But circumstances seemed so heavily on Deriabin's side that the head of the Special Inspection Section and the Party leaders let him off with the lightest of reprimands. The matter was resolved in April 1953. If the letter had been sent some years earlier, at the height of Stalin's power, the result might have been far more serious. As it was, Deriabin's bosses could deal lightly with him only because Stalin died one month after the investigation had begun. With this, Deriabin's slate, along with many thousands of others in the Soviet Union, was wiped clean, as far as Stalin was concerned.

The power struggle which followed was well joined by the time Deriabin left Moscow. It was the more complicated to judge for being so intense. Like the problem of the referee separating a heavy football pile-up, no one knew until the very last minute who was actually carrying the ball. Yet the veterans of the Guard Directorate were understandably far ahead of the rest of the world in their appraisals.

The steady climb of Khrushchev, for example, felt sharply in the professional Party leadership, was equally well marked inside the State Security. The Party functionary named Lenev, who had taken over the Guard Directorate command in 1953, was a creature of Khrushchev's, and his getting this post spoke volumes for Khrushchev's intra-Party influence. He had worked for Khrushchev in the Moscow Party secretariat. Equally bound to Khrushchev were the Central Committee men whom Lenev brought with him.

After the death of Stalin and Beria's execution, however, it was felt within the State Security that Georgiy Malenkov would get the succession. Although most of the Soviet people thought that Molotov would more likely step into Stalin's boots, or at least temporarily fill out the toes, the Party professionals had watched Malenkov sprout like a mushroom from the ranks of the lower hierarchy, in his formidable job as Stalin's chief administrative assistant. They knew also that his obvious rival, Molotov, had not held any active position in the hierarchy for the last two years.

Aloof and distant and determinedly an Old Bolshevik, he had less of a contemporary Party following than any of the other in-fighters in the current Moscow performance of *Executive Suite*. But his reputation was nonetheless impressive.

The fact that the leaders seemed closely watched at the outset was of little help to their cautious subordinates. Even answering routine Party questionnaires had become a formidable problem. Who, for instance, should a Party official put down as the world's leading Communist, now that the No. 1 man was dead? The wrong choice, e.g. Malenkov, might very easily come back from the files years later to haunt the writer long after the questionnaire might otherwise have been forgotten. The wise boys in the Kremlin and other good Party organizers throughout the country fell back on internationalism and nominated Mao Tse-tung first.

Almost no one in official life felt safe. By contrast with the Stalin days, it was impossible even to decide from which direction the blow might come. The classic story is told about the Minister of Public Works who went out to one of his districts from Moscow to check progress on the local building program. After noting the claims of all the installations in his area, he gave a huge appropriation for modernizing and beautifying the camp for "anti-Soviet" prisoners, which was located some distance from the provincial capital. To the local school, which was sadly in need of repair, he gave nothing at all. "Comrade Minister," his aide asked cautiously, "why do you do this? The school really needs the money. The prison camp improvements are not at all essential." "You fool," the Minister replied, "where do you think I will be going next year, the camp or the school?"

How did Deriabin himself fare in all this upheaval? The answer is that he survived and even found promotion, through a combination of luck, native caution, and his highly-placed friend in the Deputy Minister's office. In 1951, shortly after the arrest of Abakumov, he had been given the choice of two new assignments: chief of the personnel office inside the Kremlin Guard or Party boss for the entire Guard Directorate's Personnel Section. Either of these assignments, at that moment in history, was enough to send shivers down a man's back. For the incumbent of each office would at some moment have to make his choice between the struggling factions at the top of the Party.

Deriabin went for advice to his reliable fixer friend, who was still securely dispensing censures and favors from the shelter of the Deputy Minister's office. Pavel advised caution and delay, the while commenting that the two jobs held equally immediate potentialities for their holder's spending the next five years in a labor camp. As an alternative Deriabin brought up the possibility of a post in the Foreign Intelligence Directorate. Pavel made a few telephone calls.

The comparative safety of foreign intelligence was obvious. The Second Directorate officers, most of whom used the cover of working for the Foreign Ministry, generally kept away from personnel in the other branches and ran correspondingly less risk of becoming involved in the Kremlin in-fighting. Foreign intelligence was the "cleanest" branch of the State Security. Here one no longer spied on friends and relatives. The contrast with the Guard Directorate sounded joyful. After five years in the Kremlin's "sacred grove" Deriabin had accumulated such a wealth of disillusionment and bitterness about the mores of the ruling party that he did not feel safe expressing his true thoughts to his wife, let alone an understanding but careerminded fellow officer like Pavel.

On a May day in 1952 Peter Deriabin ordered out his car and drove to the complex of gray buildings at 1a Tekstilshchikov Street, next door to the Agricultural Fair grounds. They were the same buildings which had once housed the offices of the Komintern. He had an introduction there to the man who was later his chief in Vienna, Colonel Evgeniy Ignatyevich Kravtsov, alias Kovalev, head of the Austro-German Section in the Second Main Directorate of the State Security.

CHAPTER XV

Foreign Intelligence

KRAVTSOV, A WELL-BUILT, dark-complexioned man of forty-five, was typical of a breed of State Security officer which Deriabin had rarely met before: the foreign specialist with quite a few travel stickers on his luggage. A native of Leningrad, he had found his way into intelligence in the late thirties and served as Resident[1] in Latvia before the Soviet annexation. During the war he stayed in Moscow, as Party secretary of the Foreign Intelligence Directorate. In 1946 he did some State Security work in Switzerland, posing as a First Secretary of the local Soviet Embassy. In 1947 he spent some time in Turkey as State Security representative on the Soviet repatriation commission, after which he was posted to Berlin. After two years as Resident in Berlin he came back to Moscow, where he became the chief of the Austro-German Section of the Foreign Intelligence Directorate in 1951.

This undercover cosmopolite questioned Deriabin only briefly on his language background. This was fortunate, since it consisted of a bare working knowledge of German, derived from the counter-intelligence school and front-line

---

[1] The terms "Resident" and "Residency," translations of the Russian *Rezident* and *Rezidentura*, are not to be confused either with U.S. legal terminology or the British colonial outposts on which the sun never sets. They are merely technical descriptions for the intelligence chief of a particular jurisdiction in foreign service, and his establishment.

prisoner-of-war interrogations. Kravtsov was far more interested in the new officer's ability to write a report.
"Here," he said, handing him a dossier, "is a report just
received from Germany about the arrest of some Western
agents. Write it up as if you were writing a report for the
Central Committee." Deriabin had seen enough paper-
juggling in the Kremlin to know how important was this
final phase of intelligence work. But he needed some information about the Foreign Intelligence Directorate's procedures.

Kravtsov's bare description of the routing mechanism remains a revealing explanation of the wheels within wheels
that rule the Soviet Union. In the first place, he noted,
there was to be no written notation like "Confidential" or
"Secret" on any report. ("The people who read this are
presumed to have access to everything.") There were four
varieties of reports. The first, with thirteen copies, was for
routing to all members of the Praesidium of the Party Central Committee, with additional copies generally forwarded
to the Foreign Ministry and the Ministry of Defense. Type
No. 2, a limited-edition version of the first, was intended
for the seven most powerful members of the Praesidium.[2]
The third type of report had only three copies. In that day
one would go to Stalin, one to Malenkov, as ranking Party
Secretary, and one to whatever member of the inner circle
it most concerned, e.g. Bulganin (military affairs), Beria
(internal security and atomic energy), or Molotov (foreign
affairs).

The last kind of report, really more of a working paper,
went to one man only: the Secretary of the Central Committee of the Party. Malenkov then held this office.

The reports were not addressed by the Praesidium members' formal titles, but simply, "Comrade Bulganin" or
"Comrade Beria." They were to be purposefully short.
"Let's have none of these fifteen-page documents," Kravtsov told Deriabin, as his parting shot. "These people don't
like to read anything longer than a page, so keep out the
details. If you can make it less than a page all the better."
But in the bare scheme of the routing a man could see

[2] At the time these were Stalin, Malenkov, Beria, Molotov,
Bulganin, Kaganovich, and Mikoyan.

the skeletal outline of the power structure in the Soviet Union and its intimate connection with the police, intelligence, and terror activities of the State Security.

It goes without saying that no other agency of the Soviet state has such an intimate contact with the leaders of the régime as the State Security. As Deriabin quickly found out, no major decision on an intelligence or terror operation abroad could be taken without the direct permission either of the full Praesidium, the First Secretary, or one or two specially delegated other members. Working through the Central Committee, the State Security's recommendations become fact in the orders passed on to the Army, Foreign Ministry, or other arms of the Soviet state.

Deriabin's first trial bit of report writing for the State Security came back with the equivalent of a B-plus from Kravtsov. His transfer from the Guard Directorate was managed in a few days' time, and he moved into a corner desk in Room 223 of the Tekstilshchikov Street offices, the home of Kravtsov's highly sensitive Austro-German Section.

The externals of Deriabin's life were not much changed by this move, aside from the novelty of less of the regular night duty which had been the rule in the Kremlin offices. He and his family retained their flat in the ten-story apartment house on Chkalova Street, reserved for State Security functionaries. By this time they enjoyed the added luxury of a private phone. His Party duties continued in the new atmosphere as before, except that the elite corps of the Foreign Intelligence Directorate cultivated a far more informal working atmosphere than other Moscow bureaucrats could imagine. Kravtsov ran his eighty-one officers with the ease of long practice. Instead of the stiff salutes prevalent in sections of the Guard Directorate, his juniors greeted the Colonel with a cheery "Hallo, boss" in English and habitually referred to him, also in English, as the "Chief."

The smooth transition in Deriabin's physical existence bore no relation to the vastly changed character of the work he was to do. For all its political nuances work in the Guard Directorate was essentially that of a night watchman with a twenty-four-hour day. The officers of the Guard are, in the literal sense of the word, caretakers. They need imagination and initiative in their jobs only inci-

dentally, although a Guard officer may on occasion display prodigies of inventiveness in the process of saving his
own skin at purge time.

The intelligence officer, by contrast, is expected to devise plans and operations of his own; within the limits, that
is, of a society that views too much initiative darkly. He is
a part of an aggressive operational organization which relies more on its wits than its weapons. His area of the State
Security's secret world is the most compact of all and the
most carefully concealed. To join an organization like this
was an obvious mental relief to a man who had had to send
his imagination on holiday throughout his tour with the
Guard.

The center of the Soviet intelligence network is smaller
than its far-flung operations might suggest. In 1952 there
were some three thousand officers in the Foreign Intelligence Directorate headquarters, charged with the State Security's foreign intelligence and counter-intelligence work
abroad, and this figure has remained more or less constant.
There were an additional 15,000 officers and agents at
work in foreign countries outside the Soviet Union, including thousands of non-Soviet citizens, traitors to their own
countries. The trained Soviet officers generally rotate regularly between Moscow and duty in the field; although a
few of them, generally those engaged in deep-cover "illegal" work, come to the Soviet Union only for infrequent
vacations.

For such a small group the Second Directorate's officers
have a disturbing omnipresence. The record of their activities, although it comes to public view only piecemeal,
shows an aggravating consistency. Almost no country in the
world has escaped the depredations of Soviet agents, either
the State Security's or those of the companion military
intelligence services. The United States and the British
Commonwealth have come to know their work well, from
incidents like the Fuchs disclosures, the Rosenberg case,
and the Gouzenko exposé to the more recent trials of Col-
nel Abel and the agents Jack and Myra Soble. The suspicion that Soviet intelligence agents made off with some of
the West's early atomic secrets has long been established as
a fact. Shortly after he began in the Foreign Intelligence
Directorate, Deriabin heard Kravtsov chatting about this

with Lieutenant General Petr V. Fedotov, the deputy head of the Directorate. "If it weren't for our work in Canada and the U.S.," Fedotov noted, "the Soviet Union would still not have the atom bomb." This remark was made some seven years after the 1945 defection of Igor Gouzenko, the code clerk in the Soviet Embassy in Canada, had uncovered at least a part of this atomic espionage. "If I could get my hands on Gouzenko," Kravtsov said, "I'd string him up myself."[3]

There is no indication that Soviet scientific and political successes then or since have caused the State Security to relax its intelligence efforts. Quite to the contrary. A curious but almost unfailing barometer of Soviet spying activity, consonant with the double-think used by Moscow in most of its international dealings, is the heavy Soviet outcry against the "espionage mania" of the Western powers, particularly the U.S. in 1958 and 1959. Whenever Soviet agents are captured or seem likely to be, if for no other reason than their widespread activity, Moscow prepares for this eventuality with a spirited propaganda campaign denouncing "imperialist agents" at work inside the Soviet Union.

Not only do the State Security leaders control the work of espionage as such, but they supervise all connections of Soviet citizens with the outside world. Such a statement may seem farfetched in our age of visiting "student delegations," extensive tours of Europe and even the U.S. by "typical Soviet citizens," or Soviet participation in world scientific meetings. But the supervision sticks. It may be carried out through a judicious assortment of "cultural advisors," "interpreters," "engineers," "assistant production managers" with Soviet delegations or artists traveling abroad. It may be effected merely through the leverage of the family hostages a traveling Soviet citizen leaves behind him.

The Foreign Intelligence Directorate could hardly stretch its relatively small group of officers over such a

---

[3] Deriabin believes that at least some of the Americans involved in various spy cases were actually dupes. As the Russian phrase has it, they were agents used *v temnuyu*—in the dark (i.e. as unwitting agents).

multitude of missions, if they were not members of an elite corps. In fact, their numbers include some of the most intelligent, technically accomplished, and sophisticated members of Soviet society. Their level of education is the highest in the country, generally including years of graduate as well as normal Soviet university study. Colonel Aleksandr M. Korotkov, a former deputy to the chief of the Directorate, and head of the Illegal Section,[4] studied for two years at the Sorbonne and previously in Germany (a fact which doubtless facilitated his successful year-long impersonation at *Wehrmacht* staff headquarters in World War II). Major Ivan E. Kamenev, of the Scientific and Technical Section, got his foreign degree at Columbia, as did Lieutenant Colonel Aleksandr G. Egurnov, who more recently established working State Security illegal networks in West Germany and Poland.

An unusually high number of the Directorate's officers possess technical degrees in engineering or the sciences. Kravtsov himself was a graduate of the Leningrad Higher Technical Institute. Colonel Ivan A. Raina, another deputy to the chief of the Foreign Intelligence Directorate, who later went on to advise Mao Tse-tung in intelligence matters, is an aviation specialist. But culture, even in the line of business, is not forgotten. A casual hobby in private life can easily turn into an intelligence sideline or even a cover occupation. The head of the Directorate's Western European Section in Moscow, Colonel Ivan I. Agayants, is an Armenian with some modest *expertise* in French art and literature. He used this to good advantage in the years immediately after World War II, when he served as State Security Resident in France, with the covering diplomatic rank of First Secretary of the Soviet Embassy. Colonel Petr I. Leonov, at that time State Security officer in the Netherlands, found his life-long fascination for ships of great value in his cover job as head of the Soviet Maritime Mission there.

---

[4] In Soviet intelligence usage, the term "illegal" describes deep-cover personnel, usually residing in an area illegally under an assumed name and having no overt Soviet connections. The "legal" personnel, on the other hand, are normally Soviet officers working under an official, usually diplomatic, cover.

THE SECRET WORLD 213

As can easily be imagined these well-selected sophisti-
cates, who read the Western press far more assiduously
than they read *Pravda*, have few illusions about the Soviet
system. The average Party secretary exhorting a Party
meeting in the Second Directorate with the usual sloganeer-
ing about "socialist legality" and "Marxist-Leninist idealism" would feel a little like the proprietor of a tent show
trying to interest the between-acts crowd at the Metropolitan Opera. Such exhortations were rarely attempted. Adequate loyalty to the régime is insured by rank, comforts,
and the interesting nature of the work.

The perquisites of the Directorate's members and their
rank in Soviet society are enough to justify almost any
amount of cynicism about the régime's workings. Their
handling contrasts sharply with that of their opposite numbers in the U.S. if not most other Western countries, where
the career intelligence officer has, at least until recently,
operated under an excessive professional shadow. It has
long been the tradition in U.S. government service, especially among the military, that the intelligence specialist is
the man who never makes general, admiral, or ambassador;
on the contrary he is condemned to a small eternity of having his views overridden by younger colonels or captains in
"operations."

In the Soviet Union the opposite is true. The State Security officer, whether on foreign or domestic intelligence
duty, is the aristocrat of the services. He wears better
clothes, eats better food, lives in a better apartment house
than his counterparts in any but the very top rungs of
Soviet society. The State Security Club on Dzerzhinsky
Square is sumptuous. Even the billiard tables are the most
massive in Moscow. Actual rank in the Foreign Intelligence Directorate, as with other branches of the State Security, is not important. The very fact of an officer's con-
netcion insures him primacy over all the other arms of the
Soviet service. When Stalin made his often-quoted statement in March 1937 about raising the level of the Soviet
armed services, he put intelligence on the same footing
with the Army and Navy. It is not enough emphasized in
the West that he mentioned intelligence first.

To understand this primacy of the intelligence services
we must first go back to the meaning of "intelligence" in

the Soviet world. It is as different from the common Western concept of the word as the local investigators of the State Security inside the Soviet Union are different from a U.S. city police force. Ask any American or Western European what the word "intelligence" means to him, and he will give a definition something like "the securing of military, political, scientific, or economic information about the activites or capabilities of a foreign power." Thus he refers to a useful but generally static occupation whose practitioners inform on policy, but do not make policy.

Even a probationary lieutenant in the current KGB, serving out a few months' active apprenticeship as a Soviet Embassy "chauffeur," would laugh at this limited definition as hopelessly outmoded and reactionary. To the Soviet mind, intelligence makes policy, or at least the State Security does. It is an active, agressive political arm of the régime. Its purpose is not only to acquire information and to prevent others from acquiring information, but to manufacture information, destroy sources of foreign information, terrorize, assassinate, and proselytize, as occasion demands. In short, Soviet intelligence sets out to subvert the political and social life of a foreign country, while at the same time taking utmost pains to see that no foreigners succeed in penetrating the international curtain which the KGB throws around Soviet citizens inside and outside their country. The American mind may still picture "intelligence" as a combination of Mata Hari in her boudoir, a sinister oriental taking pictures, and Allen Dulles listening at a Kremlin keyhole while J. Edgar Hoover watches the corridors. The Soviets are quicker to conceptualize "intelligence" as an agent with a bomb in his brief case, waiting to blow up an American radio station.[5]

The word "agent," i.e. non-officer, is used purposely in this connection. Although some of the darkest deeds of Soviet espionage have been performed by State Security staff officers, the dirty jobs abroad are, if at all possible, given

[5] This is no figment of the imagination. While Deriabin was in Moscow at least two plans were outlined for blowing up key U.S. radio installations in Europe, Radio Free Europe in Munich and RIAS in Berlin. Both were discarded, but only for technical reasons.

to either Russian or foreign agents. The State Security is very cautious about the safety of its officer personnel. If a job promises any risk of violence an officer is rarely sent without some reinforcement.

The Foreign Intelligence Directorate is divided along obvious lines of area and work differences, although the operations of it sections necessarily interlock on several levels. When Deriabin was in Moscow the First Section was the American, including all espionage and counter-intelligence work in the Western Hemisphere. The Second Section[6] was the British, responsible for all Soviet undercover work in the United Kingdom, its colonies and dominions, Canada excepted. The Austro-German Section was the Third. The Fourth had responsibility for all Western European countries—and Yugoslavia, since 1948. The Sixth covered Asia. (Africa, until recently at least, has been divided among the Middle East and various colonial sections.)

These were simple area divisions, like those in most other intelligence organizations. It is the other, more complex units in the State Security command scheme that give a clue to its peculiarly aggressive function as a fighting arm of the Soviet service. The Fifth Section dealt with the Russian émigrés. Behind this harmless title is concealed an organization whose functions are: (1) to infiltrate, sabotage, and destroy all active organizations of Soviet citizens who have managed to escape their native country; (2) to persuade or bludgeon as many groups and individuals as possible to return to the Soviet Union. The Fifth Section has sponsored the so-called "Committee for the Return to the Fatherland," a "front" organization for engineering the "re-defection" of former Soviet citizens. It also organized the return to the Soviet Union in 1948–49 of some fifteen thousand White Russian refugees in China and Manchuria. Deriabin remembers acutely the rough jokes that went around the offices of domestic State Security officials then, as they prepared to take over the White Russians' files. "What smart ones they were to come back," one of his friends said, with an ironic smile. "Well, we have

[6] As with other units of the State Security, the exact numbering of these sections may have been switched in later reorganizations, but not their functions.

plenty of room for them," answered his Section chief, "in Siberia."

The Seventh Section, as it was called, had an even more innocent title: Advisory. This is the department directly concerned with the surveillance of every satellite country from North Korea to Czechoslovakia (except for East Germany, which is run separately). State Security officers of the Advisory Section have trained security forces in each of the satellite countries, and they continue to direct them.

Their officers in this group had the corollary job of spying on the local Communist leaders of the satellites, piling up enough incriminating evidence in their Moscow dossiers so that they could be conveniently dumped when, as, and if Moscow wanted to change its policy. It was this Section that supervised purge trials, like that of the executed Czech leaders, Rudolph Slansky and Bedrich Geminder, Kostov in Bulgaria, Rajk in Hungary, etc.

For all the importance of their jobs, the State Security officers in the Seventh Section were conspicuously unenvied. Their foreign assignments took them only to satellite countries where the Russians were generally hated by the subject populations far more than they were in the West. Poland was by all odds the most unpopular, almost the equivalent of garrison duty in the poorer Siberian provinces. But aside from a few years of good pickings in Prague and Bucharest, there were no compensating material advantages in any of these countries, whose theadbare economies were already picked clean by organized Soviet plundering. Ultimately hardship allowances were given for most of the satellite stations.

Duty in Western Europe, on the contrary, has always been a real prize. Paris was the universal State Security favorite, and Rome offered almost equivalent opportunity for picking up happy capitalist luxuries. One friend of Deriabin's came back to Moscow after only two years' service in Italy with what by Soviet standards was a small fortune. He and his wife bought enough clothes in Rome to equip themselves for life and sold everything else back in Moscow. His wife disposed of twenty Italian bedspreads at 2000 rubles apiece, which amounted to half the officer's monthly salary. Another 80,000 rubles worth of negotiable goods was enough to purchase that goal of all Soviet officialdom, a summer *dacha* near Moscow.

The Tenth Section concerned itself, like the Fifth, with Soviet nationals. Where the Fifth concentrated on getting escaped Soviet citizens back to the Soviet Union, the Tenth did its best to see that no one escaped for good in the process of a temporary foreign visit. It was called the Delegations and Merchant Marine Section. Its officers are the men who accompany every Soviet delegation going overseas and closely watch the activities of the crews of all Soviet ships and aircraft that visit foreign ports.

The Eighth Section, as it was then known, is the "illegal" apparatus of Soviet intelligence. All of the previously named units send their men overseas under the cover of Soviet diplomats, members of trade missions or other official representatives. The worst that can happen to one of these legal spies is deportation from the country where he is caught. This was the fate of Valentin A. Gubichev, the personable "attaché" at the Soviet Mission to the U.N. who was publicly implicated in the 1951 espionage case of Judith Coplon, in New York.

The Illegal Section of Foreign Intelligence sends its men abroad as spies pure and simple. Their communications with the "Center" in Moscow are a matter of the highest security. They rarely if ever attempt to make contact with Soviet consulates or diplomatic missions. The Illegal Section uses foreign nationals as much as possible in its work. Most of the exposed bits of Communist espionage in the West, from the Whittaker Chambers case to the well-publicized counter-agentry of Boris Morros, were those directed by the Illegal Section.

The organization of the illegal residencies in foreign countries parallels the system of residents and agents used by the legal offices. Each is headed by a veteran State Security officer, generally with the rank of colonel or above, although in rare cases the illegal resident may be a native of the country in which he works. (In Deriabin's time the illegal residencies both in Munich and Düsseldorf were run by native Germans.) But the illegal resident knows that neither he nor his agents can expect any help or even communication from local Soviet missions in the event they are caught.

A good example of an active illegal resident, in this case one who stubbed his toe slightly, was Colonel Rudolf Abel, the Soviet spy who was caught and convicted in 1957 in New York City.[7] All of Abel's communications with Moscow and with his agents were through the most devious kind of message transmissions, from radio to hollowed-out tree trunks, although some of the actual codes used were disarmingly simple.

When an agent like Abel is captured, however, Soviet intelligence uses every covert means at its disposal to get him back. It is not unusual for the Soviets to propose half-secret "deals" in which they will get back their agent in return for foreign nationals held inside the Soviet Union. This is one reason why the Soviets and their satellites makes hostages of foreigners at the slightest excuse, even though their alleged "border violations" or transgressions of "Soviet security" were most patently innocent.

The last and most sinister office on the long dark hall of the State Security's Foreign Intelligence Directorate was the "Special Bureau No. 1." The Russians with their penchant for serviceable abbreviations called it the Spetsburo. Until 1953, when it moved to the Foreign Intelligence Directorate, it worked directly under the Minister of State Security. Its importance was suggested by the high rank of its officers. Where Deriabin found most other sections of the Directorate commanded by senior colonels, the Spetsburo was in the charge of Lieutenant General Pavel A. Sudoplatov. His deputy, Leonid A. Eitingon, was a major general. Their salaries—always an index of importance in the Soviet non-capitalist system—were as high as the 30,000 rubles monthly paid to a government Minister.

The Spetsburo, in a word, was in charge of "terror." It was responsible for acts of violence: murder, assassination, what the Soviet intelligence professionals call "big operations." Wherever possible the State Security gets local gangsters to do its overseas dirty work. But in delicate cases one or two Spetsburo officers are dispatched from Moscow to do the régime's job. It was the Spetsburo which arranged the assassination of Leon Trotsky in 1940. Spets-

---

[7] The fullest account of the Abel case thus far published is an article in the November 11, 1957, issue of *Life*.

buro officers killed the White Russian General Aleksandr
P. Kutepov in Paris in 1930 and were implicated in the
1941 killing of the military intelligence (GRU) refugee,
General Walter Krivitsky. They made several attempts on
the life of General Walter Orlov, a one-time friend of Stalin's who published in the U.S. the true story of Stalin's
purges. In 1954 one such officer defected to the West before carrying out a planned assassination in Frankfurt. He
is Captain Nikolay Khokhlov, who refused to go through
with the murder of an official in the NTS (the Union of
Russian Solidarists), a strongly anti-Soviet Russian refugee
organization.

During the war the Spetsburo had been called the Partisan Directorate, in charge of guerilla activity behind the
German lines. When it resumed its old functions in 1945,
its offices were put in the main headquarters of the State
Security; but there was little lateral contact between it and
the other bureaus.

CHAPTER XVI

The Hidden War In Germany

BY COMPARISON WITH the activities of the Spetsburo, Peter Deriabin's work was clean. Or so it looked at first. The Austro-German Section was the second largest unit of the foreign intelligence setup, after the American. With all their involvements in Asia the Russians have never ceased to regard the German problem as central to Soviet security. Long before World War II, Soviet intelligence had built up from the ruins of the German Communist Party one of the world's most deadly and efficient intelligence networks. The German invasion of World War II most graphically reinforced the Soviet determination to keep the Germany of the future weak and divided. It also gave the Russians a springboard for intelligence operations in the future, through the German documents captured aftter the Nazi defeat and the hundreds of thousands of German war prisoners captured, many of whom were recruited as Soviet agents.

In 1952 the situation in Germany, as seen from Moscow, was going badly. No one inside the State Security attempted to disguise the blow given to the Soviet cause by the successful Berlin airlift of 1948, which ranked with the formation of NATO and the resistance in Korea as the most effective American counters to the aggression of the U.S.S.R. (It goes without saying that members of the Foreign Intelligence Directorate, whose associates periodically returned from duty in the Far East, held no illusions about who committed the aggression in Korea.) With hope lost of directing or even influencing the government policies of the Federal German Republic or Austria, the Soviet strategists concentrated first on preserving, later on strengthening, the hold of the Communist Party inside the East German satellite.

Already the angry German resistance was making itself felt which finally flared up in the June 1953 revolt. The resistance spirit was encouraged by a certain animal sense of the uncertainty and indecision at the top in Moscow, which began to spread among the satellites in the closing days of Stalin's rule.

The job of Soviet intelligence at this juncture was twofold: (1) an orthodox intelligence effort, although using very unorthodox methods, to penetrate the plans and councils of the Austrian and Federal German governments; and (2) an all-out counter-intelligence operation to diminish the growing centers of resistance to Soviet rule in East Germany.

Colonel Kravtsov's men were divided into three main departments: counter-intelligence for Germany, intelligence for Germany, and a combined intelligence and counter-intelligence for Austria. To these were added a special "SK" section for dealing with Soviet personnel in both Austria and Germany, another group designed for the "penetration" of U.S., British, and French intelligence operations in the area, and special "advisory" subsections for the surveillance of the East German government and the East German police and army.

At different times Deriabin worked in all these branches, and he was cognizant with most of their activities through his added importance as Communist Party secretary of the entire Section. But his first big job came in the field of counter-intelligence, ax the Russians euphemistically classified this operation. It involved him, ultimately, in the kidnapping of Dr. Walter Linse, a respected lawyer in West Berlin who at the time Deriabin came to the Austro-German Section was acting chief of the Association of Free German Jurists, then one of the most effective anti-Communist organizations operating on both sides of the unnatural German border.

It is worth recounting the Linse kidnapping in detail. In July 1952, when it happened, the news broke with startling impact and was detailed throughout the Western press. The Russians were immediately suspected of complicity and repeated diplomatic protests dispatched to Soviet occupation authorities in Berlin and to Moscow. Nothing but indignant denials came from the side of the Soviet Union, When the U.S. High Commissioner John McCloy asked his Russian opposite number about the crime, General Vasiliy Chuikov, the same man who had commanded the Siberian 64th Army at Stalingrad, answered with astonished indignation: "You do not think, I hope, that the Soviet Union would have had any complicity in this plot." As late as 1957 the International Jurists Association sent a cable to Moscow pleading for information on Linse's whereabouts. There was no reply. In so many cases like this the echoing rectitude of the Soviet denials has persuaded people in the West that the accusations were in fact groundless. It should be instructive to detail here, step by step, the manner in which the Soviet forces perpetrated this crime, then denied it, just as they have done in hundreds of cases before and since.

In early 1952 Soviet intelligence found out that the president of the Free Jurists, Dr. Theo Friedenau, planned to run a world congress of free jurists in Berlin that July. The Soviet régime had been suffering considerably from his activities, since in the course of reporting Soviet illegalities throughout East Germany, he had built up a very efficient intelligence network. With consistent success the Free German Jurists had a habit of finding out very quickly who was being tried on faked charges in East Germany. Often they were able to use their influence inside the East German courts to free those unjustly accused. The project of a world congress in Berlin, focusing attention on the criminal activities of the East German satellite, was in the nature of a last straw for Moscow.

By this time Deriabin had become an accomplished report writer. On the basis of a report from him outlining the activities of the Free German Jurists, Kravtsov recommended that the coming congress be wrecked, preferably by taking action against its organizers. Lieutenant General Fedotov, then deputy head of the Foreign Intelligence Directorate, approved the recommendation. He ordered Major General Mikhail Kaverznev, officer in charge of the huge State Security headquarters at the Karlshorst compound in East Berlin, to organize a task force to kidnap Friedenau and bring him into the Soviet area. The direct order was signed by Lieutenant General Sergey R. Savchenko, the head of the Directorate. As with all such orders, it was written by hand. Deriabin drafted it, and Kravtsov and Fedotov approved it. Outside of these four men no one in Moscow saw the actual order—in itself an interesting commentary on the curious combination of conspiratorial efficiency and half-submerged guilty conscience organic to the upper echelons of the State Security.

A month later, after repeated calls to Karlshorst from Moscow (it was always necessary for Moscow to heckle the "field" on such matters), Kaverznev reported that the plans for kidnapping Friedenau were ready. Then suddenly Friedenau left on an unannounced trip to Sweden, leaving behind as his deputy Dr. Linse, a dry, efficient barrister who had headed Friedenau's Economic section.

Kaverznev recommended that Linse be kidnaped instead. On receipt of his telegram Deriabin telephoned his superiors and promptly drafted an answering wire: "Under orders of Savchenko take all measures to sabotage the congress." He got an immediate answer from Berlin: "Operational group for Friedenau has all information against Linse. Request permission." Permission was granted on July 2.

A few minutes after seven, on the morning of July 8, 1952, the residents of Lichterfelde-West, a respectable residential suburb of West Berlin, were startled by the sounds of a struggle on the sidewalk outside Dr. Linse's home. There was a shout for help, a shot, and the sound of a car shifting suddenly into high speed. One or two passers-by, running toward the noise, saw a man being thrown into the rear seat of what looked like a West Berlin taxi-cab. A truck driver, seeing the cab flee, tried to give chase; but his vehicle was effectively stopped by a flurry of nails and large tacks which the car's occupants dropped on the pavement. The cab, speeding at sixty-five miles an hour, roared across the boundary into the East zone, where the barrier had been thoughtfully raised beforehand. All that was left of Dr. Linse was a shoe that had fallen on the pavement in Gerichtsstrasse during the fight to get him into the car.

Kaverznev's plot had been well prepared. The night before, East German agents of the State Security had stopped a cab driver in East Berlin, held him for several hours on allegations of black-market activity, and transferred his car's West Berlin license plates to the kidnappers' vehicle. The next morning's pickup was arranged after a careful prior study of Linse's movements. He was, unfortunately, an early riser. Three East German muscle-men, one of them a former Nazi party member, rode in the kidnap car and parked near his house.

When Linse came out on his way to the office, one of them asked him for a light. While he was fumbling for a match the other pinioned his arms behind him and tried to throw him in the car. The struggle that followed was bitter. Linse broke away briefly and kept fighting in the back of the car. In order to get his kicking foot inside the door one of the agents calmly shot him in the leg.

A second car with two Soviet State Security officers met the kidnap car at the border and escorted it to the Karlshorst State Security compound. There the Russians interrogated Linse immediately. Wounded and terrified, he was no match for them. Within twenty-four hours after Linse's kidnapping, Soviet Security had begun widespread operations against known and suspected members of the Free Jurists organization in East Germany.

Within the next few days twenty-seven of them were arrested and held in custody, the others either hunted or under surveillance. So much for General Kaverznev's efficient "intelligence" operation.

Back in Moscow, however, the work on the Linse case was only half finished. The day after the kidnapping, which shocked West Berlin and brought immediate Western protests, the State Security received an inter-office communication from the Soviet Foreign Ministry: "With regard to the disappearance of Dr. Linse we would like to know how we should reply or react." The humble tone was in itself proof of the supremacy enjoyed by the State Security over other elements of the Soviet bureaucracy. After checking with his superiors Deriabin sent back a rather thin guidance reply: "We know nothing about this matter."

But while this exchange was going over the official ministerial wires the former Paris Resident, Colonel Agayants, telephoned a friend of his, the Deputy Minister of Foreign Affairs, Boris F. Podtserob. Said the Colonel: "I think that it would be best to answer in this way regarding the Linse affair. Although they found his shoe in the Western sector, this proves nothing. There is no other evidence. As for the car, it had a West Berlin license plate. So the whole business must have been instigated by people inside West Berlin." Podtserob thought this over for a minute and then said slowly, "Yes, Ivan Ivanovich, I think it will come off." On July 10, the Soviet Foreign Ministry, answering through its High Commissioner in Germany, disclaimed any knowledge of the Linse kidnapping in notes replying to the American and German protests. The notes said almost exactly what the State Security had instructed.

The Foreign Ministry suitably briefed, Deriabin sharpened his pencil again and prepared a report of seven copies (to Malenkov and the key Praesidium members) about the Linse operation. He noted that the Free German Jurists had been found engaged in espionage in East Germany against Soviet forces. They were publishing false information about "Soviet methods of justice," under the guidance of U.S. intelligence. To cut off the effectiveness of this organization, his report continued, one of its leaders was brought to East Berlin and arrested. The words "kidnapping" or "abduction" were scrupulously avoided. It was not that the Central Committee would have criticized the fact of the kidnapping. They would have insisted on a "better word" being used to describe it.

The report to the Praesidium mentioned the arrests of Free Jurists agents and noted their preliminary "confessions." Further investigations, Deriabin added, were proceeding and would be reported. Everyone in the régime was satisfied.

Dr. Linse was put in a German jail near Berlin. After the preliminary interrogation was finished his wound was given medical treatment. General Kaverznev at first mulled over the possibility of putting him on public trial in East Berlin—presumably for "treason" (he had fled East Germany in 1947). But in view of the furor over his capture this was thought too risky. He was, however, returned to Soviet control at Karlshorst and eventually transferred to a prison in the Soviet Union. His sentence was probably the

standard twenty-five years then meted out to "political of-
fenders." No one outside the Soviet Union knows exactly
where he was sent.[1]

Deriabin was congratulated by Kravtsov on the success
of his first big job. At the time he felt no particular pangs
at his own part in the operation. Acting against the Germans, a race for whom he had no special love, was preferable to the constant surveillance of his fellow Russians,
while working in the Guard or in the domestic service of
the State Security. But he did begin to have doubts about
how "clean" it really was, working for the Foreign Intelligence Directorate of the State Security.

The offensive plans of the State Security did not stop at
kidnappings. They included assassination, terror, and sabotage of a variety that would have made a detective villain
admiringly envious. Each plan had the sanction, if not the
inspiration, of higher authority, and action continued to
concentrate on German organizations opposed to Communism. But the plans did not always work. In October
1952, when Moscow ordered the Berlin office to take action against another refugee organization in Germany,
General Kaverznev replied that kidnapping any of its leaders
would be difficult. His chief General Savchenko sent this
order: "If it is impossible to kidnap, undertake 'terror'
against them in every form possible." "Terror" in this context was the usual State Security synonym for assassination,
the details being left up to the plan's operational executors.

The ensuing attempt miscarried. So did another kidnapping effort, this time against a leader of the Free Democratic Party in West Berlin, despite the fact that the man's
friend and political confidant, an ex-Nazi officer, was a
Soviet agent. The agent was known in Moscow by the code
name "Siegfried." His operation was to have run along the
lines of the Linse Kidnapping. After a night of visiting the
West Berlin night clubs Siegfried suggested to his boss that
they might take a taxi home. A "taxi" from East Berlin,
with West Berlin license plates on the outside and a crew

[1] In 1955 Linse was encountered in the Soviet slave labor
camp at Vorkuta, by a group of German war prisoners who
were later repatriated.

of East German agents waiting in the back seat, was providentially at hand for the purpose. But the Free Democrat, although half inebriated, prudently said he would walk.

At this same period, Lieutenant Colonel Aleksandr Egurnov, the State Security's leading Columbia University alumnus, and one Major Nikolay Budakhin, a state security officer with the rather thin cover of *Tass* correspondent,[2] hatched a really ambitious project for blowing up the reservoir which served as the principal source of water for the people of Berlin. The purpose of this operation, as outlined, was to create panic in the West Berlin population in the hope that the Western occupying forces could be quickly driven out in the chaos that would follow. This plan was long discussed by the heads of the Foreign Intelligence Directorate, but, like earlier planned bombings of Western radio stations, it was finally turned down as impractical.

Even to the most self-confident of the State Security's directors it was clear that operations on the "terror" front were not going well. For the Linse operation, while a tactical success, was also a strategic failure. The kidnapping alerted the population of West Berlin and, for that matter, of the entire *Bundes republik* to the underground war the Soviets were waging against them. It was stupid to attempt the same tactic over again, and so the State Security men in the field tried very tactfully to point out. But in overruling their objections, as so often, Moscow showed its one big intelligence failing: an inability to understand local peculiarities and appreciate the feelings of local populations. If the Central Committee's hand is strong it is also very heavy.

There was another factor even more responsible for the canceled plans and aborted missions of the Foreign Intelligence Directorate. This was the death of Stalin and the subsequent fall of Lavrentiy Beria. By July 1953 the command apparatus inside the Central Committee was paralyzed by mistrust and factional disputes. Since almost all of the State Security's offensive operations needed Central Committee sanction this part of the Directorate's activities

[2] The proportion of *bona fide* newsmen in the *Tass* and *Pravda* overseas operation is small.

slowed to a shaky walk. It was not until September, after Malenkov's emergence had temporarily stablized the power base, that the Central Committee's control mechanics started up once more.

In more orthodox intelligence activity, however, where the constant sanction of Central Committee members was not needed, the Directorate was more successful. There was no busier corner of it than the low-ceilinged rooms on Tekstilshchikov Street, where the Austro-German Section kept its headquarters before moving into the main State Security building on Dzerzhinsky Square in 1953. In this period, as in the years immediately preceding, the Directorate continued its work of infiltrating agents into every stratum of society in Austria and the divided Germanies, some of them active workers in intelligence or counter-intelligence, others buried in "deep cover" against the day when they would prove useful.

As deputy head of a "sector," Deriabin had the sole custody of a large group of files. Each contained a handy two- or three-page summary, for quick reference,[3] of the life and activities of the most important Soviet agents in West Germany. Security was rigid. Every evening he would seal his working documents in a small brief case, which he would in turn put into a safe also sealed with his personal stamp. No one could open the safe without his observance. If higher authority wanted sudden access to the files Deriabin had to be routed out to provide it.

As Deriabin had found out in the domestic service, the State Security acted with the efficiency of a gigantic vacuum cleaner in its search for agent material. The Foreign Intelligence Directorate used the same inclusive recruiting methods and showed the same lack of scruple about the origins and habits of its people, as long as they were useful. Fascists, monarchists, socialists, businessmen, barmaids or clergymen—the State Security used them all. In some countries such a variety of talent was hard to recruit, especially after a later ban against using native Communists. But the Austro-German Section, thanks to the fortunes of

---

[3] As far as can be known, Soviet intelligence sifters and evaluators have yet to sample the joys of IBM-type automatic filing systems.

World War II, was peculiarly well-supplied with promising native German and Austrian informers.

Each day a corps of translators and officers from Kravtsov's Section would go out to a group of boxcars on a railroad siding near Moscow, where literally tons of captured German documents were stored, including priceless records of the Gestapo, the S.S., and the German Foreign Office. These they took back to the eighth floor of 2 Dzerzhinsky Square for sorting and translation. Through them the Soviets accumulated a mass of provocative information on various influential, or potentially influential, Germans; everything from records of secret Gestapo service as spies or informers to embarrassing bits of personal history. As fast as the documents were translated they were put at the service of Soviet agents in Germany and Austria, who lost no time in making contact with the people mentioned in the files.

There is no more dramatic, nor more tantalizing suggestion of how such blackmail did its work than the sequel which Deriabin was able to add to the mysterious defection of Dr. Otto John. John fled suddenly to East Berlin on July 22, 1954, while serving as head of the Office for the Defense of the Constitution, the West German equivalent of the FBI. After making a series of propaganda statements for the East German satellite government and presumably telling all he knew to the Communists, John later redefected to the West. He was tried before a West German court on charges of treason on December 22, 1956, and sentenced to five years imprisonment. (He was released for good behavior in 1958.)

The only explanation given for his action was "emotional stress." He had been active in the July 20, 1944, plot against Hitler, and his brother was executed by the Nazis for his part in it. John's flight to the Communists, according to his own public announcement, was prompted by the employment of former Nazis in the West German government.

In Deriabin's reconstruction the Otto John defection was no mystery, merely a good case job by the Austro-German Section. The work began in 1951. On coming to his new job, Deriabin inherited a thin file about John and his organization. The file grew with the passage of time. One of its principal ornaments was the name of Wolfgang Wohlgemuth, a fashionable Berlin doctor who had been used by the State Security since early in 1950.

In 1952 a Soviet agent who had been planted inside the Office for the Defense of the Constitution came up with further tantalizing information. He suggested that John, the well-known resistance fighter, had actually had some dealings with the Nazis during World War II. Kravtsov ordered an intensive search of the captured Nazi archives for confirmatory evidence.

Now comes the tantalizing part of the story. Exactly what was John's connection with the Nazis—and how sincere it was—the archives did not reveal, at least up to the time of Deriabin's departure. But they did tell the State Security enough to start an operation against him. When Deriabin left Moscow in September 1953 the Austro-German Section was continuing work on John's organization. It appears probable that John's defection to the East followed a Soviet threat to expose him, made after the investigation had got under way.[4]

Many Soviet agents in Germany and Austria had been recruited in a similarly compromising if more direct fashion. Many became highly valuable properties. Only a small portion of Moscow's German agents, however, were actually picked up in Germany or through use of the captured files. For most of them the path to becoming a Soviet informer began in a prison camp inside the Soviet Union, one of the scores at which German prisoners-of-war were held. Before their release from the camps hundreds of Germans were forced to sign papers attesting their willingness to work for the State Security. Some repudiated these forced agreements as soon as they crossed the West Ger-

---

[4] As the legal advisor to the old German Lufthansa civil air line, John was in an excellent position to further the work of Admiral Canaris's *Abwehr* intelligence network, an organization which was strongly anti-Hitler until it was absorbed by the Gestapo after Canaris's arrest and execution. It is most probable that John may have given frequent public protest of his loyalty to Hitler as a cover for his real anti-Nazi work. Quite possibly, this sort of documentary lip service—embarrassing if published by itself—is what Moscow found.

man border. But for others it was not so easy. Again the
blackmail technique was used against them.

A few months before Deriabin arrived there the Austro-
German Section was assigned the job of selecting a hard-
core group of agents from the prisoners remaining in Soviet
hands. By this time, seven years after the war, most of the
surviving unrepatriated prisoners remained in the U.S.S.R.
for some purpose. They included high Nazi party or German army officers and war criminals (a broad category by
Soviet definition), but there were also others whose luck
had not been good. There were only a few remaining members of the original Soviet-sponsored wartime Committee of
German Freedom, which was created after the German
disaster at Stalingrad. (The Committee's nominal leader
was Field Marshal von Paulus, whom the State Security
later had installed as commander-in-chief of the new East
German Army.) The State Security reasoned that the
Committee members were too distinctively earmarked as
Communists or Communist sympathizers to make good
agents back home. But others, including informers and un-
regenerate Nazis, were regarded as fine agent material.
The more crimes recorded against them, the better.

In 1952 a careful survey of agent possibilities was conducted by sixty State Security officers, who combed every
prison camp in the Soviet Union. As in past surveys of this
sort, they looked for prisoners in four broad categories:
(1) men who had informed against their fellow prisoners
while in camp; (2) men with good connections back home
in Germany or in any other of the NATO countries. Strenuous though unsuccessful efforts, for instance, were made
to compromise and use Harald Krupp von Bohlen, the
younger brother of Alfred Krupp, before his release; (3)
long-time prisoners convicted of war crimes, real or fancied, by Soviet courts. Most of these men had been sentenced to twenty-five years in jail, so they were understandably eager in their promises to work for Soviet
intelligence if released. The State Security took every pre-
caution, through its network of informers and agents in
Germany, to see that such fair-weather agents continued to
work after their return. The last category (4), included
members of Nazi intelligence or counter-intelligence
groups.

The sixty officers brought four hundred files back to Moscow with them after one such exhaustive screening of men in these groups. Further checking in Moscow whittled the list down to seventy, an interviewing brought it to thirty. Of these thirty, ten were finally chosen. The same process went on over and over again. Throughout the year over one hundred German agents were thus selected and sent back to develop "contacts" at home.

When a good agent possibility offered itself, the State Security spared no efforts to find him and make his new bargain as tempting as possible. Deriabin's colleague, Captain Litovkin, spent six months tracking down one Captain Kurt Hartmann, a wartime German intelligence officer whose fluency in Russian and Polish had landed him for a time in a camp for "anti-Soviet" Russians instead of with the other foreign prisoners. When found, Hartmann proved to have an interesting story. In 1944 his unit had captured a Russian partisan agent, an attractive girl named Marusya. Hartmann kept her with him, and they lived together for several months. Later Marusya escaped and made her way back to the Russian lines, where her grateful fellow countrymen gave her fifteen years for consorting with the enemy. Hartmann was himself captured and eventually confined in a German prisoner-of-war camp at Yaroslavl.

Hartmann agreed to work for the Soviet Union. He was brought back to Moscow, given a large room at a good hotel, all the money he needed, and the free run of the city, subject only to some unobtrusive State Security surveillance. By day the Austro-German Section put him through further intensive interrogation about his origins in Germany besides instructing him in Soviet intelligence techniques. Yet nothing was spared to make his stay enjoyable, including the company of various party girls on the State Security payroll.[5] As a final gesture of good fellowship

[5] Prostitution, in various degrees of blatancy, has always been one of the principal weapons of the State Security. It is used both as a provocation to ensnare the unwary in a blackmail game or as a means of keeping faithful agents happy and relatively carefree during certain periods. Few of the girls involved are on the regular State Security payroll, but they are obtained through the militia from a pool of available talent, mostly persons who are picked up off the streets for prostitu-

the State Security had Hartmann's old partisan girl-friend
released temporarily from her prison to pass a few months
with him in Moscow.

Before releasing Hartmann the Sate Security ostentatiously put him into solitary at another German prisoner-
of-war camp on the pretext that he had resisted interrogation and tried to escape. He was ordered to tell his fellow
Germans that the Russians had tried to recruit him, but
had withdrawn their offer after his attempted break. After
this preparation Hartmann was to be quietly released with
the next group of prisoners returning to West Germany in
November 1953, a full-fledged agent of the Foreign Intelligence Directorate.

Often the agent-recruiting processes were not this direct,
but concentrated on friends and relatives of men still held
in Soviet camps. This was a surer and more desirable way
of using the prisoners, since the State Security always preferred a bird locked up in jail to any number in the bush.
Many of the high-ranking German officers, like other Soviet prisoners, were destined never to leave Russia. But
Deriabin and his fellow officers kept up constant efforts to
recruit their relatives.

Colonel Karl Schildknecht, a German intelligence officer in World War II, was regarded as of special value because of his wartime connections with General Reinhold
Gehlen, the West German intelligence director. Although
not attempt was made to recruit him, the results of his interrogations by Soviet intelligence produced valuable information on personalities now in the West German intelligence service. Another former member of the German
army intelligence, who also received a twenty-five-year
sentence, was Colonel Alfred Dieckenbrock, who had been
assistant head of the *Abwehr* under the famous Admiral
Canaris. With him the bait failed. State Security agents
sought out his wife Renate, who lived quietly in the Federal German Republic, and arranged a meeting with a man
who said he had just left the general in a camp in Vladimir,
near Moscow. The agent asked her to write her husband,
using the services of a friendly Russian officer (also a

---

tion. A very small number of semi-agents, in the call-girl category, do have direct State Security connections.

member of the Foreign Intelligence Directorate). But when she did Dieckenbrock refused to open contact with her. "I am an old man, and I know I will die in your prison," he said. "I want no part of these games."

After this refusal Deriabin ordered the State Security "laboratory" to forge a letter to the wife in the general's handwriting. In answer to the letter she sent along a medallion, some British cigarettes, and a few books, including Clausewitz's *On War* (which he seemed to be reading a bit belatedly). But far from being taken in by these beginnings of Soviet recruiting, she told her story to West German authorities.

Since the supply of German agents was relatively plentiful the KGB used them for work elsewhere than in Germany. In 1953 Colonel Evgeniy K. Galuzin, Kravtsov's deputy in the Austro-German Section, went to East Germany on a mission connected with the imminent dispatch of a shipment of textile machines to Turkey. Turkey has one of the most difficult climates for Soviet intelligence operations, and it is extremly hard work to get a native Soviet agent into the country. Galuzin planned to recruit some of the ten East German instructors who were bound for Turkey along with their machines. In two months of intensive checking work he did manage to sign up four on whom Moscow could reasonably expect to depend.

Another agent in West Germany, compromised because of his prison-camp record, was recruited in Kiel to act as a communications channel for Soviet intelligence work in Holland. The State Security officer in the Netherlands, Colonel Leonov, sometimes had difficulty getting messages through, despite his comfortable cover as head of the Soviet Merchant Marine control group there. This agent, following the Soviet usage, was known as "Gollandets," the Dutchman.

At the time of his Turkish inspection trip Colonel Galuzin also took three or four trained German agents from East Germany, fitted them out with forged Austrian passports, birth certificates, and other credentials, and sent them into Austria as "journalists" to act as agent-recruiters. The Soviet Army was about to leave Austria, and the State Security was bending every effort to get agents strategically re-situated there for the far more difficult job of sending back intelligence from an independent country.

In this, as in all its operations, the State Security kept step with political developments, always anticipating and strengthening Soviet diplomatic or military maneuvers with intelligence preparation. In the Austro-German Section, as everywhere, it was regarded not as a scouting or information force, but as the first aggressive arm of the Soviet political offensive.

CHAPTER XVII

Cold Storage Agents And Satellites

___

IN 1955 SOME newspapers in the U.S. and Europe carried the account of the "flight to freedom" by one Mikhail Baranov,[1] a heroic Russian ex-soldier in his early thirties. Some months before, Baranov had escaped from a Siberian labor camp near Omsk, where he was an electrician, after short-circuiting the camp's electircal system. It had taken him four and a half months to make his way across the entire breadth of the Soviet Union, Poland, and Czechoslovakia before he reached safety in the U.S. sector of Vienna. His privations were extreme. Dramatically Baranov recounted to reporters how he had used his electrician's pliers to cut through the trip-wire alarm system on the Soviet border before swimming across the icy Bug River into Poland.

"Friendly farmers" both in Poland and Czechoslovakia had helped him on his escape, but it was hard going nonetheless. At one point, he said, "I took wheat grains from the growing crop, rubbed them in my hands, and ate them." Finally, after vainly trying to reach West Germany, he found a "weak spot" in the Czech border system facing Austria, and got across. An Austrian who befriended him gave him money to get to Vienna. Baranov broke through the Iron Curtain, he told his interviewers, because life as a German prisoner during World War II had shown him the great disparity of living standards between Russia and the West—

___

[1] This is not his real name.

an impression reinforced by his two years' occupation duty in Austria and Czechoslovakia with the Red Army. He had tried to escape once before, in 1947, after listening to a Voice of America broadcast, but he had been captured by Czech police and sentenced to twenty-five years at the labor camp near Omsk. The West, or that part of it which heard about Baranov, was captivated by his story.

Baranov was a fake. He was not a refugee, but a trained State Security agent whose entire escape had been planned by the Austro-German Section in Moscow. His first attempted escape from the Soviet Union, prompted by his "listening to the Voice of America," was a complete fiction. It was supplied for him by the Austro-German Section as part of his "legend," the technical name for the fictitious history, background, and circumstances of the character whom an agent is representing. The second escape had a touch of reality to it. Baranov *was* sent to the labor camp near Omsk, for which he was in Soviet eyes a legitimate candidate—all prisoners of war were treated with suspicion as at least potential enemies of the state. To get his freedom and to save his relatives he had agreed to serve as a State Security agent, and he had received intensive preliminary indoctrination in this role. State Security officers had planned his escape from the prison camp without the knowledge of the camp authorities. On his "flight" through the Soviet Union, Poland, and Czechoslovakia, State Security officers met him at convenient points to give him food, clothes, and sailing directions to the next point of contact.

The Baranov operation had been planned for almost two years before his actual "escape." Deriabin had opposed this scheme as long as he was in the Austro-German Section. He felt that the "escape" was too absurd to be believable. No one who knew anything about the Soviet Union, he argued, would accept the story of an individual's unassisted "escape" across 4500 miles of Soviet-held territory, still less the allegation that a former war prisoner would ever have been allowed to do foreign duty in the Soviet Army.

For a while his objections were considered. But in the end they were overthrown by the insistence of other officers that one more such operation as Baranov's was needed to fill the Section's "norm," as it were. Even the Foreign Intelligence officers were not immune from the general Soviet insistence on constantly bigger production figures, at whatever incidental cost to quality and long-term operating efficiency.

What was the purpose of this elaborate failure which cost the KGB a heavy investment in man-hours? It was not for normal intelligence information-seeking; a Russian refugee could hardly hope for access to political secrets, which were in any case well taken care of by other State Security sources. Baranov had been sent to the West for the sole purpose of getting information on the U.S. and German intelligence agencies who would be expected to question him.

The attention given to his mission—far from the only attempt of its kind in recent years—is an index of the importance the State Security attaches to finding out everything possible about the workings of its rival, U.S. intelligence. "Penetration" is the technical term given to the act of inserting one's own man inside the enemy intelligence forces as a trusted operative. Simple infiltration is the act of making contact with these intelligence forces and reporting on their activites. No service in the world so concerns itself with these two aspects of intelligence as the Soviet Union. This concern of the State Security harks back to the involved conspiratorial beginnings of Communism in Russia, a welter of Czarist and Communist spies, counter-spies, and double-agents cubed. In its operation it is an outgrowth of the classic technique of "provocation," used so frequently in counter-intelligence operations inside the U.S.S.R., in which an agent deliberately induces a suspect to discuss or perform anti-Soviet acts after his confidence. (See Appendix II.)

Living in its own web of suspicion, the Soviet leadership has an almost pathological desire to find out what others know, and want to know, about it. If the world-wide battle of the intelligence services did not exist Moscow would have invented it.

The major enemy of Soviet intelligence is, of course, the Central Intelligence Agency of the U.S. Technically speaking, the State Security officers have a somewhat higher opinion of British intelligence. The American service, the State Security technicians used to say, has too many officers for efficient operation, and they are often young and

inexperienced. Nonetheless, Central Intelligence agents—
and the hundreds of real or fancied spies who are wrong-
fully accused by the Soviets of Central Intelligence contacts—are the object of the most intense competitive study.

Inside the corridors of the State Security offices the
name of Allen Dulles, the CIA Director, is the next thing
to a household term. "Yes, Sergey" a case officer will say,
discussing some foreign project, "that Allen Dulles let us
down this time. But he's given the boys on the desk downstairs a very ticklish problem." Soviet intelligence keeps a
day-by-day record of Dulles's activities as they can be covered both from agent reports and the U.S. and foreign
press. In his dossier each area he visits is noted in detail,
along with accounts of his public reports, speeches, lectures, attendance at diplomatic receptions, or even cocktail
parties.

Peter Deriabin first heard of Dulles in 1944 as a student
in the SMERSH Counter-Intelligence School. In lectures
on the Western powers' intelligence networks Dulles was
mentioned as a leading American intelligence personality
in Central Europe. He was, the students learned, a capable
and experienced intelligence officer with a capacity for imag-
inative future planning and there was some speculation
about his possibly taking over U.S. intelligence in Europe
in the postwar period. Just nine years later Deriabin had
occasion to edit a small but highly secret booklet published
by the State Security in Moscow for limited distribution:
*Concerning the Activities of U.S. Intelligence Services in
Western Europe.* Here again was a thick section on Dulles's past history and some discussion of his thinking and
habits, as the Soviets imagined it. "A medium-sized man in
civilian clothes," the book began its record, "who lived during the war in a small brown house in a quiet street, Heron
Street, in Berne, Switzerland, far from the front. In 1944
Dulles already foresaw the breakdown of the anti-Hitler co-
alition, and he began to make plans for intelligence activity
against the Soviet state. . . ."

These admiring evaluations of Dulles were only for inner
State Security consumption, however. The official secret
booklet on U.S. intelligence activities (*Orientation on Central Intelligence Organs of the U.S.A.*) signed by the then
Minister of State Security, Ignat'ev, was prefaced by a

rousing propaganda foreword. The U.S., it ran, betrayed the Allied cause in World War II by violating the Potsdam agreement and beginning preparations for a new war. A leading role in the preparation of this war was being played by the intelligence organs of the U.S. These groups were in the service of the Wall Street capitalists and financed by the Ford Foundation (sic) as well as by other American millionaires. Their chief, Allen Dulles, was a brother of the well-known warmonger, Secretary of State John Foster Dulles. Both brothers, the report added, represented powerful monopoly circles inside the U.S.

The official view of American intelligence was interesting, although confused in the details of its announced "orientation." The most complete organizational description, in fact, was given not about CIA, but about a unit of U.S. military intelligence, the Counter-Intelligence Corps, with which the Russians had grown familiar through its free-wheeling operations in Europe. There was some scanty information added about other U.S. intelligence organizations, including the Office of Naval Intelligence, Air Force Intelligence, and the Federal Bureau of Investigation. All were regarded as divisions of the same office. Understandably enough the heavily centralized Soviet foreign intelligence believed that all U.S. intelligence, although differing in type and function, was united under a single authority.

When the orientation booklet was issued it was read to members of the Austro-German Section by Colonel Kravtsov during an operational briefing. In Kravtsov's reading he highlighted the necessity for improving Soviet detection facilities against what was asserted to be a new wave of "American agents" who were being infiltrated into the Soviet Union.

It is characteristic of the State Security's way of thinking that in the war with U.S. intelligence, it would try to make capital out of the inevitable by-product of the Soviet slave system: the people who try to escape it. The case of Baranov was simple and straightforward by comparison with the devious planning behind some others. One such operation, which took in even more ground than Baranov's, was the recruiting for foreign duty of a man named "Jan."

"Jan" (the code name by which he was known) was a resident of Vladivostok, ostensibly a purchasing agent for the Soviet Fishing Monopoly, but actually an agent of some ten years' standing, with an encyclopedic knowledge of the Manchurian border areas. In World War II Jan had brought back valuable information about Japanese military activities. His mission now was to find out how the United States "introduced its agents into Siberia."

For a long time the State Security had worried about this problem, which probably has little basis in fact. Convinced that some "American agents" were being smuggled into Soviet Asia from Far Eastern bases, Moscow decided to inject a double-agent into the imagined U.S. operations, to find out their secret. To this end Jan was summoned to Dzerzhinsky Square. He told his neighbors that he was going to visit an influential uncle in Moscow, in search of another and better position.

After a preliminary screening he returned once more to Vladivostok and announced that he had been successful. He and his wife told their friends that he was to be transferred for a year or two to duty with a special supply mission in the Arctic Ocean. His wife signed an agreement to receive 1200 rubles monthly from the State Security (400 rubles more than Jan's original salary) while he was absent. She was to make no mention of his intelligence job. She would receive no letters from him, except for a few forged notes from Moscow headquarters, to keep up the fiction of his Arctic mission. These matters concluded, he said good-by to his family and left Vladivostok.

When Jan arrived at the Balchug Hotel in Moscow he was understandably surprised to find himself greeted by Deriabin and other officers from the Austro-German Section instead of the Far East or American departments. In this case, the State Security reasoned that any rigged "defection" to the Americans in the Far East would smack of the obvious. So to penetrate American spying methods in the East they had prepared an elaborate little plot to be acted out in Germany.

After his training in Moscow, Jan was to go to Rostock, in East Germany. His "legend" involved posing again as a purchasing agent of the Soviet Fishing Monopoly there, a relaxed, garrulous Russian, overfond of drinking and German girls. Through nine months of conspicuously inefficient work and ostentatious play he was to remain in Rostock, after which he would be recalled to the Soviet Union for disciplining. Visibly afraid, Jan would then go to East Berlin on a "visit" and escape to the Western sector, giving himself up to the Americans.

With the Americans he was to pose as an embittered Soviet citizen who came from the Ukraine. This was done so that he would not be sent back into that area as an agent, but rather to that quarter of the Soviet Union where he would presumably be least apt to run into friends or acquaintances, i.e. eastern Siberia. He was thoroughly drilled in this legend and the purpose of his mission, which was of a purely counter-intelligence nature. Shortly before Deriabin left Moscow in 1953 Jan went off to Germany, hoping in the course of the next two years or so to find out something about U.S. intelligence methods.

The complications of Jan's assignments make their own commentary on the strength and weakness of Soviet intelligence. The planning of his mission was elaborate, cunning, and most complete. Yet here, as in the Baranov case, the Second Directorate was presuming a great deal on its own predictions of American behavior. The presumptions were: (1) that the Americans were sending agents into the Far East by a new and secret route; (2) that a "Ukrainian" Soviet agent "defecting" in Germany would be recruited by U.S. intelligence and sent to the Far Eastern theater; and (3) that he would be made privy to U.S. operations before he got there. In such detailed scheming the Directorate resembled the traditional overconfident chess player who works out what he thinks his opponent will do six or seven moves in advance and predicates all his own moves accordingly. This thought occurred to Deriabin at the time, although he himself was always an indifferent chess player.

In some cases such advance planning was technically sound. This was notably so in the "deep-cover" assignments. One of Deriabin's first jobs in the Austro-German Section was to meet an attractive young schoolteacher from Kiev and escort her to the Dnepr Hotel, a medium-fashionable Moscow hostelry which the State Security used for its peculiar variety of visiting firemen. The teacher, Mariya, was an instructor of English at a high school. Others in the Second Directorate were to make extensive testings of her facility in that language during the next three months; for Mariya's proficiency in English was one part of a peculiarly long-range intelligence project.

Mariya had been selected as a "deep-cover" agent to operate in East Germany. Besides her good Party record and a past history as a State Security informer in the Ukraine her knowledge of English was essential. She was to pose as an Englishwoman married to an Austrian, but in an area where English-speaking visitors had seldom ventured. Her "husband" was to be another schoolteacher from the same Kiev area. He was thought able to pose as an Austrian because of his fluent knowledge of German. (He was, to make the story complete, a German teacher.) Like Mariya, Igor, the German teacher, had a good Party and State Security record, and he was a man of patience.

Mariya and Igor went through an intensive course in the storied but still essential apparatus of an underground intelligence operative: codes, ciphers, invisible ink, et al. With great care the headquarters officers constructed a "legend" for them, in this case a simple one. Most good ones are. The couple from Kiev were to go to a country area of East Germany in search of some "relatives" displaced during the war. On finding no trace of them they were to "decide to stay in East Germany, where work was eaiser to find." To make their past connections seem plausible Igor was drilled intensively in both the Viennese and the Berlin dialects of German.

After this detailed preparation the two new agents were assigned no specific mission at all. On the contrary, after arriving in Germany they were to live quietly and obscurely, patiently building up local confidence in their assumed legend. They were to make no contacts with any Soviet agents and could expect none for from two to five years. Only when they were needed would any espionage mission be disclosed to them.

The couple from Kiev were examples of the "deep-cover" operations of Soviet intelligence. As such, they went beyond the functions of simple *Zakonservirovany*—freely translated as agents "held in cold storage," i.e. active agents who are temporarily ordered to suspend work. In putting this sort of agent into East Germany the State Security leaders were also hedging their bets against the eventuality that the puppet East German province will be some day merged in a greater Germany, thus changing in the Soviet intelligence reckoning from a friendly "base zone" to a hostile "sector."

There was one obstacle involved in the couple's dispatch to the West. Igor, the German teacher, already had a wife in Kiev, the mother of his two children, who took most unkindly to this transfer. Mariya, the comely English teacher, did not at all mind. (Igor, as a good Soviet citizen, was equivocal.) In any other intelligence organization this crudely-constructed triangle might have proved unworkable. For the State Security it required only a sharp talk with Igor's wife by one of the domestic State Security representatives to silence her protests. She was given a small government allowance to compensate for the loss of her husband.

At different times during the next few years Deriabin wondered how these variously-chosen agents had fared in their assignments. As he grew to know foreign-intelligence operations better he appreciated the really small nature of the gamble involved in people like Baranov, "Jan," or the artificial couple from Kiev, against even the 100-to-1 possibility that their deceptions might pay off. Agents were expendable. Recruited for their jobs through combinations of fear and greed, they had neither intercessors to help them nor mourners if they failed.

In the larger political sense the leaders of satellite governments were regarded as only slightly less expendable than high-priced agents. Their degree of expendability depended, of course, on the trouble it might take to replace them. But they were universally regarded with suspicion within the State Security.

The least reliable, as noted, were the Poles. When Wladyslaw Gomulka was first arrested by the Stalinist faction in the Polish Party a high-ranking officer of the Advisory Section remarked that even the Stalinist Poles could not be trusted. "Those people on the Polish Politburo would prefer Pilsudski to an alliance with the Soviet Union," he added, "if they had the choice."

Nor were the East Germans given any unnecessary rope in their activities, as far as the State Security was concerned. There was derogatory information in the State Security files on, among other trusted German Communists,

Heinrich Rau, one of the Premier Otto Grotewohl's deputies, and the German Communist boss Walter Ulbricht himself. Rau was under suspicion as an old Communist who had fought in Spain. His first wife was allegedly "anti-Soviet." Rau himself, according to one report, had informed for the Gestapo during his term in a World War II Nazi concentration camp. Ulbricht was alleged to have money deposited in an American bank. His intermediary in this transaction, again according to the report, was a niece living in the United States.

Deriabin had no way of checking the truth of such reports, which he would run across at various times in his own work with the files. But they were not put there, in any case, for the sake of accuracy. Every bit of unfavorable or possibly damaging information on the satellite leaders was collected indiscriminately in their files, for use whenever or if ever the State Security found it necessary to start building a case against them.

It was not until 1953 that the East German leaders were even permitted to move their residences from the Soviet-controlled Karlshorst compound, where surveillance of their movements was easy. In that year Colonel Medvyedev, the State Security "advisor" to the East German secret police forces, recommended to Moscow that they be allowed to live elsewhere, since Karlshorst proved not only confining but embarrassing as a dwelling place for allegedly "free democratic" Germans. Permission was granted, but it was stipulated that a Soviet advisor be sent along to supervise suitable guard dispositions for the new residences.

When Klement Gottwald, the Communist President of Czechoslovakia, died in 1953 the State Security headquarters took a very dim view of his successors in power, President Antonin Zapotocky and Premier Viliam Siroky. "We have a big file on them," one of Deriabin's friends in the Advisory Section told him, "and we don't trust them. Gottwald held them in his hand when he was alive. Now it's different."

Only once in Deriabin's memory did a local satellite Communist boss turn on his supervisors with any success. It was Matyas Rakosi, until his overthrow in 1956 the supremely Stalinist Secretary of the Hungarian Communist

Party. In 1952 Colonel Evdokimenko, the State Security's "advisor" in Hungary, was busy—as is normal with men in his position—recruiting key men in the local Party and government apparatus to inform on their colleagues to the Soviet mission. One of the Party officials Evdokimenko approached scuttled off to Rakosi and asked for his instruction in this matter. The divided loyalties puzzled him. Rakosi was furious. He called the Colonel in and screeched at him, "I am the first agent of the Soviet Union in this country. What are you trying to do behind my back?" Then he telephoned the Kremlin direct. Two days later Evdokimenko was homeward bound on the Moscow plane, en route to his new post as State Security section chief in Khabarovsk, near Vladivostok. "Too clumsy," was the verdict inside the offices at 2 Dzerzhinsky Square.

The Colonel's mistake was not irreparable, however. Rakosi's principal strength was his connection with Stalin. Less than a week after Stalin's death Evdokimenko was back in Moscow as deputy chief of the Austro-German Section.

The only State Security advisors who ever got into real trouble were the luckless group assigned to Yugoslavia before the break with Tito. Major General Dmitri N. Shadrin, who later supervised the protection of Politburo members for the Guard Directorate, had gone to Yugoslavia to organize a suitable guard for Tito. This was in 1945 and 1946, in the days of Tito's honeymoon with the Soviet Union. Shadrin's house was full of autographed photographs of Tito and valuable presents which Tito had given him for his services. When Tito made his break with Moscow in 1948 Shadrin was removed from his post, accused of giving valuable security information to Tito, and sent in disgrace to the Kuibyshev provincial offices of the State Security. He narrowly escaped worse punishment. Every member of the Guard who had served on the Yugoslav mission was similarly accused of "Titoism" and disciplined.

Through all the work of the Foreign Intelligence Directorate, whether abroad or in Moscow, ran a curious mixture of extreme competence and extreme shortsightedness. Its workings often seemed odd and inexplicable to Deriabin himself—that is, until he would think about them in their Communist context. At its best Soviet intelligence works quickly and decisively. Orders are confirmed and instructions executed with an efficiency that probably exceeds that of any comparable organization in the West. Yet, in the middle of its best-laid plans, there are unexplainable halts and incomprehensible lapses. How does this happen?

The answer to both the defects and virtues of Soviet intelligence is simple: its tactical successes and failures are nothing more than the extreme projection of a society's habits. The centralization of the Soviet system makes itself felt in the rapidity with which commands are executed. A Soviet State Security officer, accustomed to a system where everything begins and ends at one "Center," would find it almost incomprehensible, for example, that intelligence operations in the United States are not only divided between various organizations, but necessarily supervised by a complex of authorities: State Department officials, congressmen, the military, to say nothing of the pressure of public opinion. To the Soviet mind such a division of authority represents the grossest inefficiency. In intelligence operations, even judged by Western standards, it often does work out this way.

The State Security officer is also first and last a bureaucrat in the highest sense: that is to say, he is a member of a career service. If he is at all competent and experienced he will be unable to leave the State Security for any other sort of gainful work. The higher the rank, the more a man is bound to his service. As the old Russian expression goes, "First you sell your soul to the devil, then you sell yourself." It is inconceivable to the career officer in the KGB that people in the Western countries may enter the intelligence service and then leave it after a short period. In the Soviet system this is the worst kind of waste.

So on its plus side the State Security can mobilize a dedicated career service with officers bound willy-nilly to a lifetime task of espionage and working under the orders of a single centralized authority. But this very centralization carries within it its own glaring defects, even aside from the occupational risk inherent in the periodic changes within the Soviet leadership.

The very fact that the KGB man is a bureaucrat makes him exceptionally cautious. "When in doubt, cable Moscow" is the unspoken watchword of the service.[2]

At the same time, the ominipotence of Moscow's authority forces an almost slavish dependence on executing orders as they come. What Moscow orders must be done. One cannot answer "impossible." For the State Security man who criticizes an order automatically puts himself in the position of criticizing the entire system.

This leads to the crowning defect of the State Security system, which duplicates the big efficiency defect in all Soviet society: the only way not to execute an order is to blame the failure on somebody else. As can be imagined, this produces phenomenal exercises in verbal gymnastics in the reports passing daily from the operational officers to the Directorate's headquarters in Moscow. If Moscow orders something ridiculous it cannot be argued with. Therefore, if the KGB officer cannot explain, he must lie.

The second failing of Soviet intelligence is to overstress the normal intelligence virtue of healthy suspicion. Countless schemes of State Security officers in the field have failed because the officers involved felt they could not trust their own agents. There is no such thing as *carte blanche* in the Soviet intelligence system. Even for the most

[2] This maxim is sometimes carried to the depths of absurdity. In Vienna in 1953 local State Security officers suspected the wife of an Austrian Communist Party leader of giving information to the Western powers. In the course of a large party at the Soviet officers' club Lieutenant Colonel Pribytkov, Deriabin's immediate superior, had a long and cozy tête-à-tête with the lady. He artfully edged the conversation around to the subject of her Western contacts. Bibulous and romantically inclined, the lady suggested that they talk the matter over in a private room upstairs. "I will tell you a lot," she said. Pribytkov was escorting her there when he was stopped by his boss, the Resident. "I don't want you to take the chance," Kravtsov said, "we'd better check with Moscow first."

They did check with Moscow, which replied that Pribytkov was free to go ahead with the lady's seduction. There was only a forty-eight-hour delay involved in this strangely Ruritanian maneuver. As it turned out, this bothered the lady not at all.

trusted of officers there is no assurance that he is not being watched himself in the middle of a highly sensitive operation.

These inhibitions have time and time again canceled the effectiveness of the State Security's overseas operatives. It is just as well that they have. Without such built-in defects this organization, so assured in its command structure and skilled in its peculiarly evil tradition, could wreak havoc in the world outside the U.S.S.R.

CHAPTER XVIII

Moscow Executive Suite

THE FOREIGN INTELLIGENCE Directorate, among its other attributes, contained one of the few freely-circulating libraries of Western books and periodicals in the Soviet Union. Circulation was, of course, for a defined purpose. But any qualified State Security officer looking over Western news and comments for clues to intelligence policy could also derive a well-rounded if vicarious education in what was being done and thought outside the Soviet Union.

Deriabin was well acquainted with the Western press. (One of his first duties in reporting to the Central Committee on the Linse case was to submit a detailed commentary on the news treatment of the kidnapping in *Life*.) He had some appreciation that a less constrained life existed outside the Soviet Union, and he occasionally speculated on its exact nature. Private speculation is a Soviet citizen's most zealousy guarded piece of personal property; so he shared his thoughts with no one, not even his wife. But it was sometime in 1953, when he was walking out to his waiting car on one of the long-light evenings of the short Moscow summer, that the thought first occurred to him: "What would it be like to go to the United States?"

Many years ago his father had brought up the subject. "The best country and the richest country in the world is America," he used to say. "I have heard that it is possible there to go to see the President, knock on his door, and have him open it for you. It is a free country." Deriabin had never forgotten this information, although he never knew

251

where his father had got the idea. Sergey Deriabin had never been further away from the Soviet Union than his garrison duty on Russian Island, off Vladivostok.

Peter himself had read a great deal, comparatively speaking, about foreign countries. Fom his school days, when he had sought out books at his teachers' homes, he had sustained his father's curiosity about the world outside.

One of his teachers, the former Czarist officer, had managed to keep a large library from the old days, full of the classics that meant America to so many European children of an earlier generation. So it was that *The Last of the Mohicans, Tom Sawyer,* and *Huckleberry Finn* became a part of one young Russian's education, although he scarcely included them on his Komsomol reading lists. Then and later he kept up, also, his reading of the classic Russians, the free and sometimes brilliant writers of the early Soviet era, and many of the nineteenth-century Europeans.

How far this slightly ventilated education led to Deriabin's final escape, no man can say, least of all Peter Deriabin. But it did give him some thinking alternative to the official Soviet readers, from primers to *Pravda* to Party novelists, which were the only channel of news, art, and education for so many of his slightly younger contemporaries. The Revolution had come to Siberia as soon as it had come elsewhere; but because of the remoteness of the land the Bolshevization that followed the Revolution, and muzzled it, was later in settling. Because of this too, Deriabin had gone through his later Soviet education equipped with a slightly critical yardstick for judging it. His unspoken criticism had grown stronger, the more he saw of Soviet Communism. But as long as he was in the service of the domestic State Security he saw no hope of ever separating himself from it. He became in his own mind, therefore, just another of the many Party functionaries who know the exhortations they make to their charges are hollow, but go on making them.

The situation inside Moscow in 1953 was made to order for such wistful escapism, for escapism was what these thoughts seemed at the time. Although Deriabin had escaped the consequences of working for the Guard Directorate at the time of Stalin's death, the repercussions of this and the Beria turnover were felt strongly inside the Foreign Intelligence Directorate as well. Meetings were held in which for the first time officers openly questioned and criticized their superiors without any pretense at the usual bootlicking. "Why did General Savchenko not report on the Beria meetings to the Central Committee?" "What was the special assignment to visit Tito which Beria gave Colonel Fedoseyev?" Questions like this made a shambles of the hastily arranged assembly at which Party leaders tried to explain the arrest of Beria.

Yet all the released indignation did little but underscore the complicity of the high-ranking leaders in the abuses which they were now so busy denouncing. The angry meetings resembled the hasty lifting of a large flat rock which it was quite apparent the next régime would quickly replace. Deriabin's boss once said as much. At the same Directorate meeting Colonel Kravtsov brought out the fact that the Austro-German Section alone had been reorganized five times in two years and had suffered seven changes in its command. But no one could budge inefficient higher-ups (unless they were high enough up to warrant disposal by a rival faction). "I would like to see this rock at the top turned over," Kravtsov snapped. "Then perhaps our work would progress better."

This Time of Troubles in 1953, with its cycle of impeccable authorities publicly denounced, powers replaced, and dogma recanted, was a solvent capable of dissolving whatever remaining illusions a man held about the good purpose of the Soviet leadership. There was no longer any pretense of idealism involved in the maneuverings of the Soviet Executive Suite—just a tightly joined battle for self-preservation. Moscow itself, or at least the city of Soviet officialdom within it, resembled a closed and tightly guarded gladiatorial pit where the fighting was deadly and without quarter, limited only by the long-standing rule that the combatants sing out some slogans of workers' solidarity every few rounds.

Officers deliberately sabotaged the efficiency of their departments in the hope of getting rid of an unpopular section head on whom the faulty work could be blamed. In this way, for example, some of the case officers in the Foreign Intelligence Directorate succeeded in deposing at least one unpopular Beria appointee before the general denunciation.

Lieutenant General Ryasnoy, whom Beria had placed in charge of the Directorate, was a former official in the Party with no experience in intelligence. To unseat him his subordinates used an old "ploy" in Soviet gamesmanship. A case officer or section chief would come to Ryasnoy's office with an important cable which needed an immediate answer by the Director. When an officious secretary refused the officer admission he would make no more than a perfunctory protest, then leave the cable on the secretary's desk with the date of his submission unobtrusively scribbled on the rear side. Submerged beneath a pile of routine documents, the cable might take several days to get action, by which time the contact or the case would have been lost. The resulting inquiry would have to clear the case officer and lay the blame at the door of the Director's office. After a collection of such incidents, most of them highly beneficial to Western intelligence services, the Central Committee intervened and removed him. He had lasted three months.

Even in normal times such tactics are a commonplace inside the régime's inner world. It is a world sealed off from the reach of any law, outside the lopsided law of the Party. It is also a world, unlike the capitalist corporation, from which a man cannot escape. Since the Communist Party is everywhere there is little hope that a man who is forced out of one ministry can make his way in another. Hence the only way to right a wrong or redress a grievance is by maneuvering an opponent into an impossible position and purchasing your own advancement by his downfall. Deriabin saw the dismissal of Ryasnoy enacted time and time again in New Class society. People would pigeonhole important documents, write out vital reports in language which a newly-appointed boss could be calculated to misunderstand, or malign the character of a co-worker or a superior by direct informing tactics, or by a judicious use of veiled hints, or anonymous letters.

Sometimes such efforts failed completely, as in the classic case of one State Security officer, a Major General Karpenko on duty in the Altai Kray. The general had a falling out with one Lobanov, then the second-ranking man for that region in the Party. Lobanov had unjustly invoked Party disciplinary measures against a friend of Karpenko's, the author of a briefly celebrated novel called *First Love* (about life on a collective). Friction continued between the two and was growing serious when Lobanov was suddenly recalled and transferred. The immediate cause of his transfer was a series of anonymous letters reflecting on his loyalty and abilities. These had been sent to his boss, the Party secretary, and to the Central Committee in Moscow.

After this action was taken the letters were relayed to the chief of the Section for Anonymous Letters and Leaflets in the State Security, who ordered an intensive investigation of their source. After a month's work in Barnaul the case officers who were sent there reported that Karpenko was under suspicion. The State Security ordered him back to Moscow briefly for consultations, long enough for the investigating officers to open his safe and discover several more poison-pen letters against Lobanov.

The general was dismissed from his post and given a "strong" reprimand by the Central Committee of the Party for so attacking a fellow Party member. But since he already had accumulated twenty-five years of service he was allowed to retire. Lobanov, on the other hand, was not reinstated. Even after the poison-pen letters were exposed he remained tainted by false accusations, unwitting evidence of the paranoid suspicions of the régime. That is the most significant and most typical part of the story.

Marshal Zhukov's postwar travels to and from Moscow make another illustration of the precarious footing at the summit of the Soviet leadership. They began during World War II, when Zhukov already showed a tendency to make decisions himself without co-ordinating them with Party authorities. Nor did he take much pains to hide his criticism of the Political Department of the Soviet Army. At that time Stalin put his political marshal, Bulganin, on the Party committee supervising the front which Zhukov commanded, so that Bulganin became in effect Zhukov's political commissar.

Relations between them were very bad. When Bulganin tried to assert his own authority in strategic decisions Zhukov would invariably cut him short with a reminder of his professional ignorance in military matters. This friction was made known to the Politburo in Moscow, but Stalin took no move against Zhukov during the war, because he was such a good military commander. In 1944, however, Zhukov was put under the "protection" of the Guard Directorate. Personal bodyguards from the State Security appeared around him. He received virtually an entire new staff—cook, butler, housemaids—from State Security headquarters.

At first the Marshal thought this was a sign of Stalin's trust in him. Only slowly did it dawn on him that the new large staff had been installed principally to watch him.

In 1946, after running the occupation of Germany, Zhukov was recalled to Moscow and shipped off to the stunningly minor post of Commander of the Odessa Military District. His appointment reflected the anxiety of Stalin, Bulganin, *et al.* about his popularity and his relative spirit of independence. The State Security household went with him, and it became ever more evident that they were guards, not henchmen. Zhukov objected that his guards could travel back and forth to Moscow, when he, a Marshal of the Soviet Union, could not. But he grew more careful in what he did and said. He was visibly nervous.

After only a short time in Odessa, Zhukov was transferred to the command of the Ural Military District in the city of Sverdlovsk. He quarreled with members of the guard around him. He would turn suddenly on a waitress in his mess and shout, "What are you watching me for?" Or he would cause a scene at headquarters when the State Security officer commanding the motor pool was unable to find enough cars for his many girl-friends. He had the chief of his guard fired on the charge of insubordination. But he remained a prisoner.

In 1950 he went to the provincial Party conference at Sverdlovsk (he has been a Party member since 1920) and made a short speech. The delegates applauded him for five minutes, ignoring for once the orders of their Party secretaries. This little index of his popularity in the middle of political exile worried Moscow profoundly. He was forbidden to attend any large meetings in the future.

Immediately after the death of Stalin, Zhukov was appointed First Deputy Minister of Defense, the job he had relinquished in 1946. He recognized that Bulganin and Malenkov, however, remained hostile to him, and he attributed his exile to their influence as much as to Stalin's. So it was natural that he become an ally of Khrushchev's. In the sticky crisis before Beria's arrest he gave the anti-Beria combination the decisive support of the armed forces, a fact which swung the scales irretrievably against Beria. For this he was promoted from a candidate to a full member of the Party's Central Committee, on Khrushchev's own motion. The rest is history repeated.

Of the thirty-four personages whom the Guard Directorate had protected during Deriabin's time there, fully twenty-four are now dead, imprisoned, or languishing in figurative, if not literal, "cold storage" in the provinces. Deriabin, reckoning the march of events, has to confess a backhanded professional admiration for the keen Armenian, Anastas Mikoyan, who then as now managed to throw out an effective sea anchor in every storm that shook the Kremlin.

The secret of his success, aside from his tremendous ability, was a special one. As an Armenian, he would never be allowed to rule the Soviet Union, a state now governed by a small group of Russians and Ukrainians who would never permit another Caucasian dictator after Stalin.

Throughout the Soviet era, however, members of minority groups have been able to assert themselves with consistency in the ranks of the higher leadership, despite the fact (or perhaps because of the fact) that the Great Russian racial consciousness is unfriendly to Jews, Georgians, and Poles. In the Stalin era, especially during its later days, the number of Georgians proliferated, and prejudice began to be shown against the Jewish members of the leadership who had long been prominent in Moscow. "First the Kremlin smelled of garlic," ran the crude Russian joke. "Now it smells of *shashlik*"—(the Georgian national dish). The reaction against the Georgians after the Beria purge coincided with a fresh outbreak of anti-Semitism. Mikoyan claims to have more than filled the resultant gap with some well-placed Armenians, a race known for its sharpness at trading. "It would take two Jews," he is fond of saying, "to do what I do."

It would be hard to find a more successful and more cynical example than Mikoyan of that breed of self-seeking Communist official whom Milovan Djilas so aptly termed "the New Class." During those days after the Beria exposure Deriabin thought a great deal about the doings of the New Class and its evil hold on his native Russia. His reflections formed the basis of his later flight from Soviet power, and they are worth examining in detail.

CHAPTER XIX

The New Class

ON THE EVE of the Russian Revolution, Czarist Russia appeared to be one of the world's more hidebound class societies, a ponderous scaffolding whose structure was fatally weakened by rigid horizontal compartments. Going down the social ladder, there were the nobility, formally a part of the mass of the landowning gentry or *dvoryane*, the merchants or *kuptsy*, the priesthood (*dukhovnyye*), the town bourgeoisie (*meshchane*). These categories formed some twenty percent of the population. Far below them were the other eighty percent: the peasants or *krestyane*. Permeating these sandwich layers were the intelligentsia, the professional people and the serious thinkers of varying social background who, in the last analysis, made the Revolution.

This, however, was the formalistic picture popularized by the 1812 background of *War and Peace*. Attractive as its romantic simplicity might be to a Western observer, it had very little resemblance to the real situation: a tense interplay of forces in a society undergoing continuous change ever since the liberation of the serfs in 1861. With the dawn of the twentieth century, class distinctions were becoming more and more blurred. The importance of belonging to one class rather than another had lost its old meaning.

The make-up of the classes was changing as well. A patent of "personal" (non-hereditary) nobility, for example, was awarded upon being commissioned in the Army, upon being appointed to any (white-collar) civil service job, upon graduation from any institution of higher learning (except a seminary). Thus the formal ranks of "nobility" increased by thousands every year. Hereditary nobility was awarded automatically to all who had reached the rank of colonel or its equivalent in the civil service or who had been awarded the Order of St. Vladimir. It is a historical paradox that the celebrated Count Witte, who negotiated the peace with Japan in 1905 and became the leading political figure in pre-Revolutionary Russia, began his career as a telegraph clerk, while Lenin's family, the Ulyanovs, were members of the old landowning nobility.

It is interesting also to compare the leaders of the two factions in the civil war of 1918–22. The future Red Marshal Tukhachevsky waw an officer of the elite Semenovsky regiment of the Imperial Russian Guard. Another future Red Marshal, Sergey Kamenev, was an Imperial Army colonel, as was General Staff Colonel Shaposhnikov, later a marshal and Stalin's Chief of Staff in World War II. While these men were the leaders and organizers of the Red Army, only one among the White Army leaders, Baron Wrangel, was a bona fide aristocrat of the type usually associated with Czarist Russia. Generals Alekseyev, Kornilov, and Denikin, the organizers and creators of the four-year armed resistance to the Communist takeover, were all of peasant stock.

The Bolsheviks shrewdly recognized the nature of the task they had on hand and the forces they had to overwhelm before they could win. The "bourgeoisie," i.e. the shopkeepers, the small businessmen, the well-off peasants, and their like, were announced to be the chief enemy of the "proletariat." While ideology or personal ambition drew many of the intelligentsia into the Party the appeal to the "proletariat" was founded on simpler and baser instincts. It was founded primarily on the hatred and the jealousy of "have nots" for "haves." *Grab nagrablennoye*—loot that which has been looted," was the war cry raised by the Party during its armed struggle for the country. The slogan was most popular among those who joined the Communist side in the civil war and undeniably the best understood.

The subsequent "classlessness" of Soviet society, stemming from the social conscience of the intelligentsia, was by and large enforced in the early days of Soviet rule. No longer was opportunity restricted to the moneyed, the titled, or other families with a tradition of education. For all the harshness of Soviet rule this principle of exalting those of low degree has had a powerful effect on the people of the Soviet Union. It accounts for the active support finally rendered the régime by Deriabin's father, who, as a collective farm leader, at least temporarily saw his station in life improve far above the level which he might have reached in Czarist society. It accounts for the wild enthusiasm with which Peter Deriabin and other children of low class background greeted enlistment in the Pioneers and the Komsomol. Close enough to the past régime to realize its stratifications, they felt almost limitless opportunity stretching before them.

The great disillusionment of Deriabin's life as a Soviet citizen came as he realized that a class society had been revived in the Soviet Union. In a social sense this class society remains less rigid than the Czarist ladder rungs of nobility, business, and virtual serfdom. It is still possible for almost anyone to become a member of the Soviet New Class, regardless of social origin, if his talents are considerable and his forebears unobjectionable. This is the one original contribution which the Soviet leaders have made to the ancient tradition of oligarchy rule. But even this is growing harder. In respect to power and privileges the Soviet New Class is more rigidly screwed onto its throne than anything in Russian history since the boyars of the Middle Ages and the dictator kings, like Ivan the Terrible, who harnessed their class power.

The activist members of the Communist Party form the leading and all-powerful class within the Soviet Union, although within their number exist formidable differences of rank and station. The next ranking class is that of the professional people: engineers, bureaucrats, journalists, professors, etc. Among them, as with the Party activists, are definite grades of rank and station, with the manager class, e.g. executives directing factories or collectives, at their head. Parallel with the managerial and professional class are the officers of the Soviet armed services.

Next come the workers, rigidly divided into skilled, non-skilled, and manual categories. The last-named are, for practical purposes, peasants. They lie at the bottom rung of the ladder, the peasantry on the land. The old Russian word for peasant was *krestyanin*, derived from "Christian," possibly on the theory that the Lord might help the peasantry, since no one else would. The modern Soviet term, derived from the name for collective farm, is *kolkhoznik*. The *kolkhozniks*, unlike their grandfathers, the *krestyane*, have not even spiritual consolation to alleviate their lot. They include a variety of talents and occupations: accountants, tractor operatives, foremen, as well as simple farmers. But the higher grades of administration on the collectives prefer to be known by other titles. In Soviet society the word *kolkhoznik* has come to have the same derogatory connotation which *mouzhik* had in an earlier day. In the workers' and peasants' paradise it is used as a term of contempt.

These classes are not organized on a professional basis, except for the simple workers and *kolkhozniks* being indisputably at the bottom. The Communist Party has so threaded its way into Soviet life that any compartmentalization, even of small groups like scientists, can be nipped in the bud by the simple device of making some of the group Party members and leaving others out. This is the reason, to use the most obvious example, why the Soviet Army has never been anything but a negative factor in the Moscow power struggles. The officer corps of any Army division—to say nothing of heavily watched groups like the General Staff—is so honeycombed with Party members that any professional organization would be almost impossible. The aspiring Red Army officer looks forward not simply to being a great general, but to becoming a great general with a good Party record and good Party connections.

This recognized Party class began to show itself in the middle thirties. At the beginning of the Revolution and for some years thereafter the majority of Party members were workers, although the reins of leadership were held by intellectuals of bourgeois or even noble background, like Lenin and Trotsky. By 1935 the percentage of workers on the Soviet Party rolls had decreased greatly. By 1941, when Deriabin was getting ready for his own Party membership, he observed that comparatively little attention was paid to the class origins of new Party members. What counted was their usefulness and their loyalty to the Central Committee.

This is not to say that class origins were forgotten. As he later discovered in the State Security, a great deal of time and effort goes into investigations to determine whether some comrade's father was actually a *kulak*, a Czarist officer, or a pre-war intellectual. But these investigations are generally revealed in the act of getting rid of a Party man, not in recruiting him. That is, they are more important as threats to hold over a man's head than as immediate disqualifiers.

Party secretaries have long since abandoned their pose as the agents of class revolution. They are now talent scouts interested in recruiting able, loyal Party members who can be taken into the lower ranks of the Soviet New Class. They look for most of their recruits in the junior ranks of the bureaucracy and what in the Czarist days was called the intelligentsia. A bona fide worker or peasant must have extraordinary powers to recommend him before he is invited into the Party, unless he is already in effect a junior executive of his *kolkhoz* or factory.

Deriabin noticed this change most sharply when he returned from the war and once more became active in relatively normal peacetime Party work. The party of the working class, which he had joined in good faith in the thirties, had become by the forties a party of bureaucrats and functionaries. The Old Bolsheviks were almost all removed. The young Party professionals who replaced them were taught to think and answer questions solely by the book. What had been for so many Old Bolsheviks a motive force of group responsibility or social conscience became in the young Party worker an insistence on personal privilege. Once a worker or peasant did enter the Party he speedily stopped thinking of himself as a worker or peasant.

The change was tacitly recognized by the Soviet leaders. The regulations of past Party Congresses used to contain the ritual phrase "the all-Union Communist Party of the Bolsheviks is the advance guard of the working class." By the time of the Nineteenth Congress, in 1952, the gap between the "ins" and the "outs" inside the U.S.S.R. had grown

so embarrassingly large that the Party leadership itself struck
out the words "advance guard of the working class" and
replaced them with the definition "a fighting union of co-
believers." The "fighting union" is restricted to the Party
leadership and their activist followers, as far as the distribution of benefits is concerned.

Before the war Deriabin had been proud to call himself
a *kolkhoznik*. If anything, he was defiant about his social
origin. By 1948 he was at one with his Party comrades in
referring to *kolkhozniks* the way a small-town American
social leader once used to talk about the-people-on-the-
other-side-of the-tracks.

"Even a cook can rule a country," Lenin once said.
After forty years of Communism a cook's only ruling privilege in the U.S.S.R. is the chance to cast a useless vote. His
highest aspiration, looking at things realistically, is to become Khrushchev's cook.

Deriabin began to appreciate the way the New Class operates when he returned to the Altai Kray after World War
II as a member of the State Security. His own life was
embarrassingly more comfortable then that of his old
friends purely by virtue of his New Class job and connections. But he saw more flagrant examples of favoritism
than the mere existence of better food and housing. In
1947 one Captain Antonov, the son of the MVD chief in
the Altai, killed another young man in a street brawl in
Barnaul. For this type of involuntary manslaughter eight
years was the prescribed sentence. Antonov got three years,
of which he spent only one year in jail. During this time he
was released every weekend to go home. For ease of travel
he was given a chauffeur-driven car by his father.

If Deriabin thought such favoritism was extraordinary
and immoral in Barnaul in 1947, by the following year,
after some months' service in the Guard Directorate in
Moscow, he would have regarded it as standard operating
procedure. The members of the State Security knew better
than anyone the monstrous double standard which by then
had been codified in the Soviet Union. The law, along with
the State Security and the Communist Party, existed for
the New Class and was an instrument of their rule.

In sharp contrast to the Spartan tastes of many early

Bolsheviks the people of the New Class use comfort as sign and seal of power. When Deriabin worked in the Guard Directorate of the State Security it contained a special directorate of state rest-homes on both the Black Sea coast and the Crimea, headed by a major general. This directorate managed the large network of luxurious estates and rest-houses, parks, citrus plantations, which are at the disposal of the Central Committee of the Party. Although called "state property" these are in fact the personal villas of members of the Praesidium and a few favored marshals and Ministers. Each is attended by scores of special guards and servants, and they duplicate the lavish facilities given to the Soviet leaders in their multiple houses and villas around Moscow. Ordinary Soviet citizens are not allowed within rifle range of such estates.

The Black Sea villas are only one example of the New Class's luxuries. In the Guard Directorate, Deriabin had observed that Soviet leaders and members of their families have unlimited ruble drawing accounts. They procure their food from special state farms (or rather their servant staffs do so for them), enjoy the medical attentions of the best state specialists, provide their families with state cars for their private use. They use special state tailors, and their children go to special state private schools. Within the circle of these privileges members of the New Class live the life of the colonial rulers they condemn in their official propaganda. Their sons and daughters intermarry, their relatives are put in high official positions. But dealings outside the ruling caste are frowned on. As far back as 1950 Khrushchev banished one of the Guard officers at his villa because this lower-class Communist had grown dangerously friendly with one of his daughters.

In May 1952, as a result of a Soviet drive against "overspending," some order was introduced in the drawing-account system for Central Committee members, Ministers, etc. A limit of 30,000 rubles per month was established for unforseen "pocket-money" expenses of Praesidium members and candidates, with scaled-down variants for lesser leaders. But these officials continue to pay no taxes, and they have no obligation to subscribe to government "loan" drives.

There was no interference, either, with their perquisites: the free provisions, clothing, and automobiles. (It has long been the fashion among the "gilded youth" (*stilyagi*), most of them children of high Soviet officials, simply to turn in their cars to the pertinent motor pool after smashing them up and requisition new ones.) Their travels, as well as their large staffs of domestics, continued to be paid for by the state. In the case of the highest leaders an almost inexhaustible source of funds is derived from the sale of their Party writings and speeches by state publishing houses.

Lesser employees of the Central Committee and the Council of Ministers of the U.S.S.R. have their own type of rewards, so-called "envelopes" in which large sums of money are placed as payment, over and above their regular salaries, to the leadership's faithful servants. On the highest levels, also, pensions are given serious consideration, in contrast to the highhanded treatment of lower-ranking officials. The widow of Feliks Dzerzhinsky, the founder of the State Security, for example, has received a heavy pension from the state since her husband's death in 1926, including a car, chauffeur, and several servants. The same courtesy is offered the families of other departed Soviet heroes like Zhdanov, Kalinin, and Ordzhonikidze.[1]

The Soviet people are not wholly ignorant of this selective plundering, but their life is so dominated and threaded by representatives of the New Class, their agents and informers, that concerted protest can only make its appeal obliquely. There is a famous Moscow joke which puts the protest well. "On Moscow TV," it runs, "there is a program called 'A Day in a Soviet Capital.' Today it is featuring A Day in Moscow. It is seven o'clock in the morning. The streets are full of tired and drab-looking people on their way to work. 'These are the masters of the country—the people,' the announcer says.

"Now it is ten o'clock in the morning. The streets are full of lush Zis 110 limousines carrying fat functionaries in

[1] One of the neater tricks in Soviet officialdom, understandably, is the process of reaching old age without either missing the special ruble allowance, getting a one-way ticket to Siberia, or treating one's wife to a premature pension.

fur hats and coats. 'And these,' the announcer says, 'are the servants of the people.' "

The men at the top of the New Class necessarily set the tone and the level of their class's behavior. In Soviet society imitation is not only the sincerest form of flattery, but the best guarantee of safety. It would be impossible, fortunately, for the business and pleasure habits of the Party leadership to be copied on a large scale. (No country in the world could stand the strain.) But the example of the leadership can be imitated on a smaller scale. Not only is the political cycle of purge and counter-purge in the Kremlin reflected in the acid in-fighting and corruption through the lower levels of Soviet official life, but the fads and foibles of high Soviet society are studiously aped by every New Class functionary. Each status symbol—the *dacha*, the chauffeur, the champagne, the imported dress—is sought and treasured, not only for the comfort it brings, but the position it implies. This is, of course, a basic human failing with which many societies are familiar. But in the Soviet Union, which is a society drained of its morality and the original springs of its idealism, it can be a peculiarly dangerous and revolting prospect.

Peter Deriabin's salary and rank—he had become a major in 1949—were his physical passport to the New Class. His surroundings, his companions, and his new Party orientation led to increasingly expensive tastes and aspirations. Half in spite of himself he had become a Soviet status seeker. His standard of living was already in another dimension from that enjoyed by most of the men he had fought the war with. In Moscow a worker or a minor bureaucrat considers himself lucky to stop into a workers' bar on payday and get for his nine rubles what is known as a "worker's norm": 150 grams of raw vodka followed by a beer chaser. Deriabin could pay fifteen rubles a drink for his vodka, generally consumed at the fashionable cocktail bars: the Metropol in Revolution Square, the Zakusochuaya two blocks down from Dzerzhinsky Square, the Pivo in Pushkin Square, a bar with a history, which the poet Mayakovsky frequented in his salad days of free expression during the twenties. He dressed well by Soviet standards. In the best European tradition he went to restaurants and bars which were patronized by people similarly dressed in conservative business suits, with hats and ties. The workers or *kolkhozniks* wore caps and never ties. A new member of the New Class was very sensitive to these minor clothing distinctions.

Summers, he and his wife went regularly in Deriabin's State Security car to the *dacha* they had rented at Mamontovka. The friends they had at the same resort were not so fortunate, not being new members of the New Class. He felt embarrassed occasionally when he thought of the three-hour trip which his neighbors made on crowded subway and bus lines and suburban trains to get to the same destination.

At the few parties they attended with non-Party friends or people in the lower Party echelons, he and his wife were treated with a solicitude that grew progressively more embarrassing. After a while, before visiting relatives or friends outside the circles of New Class society, he got into the habit of putting on his old clothes to avoid being conspicuous.

The same privileges obtained in the normal business of living. To build a small roof over an apartment-house balcony, an important factor in a city then so housing-poor as Moscow, a citizen required a fire department permit. These were notoriously hard to get and an application generally involved months of waiting. Deriabin had only to show his State Security and his Party cards for the permit to be given instantly. At a Moscow tailor shop it took three months to get a coat made, given the material. A State Security card and a few rubles flashed on the tailor's table would produce miracles. The tailor's only question: "When do you want it?"

What made Deriabin an imperfect modern Soviet status seeker was certain quality of compassion and a nagging guilty conscience. He could never bring himself to plunk down his papers on a tailor's bench. Nor could he bear to watch the desperate hungry faces of the people who shared a kitchen with him and his wife in their first Moscow apartment. The man was a retired State Security employee who had long ago been chauffeur and bodyguard to the Bulgarian Georgiy Dimitrov when he was chief of the Comintern. After his retirement he and his wife lived on the slimmest of pensions. Their connections in both the Party and State Security were gone, and no more jobs were forthcoming. So Deriabin told his wife to give them some food. This act would doubtless have been condemned by his early Party instructors as a dangerous concession to Utopian socialism.

CHAPTER XX

Socialist Immorality

ONE OF THE principal duties of the State Security is to screen the private lives of the New Class magnates and their friends from the view of the Soviet people. It is probably more merciful to do so. At least it is a service to the cause of public morality. The excesses of the New Class go far beyond cases of simple wantonness, like the son of Mikoyan who repeatedly smashed up the state cars that were given him. In fact, a clinical study of Soviet social life might easily dwarf *The Lost Weekend* and make the Kinsey Report look like a *Parents' Magazine* anthology. The few lurid revelations which have reached the outside world deal mostly with the immoral excesses practiced under "Stalinism," the implication being that such things have now been corrected. They have not. The same people are running the Soviet Union now as then, and they have the same habits.

In his duties with the State Security, Deriabin got recurrent glimpses into the private lives of the men he protected. Neither the betrayal of Party principles, as he thought he had learned them years before, nor even the unjust condemnation of the innocent revolted him so much as the gross moral double standard of his leaders. The Soviet leaders' dedicated obsession with pleasure and power illustrates as nothing else could how completely the early ideals of the Revolution have vanished.

The standard originated with Stalin. He is presumed to have murdered his beloved wife Alliluyeva in 1932 in a fit of sudden drunken rage. She had been appalled by the developing excesses of his forced collectivization campaign. He admitted his crime before a special session of the Central Committee, which was already heavily peopled with his creatures. The Committee limited its punishment to an "admonition," and the death was listed as a suicide, when it was mentioned at all. As late as 1950 Stalin used to visit the Novo Devichye cemetery daily between 5 and 6 A.M., where he would sit as long as thirty minutes at a time staring at his wife's grave.

Stalin rarely if ever took action to curb the off-duty rowdiness of his disorderly bodyguard, and he was similarly indulgent with the immoralities of higher-ups. One of the most notorious primal urges in the Soviet Union belongs to Marshal Konstantin Rokossovsky, until 1956 the Soviet proconsul in Poland. Rokossovsky was "unofficially" married several times and brought relays of girl-friends to share his quarters wherever he happened to be serving. A stream of reports and complaints about Rokossovsky's conduct landed in the files of the Central Committee, specifically with the Conduct Supervision Committee, one of the most overworked administrative bodies in the Soviet Union.

In 1948 Matvey Shkiryatov, then chairman of the Party Control Commission, asked Stalin to take action against Rokossovsky. Although he read his report Stalin refused. "I have no Suvorov," he said, "but Rokossovsky is Bagration." He said this in obvious reference to the famous statement attributed to Catherine the Great, when her ministers asked her to punish the great General Suvorov for insubordination. Reminding them of Suvorov's victories, Catherine had replied: "Conquerors do not stand trial."[1]

Marshal Zhukov was another prominent ladies' man on the General Staff, and even the chambermaids in his residences were not safe from his advances. Marshal Timoshchenko, on the other hand, was best known as a drinker. His prolonged vodka bouts were notorious, and Guard officers assigned to Timoshenko's house or *dacha* needed strong stomachs, as they were invariably commanded to partici-

---

[1] Prince Bagration was one of the ablest of Suvorov's lieutenants, with a reputation for winning battles against the heaviest of odds.

pate. The drinking sessions sometimes lasted for days. One Guard Directorate captain was hastily transferred to Moscow after hitting the Marshal with a bottle in the course of an early morning brawl.

For all-round dissipation, however, few could approach the exacting standard set by Stalin's own son, Vasiliy. For years Vasiliy's quarters on Gogolevskiy Boulevard were the scene of lavish debauches, complete with all the classic touches, down to naked dancing girls performing on the banquet table. The Guard Directorate officers assigned to Vasiliy took an incredible amount of punishment, subject as they were to constant calls for a weekend or longer of heavy wining and wenching on Vasiliy's estate. In most cases they ended as depraved as their boss.

Vasiliy broke up both of his own marriages—the second was to the daughter of Marshal Timoshenko. It was after this that his father finally took a disciplinary hand to him, demoted him to the rank of colonel from lieutenant general, and cut down heavily on the scope and intensity of his entertaining. After Stalin died Vasiliy was dismissed from the Air Force Staff Academy for drunkenness and misconduct. (He was once found lying insensible in a Moscow gutter.) He was finally put in a treatment center for alcoholism.

Stalin's daughter, Svetlana, on the other hand, was a plain and rather quiet girl. But she was a victim of politics. In 1948 she was forced to divorce her first husband. He was accused of being a "cosmopolite" and associating with foreigners and was sent away, never to be heard from again. In actual fact, his principal offense was being Jewish. Stalin was always a leader in the régime's recurrent anti-Semitic outbursts.

Svetlana's second husband was Yuri Zhdanov, son of Stalin's collaborator, Andrey Zhdanov, who died in 1947. After Svetlana's father died Zhdanov divorced her, anxious to weather the de-Stalinization storm. She was allowed to return to Moscow, where she retained her apartment and one of Stalin's estates in the Moscow surburbs. Her most intimate friend was the daughter of Nikolay Shvernik, the trade union boss. Aside from this she had few contacts even with other members of the New Class. Nor has she now.

At least during the dictator's declining years Lavrentiy

Beria was probably Stalin's closest friend. They often took their holidays together, happily drinking and cooking *shashlik* on one of the Caucasian estates. Beria was the most depraved of the Soviet leadership, excelling even such pillars of immorality as Viktor Abakumov, who maintained a string of private brothels, or Lieutenant General Vlasik, the brutal head of Stalin's personal guard. The stories circulated about Beria's sex vices by Khrushchev and Co. after they got rid of him have a substantial basis in fact. He had no compunction about the women he debauched. The wives of several State Security officers, among others, were ordered at various times to spend the night with Beria, under pain of their husbands' arrest. After his arrest the names of two hundred call girls and worse were found among his personal files, and this was just the Moscow file. Whenever or wherever Beria happened to see a woman who struck his fancy he would send an officer of the Guard to "get" her for him. But his peculiar failing was a liking for very young girls.

The most egregious case of Beria's Lolita complex involved an innocent thirteen-year-old girl, a student in high school. Beria spotted her on a Moscow street while driving past in his car. He sent the chief of his personal security staff, one Colonel Sarkisov, to get her. Sarkisov followed the girl and told her that an important person wished to speak with her. Because her mother was sick and needed her the girl refused to go. At which point the Colonel produced his identification and ordered her to come with him.

Inside his house Beria gave the girl some food and liquor and asked her to sleep with him. When she refused, fighting and screaming, Beria had her drugged. The next day she woke up in his room, where she spent the next three days. She was sent home with instructions not to tell anyone of the incident unless she wanted her mother shot.

She did tell her mother on returning home. The mother rushed to Beria's house with the girl and somehow got in (the guard thinking she had returned on order). When the mother threatened Beria with a protest to the Central Committee he told her she would not live to see its outcome. So she did not report the matter until after his arrest.

The closest thing to an outdoor type among these bloated

gentry was probably Lazar Kaganovich, who has been mouldering in a provincial limbo ever since his denunciation by Khrushchev as part of the "anti-Party" group. Kaganovich was fond of taking long walks in the country. It was not unusual for him to walk for several miles along a country road, followed at a respecful distance by a car full of his State Security bodyguard. He did not go overboard completely for the rugged life; whenever he got a sharp pebble in his shoe the Guard had to make a breakneck automobile dash back to his *dacha* to procure another pair. He was also something of a do-it-yourself man, almost the only member of the leadership who occasionally took the wheel of his own car. (He once pursued a taxi-cab driver for half an hour through the streets of Moscow after the cab had hit a pedestrian without stopping. When Kaganovich caught up with him justice was swift.)

To complement his foible for exercise Kaganovich had one of the most luxurious *sauna*-baths in the Soviet Union on his estate, liberally suppled with brandy and other comforts. In the course of an inspection trip around his *dacha* a group of State Security officers, Lieutenant General Rumyantsev and three of his colonels, found the bath irresistible. They stripped, went through the birch-twig-and-stream routine with abandon, and liberally solaced themselves with the brandy and *kvas* chasers to the point where they were almost hopelessly drunk. At this moment the phone rang in the Guard headquarters on the estate. A worried voice conveyed a message: "The owner is coming home. He'll be there in five minutes." There was nothing for it but to bundle the General and the colonels, clothed only in towels and brandy fumes, into a car, throwing their uniforms in after them. Kaganovich, as it happened, was never the wiser.

It was in fact almost impossible for a member of the State Security to avoid tasting the forbidden fruit in one way or another. One who tasted well was a girl named Tonya Smirnova. At the start of her career Tonya was working in the Personnel Section of the First Main Directorate. Deriabin knew her casually in his early bachelor days in Moscow and, since she was an attractive, vivacious comrade, desired to know her better. He called on her one evening, drank a few vodkas, and was looking forward to the Moscow equivalent of an evening on the town when she suddenly looked at her watch and told him with uncommon bluntness that it was time to go. "Why?" he asked. "You can stay," she countered, "if you'd like to meet Viktor Semenovich." This was Abakumov's name. It dawned on Deriabin that the then all-powerful boss of the State Security was about to take Tonya under his wing.

He left the apartment in a hurry, thus managing to escape the fate of Tonya's former boy friend, a captain in the State Security whom Abakumov had recently sent to the district office on Sakhalin Island, some three thousand miles to the east. In the next few weeks, as Abakumov pursued his court, Deriabin noticed coming over Tonya the social sea change that accompanies the transition of most Soviet women to the New Class aristocracy. Her dress and mannerisms improved spectacularly. She never spoke to him again and avoided anything more than the most necessary contacts even with her co-workers in the Personnel Section.

So great were Tonya's charms that Abakumov married her. It was for her that he shortly after ordered a 70,000-ruble baby carriage and a 30,000-ruble robe from Vienna. Tonya grew quickly accustomed to her new town house in Moscow and the attractive Black Sea villa at Sochi, the New Class Côte d'Azur. It was at Sochi, late in 1951, that Tonya received a mysterious telegram. It read: "Take plane immediately and return to Moscow"—and it was signed Abakumov. She obeyed, wondering a little at the lack of notice. The telegram had been sent by the State Security just a day after Abakumov had been arrested. He was executed, after a long period of confinement, in December 1954. No one in Moscow knew what happened to poor Tonya.

Stories like this are only fragments of the spectrum of New Class society, as seen by one observer from his vantage point. Among the Communist Party initiates, to say nothing of the State Security itself, such stories multiply, and they lose nothing in the telling. It is safe to assume that no matter how zealously the New Class tries to keep its high living a secret, at least some of the details are known to the Party insiders—that is to say, the people on whom the New Class leadership depends to run Soviet society. However, it is in the interests of all concerned, *within* the circle of Party activists, that as little knowledge as possible of the rulers' living habits reaches the populace.

It is safe to say, also, that the big-time immoralities of a Beria or an Abakumov are not reproduced among the lower ranks of the Party, partly owing to obvious limitations of resources, partly to the fact that the lower ranks are still within the reach of Party discipline. "Immorality," or more precisely, "action against socialist morality" makes an excellent pretext for removing a troublesome rival or settling a grudge. What does exist and magnifies itself is a perpetual grayness of moral distinction. The closer one gets to the core of Soviet society, the greater the realization that it is every man for himself, and no holds barred as long as they are not too readily detected.

It is worth recounting one such grudge-settling in detail to illustrate how the quick-thinking Soviet bureaucrat can capitalize on an opponent's vices. One day while Deriabin was serving in the Guard Directorate the officer in charge of one of the Guard's surveillance sections in Moscow, one Colonel Komarov, telephoned him about a very attractive secretary whom Komarov thought would be a great asset in the Guard's offices. Deriabin took down her name and address and dutifully wrote her, asking her to come to the office for an interview. A very attractive girl, she quickly passed the requisite tests. Security checks and surveillance were instituted on her to test her reliability.

The security check quickly established the fact that the attractive secretary was Komarov's girl friend. Wherever the secretary went after working hours, Komarov seemed to go also. The security report with this information on it reached the desk of Colonel Goryshev, Deriabin's immediate superior. In accordance with standard State Security procedure Komarov's name appeared prominently in block letters.

Goryshev called in Deriabin and asked him to conduct further surveillance. "Komarov," he said, "is a stupid son-of-a-bitch, and I want to get rid of him. This is the way we'll do it. He's married, you know. Write me a report about how they're carrying on." The report was written, and Deriabin had to confirm it in the presence of two State Security generals called in to decide on Komarov's fitness for his job. Several nights later—since this was in the Stalin period all high-ranking officers in the State Security worked late at night and far into the morning—Deriabin received an order to pick up the pretty secretary and bring her in to headquarters. He objected that it was midnight, but to no purpose. So he took two officers with him and drove out to the girl's apartment—in fact, a room she rented in a small house.

The girl recognized him, but literally shrank back in terror when he asked her to come along with him. After much parleying she agreed to come quietly. He gave her his word that she would be returned that same night.

At headquarters the pretty secretary, still trembling and barely coherent at the thought of a State Security investigation, was led into Goryshev's office, to which Komarov had already been summoned. She and Komarov confessed their liaison, whereupon Goryshev dismissed her, warning her only never to say that she had been there. "All connection you have with this office," he said, "is now ended." Then Goryshev turned to Komarov. "Now suppose I call your wife on the telephone and bring her down here, too. . . ."

Komarov begged for mercy, of whatever variety was available. He received a demotion to the deputy command of a Moscow militia detachment. This made him in effect captain of a run-down precinct in the local police department. Goryshev filled Komarov's job with his own appointee. Deriabin went home with a troubled conscience.

It was not much later that Goryshev had his own moment of disgrace. En route to his new post at the labor camp in Molotov, he called Deriabin on the telephone to say good-by. "Don't come down to the station to see me. I understand," he said. "And watch yourself." (The last group of subordinates to see a disgraced commander off at the station had been fired the moment they returned to the offices.) Deriabin said, "Good-by" in turn and wondered if anyone had tapped the line.

Mindful of pitfalls such as this, the lesser comrades have their modest version of dancing girls and vodka bouts and the rented upper floor of a leaky summer house serves the purpose of a *dacha*. What they share in undiminished intensity with their betters is an idea that the state is the property of the New Class and hence ripe for the plucking. An indispensable tool of this mentality is what the Soviet citizen calls *blat*.

Blat in the original Russian meant "thievery." In the Soviet era it has come to mean a hybrid of graft, theft, and friendship. The brotherhood of the New Class is, in the first instance, divided by its very prosperity from the bulk of the nation and, in the second instance, divided against itself by its own power rivalries. The system which it operates is, on its face, inefficient, because it demands a nonproductive bureaucracy as a condition of life. Every file needs a keeper, every file on the keepers of files needs another keeper, and so on.[2]

The way to get things done through this combination of inefficiency and suspicion is *blat*. As the prizes grow richer in Soviet society the incidence of *blat* increases. "*Blat*"— runs a contemporary Soviet saying—"is stronger than the city Soviet." Or, "One hundred rubles is now worth anything like one hundred friends." Doing favors is a factor in any kind of political organization; in the Soviet Union, with its cumbersome system of Party oligarchy, mutual favors are almost the only way to get things done. The story is told of the Minister approached by a woman who wanted her son put in a university. "Who asks that I do this?" was his first reply. "No one," the woman said. "Then why do you ask me?"

Blat in the form of money is a commonplace in Soviet life. Given the shortage of educational institutions, for example, there is a formidable competition for places in universities and institutes. One sure way to matriculate in them is to pay off the secretaries or administrative assistants in a high school in order to assure good marks in the final examination. On the lower levels especially Party sec-

---

[2] Deriabin had this brought home to him when he was a teen-ager, in the very first days of collectivization, although he did not then see it as evidence of the system's illogicality. Where before there had been twenty farmers tending their plots there was now a *kolkhoz*, which demanded a chief, an accountant, a deputy chief, and at least one guard. This left sixteen men to till the same acreage. From this number subtract three deported *kulaks* and two subsequently discovered "enemies of the people." So the collective starts with eleven.

retaries can easily be reached with gifts of money or goods to facilitate a candidate's entrance into the Party. Or they can use their influence in obtaining allocations of material for a small factory, getting a book published, or getting tickets to a state vacation resort. As one gets higher up the scale *blat* grows more complex.

The craving of the Soviet people for goods, from wrist-watches to country *dachas,* has become an object of inter-national notoriety. Their greed for the good things of life has been fostered by the traditionally uncertain political conditions under which they live. "If there have been three shake-ups since 1951 there may be a fourth any day; so load up on foreign goods if you happen to be overseas, bor-row money from your agents, acquire negotiable objects for the inevitable return to Moscow." Such was the philosophy which Deriabin learned in the State Security.

The higher up the ladder a Communist goes, the more *blat* becomes not so much a matter of money bribes as a trading of power and influence. Deriabin, for example, was an able officer of the State Security. But he owed every significant transfer and improvement in his condition not to ability, but to well-placed friends. Most of his friends, similarly, owed their stations to other friends.

Almost to the end of his stay in the Soviet Union he kept trying to find some form of justice. He discovered nothing but varying equations of power. Once when a friend was arrested for a trifling prank he made the rounds of the Moscow prosecutor's offices in an effort to have his sen-tence curtailed or commuted. He was turned down by both the prosecutor and the judge, the former saying merely that he had applied too late to exert the proper influence. A sentence in Soviet law, the judge maintained, was irrevoca-ble.

Deriabin's superior in the State Security, then General Petr Gladkov, heard immediately of his representations in the form of confidential reports from the judge and the prosecutor. He asked him why he bothered to use his own influence. As it happened, Deriabin and Gladkov got along well and the latter was happy to do a small favor. The General merely telephoned the prosecutor's office and ordered the prisoner released as of that afternoon. He appeared within two hours, a free man. Such is the rule of law in the Soviet Union.

Deriabin continued to keep his thoughts on such matters to himself. But the possibility of a better life kept recurring to him—a better life somewhere, anywhere beyond the reach of the system that the State Security so sharply symbolized. There was no turning point around which his thought crystallized into a firm decision. But in the spring of 1953 one excellent opportunity for escape in the form of foreign duty materialized for him.

Some months before he had tried to get a temporary assignment to East Berlin. It would be nice, he reasoned at the time, just to take a walk in the Western sector and see what it was like. The assignment fell through. Now his boss, Colonel Kravtsov, offered him a chance to go to Vienna.

The Vienna job resulted partly from his friendship with Kravtsov, partly from the fortuitious interlocking of their two responsibilities. As a member of the State Security Major Deriabin worked directly under the Colonel as one of his deputies. But in the subsurface hierarchy of the organization it was Deriabin who was in one sense the senior. Because of his precocious Party experience Deriabin had been appointed ("elected" was the word used) Party secretary of the Austro-German Section.

This duty, among other things, put him in charge of all disciplinary actions inside the unit—since every officer in it was a Party member. When a man was accused of immoral living or blackmarketeering in Moscow or while on an overseas mission, it was the Party secretary, rather than his official superior, who judged his behavior. But it also included reporting on the Political fitness of Section members for their jobs.

In the course of their conversations Kravtsov had already suggested to Deriabin the possibility that he might like a job in Vienna. Deriabin objected that he would be automatically disqualified for this duty as a former member of the Guard Directorate. But Kravtsov assured him that the new and confused post-Stalin administration would in all probability not notice the fact on his record. Informally speaking, the bargain was made. When the subject of

Kravtsov's appointment to the Vienna Residency came up before the Party committee Deriabin gave a glowing report on his Party resourcefulness and reliability. In turn Kravtsov asked for Deriabin to be posted to Vienna as a key man in rebuilding an efficient apparatus.

In an atomsphere of mutually profitable back-scratching both recommendations were approved. On September 28, 1953, Peter Deriabin arrived in Vienna, after his first trip across territory that was not actually part of the Soviet Union.

CHAPTER XXI

Vienna

DERIABIN TRAVELED BY train to Vienna with his wife and daughter. An assignment like his lasted at least two or three years, and State Security personnel of his rank were generally allowed immediate transportation for their dependents. The trip was in itself something of an outing. The glimpses they got of the Hungarian and Austrian countryside were their first actual look at the countries which Deriabin was accustomed to use as counters in his Moscow State Security work. When they detrained at the Ostbahnhof it was the first time in his life that Deriabin had stepped on non-Soviet soil.

After the State Security Party committees had passed on his assignment he obviously needed no special training for his work abroad other than a few admonitions from the other officers in the Section to brush up his tattered German and save his money for Vienna. ("Don't buy anything in Moscow," said one man who had just returned, "you can get it all cheaper and better outside.") One of his duties in Moscow had been to run some of the weekly briefing sessions for Soviet personnel going abroad. These sessions were not complicated. In their specific instructions—avoid talking to foreigners unless on business, never go out touring unless in the company of other Soviet personnel, etc.— they resembled an American mother's admonitions to a working girl of the 1890s about to leave her country home for the company of rich but dangerous city slickers. It was presumed that a deputy section head from the Second Directorate needed no further briefing of this sort.

The first look at Vienna was a shock—even for someone accustomed by now to reading in reports and press clippings of a world far sleeker, easier, and more self-assured than the garrison society of the Soviet Union. In the fall of 1953 Vienna showed many scars of the war and the four-power occupation of Austria; but most of them were on the way to being healed. The spire of *Stefansdom* was still battered and truncated, not yet enclosed in its reconstruction scaffolding, but the shops on Kärntnerstrasse and the Graben were well lit and very busy. The darkened hulk of the Opera still lowered over the Opernring, awaiting its eventual reconstruction, but placards on almost every street corner announced that the world of sugar-voiced tenors and barrel-chested sopranos was back in order, performing temporarily at other theaters through the town. The sun made baroque shadows on the statues of unsuccessful Hapsburg generals, and the width of the Ring streets still managed to dwarf the traffic of streetcars, bicycles, military jeeps, and new American cars that whizzed along them. Restaurants and *Weinstuben* were full of customers, and only a few of them in uniform. There were full groceries and butcher shops, and no queues. No matter how well one had prepared oneself for it Vienna was a sudden awakening after Moscow.

For a man who was already a secret iconoclast inside Soviet society, the very sight of this relatively open city was further incitement to sedition. It was high irony that Deriabin's job in Vienna was to safeguard his fellow Soviet proconsuls, their subordinates, and their families from any contamination through contact with this window on the West. The "Soviet Colony" officer of any State Security residency is a trusted man of high rank. The initials SK (for the Russian *Sovetskaya Kolonia*) denote his job: the security of every Soviet national in his area. It was the duty of Deriabin and his assistants, who arrived later, to investigate any suspicion of disloyalty and contacts with the West against any Soviet citizen in Vienna, from the High Commissioner down.

One adverse report from Deriabin would be enough to send the average Soviet officer packing to Moscow on his way to anything from a reprimand to a twenty-five-year sentence as an "enemy of the people." (In the case of high-ranking officers the only difference in the procedure was the time and the degree of proof and caution required.) In the Soviet Union suspicion is enough to convict. Even if a Moscow returnee successfully established his innocence the shadow of a bad SK report would prevent his ever again getting a job of importance in the U.S.S.R.

Deriabin was also responsible for the security of visiting Soviet missions and special officials who came to Vienna. He was the sole channel of communication between the Soviet State Security and the various junior G-men of the satellite security forces which were stationed in the area. If the State Security decided to assist the Czechs or the Bulgarians on some operations of their own, it would act only through Deriabin's office.

The job of an SK officer anywhere in the State Security is exacting. In Vienna the comparative looseness of the four-power occupation scheme, by contrast with the rigid sector demarcations in Berlin, offered a rich breeding ground for contacts between Soviet people and the West. Espionage and counter-espionage activities thrived, made all the more complicated by the ease with which so many local citizens entered into an agent's or informer's relationship. (It was not for nothing that Graham Greene set *The Third Man* in Vienna.) Deriabin found out that is was often necessary to dig through layers of contacts before one could discover exactly for whom an agent was really working.

At the time he arrived the problems of counter-intelligence from the Soviet side were genuinely difficult. Like every arm of the Soviet power, the intelligence service lived in an atmosphere of continual apprehension that it was being encircled by a far bigger force of plotters and conspirators working against it, mainly American. The concern was almost always imaginary. It is part of the Communist syndrome, as we have seen, to regard the Soviet world as the *victim* of the very conspiracies it itself perpetrates. But for a moment, in the fall of 1953, this feeling of being encircled and outnumbered may have had some foundation in fact. The hammer blows of Stalin's death and the attempted Beria power seizure had been felt, by that time, in Moscow's lack of attention to its "field" operations. For a month Deriabin and his immediate boss, Lieutenant Colonel Vladimir N. Pribytkov, were the only two working officers of the State Security on duty in Vienna. Kravtsov did not arrive until the end of October.

This is not to say that Soviet intelligence was wholly absent from the Austrian scene. More than 250 officers and agents of military intelligence and counter-intelligence, operating from the Red Army occupation headquarters at Baden, twenty miles out of Vienna, and various offices within the city, continued their work almost without interruption. As Austria was still a zone of military occupation they were authorized to operate on almost as broad a level as the State Security.

The presence in Vienna of such a large component of military intelligence was no accident. The *Glavnoye Razvedovatel'noye Upravleniye* (GRU), or Chief Intelligence Directorate of the Soviet General Staff, was and is an organization which hulks as large as the State Security's Foreign Intelligence Directorate in the business of information-gathering, subversion, and terror outside the Soviet Union. In fact, the GRU is far larger in size than the Second Directorate. It has often proved more formidable to the West from the sheer comprehensiveness of its activities. With a history virtually as old as that of the Soviet Army it reached its greatest importance, quite naturally, during World War II and the immediate postwar years, when military intelligence-gathering was of the essence. (Some of the most damaging of the Soviet discoveries about the West's nuclear armaments were the result of GRU activity.)

Although the GRU concentrates on military rather than political intelligence its organization and the scope of its operations in foreign countries more or less exactly parallel that of the State Security. The rivalry between the two organizations is as old as their history. Each has its respective lobbyists within the Central Committee of the CPSU in Moscow, who engage in trying to persuade the current régime that the opposition's intelligence service is comparatively useless.

The peculiar ubiquitousness of the State Security, however, makes such policy disputes in actual practice academic. Through its own personnel in military counter-intellegence the KGB enjoys a one-way window on the

activities of the GRU. The highest officers of the GRU
are accordingly under KGB surveillance. Their private
lives, loyalty to the Party, and local intelligence activities
are sifted with equal thoroughness by KGB agents within
their organization, for forwarding to the Central Committee at the State Security's discretion.

In Vienna several highly placed GRU officers had to
play the dual and uncomfortable role of informers for the
KGB. Some of this work involved an impressive amount of
personality-splitting. The deputy chief of the Economic
Section at the Soviet Embassy, for example, Colonel A. A.
Nevsorov, was actually an officer of the GRU and used
the Embassy post only as cover. Yet Nevsorov had also
been compromised by the State Security and forced into
service as an informant on his fellow Army intelligence officers. Through the services of Nevsorov and others (including the assistant military attaché) the State Security
Residency had a constant flow of information on the activities of its sister service.

As the SK officer, Deriabin was intimately concerned
with this GRU surveillance. His standing order was a short
but specific directive from the Resident: "You must always keep your eye on any GRU personnel."

The few State Security officers on duty in Vienna had,
however, grown rather sloppy. Pribytkov, then acting Resident, was a powerful stumbling block to good intelligence
work, regardless of staff shortages. A large and visibly fun-
loving fellow about thirty-four years old, he had a long record both in the State Security and the Party. On his last
domestic assignment, in Krasnodar, he had got into trouble
with local authorities by beating a suspect so hard in the
course of "investigation" that the man almost died. With
unconscious irony the Party secretary of the locality had
written a formal censure into his record because "he used
the wrong investigative methods."

This was in 1950. By the time Deriabin arrived to join
him two years of duty in the *gemütlich* city of Vienna had
mellowed Pribytkov's zeal almost to the point of extinction.
"There are two ways to be a good intelligence officer," he
told his new deputy, "drink every day or work very hard. I
chose the first." But Pribytkov was not foolish enough to
let his laxity come to Moscow's attention. He covered up

his high living with a constant flurry of report-writing, which gave him in State Security circles the name of *kombinator*—Soviet slang for an "operator." Each month the officers at Dzerzhinsky Square would be favored with a harvest of splendidly written accounts of Pribytkov's activities in Austria. The accomplishments, while not actual deceptions, were never quite tangible. Agents would be recruited in the very heart of U.S. headquarters, only to be transferred to Salzburg just as the contacts were developing. A monster network of infiltration within the Soviet colony would be barely disclosed, only to have its principals flee suddenly to the West.

Behind this official screen Pribytkov pursued pleasure consistently, to the point where some of his female agents complained to Deriabin about his non-intelligence activities. In the office, however, he continued to be a merry companion and a most relaxing superior. "Quick, let's write a report," he would say to Peter of a morning. The report, suitably embellished, would go off in the afternoon pouch to Moscow. Whereupon Pribytkov and his assistant would go out fishing.

Such dalliance was one kind of reaction to the spiritual attrition of working for the State Security, and in the field it was not uncommon. But it was apt to involve both his superiors and subordinates in serious trouble. Deriabin was notably relieved when his boss was ordered back to Moscow. For the rest of his Vienna service he had complete control of the SK Group.

The legal State Security Residency in Vienna was divided into some fourteen subsections or "groups." They included Anglo-American, French, Austrian, Yugoslav, West German, Russian émigrés, and a special Illegal Group, not to mention technical and code units and a photo-laboratory. Each of the State Security officers had his own cover either as a staff member of the High Commissioner's office—soon to become the Soviet Embassy—an official of the various Soviet-run businesses in Austria, or a Soviet newspaper correspondent. Major Budakhin, for example, did extra cover duty as a *Tass* correspondent, and Colonel Boris Y. Mikhailov was a "correspondent" for *Pravda*. Even the traveling correspondent for the Soviet magazine *Ogonek* had State Security credentials. A highly active agent named Karl Nepomnyashchiy, he specialized in working up interest in various Soviet international "peace" campaigns and congresses.

Major Deriabin was given a high-sounding title, to approximate his State Security and Party rank, as Assistant to General Sergey E. Maslov, the chief administrative officer of the Embassy and allied installations. His office, next door to Maslov's, was Room 19 in the Imperial Hotel, the elegant former archducal palace which the Russians used as their administrative headquarters. A bare gray room with a faded picture of Vienna on the wall, it was no different in its furnishings from the typical institutional four-wall atmosphere of any Soviet headquarters, with a few significant exceptions. There was a large Austrian safe in the corner with only a few documents in it (it is SOP in all Soviet embassies and consulates to store most important and confidential paperwork in the code room), but containing a young arsenal of some twenty weapons: machine pistols, automatics, and a few carbines.

There were four telephones, which were kept unplugged when not in use. Since the telephone exchange on the Schillerplatz was in the international sector of the city the Russians constantly suspected the Americans of organizing ingenious wire-tapping schemes through the phone lines. One of the phones was on the regular city exchange, another led to the Embassy and the Grand Hotel, a third was a special intercom system for the sixteen officers in the Embassy: the High Commissioner, counselors, etc. The fourth was a direct wire to Soviet military headquarters in Baden. When using this phone the week's password had to be given before any conversation.

There was also, most importantly for the SK chief's physical comfort, a commodious couch in one corner of the room. Deriabin used this for afternoon naps, since so many of his rendezvous with agents were relatively late at night. The agents, as he recalls, were almost unanimously heavy drinkers (except for a few female agents, who excelled in other vices). Experience had shown Deriabin that a few hours' rest before a night meeting would result in his retaining his normal clear-headed concept of the intelligence mission.

One door from Room 19 led to the office of the secretary Deriabin shared with General Maslov. Through this door he received his few official callers. These were just enough to justify his cover as a member of the Embassy staff: routine document checks of Austrians scheduled to give a ballet concert, Austrian repairmen at work in Soviet buildings, investigations of defective food supplies and materials bought on the Austrian market, etc.

The other door led directly to the well-traveled corridor outside. Through it entered people on State Security business, notably his officers, and a few other State Security personnel. To help him Deriabin had five officers regularly assigned, each with his peculiar cover. Captain Nikolay P. Bulayev, his chief assistant, was the chief of personnel in the Danube Shipping Administration; Senior Lieutenant Aleksandr A. Petrov was in charge of the Fire Department of the Soviet Petroleum Administration.[1] Three others were in the Embassy: Lieutenant Aleksandr V. Maurin in the Personnel Section, Lieutenant Anatoliy V. Zuyev in the Supply Section, and Lieutenant Boris Svetlitchny, the High Commissioner's interpreter. The three junior officers, who spoke fluent German, were all graduates of the Leningrad Foreign Languages Institute.

When Deriabin had arrived at the Vienna station he was amused, but not surprised, to find two welcoming parties. The first to meet him was Mr. Rybalko, an attaché of the High Commissioner's Office. Rybalko welcomed him to Vienna, gave him the key to his family's quarters at the Grand Hotel, and offered them an Embassy car. A few minutes later Pribytkov appeared, gave him another key, and told him *his* car was around the corner. Deriabin thanked the attaché for his trouble, declined his car; then walked over to his State Security superior. "What about the two keys?" he asked. "Try both rooms and see which is better," Pribytkov said. The quarters provided for Deriabin's Embassy cover amounted to a single room, without bath, for a whole family. The State Security facilities, which they

---

[1] The official German title of the latter was *Sovietische Mineralöl Verwaltung* and the former simply *Donaudampfschifffahrtsgesellschaft*—a well-used title that happens to be one of the longest words in the German lanugage. The Russians, who like long words themselves, kept this one.

quickly occupied, were a two-room suite, with as many modern conveniences as the Grand Hotel could muster. For a Soviet officer abroad this was luxury.

Although Deriabin was not at first identified as a State Security officer the word quickly got around. He was given at that time to listening to the broadcasts of the Voice of America and Radio Liberation on his new Austrian radio, a fact quickly noticed by the occupant of the next room, the chief of the Embassy's Finance Section. Shortly after the Deriabins moved in he reported them for this anti-Soviet activity to the building officer, an Army major named Zatsepin. The report was rebuffed (since the major was one of Deriabin's agents), but the Finance Officer continued to look angrily at his new floormates. One day his attitude suddenly changed. By the low bows with which he was greeted Deriabin deduced that one more of his fellow citizens had tumbled to his patently thin "cover."

From the beginning the better-informed members of the Soviet colony in Vienna had little doubt but that Peter Deriabin was a member of the State Security. Even privately this fact was not held against him. On the contrary, the eminence of the State Security in Soviet society surrounds its representatives with something like awe instead of the half-disdain with which free societies regard the members of a security police force. Deriabin was a gregarious man who made friends easily whatever his situation. His Party seniority, also, was well known and made him doubly acceptable in the local Soviet social circles.

His fellow officials would not have been so cordial, and the Finance Officer would have been even more awed, had they known that his specific State Security job was directly involved with their own day-to-day surveillance. Every Soviet citizen faces up to the fact that he is watched. But the details of the watching, which bear witness to its effectiveness, are the State Security's internal secret.

Excepting the High Commissioner, the State Security Resident, and his staff, all Soviet officials of the High Commission had their apartments either in the Grand Hotel or specially requisitioned apartments. (It is a cardinal rule of the State Security that Soviet citizens abroad be quartered wherever possible in one definite area, easy to reach and easy to watch.) The Grand Hotel could only be entered officially through the main door on Kärntnerring. All the people quartered there used this entrance and had to sign in with the duty officer whenever they returned at night, after the curfew hour of 10 P.M. Deriabin, the Resident, and a few others had also a key to a rear entrance; but they were the only people so privileged.

The officers on duty at the desk were responsible to Deriabin's agent, Zatsepin. The SK Group could thus accumulate handy records on arrivals and departures. Other well-placed agents of his were the chief of the Communications Section, an Army lieutenant colonel, the lieutenant in charge of the Embassy motor pool near the Parkring, and the officer in charge of the Embassy garage. Through them Deriabin could keep intimate track of the movements of any member of the High Commission without leaving his desk in the Imperial. Every bit of personal information was useful to him, the more damaging to an individual, the better for the State Security. For, if the State Security had no interest in Comrade X at the moment, the knowledge of Comrad X's dalliance with the wife of Comrad Y inside the hotel or a secluded redezvous in the city was bound to come in handy some day. It would be duly filed and reported.

The slightest contact of any Soviet citizen with foreigners is on its face grounds for suspicion and has to be investigated. For such individual investigations Deriabin's section recruited amateur "informants" from among the subject's close personal friends. In some cases these informants were formally hired as State Security agents; at other times they were merely questioned closely about their friend or neighbor. When anyone's co-operation was needed the "informant" had to sign an official security oath, swearing never to reveal to anyone, under any circumstances, anything he might know about the work of the State Security in Austria.

In November 1953 an agent in the State Security Residency's Emigré Group told the officer working with him that a Georgian named Okreshidze, the director of one of the Soviet business firms in Vienna, had made a statement that it would not be difficult for someone in his position to transfer a million Austrian schillings to a Swiss account and escape to the West. This information was immediately passed on to Deriabin. On the strength of this unconfirmed report, from a man by no means esteemed as trustworthy, Okreshidze and the informant were put under a long period of surveillance. A neighbor's apartment was used as a listening post to monitor their conversations. A trio of officers from Major Leonov's Technical Group at military counter-intelligence headquarters in Baden manned the listening post after the apartment under suspicion had been "bugged" with listening devices. Here again nothing concrete was turned up to justify the charges. But the case was marked as continuing, and a file was entered on Okreshidze. Its very existence would probably bar any further advancement for him in the Soviet service.

The biggest fish up for frying was the chief of the High Commissioner's Foreign Political Section, later Counselor of the Soviet Embassy in Vienna, Andrey M. Timoshchenko. Timoshchenko was known as an individualist in Soviet diplomatic circles, famed for his sloppiness of dress. (In Ethiopia, where he was formerly Minister, the Emperor had pointedly asked him not to attend official receptions in his customarily rumpled attire.) He was given to leaving official documents lying about on his desk, in full view of foreign visitors. He was suspected of even more studied security breaches.

In 1939, when Timoshchenko was at the London Embassy, he reported to the then Soviet Ambassador Ivan Maysky that British intelligence had offered him £500 a month to work for them. No action was taken against Timoshchenko at the time. But when Maysky himself was arrested in 1951 as a British agent the Timoshchenko file was brought out and reviewed again. Perhaps he had used the report of this rejected British recruitment offer as a blind for his acceptance of another one. After Maysky's conviction Deriabin himself asked Vienna State Security headquarters for a report on Timoshchenko's activites. No action was taken. But he went to Vienna a few months later with explicit orders to reopen the case.

Timoshchenko was a high-ranking diplomat whose appointment had been approved by the Central Committee in Moscow, so Deriabin had to move with caution. But the network of agents he set up shows Soviet thoroughness in such matters. Several State Security officers were already using Timoshchenko's Political Section as their cover; among them, Colonel Vasily R. Sitnikov, chief of the Anglo-American Group in Vienna, Major Ivan Guskov of the Emigré Group, and Lieutenant Colonel Gorchakov. Deriabin recruited another of the Counselor's close subordinates for special informing work. He collected reports from the Embassy chauffeurs that Timoshchenko and his wife were in the habit of frequenting restaurants and stores in the Western sectors of Vienna. Moscow was asked to authorize close surveillance procedures, e.g. wire tapping, "bugging" Timoshchenko's office, and rifling his safes. By this time the net around Timoshchenko was tightening. But Deriabin left before he had time to complete the case.[2]

At the other pole from a matter like Timoshchenko's, no case was too small for the attention of the SK officer. On January 28, 1954, Deriabin was ordered by Moscow to meet in person one German G. Kitayev, the chauffeur of the Soviet Embassy in Beirut, who was returning to the Soviet Union with his wife via Vienna. He met them at the station, arranged for their housing and per diem allowances until they could be booked on a train for Moscow, and allotted them the princely allowance of 13.3 rubles a day ($1.30 at the international exchange rate). Even such a minor employee rated his own protective custody to forestall any possibility of his acquiring unhealthy associations.

Natasha was a non-political problem. The censors notified the Vienna State Security that she had been sending an unusual number of packages home to her relatives in U.S.S.R., wallets, purses and various small but highly negotiable articles of Austrian manufacture. This case was turned over to the SK Group. On investigation the girl, a secretary in the Internal Political Section of the High Commissioner's Office, was proved to have succumbed to the lure which entices even star Soviet athletes when faced with the fleshpots of the West: shoplifting. She was otherwise unobjectionable, politically speaking, and the disposition of her case was simple. Escorted by one of Deriabin's officers, she was put on the next train for Moscow.

---

[2] The diplomat seems to have survived this informal local investigation. In June 1959, he appeared in Bonn as Soviet ambassador to the Bundesrepublik.

These were only a few of the jobs which fell to Deriabin at the very beginning of his tour of duty. Policeman, spy, judge, unofficial hotel manager, social arbiter, watchman, and Inspector General—such were the joys of being an SK officer.

In carrying out these activities there were remarkably few clashes of authority between the regular Embassy and the underground embassy of the State Security in Vienna. Every Soviet citizen lives with the fact of the State Security's power at the back of his consciousness. The very mention of the name is enough to send the average Russian official back-pedalling frantically away from any possible involvement with the Security arm, like one of Pavlov's dogs traveling in reverse. In Vienna, also, the High Commissioner, Ivan I. Ilyichev, was himself a lieutenant general in the GRU. Ilyichev worked closely with his Resident, Kravtsov, and backed up the State Security in any of the rare conflicts of authority.

One such conflict occurred not long after Deriabin's arrival, with his nominal boss, General Maslov. A Red Army major general, Maslov ran the purely administrative side of the High Commissioner's Office with a minimum of efficiency and a maximum of vodka. He was another old-timer of the Soviet occupation, who realized that he could go no further in his career, so decided to make his own niche as comfortable and permanent as possible.

His argument with Deriabin sprang from the non-attendance of Deriabin's State Security chauffeurs at the regular Party meetings inside the Embassy. Maslov demanded that they be present at all meetings. Deriabin objected, not only because they had a lot of night work to do, but because the very controversy was calling attention to men the State Security liked to keep quietly faceless.

The General was adamant, and strong words followed. So Deriabin called the High Commissioner to ask for an appointment. What followed was an interesting restatement of the State Security's senior role in Soviet society. Major General Maslov stood at attention before Ilyichev's desk for an hour while the High Commissioner ranted and screamed about his interference with the work of a State Security major. "You should be as mute as a scarecrow," he said. "You have no other function in connection with this man's duties."

Unfortunately Maslov continued to harass the State Security detachment in petty ways by interfering with their cars, room assignments, etc. So Deriabin, not wishing to bother the High Commissioner again, took steps on his own. He asked one of his key agents, the chief telephone operator at the Grand Hotel, if Maslov had any girl-friends whom he was in the habit of visiting. The operator knew of one, a personable stenographer named Katerina, who was very close to the General. Deriabin ordered her to advise him the instant Maslov telephoned Katerina to fix a rendezvous.

So it was that on a certain winter evening Peter Deriabin answered his own telephone, put on his coat, took a camera out of his closet, and marched upstairs to the room where Katerina and Maslov were visiting. After one loud knock he opened the door with his pass key to find Katerina and the General in a most embarrassing situation. "Well, General," said Deriabin. "I think we had better talk about this downstairs. Highly irregular procedure . . ."

The very next day the State Security chauffeurs received by direct order of General Maslov the pick of the Embassy motor pool: a new Czech Tatra and a highly-prized 1949 Buick.

CHAPTER XXII

Agents And Escape

STRIPPED OF THE organizational superstructure, the day-to-day operations of a Soviet intelligence officer seem rather conservative, untouched by the technological modernization that has revolutionized most other branches of warfare. The cornerstone of the State Security information network is the individual case officer working through the group of agents for which he is responsible. Almost every day the case officer makes his rounds, like a cop watching over an illicit beat, thumbing through his notebook for the time and place of meeting Agent X, telephoning to change the manner of his meeting with Agent Y, wondering after a missed rendezvous whether Agent Z has been arrested, or even worse, compromised.

The notebook Peter Deriabin kept, giving the cryptic details of such meetings, looks surprisingly enough as if Ian Fleming had planned it for a mystery novel. "January 6: The Uruguayan at 2000; January 7: Sinilov at 1300; January 8: Arefyev at 2100; January 9: Smirnova at 2000. . . ." The telephone calls, made only when necessary, used the simple codes that have so long been favored by fictional and real-life spy systems. "Listen," Deriabin would say when his agent Feoktistov (the "Builder") answered, "my bath that you fixed yesterday needs more repairs. The water still leaks. Can you come over at six and do the job?" In that particular case the message conveyed to the Builder was crystal clear: "We have some unfin-

297

ished business after yesterday's exchange of information. I will meet you at six in the Naschmarkt."

The Naschmarkt, at the border of the Soviet and the French sectors, was a favorite rendezvous of Deriabin and his agents, as was Feoktistov's seedy, but well-populated hang-out, the Graben Café. Good intelligence officers shun back alleys, sewers, and deserted streets like the plague. The most inconspicuous cover possible is a profusion of bright lights and a lot of people; that is, if a rendezvous is carried out in a public place. For longer sessions with their agents the State Security officers in Vienna, as everywhere else, had a small network of "safe houses." These were apartments or houses, always in the Soviet sector, nominally used as dwellings by agents or State Security officers, but dedicated principally to the function of meeting places.

The safe houses were furnished by the State Security through a central clearing house, the office of the chief of the Soviet Housing Section in Vienna. But they were effectively scattered through the city: 1a Untere Donaustrasse, a gathering place for Major Georgiy Litovkin and agents of the West German Group; 19 Mühlgasse, where Deriabin had many of his more important meetings; 23 Böchlinstrasse, the modern-looking ten-room villa in the Prater which had long been consecrated as a State Security operating area.

The State Security was well aware that the best agent in the world is of little value unless an intelligence service can be sure that it controls him. In the Soviet service, where xenophobia is king, a good deal of a case officer's time was consumed in checking on the very agents who supplied his information. While the agent Feoktistov, for instance, was watching certain Austrian contacts, another of Deriabin's agents, Nekrasov, was watching Feoktistov. The deadliest enemy of all was the "penetrator" or "provocateur," an agent of an enemy intelligence service which has been successfully infiltrated into your own.

The "double agent," a man who actually sought and gave information on both sides of the fence, was often tolerated, depending on the information he produced, for he was a window on the operations of the other side. Before coming to Vienna, Deriabin had successfully manipulated the activities of one Polish double agent, a man known by his cryptonym of "Serezha,"–"little Sergey," who was sent into Poland from West Germany by one of the NATO powers to gather military information. When Serezha was nabbed at the East German border State Security officers there cabled Moscow, as usual, for permission to recruit him as a double. Permission was granted, and Serezha was furnished enough slightly doctored infomation about Red Army installations in Poland to make his trip seem worthwhile to his original employers. Meanwhile the State Security had prepared an informational shopping list of its own which Serezha was to supply as soon as he returned to his base.

In Vienna itself the State Security had had a less fortunate experience. One of its best Austrian agents, an alert and physically powerful ex-Nazi, Armin Rentmeister, was discovered to be working for the West. Rentmeister was lured to a safe house in the Soviet sector to meet a State Security lieutenant colonel named Antropov. Antropov, especially selected for his brawn, was expected to subdue and arrest him. Why such primitive methods were necessary is something of a mystery. It is true, however, that the State Security avoids actual bloodshed or public violence whenever possible (it is too conspicuous) if Soviet personnel are involved in an operation. Rentmeister was finally subdued by Antropov and two other officers after five quarts of vodka had been expended in an initial softening-up process. He was thrown into a car and taken to the Soviet military headquarters at Baden, where he received the usual twenty-five-year sentence.

The experience with Rentmeister made Colonel Kravtsov's Residency all the more cautious about the credentials of its agents. But until the very end there was at least one known double agent in Deriabin's particular network.

At the outset Deriabin was given the files of forty agents in Vienna with whom he was supposed to keep in regular contact. There were originally more, but changing circumstances had reduced the number considerably, notably a significant directive which the Deputy Resident, Colonel Galuzin, brought with him from Moscow in December 1953. From that time on, all State Security residencies were ordered to avoid recruiting agents with any local

Communist Party connections and to trim foreign Communist Party agents from their payrolls, with only a few exceptions. The directive was issued for several reasons: (1) Moscow's recognition that the high-water mark of Communism in Western Europe, at least, had passed. With native Communists increasingly pruned from sensitive positions their usefulness for intelligence purposes diminished. (2) For this very reason any local Communists caught in espionage operations would make things that much more difficult for their hard-pressed fellows. (3) The third reason was not stated, but was implicit in Moscow's growing suspicion of national Communist tendencies. It was becoming a sticky question whether a foreign Communist would not place his own country's interests before Moscow's, or at least his interpretation of them.

The new directive cost the Vienna Residency some promising recruits among local Party members. (Only a few Communists, including three members of the Vienna police force, were kept on.) But it simplified the problem from a professional point of view. At different times in its foreign operations the State Security had run into some embarrassing road blocks through ideological or jurisdictional disputes with native Communist leaders. Most of the professionals preferred the simpler recruitment of agents through bribes, cajolery, or blackmail.

As the SK officer, Deriabin's job was almost totally one of counter-intelligence. Active spying was done by the other sections of the apparatus. His overriding concern was to see that no Soviet citizens developed, or even risked, any undue contact with foreigners. So the bits of information he picked up in his rounds were almost always secondary and in themselves unimportant. Comrade X in the Economic section had been seen talking with some Swiss businessman. The wife of Comrade Y in the Soviet Petroleum Administration was getting into debt at non-Soviet shops. A friend of a known American agent was seen talking to Comrade Z. A suspicious-looking Austrian had been taking pictures of Soviet personnel in front of the Hotel Imperial. An agent of the Emigré Group might have been recruited by the British.

Each scrap of suspicion had to be weighed, sifted, and assayed. The carefulness of this process generally served to magnify the doubts instead of settling them. So the SK officer's notebook was always full. Deriabin's round of night visits never ceased. The State Security chauffeurs kept the Buick and the Tatra in constant motion.

Few, if any, of the agents knew Deriabin by his real name. His real name, in fact, would not even have been used in his official Embassy cover if his orders to Austria had not come through too swiftly for the usual State Security name-changing operation, done before a man goes overseas. There was not enough time to prepare new documents and a "legend," although he assumed his code name of Konstantin for purposes of official correspondence with the Second Directorate in Moscow. Some of his agents knew him as Korobov, a chief of section of the Soviet Commercial Administration (USIA) in Austria. For others he had the name and, of course, the documents of one Voronov, a clerical employee in the High Commissioner's Office. There was also the name of Smirnov, another mythical USIA employee, which he used frequently.

Of the thirty agents remaining after the State Security purged the Communists from its ranks, less than half were Soviet citizens, most of them the officers in the sensitive posts already mentioned. The others were an odd mixture: a few Austrians, some Russian émigrés, a Greek citizen long resident in Vienna. They had been recruited for the usual variety of reasons. But their individual stories were sometimes strangely involved and pathetic.

There was Irina Kotomkina, the French-born daughter of a Russian émigré, who worked as a translator and secretary for the Communist-sponsored World Federation of Trade Unions, which has its headquarters in Vienna. Kotomkina had married a senior lieutenant named Uksov, in the Soviet Air Force, when she first came to the WFTU, and settled down in his quarters. They had one child. As soon as Uksov's superiors found this out, he was shipped home. Kotomkina was shortly after approached by the State Security and recruited after a State Security officer promised to help get them together again. She worked faithfully for the State Security thereafter. She reported on the friends and the movements of WFTU officials, in particular its French chief, Louis Saillant, who, like most foreign Communists, the State Security trusted not at all. Often Kotomkina asked about her husband. "Soon," Deriabin regularly promised her, "we will write to Moscow. We can arrange it. But first we would like to know . . ."

Sergey P. Feoktistov was also an émigré and an improbable choice for agent work. Not only had his father been a Czarist lieutenant general, Feoktistov had himself fought in Wrangel's White Army after the Revolution and worked in Czechoslovakia as an engineer between the wars. His family had remained in Czechoslovakia after the Communist take-over there, thus making them excellent hostage material. So Feoktistov had little choice about working for Soviet intelligence. He received good money, also, for his professional work as manager of a Soviet-controlled Austrian factory.

Probably the most involved origins of any agent's recruitment lay behind the code designation for one useful man in Deriabin's notebook, the "Uruguayan." Evlampiy S. Shvedov was a Ukrainian with a Uruguayan passport who worked as a driver in the headquarters of the Soviet-controlled Danube Steamship Company. He had come to Vienna originally, on the way to Moscow, because of his sister's peculiarly unfortunate marriage back in Uruguay. The story behind the marriage and his arrival is an almost incredible illustration of how far and how fine the State Security spreads its nets.

Shvedov and his sister Anna were reasonably prosperous farming people in Uruguay, where their family had emigrated some years after the Russian Revolution. After World War II Anna began to get letters from her aunt, telling about the wonderful, abundant life in the U.S.S.R., her own loneliness, and her great desire to see her only two surviving relatives. The aunt's signature on the letters was authentic, but everything she said in them had been "organized" by the domestic branch of the State Security. At the same time that the aunt's correspondence grew intense the Shvedovs made the acquaintance of a former Soviet soldier named Kolomiyets. The soldier had been proscribed by the State Security for "traitorous activities" (he had been taken prisoner by the Germans and co-operated with them). After considerable hardship he had got to Uruguay illegally, but he found a good job as a musician in the town of Paysandu, where there was a sizable Russian and Ukrainian colony.

The fugitive musician fell in love with Shvedov's sister about the same time that Captain Pavel Kotik, the State Security Resident for Uruguay, received a report about him from Moscow with the order: "Take all necessary measures to induce Kolomiyets to return to the U.S.S.R." Captain Kotik, who was better known to Uruguayans as the Soviet consul in Montevideo, was aware of the organized correspondence between the girl and her aunt, and Anna's growing desire to come to the Soviet Union. He talked with her at length and took applications from her and her brother to visit the Soviet Union. When the visas were not forthcoming Kotik obligingly explained that it might be far easier to get a visa if she were married to a Soviet citizen. The musician's love for Anna Shvedova was well known, and "Consul" Kotik dropped a few gentle hints. Why not marry the musician and persuade him, too, to return to the Soviet fatherland?

Going all the way down the garden path, Shvedova agreed. She married the musician, and by a happy coincidence the visas to the Soviet Union came right along. In 1951 the bride and groom boarded a Soviet ship in Montevideo. Just before the departure a last-minute "examination' of documents revealed some "irregularities" in the woman's. She was put off the ship, to stay in Uruguay. Her luckless new husband was kept on and sailed away to a twenty-five-year sentence at hard labor for his "traitorous activities."

With a gullibility apparently peculiar to overseas Soviet sympathizers in situations like this one, Shvedov himself took ship en route to Moscow in search of his sister's husband. He came to Vienna in his search for a Soviet visa, and there the State Security recruited him. "Any day now," the case officers would tell him with assurance, "and the visa will come through. We want to help you."

It fell to Deriabin, as the senior SK officer, to feed the illusions of unfortunates like Shvedov and Kotomkina, as part of his daily round. Shvedov, incredibly, still looked forward with hope and satisfaction to his "new life" in the fatherland. He would have been shocked if he ever found

out how attracted was Deriabin by descriptions of his old
life in Uruguay. Even Feoktistov, the ex-White Guardist,
talked about placing his sons in a Soviet scientific institute.
Deriabin gave them all constant reassurance. Sitting in a
café on Vienna's Argentinastrasse, he listened to Shvedov's plans to buy a tractor as soon as he got to the
U.S.S.R., where "all the land belonged to the people." Then
he would tour the world as a Soviet citizen and see China,
where he had always longed to go. "Poor bastard," mut-
tered Deriabin to himself after one such meeting, "you go
to the Soviet Union, and they will put you in front of a
tractor."

When he came home from work at night, driving with
his silent chauffeur past the rows of trees along the Ring-
strasse, his own assurances came back to stick in his throat.
"It was not exactly lying," he argued to himself. "It is my
job to give answers. I gave them." But what was left of his
original Communist dedication was fast crumbling. No one
had such a clear view of the pathological desire of the Soviet régime to still every contrary voice, to get every dis-
senting thought back inside its borders, so the thought can
be killed. He continued to do his job. When Shvedov
showed him his Uruguayan passport he asked if he could
borrow it. He kept it or ten days, during which time it was
sent back to Moscow for copying, and then returned it.

The last straw for Deriabin, as it turned out, was what
he saw during the two important events for which every
State Security officer in the area was mobilized: the World
Congress of the World Federation of Trade Unions in October and the session of the World Peace Council in November 1953. The staff was still shorthanded and suffering
from more than the usual State Security paranoia. "A fine
thing," said Colonel Kravtsov at a meeting just before the
Peace Council. "Over two thousand American agents
swarming around the city and they give us seventy-one officers to fight them with."

A few specialized reinforcements did come from Moscow for conference time. The most important State Security visitor was Aleksandr Panyushkin's deputy in charge
of the Second Directorate, Colonel Sergey L. Tikhvinsky.
Tikhvinsky had previously served as consul-general in New
York and done some years of duty in Nationalist-held

China. Tikhvinsky was one of the State Security's leading eggheads. In 1952 he dropped into the Academy of Science to get a doctorate of philosophy and history. Possibly because of his intellectual concerns he was particularly interested in keeping the more intellectual of the Soviet delegates to the Peace Council under close surveillance. He told Deriabin to put a tail on Ilya Ehrenburg, the veteran Soviet littérateur and propagandist, known in Moscow for his contacts in the West. "We have a big file on him," said Tikhvinsky, "so keep a good watch. We do the same with that fellow Zaslavsky[1] in Moscow."

Deriabin was too shorthanded to put any man on Ehrenburg. And he was having his own troubles keeping tabs on one Nazim Khikmet, a veteran Turkish Communist writer, briefly in Vienna from his Moscow exile. Khikmet was allegedly in danger of kidnapping by Turkish agents, who never materialized. But he was important to Soviet intelligence as a point of contact with Communist underground agents in Turkey. Despite warnings to stay put he had an irritating habit of straying away from his room in the Grand Hotel for extended dalliance with the hostesses at the Moulin Rouge nitery around the corner.

The Council lasted a week. For Deriabin and the SK Group it was a blur of steady activity, for their office was responsible for the safety of each delegate. Despite the few extra men from Moscow, Deriabin himself had to put in an appearance at all the principal official functions as well as keeping tabs on the extracurricular movements of the delegates. (He had to escort Tikhvinsky, for example, to a private meeting with James Endicott, the Canadian former clergyman who had committed himself to belief in the evidence of U.S. atrocities and use of germ warfare in Korea. The Soviets hoped to get from him an informal briefing about British and Canadian objectives at the Berlin foreign ministers conference soon to be convened.) Spiritually it was hardly an ennobling experience. Every screaming slogan about the "glorious peace movement" inspired by the Soviet Union brought its own contrapuntal reflection on

[1] David Zaslavsky, the obedient *Pravda* editorialist who in 1958 delivered one of the more venomous poison-pen attacks on the Nobel Prize winner, Boris Pasternak.

the Soviet system's dishonesty, and how deeply it bit into its own officials.

Through his years of Party indoctrination Deriabin retained at least a traditional feeling of reverence for the Orthodox Church, in which his parents had had him baptized. It was with particular disgust, therefore, that he participated in the attempts at recruitment of Father Arseniy Shilovskiy, an Orthodox priest in Vienna. In World War II Father Arseniy had preached repeated sermons against Communism, a fact which the State Security had only recently uncovered.

The Vienna Residency hoped to use this record as a lever for recruiting him; the Soviet mission could officially make life very uncomfortable for an émigré anti-Communist still behind the Soviet line. A State Security officer approached him in 1953, hinting that all would be forgotten should he co-operate. Although frightened and in an impossible situation, the priest resisted all efforts at turning him into an agent. Even the Metropolitan Nikolay's visit, with a friendly invitation to return with him to Moscow for an ecclesiastical meeting, failed to bear fruit. Nikolay, the second highest ranking churchman in the Soviet Union, was in Vienna with the other Soviet delegates to the Peace Council. He came several times to the little Orthodox church where Father Arseniy was pastor, to put the seal of ecclesiastical approval on the recruitment effort of the State Security. He himself had been doing the State Security's bidding for many years.

This evidence of high-level intimidation came on the heels of a more striking sign of the high-level distrust which continued unabated, if not increased, among the Kremlin hierarchy after the death of Stalin. Just a few weeks before, Deriabin had had to undertake a peculiarly delicate shadowing mission, specially ordered from Moscow. Its object was a high Soviet official named Berezin, the deputy of Nikolay M. Shvernik, then chairman of the All-Union Central Council of Trade Unions, who led the Soviet delegation to the Trade Union Congress (and spent most of his spare time buying underwear for his wife in Moscow). Each night, after the delegates had returned to their hotel, Deriabin received a written report from the head of a three-man surveillance detail, seconded for the purpose from the Red Army counter-intelligence detachment at Baden. He never knew himself what Berezin was being watched for. Neither Berezin nor Shvernik, in turn, knew anything about this surveillance. (Since that time Berezin has not left the Soviet Union.)

Paddling his way through all this organized treachery, Deriabin still had to smile answers to those of the Communist faithful who touched base in Vienna during the Congress season. At the Trade Union Congress he met a Spanish Communist who had made his way illegally from his native country to Austria. The Spaniard was impressed: "What a great country the Soviet Union is! I hope some day we can build a fine socialist country like this in Spain." "Ah yes," Deriabin said, "you must fight for this. It's a great life we have in the Soviet Union."

Every smart boy in the Soviet Union realizes early in the game at least part of the lie that he is living. He realizes, at the same time, that being privy to the big lie is the price and in a sense the reward of his talent. His ground rules are strict, and he knows they are dirty. Partly as an exercise in self-justification he joins with enthusiasm in the circumlocutions, the contrived "Marxist-Leninist" explanations, the avoidance of harsh words like murder and kidnappings to describe political murders and kidnappings. They are the only ground rules he knows, the devices with which the Lying Society sweeps its dirt under the rug. In Deriabin's case the lie was reaching the point beyond endurance.

At five o'clock in the morning of February 13, Colonel Kravtsov called Deriabin at his hotel apartment and told him to make an immediate investigation of a reported defection. An official of the Soviet Petroleum Administration named Anatoliy I. Skachkov had been reported missing by his frightened wife. He had come home drunk after an evening of revelry at the Maxim night club, where he had gone with a visiting State Security lieutenant colonel from Moscow. Bluntly, as the story went, Skachkov had told his wife he was leaving "for the Americans," taken two overcoats and two suits, and walked out.

Deriabin put on his clothes, called his driver, and set out for Skachkov's office, to talk to the Petroleum Administration security officer. On the way he pondered over the odd circumstances of the defection and the unusual fact that it had immediately followed an evening of drinking with a Moscow State Security officer. Was this another rigged "penetration," planned to insert yet another agent into the workings of U.S. intelligence? Spectacular binges were often used as a cover for such operations. He wondered. If the defection were rigged it would be perfectly normal for Moscow to tell no one in Vienna, with the possible exception of the Resident himself.

For the next twenty-four hours, however, Deriabin and one of his junior officers conducted a thorough investigation of Skachkov's business and living establishments. (It was facilitated by the fact that he had already undertaken a loose surveillance of Skachkov's wife, for another reason.) They collected all papers of value from the apartment and removed them to the Embassy offices. On the night of the fourteenth, Deriabin put Lieutenant Maurin on all-night guard at the Skachkov apartment, since the Resident had expressed fears that the Americans might attempt to raid it.

The problem of defection was an interesting one, and the hurly-burly of the Skachkov investigation made Peter Deriabin reflect on it rather thoroughly. The possibility of such an act had occurred to him already, for himself. On several occasions he had tried, through a known double agent, to make contact with an American intelligence officer. The half-formed impulse that struck him in Moscow was now active. It had crystallized during the last few months to the point where a desire to break with the system was now a definite and conscious thing with him. It interfered with his work. Foreign intelligence was no longer the technical pleasure it had been, a glorified mental exercise. Nor was there any pretense left that the job was "clean."

His work had suffered only slightly with the technical intensity gone from it. The agent network was still in good order. His relations were good with Kravtsov and his fellow officers. If the Skachkov defection were proved genuine he might receive a reprimand, since the matter was very much in the SK area. But he was in no danger as yet. Like the village clergyman whose services still ran smoothly after his personal doubts had become obsessive, Deriabin wondered how long the equilibrium could continue.

Late in the morning of February 15, after another night of work, he stopped in at his apartment in the Grand Hotel. His wife querulously asked him when he would be home again. He had not told her of his growing disgust with his life. They did not get along too well. She had a long Communist background, also, and might not have understood. In the Soviet Union even with wives, parents, or children one could never be sure. No one knew this better than a State Security man, whose job had so often included the intelligence exploitation of family differences. "Maybe I'll never come back," he said, and he left.

What makes a man finally jump over the wall? What causes the last moment of decision and puts the flesh of long-held thoughts into the armor of action? A man knows once, but it can never be explained. At 3:30 P.M., after a last check of Skachkov's apartment house, Deriabin left his junior officer and walked towards the Naschmarkt. It was a steel-gray day. A few snowflakes were falling, driven by the gathering wind. Deriabin put up the collar of his tweed overcoat. He stopped at one of the open-air booths and ordered a sausage and a bottle of beer.

When he had finished he hailed a taxi and ordered it to Herzmansky's department store, a large emporium on the corner of the Mariahilferstrasse and the Stiftgasse, near the borders of the French and U.S. sectors. Soviet people often visited Herzmansky's. Up to now his action was normal. When the taxi drove off he looked carefully up and down the street. No uniforms. No familiar faces among the civilians. He looked at the buildings along the Stiftgasse, trying to pick out the one he was seeking. A street-cleaner passed by, pushing his long-handled broom along the gutter. "That's the American *Kommandatura*, isn't it?" Deriabin asked him, pointing to a large entrance gate on the other side of the street, guarded by two U.S soldiers. The man nodded. Deriabin walked across the street and asked one of the sentries in German if he could see an American officer. The sentry beckoned him inside.

He walked across a court into a lobby with a high desk, like a police station. There were two U.S. soldiers sitting behind it, who paid him no attention. An Austrian attendant asked him his business. Deriabin said in his broken German: "I would like to talk to a Russian-speaking officer." The attendant disappeared and came back with an American civilian. Again Deriabin made his request: "I want to talk to a Russian-speaking officer." "Ah," the American said, "you want to speak to a Russian officer." Deriabin's evident panic showed the error of this interpretation. "Someone in intelligence," he said hastily. "Is there anyone here from CIC or CIA?" "Wait here, please," the American said and went away. He had understood.

Deriabin tried to pass the next few minutes looking at an American magazine he found on a bench. He still remembers the pictures in it: an ordinary American family having a holiday at the beach. All very normal.

Finally a U.S. Army captain who spoke good, if accented, Russian came into the room. Deriabin told him his official rank and position and requested political asylum. The captain whistled. "Look here," he said, with what might be called an excess of international tolerance, "you know what you're doing, don't you?" Deriabin assured him that he did.

The week of February 15 was one of blustery, gray weather. Intermittent snows swept over Vienna from the cold Hungarian plain, giving way only to the oddly warm winds called the Föhn. The perennial cardplayers in the Graben Café huddled over their tables longer than they had planned, reluctant to experience the changeable elements. Traffic was unpredictable, and the music lovers who wanted to hear *Die Meistersinger* that evening left home even earlier than usual to allow for transportation tie-ups.

To Deriabin, talking anxiously with American officers inside U.S. headquarters, the week of snow and wind had a special, urgent meaning. Air travel was rendered precarious—especially from the small Heiligenstädter landing strip for liaison planes, the one take-off point within the U.S. sector of the city. This narrowed his choices of an escape route through the Soviet zone of Austria to two: either wait for better weather or risk the overland journey by rail. To rely on a scheduled flight from the large airfields of Schwechat or Tulln outside the city was risky, involving possible interception at check points in the Soviet zone.

"Don't worry," the intelligence officer said. "We'll get you out in a week or so." Deriabin jumped up in the secluded interrogation room. "A week!" he said. "A week will be too late. Get me out immediately."

Less than twenty-four hours after he had walked into U.S. headquarters, Deriabin drove down to the Westbahnhof in a U.S. Army car. With two American companions and a set of skilfully forged credentials he walked into a reserved compartment on the midday train, the west-bound Orient Express. He was not a very prepossessing figure, a big-jowled man who looked a good ten years older than his age. He wore a new suit of necessarily ill-fitting Austrian clothes. He had with him, for the overnight trip, two ham sandwiches, some water, and a package of American cigarettes. For security's sake he was under orders not to leave the compartment, not that he had any desire to exhibit himself.

The train passed through the Soviet zone without incident. As it was growing dark it arrived in Linz, the beginning of the American zone of occupation. There Deriabin and his escort transferred to a waiting car, which drove them a little further on to another U.S. military headquarters.

It was the first time in his life that Peter Sergeyevich Deriabin had been outside the visible authority of the Soviet Union. He began to sense the reality of the dream of escape which he had so long enjoyed. It was as yet not very comforting. For all his theoretical acquaintance with the West, his glimpse of its standards through the reports and publications that had reached him in Moscow and Vienna, it was a great and perilous unknown. With some comfort he repeated to himself a Russian proverb: "If die we must, let's do it with music." His decision, at least, was over.

At 8 A.M. that morning Soviet troops took up positions astride every road and rail line leading out of Vienna. For a week Soviet patrols combed each vehicle leaving the city with the most stringent insistence on proper documents and identification for all travelers. Soviet authorities notified the Austrian police. "Soviet officials"—ran a United Press dispatch of February 20—"asked Austrian police to join the hunt today for two Russian factory officials who vanished after a drunken night-club spree and may try to es-

cape to the West." The Soviet announcement named Deriabin and Skachkov and accused them of carrying off
considerable quantities of Soviet government funds.[2]

The search continued within Vienna. Lights burned late
into the night at the offices of High Commissioner Ilyichev
and the Resident, who had more than their share of Moscow telegrams, while humbler members of the Soviet mission wondered what secret forces could have been at work
within such a good Communist and such a popular fellow,
to have planned an escape so successfully.

In every direction the measures for the fugitive's apprehension were swift and comprehensive. But they were too
late.

[2] At the time of his escape Deriabin had the equivalent of
eight dollars in his pockets.

CHAPTER XXIII

Khrushchev And The State Security

IN THE FIVE years since he left Soviet control, Peter Deriabin has only once had any form of contact with his old bosses in Moscow. On March 20, 1959, three days before the first account of his career in Soviet intelligence was published in *Life*, the Moscow radio, broadcasting in English, delivered itself of a loud and, to say the least, inventive denunciation, basing its remarks on fragmentary newspaper accounts of Deriabin's first public appearance before Representative Francis Walter's Congressional subcommittee in Washington.

"The other day the House Un-American Activities Committee published a report of a closed session where one Peter Deriabin gave evidence. The highlight of Deriabin's testimony was what he labeled the activity of Soviet spy organizations . . .

"The only thing we will not refute from all Deriabin said is that he really used to be a Soviet citizen, that he betrayed his country and his people five years ago. Now, who actually is Peter Deriabin? Rather, who was he before he fell into the hands of the U.S. intelligence service and became a traitor? Chairman Francis Walter of the Un-American Activities Committee calls him the highest-ranking Soviet official who ever defected to the West. Deriabin himself says he is a former Soviet intelligence officer. By the way, he never even had a high school education and never learned a single foreign lan-

guage. Both Deriabin and his U.S. inspirers claim that
five years ago, in February 1954, he deliberately crossed
over to the West while in Vienna, Austria, choosing what
he called freedom. That is the United States' version
today of Deriabin's appearance in the West.

"Five years ago, however, there was a different story.
You can read it in the European edition of the U.S.
newspaper *Stars and Stripes* of February 23, 1954. It
explained then that Deriabin disappeared from Vienna
after a drinking bout at a night club. As for his job, the
Stars and Stripes reported that he was a rank-and-file
employee of a big Russian industrial trust known as the
USIA, meaning the office of Soviet property in Austria.
The paper added that before his disappearance Deriabin
had stolen large sums of money from the organization
that employed him.

"Radio Moscow asked the U.S.S.R. Ministry of Foreign Trade about Deriabin and his activities in Austria.
We were told the following. He really went to work in
Austria in the supply department of his organization. In
February 1954 he disappeared from Vienna with a large
sum of embezzled money. Those who worked with him
in Austria report his great weakness for drink. We were
told that in a short period of time he had managed to
marry four times, living with his two last wives simulta-
neously for two years. It was revealed soon after his disappearance from Vienna that he speculated on the black
market there in property stolen from his organization.

"These facts make it clear that the U.S. intelligence in
Austria found their man utterly devoid of any concep-
tions of honor or conscience. As a result, he disappeared
in circumstances which were unclear then, to come afloat
five years later on the crest of the muddy anti-Soviet
wave in Washington. That is the real Peter Deriabin."

Thereafer Moscow remained silent. The tone of its one
broadcast and the wildness of its charges would have been
enough to assure Deriabin, without any other evidence,
that the Kremlin of Nikita Khrushchev is no different
from its predecessors. But there was ample additional evidence, which holds true despite surface appearances to the
contrary.

American tourists can come back from Moscow with stories of a society straining at its old controls. Cultural exchanges can multiply. The Soviet people can inch a few more steps forward toward a better and freer life. But in the last analysis all efforts to produce a real thaw in the U.S.S.R. will fail as long as the State Security maintains its position as the ultimate executive arm of the régime.

The present shape of the State Security, its tactics, and its leadership can be understood only in terms of the man who uses it: Nikita Sergeyevich Khrushchev. Since the beginning of 1959 Khrushchev has been able to direct the activities of the Chekist organizations as aboslutely as Stalin did, nearing the apex of his power. He is no stranger to its activities. If his method of using it differs sharply from Stalin's it is a difference of tactic, not basic intent. Khrushchev controls security organs, as Stalin did, to perpetuate his personal rule and the Party dictatorship, two elements which he strives to equate. The objective of each man is to keep the lid on. But where Stalin employed a heavy iron pot cover, Khrushchev is more apt to use a bright modern pressure cooker.

The rise of Khrushchev to power has a long and continuous history. It dates not from his long period of rule in the Ukraine, which became virtually a personal fief, but earlier, when he was first secretary of the Moscow city Party committee organization in the thirties. It was during this time that Khrushchev built up his own organization within the Party cadres of the capital. His keen ward-heeler's appreciation of people and power drew Stalin's quick attention, which he readily demonstrated. In a 1937 speech before the voters of the Stalin electoral district in Moscow, Stalin began by noting that he had not intended to talk to them that day, but had been persuaded by their "respected Nikita Sergeyevich." Given the Byzantine world of Soviet Communist etiquette, this informal mention from the leader amounted to an official laying on of hands.

Khrushchev went to the Ukraine as Party boss in 1938, thoughtfully taking with him some of his most efficient *apparatchiks* from the Moscow Party machinery. By the following year he had so well asserted his control over his huge and sensitive Russian subsidiary that he was made a full member of the Politburo at the Eighteenth Party Congress. He continued his Ukrainian responsibilities during World War II, in which he was commissioned a lieutenant general for his work in directing underground Party organizations during the German occupation of the Ukraine.

For a time in the immediate postwar period Khrushchev lost his Ukrainian job in the Kremlin in-fighting: Kaganovich was sent to replace him. But he regained it after a year. In 1949 he went back to Moscow in something like triumph as one of the secretaries on the Central Committee, as well as boss of the Moscow Party committee. By the time of Stalin's death he had become a leading contender for the succession.

That Khrushchev ultimately won the succession for himself was the result of two factors: (1) his considerable grass-roots strength among the Party activists; and (2) his intuitive ability to play off his rivals against each other. Both Malenkov and Beria strove hastily and desperately to seize power before the other could. As a result, their plans were slipshod and reckless, and their tactics open to intra-Party criticism which they were as yet too weak to silence. Khrushchev, playing the game in the finest barefoot tradition, waited in the background with his hatchet while the two big rivals weakened each other. They did. Beria's pell-mell rush for power via the State Security succeeded only in uniting the others against him. Malenkov's new soft policy in the Soviet government might have proved popular, but he did not have the chance to get his "be-kind-to-consumers" movement off the ground against the criticism of the other Party leaders.

By 1955 Khruschev had secured his own primacy in the Party and was well on his way to asserting his dictatorship. But he still moved cautiously, using colleagues and opponents with equal care as counters in his play.

Zhukov, for example, was a useful knight on Khrushchev's chess board. He was used to offset Malenkov's influence, in combination with Bulganin. After Malenkov's overthrow he became Minister of Defense. As a further reward for his services he was made a candidate for membership in the Praesidium of the Central Committee and finally a full member, the first military man ever to get this far in the Party. Zhukov visibly enjoyed his new responsibilities. Taking advantage of his new power and his

undimmed popularity, he set out to challenge Party doc-
trine by trimming the edges of the political department in
the armed forces. He was, to put it mildly, feeling his oats.

Khrushchev continued to use him. He took advantage of
Zhukov's old grudge against Bulganin to keep Bulganin
definitely the junior member of the B-and-K combination.
He used both Bulganin and Zhukov to complete the disgrace of Molotov, Malenkov, and Kaganovich as the "anti-
Party faction." At the same time, he had taken steps to
counter Zhukov's popularity with the Army. In 1955
Khrushchev secured promotions to marshal for eleven of
the most influential Soviet generals. Little doubt was left in
their minds about the source of their good fortune. Their
elevation diminished the gulf between the authority of Zhukov and lesser military leaders.

With the stage thus set Khrushchev removed Zhukov in
1957 in order to eliminate a dangerous rival and, secondar-
ily, to increase the direct influence of the Party in the
Army. His act was not so much the assertion of Party supremacy against an Army figuratively chafing at the bit.
High commanders in the Army have always been appointed by the Party, and they are Party members. As previously noted, the Army is so honeycombed with Party influences that it is hard to see how any real independence
could develop. What the commanders generally advocate is
not all professionalism and no Party, but a little more professionalism and a little less Party—quite a different object.

Principally Khrushchev's action was a virtuoso performance of New Class leadership, especially since Zhukov's
fall from grace was followed barely a year later by Bulganin's.

Khrushchev was even wary of his own closest supporters, as he showed in the case of a trusted Party henchman
named Nikolay P. Belyaev. Belyaev illustrated an ever-
present pitfall of the Soviet Executive Suite: the ascent to
Moscow and back. He became a member of the Central
Committee Praesidium in 1952, shortly after his arrival in
Moscow from the Altai Kray, and there cultivated Khrushchev's acquaintance. In 1956, as events proved, his educated guess about the winner of the Kremlin power struggle was handsomely rewarded with an appointment as one

of Khrushchev's under-secreatries at the top of the Party administration. Belyaev's name came to be reckoned with in Moscow. In 1958 he was without warning sent to Kazakhstan, as secretary of the Party for the Kazakh republic. It was a sign in turn that the man who had supported his rise to power in Moscow now found Belyaev's power growing uncomfortable.

The period of Khrushchev's rise can be divided into three clearly marked parts. The first was the actual modern Time of Troubles, from 1953 to 1956, in which the Party leaders staged their fight over the succession. Because of the fight and the obvious lack of a single master to follow Stalin, this was a time of great weakness within the Party leadership. Had the U.S.S.R. been faced with an aggressive American diplomatic policy on the international scene, the Party leaders might have been in real trouble. As it was they needed only to fend off possible discontent within the Soviet Union and deal summarily with their one foreign crisis, the East German revolt of 1953. The Soviet people they soothed with a modified program of bread and circuses, i.e. the obvious, if slight, concessions to the consumer made by the Malenkov régime. A great show was made also of weakening the State Security mechanism and erecting some safeguards for individual rights.

The second stage was the "Thaw" and reaction in 1956–57. The decision to "desanctify" Stalin was probably taken late in 1955 by Khrushchev, who was aware of the void left by the great dictator. Just as people in the early Stalin period had grumbled that "things wouldn't be like this if Lenin were alive," a tendency had grown to look wistfully back to the Stalin era whenever the régime showed shortcomings. Pushed by Mikoyan's anti-Stalin overtures, Khrushchev in his secret speech at the Twentieth Party Congress probably denounced Stalin in more sweeping terms than he had intended. But the basic intention was long planned.

The 1956 denunciations rang strangely in the ears of Party stalwarts. Two years after Nikolay Voznesensky's execution in 1949, Deriabin had attended a meeting in the State Security officers' club in Moscow. There Khrushchev, as head of the Moscow Party organization, explained in great detail the horrors of the Leningrad conspiracy. In his opinion they fully "justified the steps Comrade Stalin had taken" to eliminate the conspirators. This was only one example of Khrushchev's complicity in Stalin's decision-making.

Khrushchev's denunciations of the "cult of personality" for a time made him seem allied to generally liberal influences inside the U.S.S.R. So did his breezy manner, his well-publicized urge to travel, his sense of humor, and fondness for personal investigation. Visitors from foreign countries who met him continued to be impressed by his candor and apparent familiarity with what non-Soviet minds are thinking; a tribute, if nothing else, to his assiduous daily reading of U.S. and European press translations.

Yet Khrushchev's third period, which began in 1957, has in fact meant for the Soviet people a subtle return to the fetters of one-man rule. Much of his repression Khrushchev manages to conceal behind the billboard of a naturally outgoing personality. Like the old-fashioned American political boss of a bygone day and conspicuously unlike the recent image of Stalin, he has the knack of mingling cheerfully with crowds at the Soviet equivalent of a Sunday school picnic scant minutes after he has pulled off the most ruthless sort of political treachery or blackmail in the privacy of his own office.

Internationally he has profited by the success of the *sputniks* and the Soviet missile program. On the one hand he has used the prestige of Soviet scientific accomplishment to foster the view that the U.S.S.R. is pledged to honest international co-operation at the technical level, its scientists constantly ready to meet their foreign colleagues at international conferences (while their families remain in the Soviet Union). On the other hand he has used the threat of Soviet missile aggression as a premise for a series of international thrusts and jabs, of which the latest is the attempt to run the Western powers out of Berlin.

The scientific progress has helped strengthen his régime by its appeal to the considerable patriotic pride of the Russian people. The international adventuring has helped distract them from domestic failings like Khrushchev's sometimes disastrous experiments in agricultural production. It also continues the illusion that Communism is a vital, expanding international force. In the minds of the Soviet leadership it is vital to perpetuate this illusion among the people.

The new criminal code is hailed as a return to "revolutionary legality," although some of its provisions are more severe than the code used in Stalin's time. Soviet tourists are allowed to visit foreign countries in numbers greater than ever before permitted. The supply of available consumer goods is slightly but ostentatiously increased. A certain amount of free expression is permitted. At least surveillance has been minimized and arrest and prosecution of "anti-Soviet" elements for the moment slackened.

Such "thaw"-like phenomena are not unknown in Soviet history. It was Stalin, after all, who presided over the closing stages of the New Economic Policy and himself braked the excesses of collectivization with his memorable "dizzy with success" editorial. It is not difficult to see these outward signs as in part a response to popular pressure, in part mere popularity maneuvers made by a dictator who has not yet nailed down his job as tightly as he would like.

What are the signs of Khrushchev's hardening policy? In the first place Party rule has been enormously strengthened. For the time being Khrushchev has nipped in the bud the emerging healthy tendency of the Soviet manager class, the professionals, the official government (as opposed to the Party government) bureaucrats, and in particular the intellectuals to speak for themselves as representatives of definite class interests among the Russian people, not merely interlocking sections at the base of the New Class leadership.

In the new Seven Year Plan Khrushchev has called on the Soviet people for new sacrifices with scant return, on the Stalin model. His plan for colonizing the virgin lands in Siberia involves the resettling of one million members of the Komosomol: one way of solving the Soviet youth problem. It will be the largest forced migration in Soviet life since the death of Stalin.

Ideological censorship on the Soviet Union's writers is in some ways firmer than it has been since the days of Zhdanov's socialist-realism crusade after World War II. The Pasternak crisis in 1958 only dramatized an existing policy.

In foreign policy Khrushchev has taken anything but a "soft" line. The "revisionism" that he once supported in the satellite countries is now the deadly sin of Communism, exactly as Trotskyism was at an earlier time. "Peaceful coexistence" is no longer mentioned in international conferences. Tito, once Khrushchev's friend, is branded an enemy. Nagy is dead. Gomulka is under fearful pressure.

It would be foolish to confuse Khrushchev's practicality, in this connection, with any substantial shift in Soviet thinking. He has inaugurated a new era of economic cooperation with the East European satellites, for instance, because he keenly realizes that the events culminating in the 1956 Hungarian and Polish revolutions cannot be completely undone. The degree of Soviet plundering tolerated by Eastern Europe in the late forties would not be tolerated today without serious internal disturbances. But he will hang on to Berlin at any cost, as long as he feels the U.S.S.R. is in a strong position militarily, because he knows how essential Berlin is to the Soviet hold over the satellites. His gestures toward West Berlin are a move to eliminate what he realizes is a great potential present Soviet weakness and potential Soviet defeat.

Neither Beria nor Malenkov were this adamant. At the time of the June 1953 revolt, Beria remarked, "I have said for a long time that the Germans love to eat white bread with butter and to drink coffee in the morning, which is the reason why we cannot force them to build socialism." Beria's tendency was to cut Soviet losses abroad wherever possible, without worrying about further expansion. And his substitution of native minority groups for Russians, as noted, indicated some liberalism on this score, whatever was behind it. Malenkov, for his part, was probably prepared to accept some kind of workable co-existence with the non-Communist world.

Not so Khrushchev, or at least not unless he is forced to. He is a Russian expansionist, and he has little truck with minority groups inside or outside the U.S.S.R.

The seal was set on Khrushchev's brand new dictatorship at the Twenty-first Party Congress of the CPSU in January 1959. The Congress was a one-man show. It was dominated by Khrushchev even more completely than the more recent congresses under Stalin. Virtually every speaker lauded the "vivid, creative Marxism-Leninism" of Nikita Sergeyevich Khrushchev, and the rounds of applause were greater than anything heard since the last dictatorship. Nikita Sergeyevich, who has already resumed the Stalinesque habit of reviewing parades in a general's uniform (a promotion to marshal will doubtless soon follow), has already become a sanctified Party theorist. The Khrushchev five-foot shelf of Party writings (headed by his most recent best-seller, *Towards Victory and Peaceful Competition with Capitalism*) is becoming as obligatory an item on Party members' bookshelves as the former collected works of Lenin and Stalin.

Khrushchev's sixty-fifth birthday celebration on April 17 was marked by a wave of "spontaneous" demonstrations, meetings, and greetings. By contrast, the eighty-eighth anniversary of Lenin's birth was celebrated quietly, with no more prominent an official than Brezhnev, one of the Central Committee secretaries, in attendance.

Yet Khrushchev is not completely the boss even inside the Communist Party. The upheavals of the post-Stalin time set off a chain reaction which has not yet ended. The rising educational level of the Soviet people has stirred a faint breath of discontent in the country, a striving for a better life.

A need to forestall dissatisfaction was noticeable even at the Party Congress in the energetic way in which Khrushchev kept circulating among the delegates, like a watchful ward heeler at an old-fashioned political clambake. This was true even after his decisive victory over the last survivals of the "anti-Party" group: Malenkov, Molotov, Kaganovich, and the self-accusing Bulganin. With him constantly were Anastas Mikoyan, the obliging Old Bolshevik, so useful as an index of a régime's continuity, and Khrushchev's new right-hand man, one Aleksey Kirichenko, the hatchet man of the régime. "Here," Nikita Sergeyevich would be saying in effect, "is the warrant of my legitimacy on one side and a representative of my new order on the other."

This explains Khrushchev's obsession with international politics. Where democratic statesmen hold their positions by virtue of elections and constitutional mandates, a Soviet leader holds his by a peculiar combination of power and prestige. Although the power element in Khrushchev's rule was increasing in 1959, he still had to depend on keeping up his prestige—or better still, his reputation as *the* member of the Soviet leadership who can run things best—and to this end his achievements on the domestic scene are daily dramatized by press and Party. They are susceptible to embarrassingly possible contradiction, however, even in the field of agriculture, where Khrushchev constantly boasts of his *expertise* but where, in fact, he is gambling heavily.[1]

The easy way, therefore, to serve himself up to public

[1] So far, the gamble seems to be paying off: Khrushchev's bold decision to open up the virgin lands, against considerable Party opposition, has been rewarded finally with good weather and a record harvest in 1958. His transfer of machinery from the tractor stations to individual collective farms, a revolutionary break with traditional Bolshevik thinking, is almost complete. At the Central Committee Plenum in December 1958, where an abject Bulganin apologized, in the name of the "anti-Party" group, for obstructing a farm program "of genius," his ebullient onetime stable-mate gave some impressive statistics on vastly increased Soviet farm production. In discrediting the "humbug" figures given by Malenkov in 1952, however, Khrushchev was almost certainly fudging his own. He is committed by the Seven Year Plan to an increase of seventy percent in agricultural production by 1965.

In order to achieve this fantastic expansion Khrushchev cannot rely on paper figures but must put real pressure on the peasants to improve their efficiency. Potential harvests are at the mercy of the weather, there is not much more land to be opened up, and there is a grave shortage of manpower because of war losses. Khrushchev has already achieved the enlargement of collective farms by mergers, and he is working hard at raising the economic level of collective farms and introducing urban communal services into the villages. His detailed proposals, however: *agrogorods,* where workers can be housed in apartment buildings with communal services, and the transfer to the collectives of privately owned garden plots and livestock, would take away not only considerable means of support but the last vestiges of independence allowed to the *kolhoznik.* So far Khrushchev has concentrated on advocating better scientific research (he has even rehabilitated some of Lysenko's less extreme ideas) and more efficient organization within the Ministry of Agriculture, but the real gamble is whether he can make a success of his ambitious program without having to abandon caution and his facsimile of popularity with the peasants.

view is as a leading patron of the sciences, i.e. *sputniks*, and
a sure-footed diplomatist who keeps world peace by frus-
trating the complex designs of the encircling capitalists.

A thrust into the Middle East, threats against Berlin,
even the diversion suggested by Khrushchev to Mao Tse-
tung in the Quemoy area, each such maneuver not only
distracts the Soviet public (and more importantly the Party
rank-and-file) from its own immediate situation, but it ce-
ments trust in Khrushchev as the one man who can handle
the job. There is also at issue here a basic urge of Russian
nationalism to get itself recognized as equal, if not superior,
to the older powers of the West. When Khrushchev goes to
the summit for a talk with the American President, for
instance, it is no small prestige victory. He can say, in effect: "Look. It is I, Nikita Sergeyevich, whom the big foreign powers want to talk with—no one else. See how they
refused summit conversations with Malenkov or Molotov or
those people. But with me and with *my* Soviet Union they
must reckon."

To an extent this can be done by the normal tempo of
Soviet drum-beating. In May 1959 Soviet embassies
throughout the world released a new official biography of
Khrushchev which showed how the destroyer of the personality cult had envolved, since he cut Stalin down to size.
Noting that he is a "Leader of the Lenin type," the biography added, without any consciousness of the irony involved, that "when Khrushchev makes a speech you get the
impression that actually he is just thinking aloud and putting your own ideas into words." His 1956 exposé of Stalin
at the Twentieth Party Congress was hailed as demonstrat-
ing "his complete frankness with the masses, even in cases
involving extremely complex political problems." (The
speech, incidentally, has never been made public in the Soviet Union, outside limited Party circles.)

The most revealing sign of Khrushchev's final grab for
power is the maneuvering inside the State Security. It was
December 25, 1958, when he replaced the veteran Chekist
General Ivan Serov with the young Communist Party
leader, Aleksey N. Shelepin, then only forty-one years old.
The replacement was far from the much-advertised down-
grading of the State Security apparatus. Quite to the con-

trary, it was the last step in consolidating the State Security's power in one man's hands.

Serov, a career officer with the confidence of the State Security professionals, had played a dangerous game during the Time of Troubles. Although generally pro-Khrushchev he was in a sense an arbitrator between Khrushchev and the opposing anti-Party faction. He manipulated the bloodless purges of Malenkov *et al.* from positions of power just as preceding heads of the State Security had rigged the purges for Stalin. Like them, Serov knew too much. His replacement by a veteran Party man exactly parallels Stalin's replacement of Yagoda with Nikolay Yezhov in 1938.

Khrushchev had done exactly the same thing two years before when he dismissed Kruglov as head of the MVD in 1956, substituting a Party functionary named Dudorov.

Shelepin's choice assures Khrushchev of a faithful functionary in a post absolutely vital to his security, a functionary who can be trusted to purge any non-Khrushchev dissidents, without evolving any new factions of his own. Shelepin's background is in youth activities. He was made First Secretary of the Komsomol in the last year of Stalin's dictatorship, and continued in that post until his KGB assignment. With a young man from the junior branch of the Party in charge the State Security will doubtless not seem so terrible.

His selection is a two-edged sword for Soviet youth. The growing restlessness of the younger Soviet generation is the great barrier in the way of reinstituting a firm one-man dictatorship. The very fact of Shelepin's background points a finger at the trend of State Security activities in the near future. The youth are target No. 1.

The following extract is taken from an article in *Leningradskaya Pravda* (March 5, 1959). Titled "They Are Losing the Dignity of Soviet Man," it is intended to justify the increasingly heavy police surveillance of the Soviet Union's younger generation, which is clearly all too susceptible to non-Party influences:

... The young workers (male and female) are devoting all their strength to the further development of industry and agriculture. However, in our harmonious and robust young family, there are people who scorn the standards of Communist morals. They do not wish to heed our rules of life. By conducting themselves in an unseemly manner, certain people lose the dignity of the Soviet man and in a number of cases put themselves on the road to crime . . .

"Preferring a parasitic existence to honest labor, these 'stilyagi' (stylish ones) humiliate the dignity of the Soviet man. Carried away by foreign films and the music of low-standard jazz, collecting reproductions of pictures of bourgeois formalist artists and even pornographic postcards, the majority of the 'stilyagi' are beginning to kneel down blindly before the flashy exterior of the Western culture. As a rule, these are morally rotten people . . . parasites, spongers and detractors of all that is dear to every Soviet person.

After citing many examples of youthful high living, *Leningradskaya Pravda* gets down to business:

Life shows that it is among such 'heroes' that people can be found who fall easily under the influence of bourgeois ideology.

In their violent anger against the Soviet Union, the imperialists are not squeamish about using any means to cause damage to our fatherland. Secret intelligence work occupies a prominent position in their arsenal. . . .

More than one instance can be cited in which people leading an amoral form of life—i.e. blindly bowing down before 'Western culture' because of their political indifference—fell into the hands of the intelligence services of the capitalist countries . . .

"We not infrequently still meet people," remarked Comrade N. S. Khrushchev in his report to the 21st Congress of the CPSU, 'who unscrupulously profit by the public labor, who are engaged in speculation, who break discipline and disturb public order. It is impossible to wait quietly for these remnants of capitalism to disappear by themselves. It is necessary to conduct a decisive battle against them, to direct public opinion against all kinds of manifestations of bourgeois views and customs and against anti-Soviet elements.'

According to our deep conviction the time has come for a wide segment of the public to take more decisive measures where the 'stilyagi' are concerned.

"During the last few years the Leningrad Directorate of the KGB under the Council of Ministers of the U.S.S.R., along with the punitive measures applied to actual enemies of the Soviet state, has widely used measures of warning and prevention against those who go astray or temporarily fall under the influence of others. This is especially the case with young people . . . We must, through our organs of the militia, courts and prosecutors, apply even more decisive measures of suppression of their anti-social activities.

To accompany the new youth activities of the State Security, there has been a steady revival in the Soviet press of laudatory references to the KGB and its "Chekists." "It is our task," as Shelepin puts it, "incessantly to strengthen the State Security organs, even more actively to catch the imperialist spies and scouts, and expose in time all the designs and political intrigue of the enemy."

At the elections to the Supreme Soviet in March 1959, at least forty-nine generals and chairmen of the State Security, MVD, and border troops were elected as deputies, an intrusion of the police arm into the formal politics of the U.S.S.R. which not even Stalin attempted. In certain border republics State Security control is complete in form as well as in practice. In Uzbekistan, for instance, half of the members of the republic's Supreme Soviet are leaders of the KGB, MVD, or border troops.

Deriabin himself has seen enough evidences that the State Security is as internationally active as ever. Shortly after the opening of the Brussels World Fair in 1958 he happened to glance at a New York Sunday newspaper article showing four typical "visitors" from the Soviet pavilion making a friendly visit to the U.S. exhibit. Two of them he recognized immediately as officers of the Foreign Intelligence Directorate. (One of them, a captain, had been at school with him in Moscow.) A month later he went to the New York appearance of the Moiseyev Folk Dancers. He was surprised to find his old friend, Lieutenant Colonel Aleksandr A. Kudryavtsev, sharing in the curtain calls. He had not displayed much zeal for dancing in his previous assignment as a State Security officer in Western Europe.

In 1957 the well-received Soviet construction delegation to the United States included another KGB acquaintance of Deriabin's, Major Sergey A. Zagorsky. The Major was listed simply as a "construction engineer," although his last previous job had been the unconstructive task of putting incriminating evidence into the dossiers of East German officials. The year before, a religious delegation sent "spontaneously" by the Russian Orthodox Patriarch of Moscow arrived in New York and Chicago on a goodwill visit to U.S. churchmen. Regrettably the leading ecclesiastic on the tour was the same Metropolitan Nikolay whom Deriabin had escorted briefly in Vienna on a previous occasion. The Metropolitan is a State Security agent of long standing. This is not surprising in view of the fact that the official spokesman for the Orthodox Church in the U.S.S.R., G. G. Karpov, is a major general in the State Security. (His title, for the record, is Chairman of the Council of Russian Orthodox Church Affairs in the U.S.S.R.)

There are rarely more than two KGB members in any Soviet (visitors) delegation abroad. Generally only one is necessary. But one is always there, and the lie implicit in these hidden ambassadors pervades every action of Soviet international relations. (Even the most intense American champions of world student co-operation have lately grown nettled at the prevalence of forty-year-old "student" leaders on exchange missions.)

In sum, the beast has changed his spots slightly, but he has not gone away. The advertised softening of the State Security has been only a prelude to its consolidation as an agent of the new dictator. Just as a restrictive personal dictatorship is the inevitable by-product of Soviet Communism, the State Security remains the necessary tool of the dictator and the Party through which he rules.

EPILOGUE

by Peter Deriabin

A READER WHO has reached this point in the book will probably have one big question in his mind: what happened to Peter Deriabin after his escape from Vienna in 1954? As the person most intimately concerned, I should like to give an answer. Because of the nature of my former work and the understandably sharp reaction of the Soviet régime to my "defection" the answer cannot include all the details I would wish. Suffice it to say that I have been living in the United States since that time, engaged in a dual kind of study.

On the one hand I have been working with various American scholars on the Soviet Union, giving them and their students the benefit of my particular experience and knowledge of how the Soviet state operates. At the same time, I have been deep in my own study of the United States. It is a study that goes far beyond the transition from one country to another. For a Soviet citizen, a product of Soviet society, finds when he enters the world outside that he must re-learn how to use certain human rights and privileges of which he has been long deprived. Parts of his soul and his character have almost atrophied from disuse—in particular, that most prized of human attributes, the workings of a man's free choice.

On the material level I was, of course, overwhelmed on my first visit to the United States. What I saw in Vienna had prepared me somewhat for it. But I could not have imagined the abundance, the cars, the colors, the supermarkets, the multitude of small services in American life. You must forgive me for suspecting at first that all this abundance I saw was some clever program arranged for my benefit. After all, I had been raised since childhood on propaganda describing the evils and misery of capitalist countries. Long before I left the Soviet Union I had begun to recognize this Soviet propaganda as such. Nonetheless, some of it sank in and unconsciously affected my judgments.

It is difficult for a native-born American to comprehend the wonder with which a former Soviet citizen views the smallest aspects of American life. The neon signs for example. Moscow has its neon signs, but a shop-keeper can only use one if he is prepared to do without electricity for something else. And why advertise anyway? If you have goods in Moscow people will buy them, because goods are always scarce.

I was startled by movies which run continuously. In Moscow going to a cinema theater is an event which must be long planned. You must make your reservations and buy a particular seat. As for an institution like the American drive-in movie, I found it fascinating. Had someone in Moscow told me it existed I would have laughed.

American TV, I know, is much attacked by American critics for its overadvertising, its saturation with westerns, etc. I for one found westerns very useful as a painless device for getting something of the atmosphere of American history. Although the advertising could be less frequent it is worth looking at some boring commercials for the privilege of turning one program off and getting another. In Moscow there is only one television station to look at. You can look at it, that is, if you are lucky enough to get a set and if you are yourself a skilled enough mechanic to keep the set in good repair.

Americans drink more than Russians, but they handle their liquor better. The Americans drink socially. Russians drink in bouts, to forget or to celebrate. "Life is very good," as the man in the Moscow story said to his friend, "let's have a drink." "Life is very bad," his friend replied, "let's have another."

American police are a far cry from their Soviet counterparts. If an American traffic cop stops a motorist he gives him a ticket. If a Soviet militiaman stops him he gives him also a monumentally boring moral pep-talk which sometimes lasts for a half-hour. To say nothing of the heavy penalties exacted for even minor transgressions.

I must be forgiven for beginning my impressions of the United States on a material level, but it is inevitable from my Soviet background. Despite all the Soviet press denunciations about materialism in the capitalist countries the fact remains that four decades of Communism have made real materialists out of the Russian people, in the most elementary sense of the word. Russians have to be materialists in a society where the supply of things necessary for a good life, or even a subsistence life, has constantly been sacrificed to the building of unproductive factories or wasteful war materials, let alone the extravagances of the Communist Party's New Class. So the average citizen is reduced to the level of constant worry about satisfying basic material wants for himself and his family. Any people would be materialists in this situation.

Yet the very choice I have observed among material products in the United States leads me to the big, overwhelming difference between this country or other free countries and the Soviet system. An individual may decide for himself. I know this is something which American politicians like to talk about in their Fourth of July speeches; freedom is a thing in which Americans take a justified pride. But no one can properly appreciate freedom unless he has been once deprived of it. When I look back on the conditions of my life in the Soviet Union I think of freedom of choice as a truly wonderful thing.

Political freedom has impressed me even more forcibly than economic freedom. For many months after I came to the United States I was afraid to criticize anything in this country for fear I might be doing wrong. Since I arrived in the U.S. during the McCarthy hearings, with all their charges and counter-charges, you can understand that I was doubly diffident. But the very fact that these hearings could be held in public amazed me. Gradually I came to understand that free criticism is at the root of the American system. It still makes me slightly nervous to hear the

President and other high American officials violently criticized—a relic of my past experience. But what a welcome
change.

The most amazing thing about this system of free choice
and questioning is that it works. From my earliest school
days in the Soviet Union I had been taught the contrary.
Private businesses do things here with ease and informality,
yet the productivity rate is astonishingly high. In the Soviet
Union workers toil hard and noisily, but their productivity
rate is low by compariosn.

Similarly I cannot forget the contrast between the behavior of American and Soviet officials. When I first visited
the Capitol in Washington I was startled to find so few
guards or security devices in operation. Even more startling
was the sight of U.S. congressmen having lunch in their
unpretentious restaurant, with a stream of visitors passing
through, or mingling with crowds of tourists in the Capitol
corridors. In the Soviet Union deputies to the Supreme Soviet or members of the Central Committee would be eating
in grand style, behind well-guarded closed doors. Yet no
Soviet citizen would believe that the U.S. Congress operates
this way unless he saw it for himself. As the old Russian
saying goes, "A Russian doesn't believe what he sees until
he touches it."

There are naturally some things in American life which
I might criticize. I never cease to be amazed at the dullness
of so much food that comes from so many spotless, mecha-
nized kitchens. Perhaps it would help if American women
spent more time there, instead of continually asserting their
independence. I must confess that American women puzzle
me. They appear to be frank and sometimes almost mascu-
line in their expression; but they conceal their inner selves
and emotions, sometimes in a highly involved manner.

On a more serious level I think that American schools
could do with more discipline and more hard work. The
students I have met too often seek out the *easiest* way to
get through school and college, instead of setting out to
learn something. Too often they are only interested in how
to earn more money. That should not be the primary purpose of an education.

This is not to say that Soviet schools are better. I have
been amused by the extreme statements of some Americans

about the virtues of Soviet education, since the *sputnik* alarm. Actually the Soviet Union puts all its energies into a few very good schools and universities. The average level of Soviet education is below that of education in the United States.

Taking the last five years as a whole, I have found the transition to life in America sometimes hard, generally fascinating. But in almost every department of life it has been easier than I had at first thought. It has been made easy, principally, by the outgoing character of the American people. Americans resemble Russians in this respect. It is easier for a Russian to feel at home in this country than anywhere in Europe.

I speak as a Russian. And some part of me will always remain with my Russian land, with the unspoiled country of the Altai, the rushing rivers coming down from the mountains, the steep gorges covered with budding birch. It is hard to blot this country from a man's memory. Its fresh beauty has a deep hold on the soul.

Had I continued as a teacher in the Altai I would have never left this land. Had I entered some other avenue of endeavor—engineering, literature, or science—and risen within this field to some prominence in Moscow, I would probably have remained, remained as millions of my countrymen today, knowing that something was wrong with their leadership and their system, but lacking the means to correct this wrong or even the voice to criticize it. But I went down a road which took me deep inside the Soviet leadership. I saw the diseased body as it really is, as very few Russians are ever permitted to see it. After this I could not remain. In a very real sense I think of myself as a counterpart of that fictional character of Chesterton's, *The Man Who Knew Too Much*.

How long the evil system of Khrushchev, like the evil system of Stalin before him, will be able to keep down the rising, but still mute feeling of the Russian people for a better life and a better world, no man can now say. It will not be indefinitely. Russia has a score to settle with Communism some day. But no one can predict just how the score will be settled. Perhaps release will only come through the long steady erosion of the Soviet system. This may take decades.

I do know that the one hope for cleansing my mother country of Communism comes from the very presence of America, the country which official Soviet propaganda denounces as the constant "enemy." I shall be content and proud if what we have written here helps the people of the United States, who directly decide their own destinies, to an understanding of how long, how complicated, but how necessary is their struggle against Khrushchev's New Class system of Soviet Communism. It is a struggle which free people can and must win. They can win only if they act seriously and with strength, in full knowledge that the friends of freedom are not so weak, its enemies not so strong.

ORIGINAL EPILOGUE

IN THE FIRST edition of this book in 1959, I told of my first impressions of the United States, above all of my wonder at its freedoms. Today, I still feel that wonder, although this has now been my own country for more than 25 years.

Today my wonder is mixed with concern. This marvelous country of ours is still deeply engaged in that war of which my coming to the West was an episode. Yet many Americans seem not to recognize it. Perhaps my book, in its time, helped people understand Soviet methods; many others came out of the Soviet Union after me with their own experiences, confirming mine. Yet, it hasn't been enough: the people of these comfortable lands still find it hard to believe what we've been telling them about their danger.

I shake my head in amazement when I read that the Cold War is over and that we live today in a different era. Clearly the words "detente" and "peaceful coexistence" mean different things to many Americans than they do to Soviet leaders. Have the latter stopped saying they are hastening our inevitable doom? Have their institutions, their weapons, their methods changed? As a former insider who has closely followed Soviet events, I can answer: No. Whatever our theorists and optimists may say, the Soviet regime has not changed and has never let up its efforts to destroy our system. It cannot: our liberties, like the "Solidarity" trade union in Poland, represent a frightening threat to the Soviet leaders' power over their own people.

For my part, during my quarter century in the West, I have never felt that I could let up in the struggle I began on that snowy February day in Vienna in 1954. Part of my fight has taken place on what the Soviets like to call "the invisible front." I long co-operated with western intelligence agencies, providing what the CIA described as "a wealth of research data of vital importance." In turn they helped keep me up to date on events and people inside the USSR.

But much of my fight against Soviet power has taken place in the fields of scholarship and publicity. After writing *The Secret World* I did a year of Soviet and American studies at the graduate school of an American university, and had opportunities there, and at other universities, to exchange knowledge and viewpoints with such distinguished American scholars as Bertram D. Wolfe. I lectured to diverse groups and organized courses in Soviet realities for a number of government agencies and private institutions. I testified four times before the U.S. Congress on the subversive operations of the Soviet state security, the KGB, and participated in television panel discussions. I wrote another book, describing those "Watchdogs of Terror," the Kremlin leaders' guards, in which I had served. Through my earlier association with Frank Gibney, I had the privilege of selecting and translating *The Penkovskiy Papers*, the legacy of a brave Soviet military intelligence officer who fought Soviet tyranny on the most dangerous front: behind the lines, on the inside. (This task had personal associations for me: I had served in the Red Army under Penkovskiy's father-in-law, General Gapanovich.) For decades, I have closely reviewed most of the Soviet books, magazines, and newspapers in my field and have talked to many who emigrated from the U.S.S.R. after I did. And I am now writing another book.

My private life in the West has been rich and fulfilling. I married happily and raised an American son of whom I have many strong reasons to be proud. I have traveled through this great and varied continent, fished off its coasts and in its lakes and rivers, tried my hand (without notable success) at sports I had never known in the U.S.S.R., and have made good and true friends. But it was not easy

at the beginning, I must admit; I didn't speak English well
and western ways are different. So much liberty confuses a
"Soviet man," who is used to having all important decisions
made for him. I drank heavily for a time. And then as my
English improved and I began to recognize the opportunities open before me, I settled down. I went to school to
improve my English—and to observe and participate in
American scholarship on the U.S.S.R. I saw there was a
place for my knowledge and skills—even a strong need for
them.

And I have never regretted for a moment my decision
for liberty. The Soviet regime condemned me to death—
although there was no other way out of the KGB—and its
murder squads have surely tracked me. That is their way;
they know only violence. As you have seen from this book,
in that milieu, I too found it natural to plan the kidnapping
and murder of opponents of Soviet Power. Here in the
West I've found tolerance and freedom from fear—a blessing
which can only be fully appreciated in its absence.

Let us look briefly at what the Soviet Government has
said about me since I left "The Secret World." As reported
in *Possev* (No. 6 for June 1977), in 1969 and 1971 the
KGB issued a top secret document entitled "List of Agents
of Foreign Intelligence Services, Traitors to the Motherland, Members of Anti-Soviet Organizations, Individuals
Who Participated in Punitive Acts and Other Wanted
Criminals" (Alfavitnyy spisok agentov inostrannykh razve-
dok, izmennikov Rodiny, uchastnikov antisovetskikh organ-
izatsiy, karateley i drugikh prestupnikov, podlezhashchikh
rosysku). The "KGB Wanted List" consists of 460 pages,
describing in alphabetical order about 2,000 persons subject
to arrest on the territory of the U.S.S.R. and abroad. There is
a brief biographical sketch of each. My name appeared on
page 115 with the following information:

Deriabin, Petr Sergeyevich, born 1919 in the Village
of Lokot', Yel'tsovka District, Altay Kray, until 1953
lived in Moscow City. Former officer of the KGB and
member of the CPSU [Communist Party of the Soviet Union]. *Education*: In 1938 was graduated from
the Teachers College in Biysk, Altay Kray. [*Description*:] Medium height, thick-set, wide shoulders, one
shoulder higher than the other, black hair, round face,

green eyes, chin with dimple, pigeon-toed, he has scars
from wounds on the leg and on the shoulder-blade.
[*Relatives*:] *Wife*: Makeyeva, Marina Semenovna, lives
in Moscow. *Sister*: Prilepskaya, Valentina Sergeyevna,
lives in Altay Kray.

Deriabin, while in Austria, on 15 February, 1954,
fled to the American Zone of occupation, established
contact with American intelligence and gave away information known to him about the work of the U.S.S.R. organs of state security. Subsequently Deriabin was taken
to the U.S.A.

On 20 September 1957, the Military Collegium of the
U.S.S.R. Supreme Court sentenced Deriabin to death in
absentia. A photograph and sample of [his] handwriting
are available. His Investigative File is in the Second
Chief Directorate of the KGB under the Council of
Ministers of the USSR. (Previously Deriabin was on the
"KGB Wanted List" for 1963, p. 362, second from top).

At least "The Wanted List" provided more or less correct information (of course with important omissions) as
compared with Moscow Radio's broadcast in English on
March 20, 1959, three days before the first installment of
The Secret World was published in *Life* magazine. The announcer provided another version of my biography. In the
twelve-year interval between the radio broadcast (1959)
and the publication of the "KGB Wanted List" (1971), the
KGB and the U.S.S.R. Supreme Court had "found out" that
I was an "officer of the KGB organs," not just "a rank-
and-file employee in the office of Soviet property in Austria," but had forgotten that I had "stolen large sums of
money" and "speculated on the black market" and had
"managed to marry four times."

Confirming that I had "graduated from the Teachers
College in Biysk City," The "KGB Wanted List" omitted
very important information about my education and active
participation in World War II. It failed to say that I
graduated from the Higher Counterintelligence School of
SMERSH and the Institute of Marxism-Leninism of the
Moscow City Party Committee and that during my work in
the KGB I also served as Komsomol and Party Secretary. (In
1959 Moscow Radio stated that Deriabin "never even had a

high school education.") The "KGB Wanted List" was accompanied by an Order signed by Major General Chebrikov, Deputy Chairman of the KGB, to all chiefs of the Republic KGBs, military counterintelligence of the Soviet Armed Forces and Border Troops of the KGB: "Take active measures to search for criminals named in the "Wanted List", according to order of the KGB No. 00103 of April 28, 1963." Dated September 14, 1971.

The "KGB Wanted List" itself was signed by Major General Siomonchuk, Deputy Chief of the Second Chief Directorate, and by Colonel Karpeyev, Deputy Chief of the 13th (Search) Department. I knew Leonid Ye. Siomonchuk very well. In 1953 he was a Lieutenant Colonel and Chief of the Austrian Sector of the Austrian-German Department, First Chief Directorate, in Moscow KGB Headquarters. He was my supervisor shortly before my departure for Austria. During World War II he was an officer in the Executive Action Department (at that time known as Spets Buro #1). After World War II he operated in Austria and successfully ran an important agent, an Austrian-Swiss millionaire.

Four weeks after I came over to the West, my old service took on a new name, its eighth: it now calls itself the KGB. But nothing else changed. What I wrote then remains valid today; my book has not become outdated.

Even the people are the same, many of them. You may be interested to learn what became of some of my KGB colleagues, some named in the pages of this book. While I was becoming an American, they went on spying and repressing—many of them in fields which an American might find surprising.

Take my old coworker Vasiliy Romanovich Sitnikov, for example. You met him as head of the KGB spy group subverting American and British officials in Vienna during my time there. Today he does his work in the "literary" field. While I've been in the West, Russian writers have been harassed, put on trial, imprisoned and tortured, many have died or have been exiled; the best among them now live in the West as emigrants. They've been defeated and driven out of their country by the Soviet regime, working through its KGB. As one weapon in this battle, the Soviet government ratified the International Copyright Convention and ever since has been manipulating copyright laws to silence and jail writers who dared stray from narrow orthodoxy. The KGB's role is clear: Sitnikov and another old colleague of mine moved into the top leadership of the Soviet Copyright Agency as soon as it was formed, in 1973.

Well, one might say, Sitnikov had some qualifications. He got into the world of books via the KGB's "Disinformation Department" (he was its deputy chief), which spent its time planting fraudulent documents in the West, sponsoring books for the lies they spread, painting swastikas on synagogues to give the impression that Nazism was reawakening in West Germany—all sorts of things to suppress and distort truth and to confuse and mislead the West.

I didn't mention in my book my old boss, Yevgeniy Petrovich Pitovranov. He's worth a note here, because in the West I've found to my astonishment that American businessmen think, when they trade with the Soviet Union, that somehow they're dealing with their own kind over there. They even cite the U.S.S.R. "Chamber of Commerce and Industry," paralleling our own in name, which helps take care of them. Some "Chamber" that is: its First Deputy Chairman is KGB Lieutenant General Pitovranov. In my time he was head of the KGB's whole internal security apparatus, where he shared responsibility for uprooting whole nations and jailing people who so much as hinted at friendly feelings for the West. After a spell in jail himself as an associate of the infamous Viktor Abakumov, former Minister of State Security, Pitovranov headed all the KGB's spying and subversive operations abroad. Well, at least he had experience with foreigners . . . and did not deny it. While attending an international conference on the protection of patents and industrial processes in Melbourne, in 1974, Pitovranov granted an exclusive interview to discuss increasing trade between Australia and the U.S.S.R. When newspapermen asked him questions about his past work in Soviet state security he stated that he had indeed "worked with the KGB. There is a ruling that each communist must obey the laws of the Party and its political decisions. If the Party orders you to one organization or another, you must obey the Party order . . ." The Party "recommended me for this work in the Chamber of Commerce and Industry and the Chamber gave me the honor of being Senior Vice-President." Pitovranov also added: "Each nation . . . requires an organization for security. Each has its own method of approach. One is not able to judge from one's own country what goes on in other countries . . . Now I bring nations closer together." (See *The Australian* for February 28, 1974.) Noble words from the old Chekist, but they sugarcoat the facts. With the Party blessing, Pitovranov has almost a whole Department of KGB officers under his command in the U.S.S.R. Chamber of Commerce and Industry. I limit myself to mentioning here only one close associate of Pitovranov. He is my former acquaintance, KGB Colonel Khachik (Khristofor) G. Oganesyan, First Deputy Chairman of International Exhibitions and the Moscow World Trade Center under the Chamber of Commerce and Industry. He used to be a senior spy in the Near East, Germany, and Austria. Now he is making speeches for foreigners, including Americans, at the opening of Exhibitions in the U.S.S.R.

It's the same with "justice." The words "supreme court" evoke in the West a vision of law independent of government and ruling the life of the land. In the Soviet Union the first deputy chairman (you might say, deputy chief justice) was my old friend and drinking companion KGB General Sergey G. Bannikov. He had legal qualifications, all right—Soviet style: he was a SMERSH and KGB interrogator and investigator in my time, and had participated in the infamous OSOs, drumhead courts run by Soviet State Security which sentenced without trial tens of thousands to camps and jails where most of them died. The disbanding of the OSOs was one of the proud accomplishments of the post-Stalin "return to socialist legality," but as you see, the people and the work continue. (By the way, this deputy chief justice had also "advised" the Bulgarian satellite of the KGB—that service which murders its emigrés with KGB weapons such as poisoned pellets shot from umbrellas.)

I think it is also appropriate to mention here what happened to my boss in Vienna, Colonel Yevgeniy I. Kovalev (Kravtsov), the KGB Rezident, i.e., Chief of Station, in Austria. Shortly after my defection he was recalled to Moscow and held responsible for my action. As is usual in such cases, it is assumed that he was severely reprimanded by the Central Committee of the Communist Party of the Soviet Union and by the KGB Chairman, demoted with a notation in his file that he was never again to be entrusted with a senior position, such as Rezident, chief of a department or higher, and more likely dismissed from the KGB. The Moscow newspaper *Moskovskaya Pravda* announced his death on 2 August 1973, stating in a short obituary that he died "after a serious and prolonged illness." The obituary was placed by the Command and Party Committee of an unidentified "military unit." "A military unit" could also be a KGB unit such as the Higher KGB School, the Illegal or Executive Actions Departments.

My close KGB associate, Colonel Sergey L. Tikhvinskiy, whom you met in my pages handling spies in Vienna, later served in London posing as a counselor of the Soviet Embassy. He is now chairman of the Society of Soviet Historians, editor-in-chief of the magazine *Modern and Contemporary History*, and chief of the History-Diplomatic Administration (the secret archives) of the USSR Foreign Ministry, with Ambassadorial rank, and a corresponding member of the U.S.S.R. Academy of Sciences. Gone straight, you suggest? Old KGB Veterans never do: the KGB's work always comes first. And a few years ago Tikhvinskiy led a delegation of Soviet "historians" to the United States, where, among other things, he delivered a speech on human rights.

Most recently, as of January 1982, it was reported that Tikhvinskiy was in Peking, allegedly to establish a dialogue between Peking and Moscow. As I stated before, an old spy never dies. Tikhvinskiy started his "diplomatic service" in China, in 1939, as a KGB officer serving first in Sinkiang province. Later he served in China as Consul General and Counsellor of the Soviet Embassy. When relations between China and the USSR began to deteriorate, Tikhvinskiy was switched to Japan where he served as Chargé d'Affaires, directing a spy network against China.

My agent Karl Nepomnyashchiy, whom you met in these pages as a specialist in Soviet "peace" campaigns, met his end when a helicopter he was riding in was shot down by Czech resisters to the Soviet invasion in 1968.

Two of my colleagues, mentioned in this book, later gained notoriety in the West: General Ivan Ivanovich Agayants, as head of the KGB's Disinformation Department (where his deputy was Sitnikov), and Anatoliy V. Gorsky, when it was revealed that he had handled top-level spies within the British Government, including Donald Maclean.

You must not think that these are exceptional cases. I have simply mentioned a few old friends and colleagues. You can find their like throughout the Soviet state running all sorts of things which westerners think have nothing to do with subversion and repression. In the U.S.S.R. they stand front and center: the Soviet rulers hold their power only by coercion, and the KGB manages that coercion for them. In all walks of life and society.

To hold on to that power and the rich privileges which go with it, the Soviet leaders must crush all opposition, everywhere. They've done it inside the U.S.S.R. and they're still doing it abroad, in every country. Like it or not, that means us. They are sworn to wipe out our liberties—which they call "ideological subversion." The KGB is their main instrument.

I hope that republishing my book will sound the tocsin once again.

Peter Deriabin
—May, 1982

APPENDIX I

The Formal Development Of A State Security Case

IN THE FORTY-TWO years of the State Security's activities the development of a case against a suspected person has come a long way from the curt watch-and-grab technique of the early Chekists. Each type of case has its own classification and peculiar rubrics. They begin with the Preliminary Operational Check (*Predvaritelnaya Operativnaya Proverka*, "POP"), a cursory examination of all material already in the case officer's possession. The next complex operation is the Preliminary Operational Elaboration (*Predvaritelnaya Agenturnaya Razrabotka*, "PAR"), which involves a thorough check of a suspect and the opening of a file on him in the KGB offices. A Preliminary Operational Elaboration[1] must be recorded in the central files of the KGB, whatever the circumstances. Once Moscow has been thus informed the suspect's chances for ultimate release diminish by something over ninety percent The Agents' Case (*Agenturnoye Delo*) is a complicated proceeding in which a group or several persons are put under surveillance, with several agents involved in the operation. The Formal Case (*Delo Formulyar*) is a case opened on one person only, but with several agents (and several filing systems) involved.

To illustrate the thoroughness of the Soviet counter-

---

[1]In translating these technical terms into English it is almost impossible to avoid reflecting the Russian language's affinity for jawbreaking vocabulary.

intelligence mechanism inside its own country we have here appended an example showing the evolution of a Formal Case (*Delo Formulyar*), on a suspect described under the code name of *Sapozhnik*, the "Shoemaker." The case is a fictitious one (obviously the files of the KGB were not opened for the purposes of this study), but it is correct in every detail, based on Deriabin's long familiarity with these proceedings.

The case officer, one Filipov, assigned to the Borets factory in the Kaluga Oblast, begins the file on "Shoemaker," a worker named V.I. Nikolayev, after one of his agents in the factory reports evidence of an "anti-Soviet" statement. Filipov orders the agent, called by his code-name Bystryy, to put Nikolayev under surveillance. He then makes inquiries about Nikolayev to various KGB authorities. As the case shows "promise," the pace of agent reports and official re-checking quickens.

REPORT

Today, at the end of the Workers' Meeting, when our branch was given the plant's Red Banner as an efficiency and production award for the first quarter of 1954, the locksmith NIKOLAYEV, Vasiliy Ivanovich, publicly stated: "Which of us actually needs this banner? It would be much better if every worker in our branch was given 50 rubles as an award. Now this banner will be on display, but we shall still be short of food in our kitchens. I am positive that from tomorrow on our Communist Party organizer will increase his pressure on us for harder work just because we have this banner."

Workers Karpov, Mikhail, and Spiridonov, Ivan, who were standing near Nikolayev, remained silent and just looked at him.

Nikolayev has been employed in our plant for two years. He seldom fulfills the norms assigned to him and constantly talks about how to get more food and work less.

April 15, 1954

BYSTRYY

DEVELOPMENTS:

This is the first report on Nikolayev.

Agent Bystryy was ordered to continue his observation of Nikolayev.

Check Nikolayev, V. I., in the central files.

April 16, 1954

Case Officer FILIPOV

REPORT

In compliance with your order, I have had several conversations with locksmith NIKO-LAYEV. From his own words I learned that he is married, has two children, and that, prior to employment in our plant, he worked as an electrician with the Artel Elektrik, from which he was dismissed for shirking and for breaking labor discipline. However, Nikolayev installed electric lights in the apartment of the Chief of the Artel and drank vodka with him, and the latter gave Nikolayev a certificate stating that he had resigned from the Artel Elektrik.

To my question as to what relatives he has in Kaluga, Nikolayev replied that all his relatives were *nieputevyye* (had taken the wrong turning in life) : one brother (I do not remember his first name) is now serving a prison term for theft, and another was a German POW and now lives some-

where in Krasnoyarskiy Kray. According to Nikolayev, his parents died in 1930.

At the end of the above conversation, Nikolayev asked me not to repeat what he had told me
to anyone. He added that he considers me his
friend.

Once, after working hours, we went into a
pivnaya (beer parlor) where Nikolayev bought
100 grams of vodka and I bought two glasses of
beer and two sandwiches. At that time Nikolayev
told me that his wife reprimands him every time
he drinks. He added that because of his continual
lack of money and disappointment with living
conditions, he frequently gets hopelessly de-
pressed, and then he drinks. According to his own
statement, he does not read Soviet newspapers because, in his opinion, there is nothing in them
worth reading.

April 29, 1954

BYSTRYY

DEVELOPMENTS:

1. Add this report to material concerning Nikolayev, V. I.
2. Get from the plant's personnel office all
   details from Nikolayev's file and his characteristics.
3. Check his reputation at his previous place
   of work.
4. Check and verify all details given by Nikolayev in his autobiography (after a copy is
   received from the personnel office).
5. Agent Bystryy was ordered to get the exact address and full name of Nikolayev's
   brother who has been a German POW.

6. Check information concerning Nikolayev's parents. It seems to me somewhat unusual that both died in 1930—maybe they were deported kulaks.

May 4, 1954

Case Officer FILIPOV

REFERENCE

Taken from Nikolayev's personnel file:

NIKOLAYEV, Vasiliy Ivanovich, born in 1910 in the town of Kimry, Smolensk Oblast, Russian, primary school education, no court record, not a Party member, employed at the Borets plant since September 15, 1952, resides in Kaluga, House No. 5, Rasin Street, married and has two children.

Parents: Father—Nikolayev, Ivan Maksimovich; and Mother—Elisabeth Petrovna. According to statements in the files, both died in Kimry in 1930. A brother, Dorofey Ivanovich, born in 1920, lives in the town of Minusinsk, where he works as a driller in the Im. Lenina plant. Another brother, Timofey Ivanovich, born in 1922, lives in the town of Kimry and is employed as a shoemaker in the Artel Krasnyy Sapozhnik.

Nikolayev's *wife*, Vera Petrovna, born in 1913 in Kaluga Oblast, housewife, lives with him.

Children: Son - Yuriy, 12 years old
Daughter - Zina, 5 years old

May 10, 1954

Chief of Personnel Office
of Borets Plant
USTINOV

DEVELOPMENTS:

1. Check files of First Special Section in Kaluga Oblast KGB and the First Special Section of KGB in Smolensk Oblast on all persons mentioned above.
2. Check social background of Nikolayev, V. I., and his parents.
3. Check both of Nikolayev's brothers at their places of employment.

May 11, 1954

_____

Case Officer FILIPOV

TO: Chief of First Special Section KGB of U.S.S.R., Moscow
Chief of First Special Section of the KGB Directorate, Smolensk Oblast, Smolensk
Chief of First Special Section of the KGB Directorate, Kaluga Oblast, Kaluga

I would like you to inform me of any compromising material known to you concerning the following persons:

1. NIKOLAYEV, Vasiliy Ivanovich, born in 1910 in the town of Kimry, Smolensk Oblast.
2. NIKOLAYEV, Ivan Maksimovich, born in Kimry, and died in 1930.
3. NIKOLAYEVA, Elisabeta Petrovna, born in Kimry, and died in 1930 also.
4. NIKOLAYEV, Dorofey Ivanovich, born in 1920 in Kimry, and at present living in Minusinsk, Krasnoyarskiy Kray.
5. NIKOLAYEV, Timofey Ivanovich, born in 1922 in Kimry, where he presently resides.

6. NIKOLAYEVA, Vera Petrovna, born in 1913 in Kaluga Oblast.

May 12, 1954

Chief of Economic Section of KGB Directorate, Kaluga Oblast
Colonel PETROV

Chief of Subsection

CASE OFFICER: Operupolnomochennyy FILIPOV

TO: Chief of Kimry Rayon Section of KGB Directorate, Smolensk Oblast, Kimry

We would like to ask you to check the social backgrounds of the following persons:

1. NIKOLAYEV, Vasiliy Ivanovich, born in 1910 in the town of Kimry, Smolensk Oblast, and residing in Kaluga at the present time.

2. NIKOLAYEV, Ivan Maksimovich (
   (both died in 1930)

3. NIKOLAYEVA, Elisabeta Petrovna (

4. NIKOLAYEV, Dorofey Ivanovich, born in 1920, and presently residing in the town of Minusinsk.

5. NIKOLAYEV, Timofrey Ivanovich, born in 1922, and residing in Kimry.

Any compromising material known to you

concerning these persons would be very much appreciated.

May 12, 1954

> **Chief of Economic Section of KGB Directorate, Kaluga Oblast**
> **Colonel PETROV**

> **Chief of Subsection**

Case Officer: _____
Operupolnomochennyy FILIPOV

ANSWER FROM THE FIRST SPECIAL SECTION OF KGB DIRECTORATE, KALUGA OBLAST

TO: Chief of Economic Section of KGB Directorate, Kaluga Oblast

Referring to your request in Letter No. . . . , dated May 12, 1954, I would like to inform you that we have no record in our files concerning any person mentioned by you.

May 15, 1954

> **Chief** _____

ANSWER FROM THE FIRST SPECIAL SECTION KGB OF U.S.S.R.

TO: Chief of Economic Section of KGB Directorate, Kaluga Oblast

In compliance with your request No. . . . , dated May 12, 1954, I can inform you that in our files the following is recorded:

NIKOLAYEV, Dorofey Ivanovich, born in 1920 in the town of Kimry, Smolensk Oblast, a German POW from 1942 to 1945, at which time he was liberated by the Soviet Army. Files on screening of Nikolayev, D. I., No. . . . , are kept in the archives of the First Special Section of the KGB Directorate of Krasnoyarskiy Kray.

We have no information concerning any other person mentioned in your request.

May 27, 1954

Chief _____

ANSWER FROM THE FIRST SPECIAL SECTION OF KGB DIRECTORATE, SMOLENSK OBLAST

TO: Chief of Economic Section of KGB Directorate, Kaluga Oblast

In compliance with your request dated May 12, 1954, I can inform you that the following is recorded in our files:

1. NIKOLAYEV, Ivan Maksimovich, born in 1885 in the town of Kimry, was deported to Vologodskaya Oblast as a former kulak in 1930.

2. NIKOLAYEV, Timofey Ivanovich, born in 1922 in the town of Kimry, was sentenced by the court in 1953 to five years' imprisonment on the grounds of paragraph 74 of the RSFSR criminal code. He is presently serving this sentence in the Smolensk Corrective Labor Camp.

We have no information concerning the other persons mentioned in your letter.

June 1, 1954

_____

Chief _____

ANSWER FROM KIMRY RAYON SECTION OF KGB DIRECTORATE, SMOLENSK OBLAST

In compliance with your request No. ...., dated May 12, 1954, I would like to inform you that:

NIKOLAYEV, Vasiliy Ivanovich, was born in the town of Kimry in 1910. He is the son of a well-to-do handicraft man, NIKOLAYEV, Ivan Maksimovich. The latter was born in 1885, and prior to the revolution of 1917 was the owner of a shoemaking shop where he employed several laborers. After the revolution and until 1930, he had a leather-processing shop. Here too he employed several workers. In 1930 he was *raskulachen* (everything he possessed was confiscated) and he and his immediate family were deported to Vologda Oblast. Later, we received information that Nikolayev, Ivan Maksimovich, and his wife, Elisabeta Petrovna, died in Vologda in 1930.

One of Nikolayev's brothers, Timofey Ivanovich, born in 1922, was sentenced in 1953 to five years of imprisonment on the basis of paragraph 74 of the RSFSR criminal code (hooliganism and knifing a man). At the present time he is serving this sentence.

The second brother, Dorofey Ivanovich, born in 1920, according to our information, was deported to Krasnoyarskiy Kray (as a former German POW), where he still lives.

We have no other information concerning the persons mentioned by you.

_____

Chief _____

Attachments:
   Your original letter and
   reference given to us by
   the Town Council

June 15, 1954

TO: Chief of Minusinsk Town Section of KGB Directorate, Krasnoyarskiy Kray, Minusinsk

In connection with a special check of NIKOLAYEV, Vasiliy Ivanovich, we would like to have information concerning his brother, Dorofey Ivanovich, born in 1920 in Smolensk Oblast.

According to a letter from the First Special Section, KGB Directorate of U.S.S.R., NIKOLAYEV, D. I., is on their records as a German POW from 1942 to 1945. This letter also indicates that Nikolayev, D. I., lives in the town of Minusinsk, where he is employed as a driller in the plant Im. Lenina.

Nikolayev, V. I., is trying to conceal the fact that his brother Dorofey was a German POW.

Any compromising material concerning Nikolayev, D. I., known to you, and confirmation of the above-mentioned information as to his residence and place of employment would be very much appreciated.

June 17, 1954

Chief of Economic Section of KGB Directorate, Kaluga Oblast
Colonel PETROV

ANSWER FROM MINUSINSK TOWN SECTION OF KGB DIRECTORATE, KRASNOYARSKIY KRAY, MINUSINSK

In compliance with your request No. . . . . , dated June 17, 1954, we can inform you that NIKOLAYEV, D. I., born in 1920 in the town of Kimry, Smolensk Oblast, is living in the town of Minusinsk, where he works as a driller in the plant Im. Lenina.

According to our records, Nikolayev, D. I., was a German POW from 1942 to 1945, when he was liberated by the Red Army. He was then sent to Soviet Screening Camp No. 12 in Poland, and on the basis of a decision by the Special Screening Committee was sent to Krasnoyarskiy Kray for permanent residence. The main reason for this decision was the fact that Nikolayev, D. I., had joined the Vlasov army.

Nikolayev, D. I., is constantly under the surveillance of our agents.

We have no other information concerning this person.

July 20, 1954

Chief _____

REPORT

After work yesterday evening, I left the plant with NIKOLAYEV, V. I., and accompanied him to the streetcar stop. On the way, Nikolayev told me he had recently received a letter from his brother, who is serving a five-year sentence for hooliganism. Nikolayev said his brother had stated in his letter that he had never knifed anyone and that he had been sentenced unjustly.

Nikolayev, V. I., while speaking of the Victory Day celebration, stated: "What a funny victory we got—we won the war but our living conditions are worse than before the war. For instance, look at the fate of my two brothers: both fought in the war, both were wounded on the battlefield, and now one is in prison and the other has been deported." To my question of why his second brother had been deported, Nikolayev answered: "Our government based its decision on the fact that my brother had been a German POW. However, nobody took into consideration the fact that my brother was captured by the Germans while wounded. Even today he limps on his right foot. Our authorities found out that he had been in the Vlasov army, but no one was interested in knowing that his only reason for joining that army was the hunger suffered by all Russians in the German POW camps. Actually, while in the Vlasov army, he worked as a cook. Now he has been deported to Siberia and there suffers from hunger and cold."

During this same conversation, I asked Nikolayev what he thinks about the arrest of Beria. He stated: "It is not worth while to talk or think about Beria because everyone sitting in the Kremlin is alike." When I said that Beria had wanted to take over the entire power of the State and become another Stalin, Nikolayev was apparently not satisfied with that explanation and said: "It is necessary to give the power to the real workers, then nobody will try to take it from them."

Shortly thereafter we came to the streetcar stop, where we parted.

July 20, 1954

BYSTRYY

DEVELOPMENTS:

1. Agent Bystryy received orders to continue surveillance of Nikolayev.
2. Because the level of Bystryy's political education is not satisfactory, I ordered Agent Krot to contact Nikolayev to study his political thinking and ideology. Krot lives in the same apartment house as Nikolayev, and therefore can easily make his acquaintance.
3. Report all material concerning Nikolayev to my superiors asking for their decision and instructions.

July 20, 1954

Case Officer FILIPOV

REPORT

Following your instructions, yesterday evening I visited NIKOLAYEV in his apartment under the pretext of asking him if he would like to go fishing next Sunday (we have fished together several times in the past).

I soon started to talk about the latest news and in particular of the latest decision by our government to improve the economic situation of workers and employees. During the conversation, Nikolayev several times stated that such decisions and regulations for improvements had been made by the thousands, but living conditions throughout the country were still very difficult. He then told me the following anecdote which he allegedly overheard in a restaurant: One Soviet citizen asked another, "Why are so many people in the Soviet Union barefooted?" The other explained that it was because of the shortage of leather. The first did not accept this explanation and stated: "Not only because we are short of leather, but because by remaining barefooted we can more easily overtake the capitalist countries in our race with them." Nikolayev added that a somewhat similar explanation could be applied to the new government regulation which actually means: "You can read this regulation, but you cannot ask for better food."

In my opinion, Nikolayev is displeased with the management of our plant. He complained that his earnings had not been increased for a long time, and criticized the labor union because it refused to give his son a free railroad ticket to go to the Pioneer camp. I have also found out that Nikolayev spreads anti-Soviet anecdotes while at work in the plant. For instance, he recently told the following story to his fellow workers: A Jew decided to escape from the Soviet Union and succeeded in getting as far as the State border line. However, at that moment he saw he had been spotted by a border guard. Therefore, he quickly lowered his trousers and squatted, pretending he wanted to relieve himself. Furthermore, he squatted directly over a spot where a dog had previously relieved himself. The border guard approached and asked what he was doing. The Jew pointed to the dog's excrement and asked: "Don't you see what I was doing?" The border guard stated that the excrement was a dog's, not a human's. The Jew then said: "Why are you surprised by that? Don't you know that life in this country is not a human's, but a dog's?" (Nikolayev told this anecdote in the presence of workers Prokop'yev and Sinitsin. I myself was standing nearby and heard every word.)

I learned that when the subscription for the State Loan was taken in our factory last May, Nikolayev, after getting home, told his wife: "Those scoundrels again forced me to subscribe to the loan."

On September 1, Nikolayev will celebrate his son's birthday and he has invited me to come for dinner. I will take advantage of this to continue similar conversations with him.

July 27, 1954

KROT

DEVELOPMENTS:

Immediately reported the above to superiors.

July 27, 1954

Case Officer FILIPOV

REFERENCE

Based on the results of a special check and preliminary information from agents concerning NIKOLAYEV, Vasiliy Ivanovich.

NIKOLAYEV, Vasiliy Ivanovich, born in 1910 in the town of Kimry, Smolenskaya Oblast, Russian, not a Party member, no court record, primary school education, locksmith employed at the Borets plant, permanent resident of Kaluga, House No. 5, Rasin Street. Married and has two children.

In the light of the preliminary information obtained from agents Krot and Bystryy, it is assumed that Nikolayev initiates among his fellow workers and neighbors malicious anti-Soviet conversations. He tells them malicious anti-Soviet anecdotes and expresses criticism of the Communist Party and Soviet Government regulations and decisions. For instance, early in April 1954, Nikolayev stated that he does not read Soviet newspapers because, in his opinion, there is nothing of interest in them.

During the same month he openly expressed dissatisfaction with the fact that the plant's periodic production award, the Red Banner, had been given to his branch. At that time he stated: "Why such great excitement about this banner? The fact that it has been placed in our recreation room will not do away with the continuous shortage of food in workers' kitchens. On the other hand, I have no doubt that our Communist Party organizer will now press for more and more productive work because this banner was given to us."

When the campaign for the subscription to the State Loan was finished, Nikolayev stated in the presence of his neighbors: "Scoundrels! They again forced us to subscribe to this loan, although everywhere it is emphasized that subscription is voluntary."

Nikolayev is concealing the fact that his father and mother were deported to and died in Siberia.

One of his brothers, NIKOLAYEV, D. I., was imprisoned by the Germans and joined Vlasov's army. At the present time he is in Kransnoyarskiy Kray, where he was deported.

A second brother, NIKOLAYEV, T. I., was sentenced by court to five years in prison for hooliganism and is now serving this term.

August 14, 1954

Case Officer FILIPOV

Decision of Chief of Section:

Immediately to open a *delo formulyar* on NIKOLAYEV, V. I., and start operational development of the case with the use of an agent network. The development of this operation should be checked.

August 15, 1954

Chief of Section

APPROVED: _____   **TOP SECRET**
              Chief of Section

DECISION

(Order to Initiate a *Delo Formulyar*)

August 17, 1954

I, Senior Lieutenant FILIPOV, Case Officer of the Second Subsection of the Economic Section of Kaluga Oblast KGB Directorate, after studying available material concerning NIKOLAYEV, Vasiliy Ivanovich, have found that:

Nikolayev, Vasiliy Ivanovich, employed at the Borets plant as a locksmith, is initiating among his fellow workers and neighbors malicious anti-Soviet conversations and spreading anti-Soviet anecdotes. This was reported by agents Krot and Bystryy.

In addition, Nikolayev, Vasiliy Ivanovich, is concealing certain details about his social background and the fact that his brother has been a prisoner of war.

On the basis of the above-stated facts I

DECIDED: to establish on Nikolayev, Vasiliy Ivanovich, the active processing (through agents) of a State Security case and to open on him a *delo formulyar*, classifying the case as anti-Soviet propaganda and anti-Soviet pronouncements.

to register this case with the First Special Section of Kaluga Oblast KGB under the cryptonym of "Shoemaker."

Case Officer FILIPOV

APPROVED: _____
Chief of Subsection

After the decision was made to open a *delo formulyar*, the investigation continued for a year. During this time not only Nikolayev but his close associates were watched carefully, for evidence of the "conspiracy" so beloved by KGB case officers. The "evidence" on Nikolayev at least was strong enough to warrant a stiff prison sentence—as noted next.

APPROVED: _____   **TOP SECRET**
Chief of Section

DECISION

(Re Transfer of File to Archives)

September 15, 1955

I, Case Officer of the Second Subsection of the Economic Section of KGB Directorate, Kaluga Oblast, Sr. Lt. FILIPOV, after study of the contents of *delo formulyar* No. . . . entitled "Sapozhnik," have found that the person with whom this case is concerned, namely NIKOLAYEV, V. I., has been arrested by the KGB Directorate, Kaluga Oblast, and sentenced by the military court of Moscow Military District to 10 years in corrective labor camp for anti-Soviet agitation and propaganda.

The contents of this file do not at this time represent any operational value for the Economic Section of the KGB Directorate, Kaluga Oblast.

Bearing these two points in mind, I have decided:

Delo Formulyar files on "Sapazhnik" concerning Nikolayev, Vasiliy Ivanovich, should be transferred to the First Special Section of the KGB Directorate, Kaluga Oblast, and deposited in the archives there.

Case Officer FILIPOV

APPROVED: _____
        Chief of Subsection

APPENDIX II

Provocation

THE DEVICE OF provocation is as old as history, if not older. Since the Serpent first interested Eve in fruit-tasting, people have sought to gain advantage by enticing antagonists to commit themselves in an atmosphere of false security. It remained for the Soviet leadership to codify this underhand technique and to reduce it as far as possible to the level of a technical operation. Almost since the beginnings of the State Security the use of provocation has been essential to the so-called *Agenturnaya Kombinatsiya,* a staple in Soviet intelligence and police work.

The following two cases illustrate the State Security's provocation methods.

I

In a *rayon* in the Karelo-Finnish Union Republic, near the Finnish border, a State Reservation guard named Trofimov[1] lived with his wife and two sons, one of whom was employed as a local forester. Hunters who had twice spent the night in Trofimov's house informed the State Security that he had expressed anti-Soviet feelings. In their opinion, he could not be considered a reliable person. On the basis of these informants' reports, the State Security decided to submit Trofimov to a secret investigation. The fact that he

[1] Pseudonyms have been used throughout this Appendix.

367

lived very close to the Finnish border doubtless influenced their decision.

It was impossible to assign an agent to this work because Trofimov and his family were the only residents in that vast forest area. The local State Security office was accordingly forced to use transients. A group of hunters was dispatched there with instructions to stay overnight in Trofimov's house to pick up confirmatory evidence. On their return, the State Security "hunters" submitted a report almost identical to that of Trofimov's previous visitors.

It was then decided to introduce an experienced and proven agent into the case, who spoke both Russian and Finnish fluently. The agent, whose name was Rylsky, was provided by the State Security with Finnish clothing, food, and other equipment. He was instructed to make the long trip on skis, approaching Trofimov's house before nighfall from the west. It was hoped this would give him the impression that Rylsky came from Finland.

As he approached the house, Rylsky was met by a barking dog. The noise at once brought Trofimov outside. When he saw the direction of Rylsky's ski tracks, he greeted him joyfully, saying, "I can see that you are our man." Inviting Rylsky into his house, Trofimov assured him he need feel no fear. Only members of his immediate family were present.

At dinner, attended by Trofimov's wife and younger son, the master of the house showed himself in excellent humor. Expansively he told Rylsky about the contrast between living conditions in the old days and at present. For his part, Rylsky offered Trofimov some Finnish cigarettes, rum, and canned food. Trofimov accepted these gifts with visible pleasure. Early the next morning the Trofimovs paid Rylsky the compliment of furnishing him with a hot bath in their *sauna*.

Before Rylsky left, Trofimov advised him as to the safest and most convenient roads and gave him the addresses of several friends in the town of Monchegorsk, stating that Rylsky could spend a night there quite comfortably and securely. Trofimov also suggested that Rylsky cease wearing Finnish clothing for fear of attracting unnecessary attention from the militia or the local population. Finally he offered Rylsky a pistol, which he had kept in a concealed place for a long time. Rylsky refused his offer, explaining that it would be better for him to continue on his way unarmed. As a last expression of their hospitality, the Trofimov family invited Rylsky to visit them again on his return trip, and the young son was told to guide him safely to Monchegorsk.

On the way, the youngster mentioned that his father occasionally used "explosives" for fishing. Questioned further, he went on to say that the explosives were part of a well-hidden cache of weapons—detonators, hand grenades, two pistols, rifles, and ammunition—which his father had hoarded in the expectation that one day he might need them. All these details Rylsky duly reported to the State Security officer in Monchegorsk.

Stimulated by this evidence, the State Security decided to develop the case further. A special *agent provocateur*, who also spoke Finnish, was carefully briefed and equipped for the mission. He too appeared on skis, in virtually the same track previously used by Rylsky. On arriving at Trofimov's house, the new agent told his host that Rylsky had reached home safely, crossing the Soviet border without incident. He gave Trofimov more Finnish cigarettes, canned food, and rum, noting that these came from Rylsky in gratitude for their hospitality.

The Trifimovs were delighted to hear that Rylsky had not forgotten them and they invited the newcomer to stay the night. The agent artfully steered the conversation to the subject of hunting, and Trofimov obligingly revealed that many of his friends from town used his house as a headquarters for their own hunting trips. They had shot an elk, an animal normally under state protection—hardly a judicious boast, coming from a game warden. Before the agent left for Monchegorsk, Trofimov went on to say that he could find a rifle in a hidden cache if he ever needed one. The agent heartily thanked him and left the following morning.

It took little deliberation for local State Security officials to decide that Trofimov and his family could be liquidated. Before their arrest, however, all people mentioned by Trofimov in his talks with the agents were put under surveillance and several were arrested. The Trofimovs were then carted off to the Monchegorsk jail.

During his interrogation, Trofimov was told that a Finnish spy had been caught on the border and confessed to Trofimov's complicity in various Finnish espionage missions. The "spy" had also admitted that Trofimov was hiding firearms. Trofimov confirmed these accusations and was sentenced to fifteen years in prison. His wife received ten years, and his sons five years each.

It is an interesting side comment on State Security procedures that at no time was Trofimov told the real identity of his *provocateurs*. As far as he knew both men were in reality Finnish agents. In this way, the accused himself was never aware that the entire case against him had been artificially developed as a result of provocation methods. It remained a moot point whether or not Trofimov actually intended to use the weapons for anti-Soviet activity. It is a further tribute to the thoroughness of Soviet punitive methods that the convicted "spy" was also found guilty of permitting illegal hunting and fishing on a state game preserve.

II

Just before World War II, the Leningrad State Security headquarters had been watching a man named Pervukhin, an employee of the city administration. Preliminary information on Pervukhin was sketchy, although he had on occasion made remarks critical of the Soviet régime. The State Security did know that Pervukhin had been seen making notations in a notebook which he kept with him at work. Informants reported that he even took the notebook with him on visits to the men's room.

The State Security was naturally eager to learn the contents of this notebook and what type of anti-Soviet activity Pervukhin was carrying on. (Any private note-taking was naturally assumed to have an anti-Soviet purpose.) But Pervukhin was an intelligent and well-educated man, who avoided any conversations and discussions, although his behavior toward authority was scrupulously correct. Therefore, it was difficult to find an agent who might logically keep him under surveillance.

For want of any of its currently employed agents, the State Security decided to engage a woman named Malysheva, who worked in Pervukhin's office. After a brief

screening, a case officer got in touch with her. Malysheva
willingly answered all his questions and told him all she
knew about Pervukhin. When he raised the point of her
actually informing on Pervukhin, however, Malysheva
flatly refused. She said, with some courage, that her religious beliefs made this impossible. Prior to the Revolution,
Malysheva explained, she had been the director of a school
restricted to children of the upper classes. Her husband
had long ago been imprisoned by the Cheka as a reactionary. She was already an old woman, she said, and no matter how powerful the State Security was, it could not force
her to do such work.

The State Security did not give up, but kept in touch
with Malysheva. In time a case officer managed to con-
vince her that it was advisable even for an old woman to
keep on good terms with the régime. Gradually she began
to give a few bits of information about Pervukhin, which
had little value. In time, however, as she became involved
in the State Security network, she developed an interest in
her work. It was, after all, flattering for an old woman to
receive so much attention.

Once the State Security gained some confidence in her,
Malysheva was ordered to watch Pervukhin carefully
throughout the office day. If ever he was to leave his notebook unguarded for a moment, Malysheva was to press a
warning button on her desk—quietly installed by the State
Security. In the course of time Pervukhin did relax his vigilance to the extent of leaving the notebook on his desk for
a few minutes. At once, Malysheva pressed the button. A
few moments later, in barely the time it takes to say "State
Security Special Surveillance" in Russian, the telephone on
Pervukhin's desk rang. He was ordered to present himself
at the personnel offices without delay. He left the room in
great excitement, forgetting to pick up the notebook. During his absence all the pages of the notebook were photo-
graphed by an agent who had been waiting for this moment.

When he returned to his office, Pervukhin was visibly
relieved to see that the notebook was still on his desk. He
put it in his pocket and continued his work. He had no way
of knowing that the State Security now knew his secret:
that he was collecting information which could be useful

for espionage purposes. Having assessed this fact, the State Security decided that Malysheva should ingratiate herself with Pervukhin. There could be no easier way than to tell him about her husband's bitter fate and all she herself had suffered because of the Soviet régime.

Pervukhin displayed cautious sympathy. He conceded that under the Soviet régime it was almost impossible to live one's life honestly and decently. Further on in their conversations he made so bold as to say it was necessary actually to fight the régime—otherwise it would be impossible for any Russian ever to maintain even simple human dignity. During all this talk, Pervukhin was careful to warn Malysheva that she must never repeat to anyone what had been said. Malysheva assured him that past experience had already taught her how to keep her lips sealed.

At this point, another agent was injected into the case by local State Security officers. This man Gurevich purported to be a political prisoner who had recently been freed from the same camp where Malysheva's husband was serving his sentence. Before his release, he claimed to have been approached by Malysheva's husband, who asked him to pass on some messages for his wife. Naturally, Malysheva suspected Gurevich's State Security connections, but in accordance with normal procedure she was not informed of his precise purpose.

It did not require Malysheva's explicit knowledge for the plan to work out very successfully. First, Gurevich gave her a package of cigarettes, advising her to check the contents very carefully, since in this way she might find an important message. On reaching her office, Malysheva immediately showed the package of cigarettes to Pervukhin and told him the entire story—as she had heard it from Gurevich.

Pervukhin was very excited about this, and that evening they looked through the cigarettes together. At first they found nothing unusual. But when they began to open the filters, they noticed that something was written on the inside of each one. On arranging the filters in the proper order, they were able to read the following message: "Dear Wife, I am in good health and treated quite well. I am now in Camp X. and I hope that in the near future I will be able to escape not only from this camp but also from the Soviet Union."

The message went on to say that as soon as he got abroad Malysheva's husband would try to send a reliable person to her in order to arrange her safe escape from the Soviet Union. He asked her to be ready for this step and gave her a password through which she would recognize his messenger.

Pervukhin considered the message to be authentic. He advised Malysheva to accept her husband's proposition. Going further, he asked if she could ask the future messenger to arrange his own transit across the border. Malysheva answered that she could not foresee what the messenger's reaction would be, but she solemnly promised to intercede with him on Pervukhin's behalf.

One evening a man supposedly sent by Malysheva's husband approached her. She immediately informed Pervukhin that the messenger had made contact with her, using the established password. After a meeting had been arranged, the "messenger" finally agreed to take Pervukhin abroad also. Pervukhin hurriedly packed some of his belongings in a small bag and declared himself ready for travel. At that very moment Malysheva feigned sickness (under orders from her State Security case officer) and said she was too ill to attempt such a hazardous thing as a border crossing. It was decided, therefore, that Pervukhin would go alone with the messenger. He and Malysheva bade each other farewell with considerable emotion, and she wished him a most successful trip.

Pervukhin and his guide made the first part of the trip by train. Shortly before reaching the border town, they left the train and walked along a narrow path through the forest. At one point the guide took a bottle containing some kind of liquid from his pocket, telling Pervukhin to rub it on his shoes and the knees of his trousers. The use of this solution, the guide explained, would make it impossible for dogs to track them down.

As they approached the alleged border line, they began to crawl on all fours, as quietly as possible. At length the guide declared they were across. Pervukhin kissed the soil, stood up, and took a very deep breath. "Now," he said, "I

am a free man." He thanked the guide and they continued
on their way, walking normally.

Suddenly they were stopped by a sharp order given them
in a foreign language. The guide told Pervukhin to raise his
hands. They were approached by a "foreign" border guard
who briefly checked them for arms and took them to a
nearby post where they were separated. Pervukhin was
treated kindly and given some foreign liquor to put him at
his ease. During the next four days, he was questioned by
"local authorities" through a translator. He took this opportunity to write down all the details of his life. He also wrote
an application to the parliament of the country, asking to
be granted the right of political asylum. He was finally
informed, however, that asylum was not possible because of
an agreement made with the Soviet Union by that country's
government. Accordingly, he would have to be returned to
the Soviet Union.

Pervukhin's intense reaction to this news can be imagined. Shortly thereafter, his hands were bound, he was
blindfolded and put into an automobile. When the car
stopped, after traveling for several hours, his blindfold was
removed and he found himself in front of Soviet State Security officers.

The extraordinary thing about this operation is the
length to which the State Security went to secure a pleni-
tude of evidence against one weak and obviously credulous
dissenter. The extensive use of *agent provocateurs*, the patient working out of a faked "escape," the simulation of a
foreign border post—all this involved net play was possible
only in a system pathologically sensitive to conspiracy. The
only justification for this minute entrapment scheme was
that the "foreign" border guards did receive a detailed account of Pervukhin's background and political associations.
But there is little doubt that this could have been elicited
equally well in a State Security interrogation cell.

APPENDIX III

Some Pitfalls Of Socialist "Legality"

ON CHRISTMAS DAY 1958, the Soviet Union presented the world with a significant revision in its entire criminal code. The revision was not formally "complete." It amounted to a statement of "basic principles" regarding criminal law and criminal procedure. Soviet jurists were quick to point out that the "principles" must be "ratified" by the individual republics.

No pebble was left unturned, however, in the effort to present these "basic principles" as a decisive, if not final, blow struck for safeguarding the liberty of the individual Soviet citizen. This was in line with the statement of the Twentieth Party Congress in February 1956, when Party units were told to "stand vigilantly on the watch for any infringements of legality, to prevent unequivocally and with determination all manifestations of lawlessness and arbitrary actions and violations of legal procedure."

Undeniably the new codes enacted have wiped from the books some of the worst bits of codified ruthlessness in Soviet practice, e.g. it is now forbidden to punish persons automatically for crimes committed by their relatives. As such, they have responded to the submerged but nonetheless insistent demand of the Soviet people, a better-fed and better-educated generation than the one preceding, for something approaching formal justice. This aspect of the codes has received most publicity in the West. It is cited as part of the new "relaxation" in the U.S.S.R. in many of the recent commentaries by just-returned American and other tourists. A visit to a "reformed" prison, for example, is now almost *de rigueur* for important foreign travelers. (It is generally the same prison.)

A close reading of the new revisions, however, shows that legal prospects are far less rosy than advertised. For behind the advance publicity about the reduced judicial role of the State Security, the rehabilitation of those unlawfully convicted, and the newly alert vigilance of Soviet prosecutors for human rights, the code conceals some new severities. If its publication reflects a popular pressure for justice, it mirrors equally well the growing problems and tensions of the Soviet leadership in the era of Khrushchev. The laws advertise a new deal in the courts for the Soviet citizen. But, paradoxically, they are designed for strengthening the hold of the one-man dictatorship on the Soviet people. If the sword is more richly covered this time, the blade is sharper underneath.

Although the new codes are as yet incomplete and comment will long continue, it seemed useful to set down here some of their distinguishing features, with both the fears and the hopes embodied in them.

Until the death of Stalin, no significant revisions had been made in the basic Criminal Codes of 1922, established for the Soviet republics. Various drafts for new codes were discussed but nothing ever came of them. But the weakened collective leadership which succeeded Stalin felt itself obliged to come up with ostentatious popular concessions, particularly since the abuses of the State Security and its allied agencies had grown so flagrant as to make the so-called "socialist legality" an open mockery.

There was another reason for legal rearrangement. The attempted coup by Beria had given the other members of the Central Committee quite a shock, depending as it did on his iron control of the State Security. It was decided that henceforth the heads of the State Security should be responsible to *all* the members of the Praesidium, insuring that no one could use the secret police arm for his own purposes. This "safeguard" is academic in 1959, Khrushchev having long since peopled the entire Praesidium with his creatures; but it looked hopeful in the immediate post-Stalin period.

Such inner administrative reshuffling was only part of a

continuing pattern of popular concessions in legal and judicial matters. In September 1953, the meeting of the Supreme Council abolished the special assemblies and notorious three-man tribunals called the *troike,* which since 1934 had carried out extra-legal measures against political opponents of the régime, real or fancied, as defined by the State Security. These boards had proved particularly useful when the KGB lacked sufficient evidence to be sure of a conviction in the courts or when the hearing of a case in public could be contrary to the régime's propaganda. Several of their members, however, were retained in the First Special Section of the KGB, in charge of central indexes— an excellent vantage point for future activity, if required.

On May 24, 1955, the Praesidium of the Supreme Soviet approved regulations governing the conduct of prosecutors. These defined the competence, rights, and obligations of prosecutors in all echelons of the Soviet legal system and increased their stature. Among other things the regulations charged the prosecutors with the task of supervising local units of the State Security. This new authority granted the prosecutors hardly went unchallenged. But it put enough of a check on the independence of most State Security units to hamper their undercover use by various factions in intra-Party quarrels.

On September 17, 1955, amnesty was granted to certain categories of Soviet citizens guilty of co-operation with the Germans during World War II. This amnesty extended to former members of the Russian "Army of Liberation" (the Vlasov formations) and some people who had served in the German army or police, who were released from their places of imprisonment. The amnesty decree also covered Soviet citizens guilty of these crimes during the same period, who had so far failed to return to the Soviet Union but who might be tempted to do so by the mercy offered in the amnesty. Its ambiguous wording makes for a highly arbitrary interpretation which may well have surprised some émigrés who took it seriously. However, the fact that it was promulgated again testified to the shifting winds behind Soviet penal policy.

On April 25, 1956, the Praesidium of the Supreme Soviet published a decree abolishing the legal accountability of workers and employees for quitting their jobs without permission or taking unauthorized leave. This decree ended the inhuman laws of 1940, under which thousands of workers had suffered. Yet these forced-labor laws had already died a natural death. In its concern about the growth of popular discontent in the postwar period, the régime had applied them increasingly rarely and by 1956 they were scarcely ever invoked.

During 1957 and 1958 supervisory commissions were created within Party executive committees for the control of places of imprisonment. The military tribunals of the MVD troops were abolished and their jurisdiction transferred to strictly military courts-martial. Conditions in some of the labor camps and prisons had become more bearable since the upheavals of 1953, when the officials in charge were uncertain whether in the future they might not find themselves working with former prisoners.

The capstone in this "reform" campaign was the long-promised revision of the criminal code.

On March 27, 1953, three weeks after the death of Stalin, the Praesidium of the Supreme Soviet of the U.S.S.R. had announced its decision to "review the criminal code of the U.S.S.R. and of the Union republics, with the prospect of substituting measures of administrative and disciplinary character instead of criminal punishment for certain administrative, social and other less dangerous crimes, and also easing the punishment for certain crimes." The Ministry of Justice of the U.S.S.R. was ordered "to prepare the necessary proposals in one month's time in order to present them for examination by the Council of Ministers of the U.S.S.R. for eventual submission to the Praesidium."

The month grew into five years. Finally, in its session of December 1958, the Supreme Soviet of the U.S.S.R. passed the following laws:

1. The principles of criminal legislation of the U.S.S.R. and the constituent republics.

2. The law abolishing the deprivation of the right to vote by court action.

3. The law on criminal responsibility for crimes against the state.

4. The law on criminal responsibility for military crimes; i.e. crimes committed while in service.

5. The principles of legislation concerning the judiciary of the U.S.S.R. and constituent and autonomous republics.

6. A law changing the procedure for the election of judges and assessors of people's courts.

7. A statute on courts-martial.

8. The principles of criminal procedure of the U.S.S.R. and constituent republics.

The two most important measures, the Principles of Criminal Legislation and the Principles of Criminal Procedure, had been published in draft six months before. It seems unlikely that the Soviet public in general had much knowledge of their contents, since publication was confined to the legal journals, as can be deduced from statements made by the chairman of the Supreme Court of the U.S.S.R., A. F. Gorkin, and of other deputies who spoke in the Supreme Soviet meeting. The laws as finally passed, however, were considerably amended as a result of discussion within the Legislative Commissions, where the "conservative" elements evidently managed to curb the zeal of the would-be reformers. The methods they used are suggested in the speech of one Deputy Zarobyan to the Supreme Soviet, where he complained that not one of the chairmen of legislative commissions in the republics' Supreme Soviets had been invited to participate in the final amendments of the drafts. Zarobyan suggested that this shortcoming should be eliminated in the future. His speech was followed, however, by the unanimous adoption of every law in question, accompanied by the usual thunderous applause.

The revised codes were significant, nonetheless. To appreciate their importance it is necessary to take into consideration the traditional Soviet theory of law itself. In Soviet theory, unlike that of the West, there is no thought of a government *under* law. Law is merely an instrument of the ruling state power. Soviet jurists dislike answering that abstract question: "What is the law?" They generally find it safest to parrot the official definition originally given by Vyshinksy: "The law is the legalized will of the ruling class, conditioned in the final analysis by the material conditions of its existence."

"Ruling class," as Soviet law has it, refers of course to

the mass of the "people." But where it is impossible for
various sections of the population either to express their
wishes or to protect their interests, the expression "will of
the people" naturally means the will of the people in
power.

Soviet writers buttress this definition by adding that the
law is essential "for protection, for the stabilization and development of social relationships and for the order pleasing
to and profitable for the ruling class."[1] Authorities often
cite Lenin's dictum that "law is nothing without the mechanism of governmental power able to ensure that its provisions are carried out." Lenin also admitted, however: "The
class which has seized political power has done so knowing
that it has seized power *for itself alone*. This is implicit in
the idea of the dictatorship of the proletariat. When we
speak of the 'dictatorship' of a class we do not mean anything at all unless we mean that this class consciously takes
all political power into its own hands and does not fool
either itself or others by any verbiage about 'a national authority elected by universal suffrage and consecrated by
the will of the whole people.' "

Ideally, as Lenin himself added, the people should right-
fully participate in the creation of law under the leadership
of the Communist Party. Soviet writers insist that the "new
law created by the Socialist state" reflects the revolutionary
consciousness "of the people." There is one obvious hitch in
this happy theory. "Vestiges of the old order" still remain
in the consciousness of the people, thus making it difficult
"to inculcate a new Socialist attitude toward work." Since
the Socialist state "bears the responsibility for the education
of the masses in the spirit of Communism," these vestiges
must be erased. One of the most important means at the
command of the Socialist state in so doing is Soviet law.

Thus Soviet legal theory operates concurrently on two
levels: the people's will and the state's convenience. Or, to
use Soviet legal language:

(1) "Soviet law expresses the will of the working class
and of all workers, and combines in itself the policy of the
Communist Party and of the Soviet government. It there-

[1] Golunsky and Strogovich *Theory of Government and Law,*
1940.

fore possesses tremendous strength of conviction as far as the working class is concerned and is held in high repute by the workers."

(2) "These provisions, which express the will of the state, are protected and implemented by the power which the state has to enforce them."[2]

Yet even with "vestiges of the old order" still in evidence, the people's will and the state's convenience are viewed in practice as one and the same. The man who disobeys a keep-off-the-grass sign is not only breaking a state ordinance, but displaying positive antagonism toward his neighbors. The same holds true for the sentences and decisions of Soviet courts. Soviet jurists note their "large educational importance, firstly because they are based on Soviet law and secondly because they stem from courts that are genuinely of the people."

They go on to explain that "with the capture of power and the establishment of the dictatorship of the proletariat, the law serves as the most important instrument existing in the creation of new Socialist relationships in society. The initiative of popular law-making is encouraged and directed by the Communist Party, which has now become the ruling party. The creation of law finds its organized and highest expression in the lawmaking activity of the Socialist state. Soviet law plays a *creative* part in the task of the organization and development of new protective relationships. Soviet law has established the strictest order in the regulation of social relationships, organizing the will of the workers into a united effort."[3]

Law, in sum, is not a body of rules for keeping public order and protecting private rights, as European and American jurisprudence has it. It is, on the contrary, a weapon aimed solely at producing and maintaining a certain kind of society. In Soviet theory, all the classic functions of law are secondary to this dominant idea.

Strictly speaking, Soviet statutes operate on the principle that the only right conduct is that specifally permitted by law. Everything not so specified is—or may be—prohibited.

[2] These quotations are taken from *Forty Years of Soviet Law*, a textbook published by Leningrad University in 1957.
[3] *Forty Years of Soviet Law*.

In the Soviet system the judicial interpretation of rights is similarly odd. Judges hold court only to evaluate the evidence, not to interpret the law. The Supreme Court of the Soviet Union is merely a Party organ, as is true of all the higher organs of the Soviet government. It puts out directives to be followed which define the freedom of interpretation of rights, but never expand it. That would mean exceeding its authority.

The new codes perform perhaps their greatest service in making something of a break with the theory behind this kind of legal system—"socialist legality," as the Soviet jurists call it—which views crime and punishment only as state or "class" problems. As an American commentator, Vladimir Gsovski, Chief of the European Law Division of the Library of Congress, put it: "The idea of ordinary human justice has scored a victory over class injustice."

This changing view is demonstrated by revisions of some obvious injustices, long welded into the Soviet legal structure. The abolition of legalized vendetta on the part of the state, i.e. the punishment of a criminal's relatives for his crime, whether they had shared in it or not, is important to a people who have lived so long with communicable terror. Yet side by side with this reform exists a restatement of one of the terror's worst features. For example, Article 26 of the law on criminal responsibility for crimes against the state, entitled "Failure to report crimes against the state" lays down that "failure to report knowledge of a planned or committed crime against the state . . . is punishable by confinement for a period of from one to three years or corrective labor of from six months to one year."[4]

The relevant article in the new Principles of Criminal Legislation is simply called "Failure to inform": "Failure to inform on a crime reliably known to be in preparation or

---

[4] The crimes to which this penalty applies are treason against the fatherland, espionage, acts of terrorism against the government or against a representative of a foreign state, subversive activity, sabotage, "organizational activities directed towards the commission of especially dangerous crimes against the state, as well as participation in anti-Sovite organizations," banditism, and the manufacture or circulation of counterfeit money.

to have been committed entails criminal responsibility only in cases specially envisaged by the criminal law."

These articles obviously admit of varying interpretations—depending on the whim of the régime. The former criminal code stated that members of the family of a person committing a counter-revolutionary crime were punishable for it whether or not they knew about the act committed or to be committed. Now, on the basis of the new article, not only can relatives of the accused be held liable for his act but also his neighbors, friends, and acquaintances. This applies not only to "counter-revolutionary" acts, but to the large variety of transgressions listed above. Thus, in Khrushchev's "reform" administration, as in Stalin's earlier time, refusal to turn informer remains a crime against the state. At least the new code does state, although in somewhat ambiguous terms, that action can be taken only against those with "reliable knowledge" of a person's crime.

In the first drafts of the revised codes it was provided that an accused was to be considered innocent until he was proven guilty. This struck very boldly at the old rule of Andrey Vyshinsky's that the most valid proof of a crime is the culprit's own confession to it. In the final amendment process this sharp break with the Soviet past was deleted. As *Pravda* noted on December 27, 1958, "it is a deep contradiction of the nature of Soviet Socialist law to attempt to bring into our theory and practice the obsolete dogma of bourgeois law, such as presumption of innocence." In commenting on the final decision, Deputy Sharkov of the Lithuanian SSR explained: "Perhaps the jurists can understand the meaning of such a complicated formula [as presumption of innocence] but great masses of the working people could hardly understand it."

The new law on criminal responsibility does away with the shameful title "enemy of the people," a staple phrase in Soviet judicial procedure since its introduction by Lenin in 1917. Since the term "counter-revolutionary crime" has been replaced by "crime against the state," however, the culprit may be called an enemy of the state instead. It is certainly a franker term.

It is significant that this law on criminal responsibility for crimes against the state was not published in advance for discussion. The attitude taken toward political offenses is at the heart of Soviet criminal legislation and the category of "especially dangerous crimes against the state" adds some new categories of crimes to those listed as counter-revolutionary under the old code: betrayal of the fatherland, espionage, terroristic activity, subversive activity, sabotage, anit-Soviet agitation and propaganda, membership in an anti-Soviet organization, etc. One of the new categories is "propaganda for war"—a handy catch-all-crime—which is punished especially severely by a term of imprisonment of from three to eight years. The category is in a way redundant, since the previous article of the law defines *any* propaganda in the Soviet Union except Communist propaganda as a crime.

At a time when most countries in the West are discussing the abolition of the death penalty, the new Principles of Criminal Legislation retain the death penalty for treason in its various forms, and extend it to apply to new categories of crimes against the government with a rider that this is an "exceptional measure of punishment until its complete abolition." Where in the past the death penalty applied only to a Soviet official who failed to return from abroad as ordered by his superiors, it is now applicable to *all* Soviet citizens who, having gone abroad, refuse to return—an ironic by-product of the new, officially permitted tourism.

The death penalty is not limited to transgressions against the Soviet state. It can apply also to acts committed against governments of other "popular democracies." Article 10 of the law on criminal responsibility says: "In line with the international solidarity of the workers particularly dangerous crimes against the state committed against another workers' state are punishable [in the same degree as for similar crimes committed against the Soviet government, i.e. by death or a long term of imprisonment]." By this token anyone participating in a civil war against Communists in a foreign country or acting against the Communist Party in that country (regardless of which country he himself happens to be a citizen) could be tried under Article 10 as soon as he came under Soviet jurisdiction—with the consequent penalties.

Article 7 of the same law reflects Soviet sensitivity to various forms of anti-Communist or pro-Western propaganda recently circulated by announcing as an especially reprehensible crime the dissemination or keeping of "slanderous fabrications discrediting the Soviet social and political order."

Another section, Article 3, provides a detailed and comprehensive definition of "an act of terroism," which D. S. Polyansky, Chairman of the Legislative Commission of the Soviet of the Union, conceded had often been broadly interpreted in the past because it had not been defined with sufficient precision. It is now defined as the killing of a statesman, public figure, or representative of government, committed in connection with his state or public activities, with the purpose of undermining or weakening Soviet power, or "grievous bodily harm" inflicted with the same intentions upon such a victim.

One undeniable major reform in the new codes is the repudiation of crime by analogy. The codes of 1922 and 1926 permitted punishment to be imposed for "socially dangerous acts" not specifically listed as crimes by applying whichever section of the code seemed to fit the act most closely. One explanation given for this concept, so alien to Western legal theory, was that the authorization to apply criminal law by analogy was necessary when the kinds of crimes changed so fast. According to the new Principles of Criminal Legislation no one may be tried for crimes not laid down by the law—a clear theoretical break with the Soviet past. Yet the loose wording of the articles permits a tremendous variety of interpretation, making one wonder how far this theoretical advance will be translated into actual practice.

According to the old law children of twelve were held responsible for certain crimes and those of fourteen could be considered as criminally responsible as an adult. Under the new provisions full criminal liability starts at sixteen, and for certain specific crimes at fourteen. The number of these specified crimes, however, is so large that not many offenses remain for which responsibility can begin at sixteen.

The deprivation of voting rights as an additional penalty for serious crimes has not been continued in the new codes. The courts are told to be very strict, however, in dealing with persons who have a criminal record.

The Principles of Criminal Legislation set the maximum term of imprisonment for serious crimes at fifteen years instead of twenty-five. In certain cases it is even reduced to ten. This is based on the fact that the practice of long-term imprisonment has not proved useful.

On the other hand, the Principles—to say nothing of the statements made by representatives of the Communist Party in the Supreme Soviet of the U.S.S.R.—provide for severer conditions in prisons and camps. Here again, Khrushchev has attempted to turn back the post-Stalin drift toward liberalization, which once seemed likely to end the forced labor system. The Chairman of the Legislative Commission Polyansky noted that the effectiveness of a sentence was often weakened as a result of the incorrect application to it of the so-called "system of accredited working days," by which a prisoner could shorten his sentence by extra work, and one of the provisions of the Principles is that people sentenced to imprisonment for serious crimes cannot have their sentences reduced for good conduct. Gorkin, the Chairman of the Supreme Court, was indignant that prisoners had been known to comment favorably on their places of imprisonment. "Isn't it possible that the conditions of life created in places of imprisonment are a little bit too good for those who break the laws and interfere with the lives of honest Soviet people? It is necessary to establish a stricter régime in the labor colonies and to educate the prisoners under condtions of heavier labor, so that their memory will not retain a favorable impression of the imprisonment. It is necessary to punish all those who break Soviet law but the law should be especially severe and relentless toward those who make crime their profession."

Some of the deputies even suggested that it might be well to call all criminal prisoners "political enemies." As the *Literaturnaya Gazeta* of January 13, 1959, has it: "These changes are fully justified since the new reduced sentences should in fact become stricter and more realistic . . . It is necessary to activate and strengthen all the agencies of the militia . . . There should be no unsolved crime. We are marching toward Communism while these people get underfoot and prevent us from moving ahead. If a criminal murders or rapes or beats up a Soviet worker or corrupts a young person, how is he different from a saboteur? In what way is he better than a saboteur? Is not an attempt on the life of a Soviet citizen an act of sabotage? The criminal despises our society, he is hostile to it, he is a very real enemy. We have the dictatorship of the proletariat. Let us remember the words of Lenin that 'the dictatorship foresees a revolutionary government which is in fact very hard and pitiless in the suppression of exploiters as well as hoodlums.' "

Pravda and *Izvestia*, describing the new laws, used almost the same language: "This weapon strikes down everything which gets in the way of our irresistible movement forward." This tone hardly accords with the frequent protestations of Soviet theorists that the essence of legal policy in a Socialist state lies not in taking vengeance against criminals but in the attempt to reform persons who have strayed from the straight path.

Comparative provisions of the new law of criminal responsibility for crimes against the state and the old criminal code:

There are some revealing comparisons to be made between individual provisions of the new and old laws. It is no accident that the penalties against treason, espionage, terroristic acts, and other "especially dangerous crimes" formerly listed far down in Articles 50 onwards are placed at the top of the list in the new law. This is done to emphasize the ever-present danger of war and the need for political "vigilance" in a Soviet Union whose population is now more susceptible than before to the lures of peaceful living and consumer comforts.

There is one more small but interesting instance of the régime's efforts to keep the judicial ranks closed throughout the scattered territories of the U.S.S.R. That is the cast-iron universality of the articles noted. Under the old dispensation the various republics were allowed at least to vary the numbering of their criminal codes. In the 1958 law not only were the same basic articles enforced throughout the Soviet Union, but all republics were ordered to give them identical numbering.

Article New Code	Article Old Code[5]
1. Treason against the fatherland	58 - 1 - A
2. Espionage	58 - 6
3. Acts of terrorism	58 - 8
4. Acts of terrorism against a representative of a foreign power	No article dealing with this subject but in general, crimes of this character were dealt with under Art. 58 - 5 which provided the same punishment as 58 - 8.
5. Subversive activity	58 - 9
6. Sabotage	58 - 7
7. Anti-Soviet agitation and propaganda	58 - 10
8. War propaganda	No article dealing with this. First Soviet law passed on this subject issued on March 2, 1951. It provided for trial of persons guilty of war propaganda as being especially dangerous criminals.
9. Activity connected with the organization of specially dangerous crimes against the state and membership in anti-Soviet organizations	58 - 11
10. Especially dangerous crimes against the state committed against another worker's state	58 - 1 - Part 2 stated that in view of the international solidarity of interests of all workers some actions are deemed to be counter-revolutionary when directed against any other state of workers, even if not a part of the U.S.S.R.

[5] The articles cited under the "old code" heading refer to the pilot criminal code of the RSFSR.

Article New Code	Article Old Code
11. Disruption of national and racial equality	59 - 7
12. Disclosure of state secrets	This was dealt with by special decree of June 9, 1947.
13. Loss of documents containing state secrets	Dealt with in special decree of June 6, 1947.
14. Banditism	59 - 3
15. Smuggling	59 - 9 and Article 83
16. Mass disorders	59 - 2
17. Evasion of military conscription	59 - 4
18. Evasion of general mobilization in emergency	193 - 10 - A
19. Evasion of payment of taxes or other obligations in wartime	59 - 6
20. Illegal departure from or entry into the U.S.S.R.	59 - 10 and Article 84
21. Violation of rules of international flights	59 - 3 - D
22. Violation of traffic rules and negligence in care of transportation	Articles 59 - 3 - V, 59 - 3 - G, and sometimes 75 - 1, 75 - 2 were used.
23. Sabotage of transport	59 - 3 - B
24. Forgeries and counterfeiting	59 - 8
25. Violation of currency regulations	59 - 12
26. Failure to report knowledge of crimes against the state	Sometimes dealt with under 58 - 1 or 58 - 12, or 29 - 13.

Earlier in 1958, the Soviet government had already passed a law dealing with punishment for failure to carry out production norms. This ordinance was designed to put teeth into the new campaign against plant and factory directors and leaders of various branches of industry whose enterprises lagged in the fulfillment of production norms. Even Ministers of the central government were threatened with punishment if enterprises under their control fell behind on their schedules.

This law was an obvious result of the need to insure the success of Khrushchev's productivity reforms of 1957, which decentralized Soviet industry and planning, against considerable opposition. It does not, however, make clear which particular branches of industry were defective or what could be construed as "full productivity." In somewhat ambiguous terms it is made clear that the "inability of interested organs to deliver certain materials and equipment on time to various republic and provincial economic councils" will be considered as a crime and those guilty will be tried and punished to the full extent of the law.

One may deduce from this that there are more ways than one of fulfilling production norms in Soviet forced labor camps, at least.

It is not surprising, in view of such stringencies, to note that the draft of the new codes, according to Chairman Polyansky, was prepared "with the active assistance of workers of the prosecutors' offices, courts, *MVD, KGB*[6] and the juridicial commission." One may have understandable doubts about the State Security's loudly announced divorce from judicial and punitive proceedings. There are more than enough loopholes in the law for the State Security's version of "administrative measures."

If the law were favorably interpreted, the advances might well outweigh the new Khrushchevian severities. Unfortunately, the régime has given few indications that it *will* be favorably interpreted—unless "favorable" is taken to mean "favorable to the state." Even behind the Iron Curtain, doubts have been expressed about the practical validity of the reformed codes. As an eminent Polish jurist put it, after a learned disquisition on the new Principles:

"It is, however, quite a different question to what extent good legal principles, once recognized, are obeyed in practical application."

---

[6] Our italics.

ORGANIZATION OF THE ORGANS OF STATE SECURITY OF U.S.S.R.

COMMITTEE OF STATE SECURITY (KGB)

COMMITTEES OF STATE SECURITY OF UNION REPUBLICS

DIRECTORATES OF STATE SECURITY FOR OBLASTS, KRAYS, AND AUTONOMOUS REPUBLICS

SECTIONS OR SUBSECTIONS OF STATE SECURITY IN URBAN RAYONS

SUBSECTIONS OF STATE SECURITY IN RURAL RAYONS

CASE OFFICERS
(villages, areas, blocks)

ORGANIZATION OF THE COMMITTEE FOR STATE SECURITY OF U.S.S.R. (THE "CENTRAL APPARATUS" IN MOSCOW)

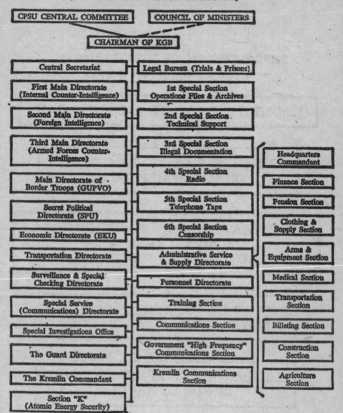

CPSU CENTRAL COMMITTEE — COUNCIL OF MINISTERS

CHAIRMAN OF KGB

Central Secretariat	Legal Bureau (Trials & Prisons)	
First Main Directorate (Internal Counter-Intelligence)	1st Special Section Operations Files & Archives	
Second Main Directorate (Foreign Intelligence)	2nd Special Section Technical Support	
Third Main Directorate (Armed Forces Counter-Intelligence)	3rd Special Section Illegal Documentation	Headquarters Commandant
Main Directorate of Border Troops (GUPVO)	4th Special Section Radio	Finance Section
Secret Political Directorate (SPU)	5th Special Section Telephone Taps	Pension Section
Economic Directorate (EKU)	6th Special Section Censorship	Clothing & Supply Section
Transportation Directorate	Administrative Service & Supply Directorate	Arms & Equipment Section
Surveillance & Special Checking Directorate	Personnel Directorate	Medical Section
Special Service (Communications) Directorate	Training Section	Transportation Section
Special Investigations Office	Communications Section	Billeting Section
The Guard Directorate	Government "High Frequency" Communications Section	Construction Section
The Kremlin Commandant	Kremlin Communications Section	Agriculture Section
Section "K" (Atomic Energy Security)		

STATE SECURITY FOREIGN INTELLIGENCE

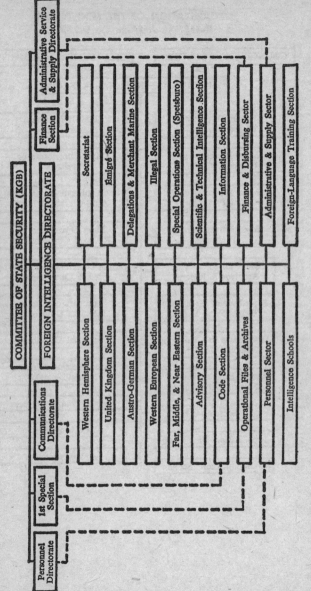

COMMITTEE OF STATE SECURITY (KGB)

| Personnel Directorate | 1st Special Section | Communications Directorate | FOREIGN INTELLIGENCE DIRECTORATE | Finance Section | Administrative Service & Supply Directorate |

- Western Hemisphere Section
- Secretariat
- United Kingdom Section
- Emigré Section
- Austro-German Section
- Delegations & Merchant Marine Section
- Western European Section
- Illegal Section
- Far, Middle, & Near Eastern Section
- Special Operations Section (Spetsburo)
- Advisory Section
- Scientific & Technical Intelligence Section
- Code Section
- Information Section
- Operational Files & Archives
- Finance & Disbursing Sector
- Personnel Sector
- Administrative & Supply Sector
- Intelligence Schools
- Foreign-Language Training Section

ORGANIZATION OF THE MINISTRY OF INTERNAL AFFAIRS OF U.S.S.R.

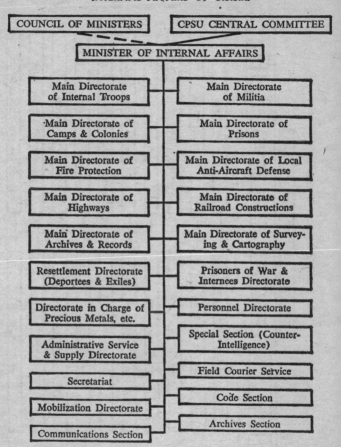

COUNCIL OF MINISTERS	CPSU CENTRAL COMMITTEE

MINISTER OF INTERNAL AFFAIRS

Main Directorate of Internal Troops	Main Directorate of Militia
Main Directorate of Camps & Colonies	Main Directorate of Prisons
Main Directorate of Fire Protection	Main Directorate of Local Anti-Aircraft Defense
Main Directorate of Highways	Main Directorate of Railroad Constructions
Main Directorate of Archives & Records	Main Directorate of Surveying & Cartography
Resettlement Directorate (Deportees & Exiles)	Prisoners of War & Internees Directorate
Directorate in Charge of Precious Metals, etc.	Personnel Directorate
Administrative Service & Supply Directorate	Special Section (Counter-Intelligence)
Secretariat	Field Courier Service
Mobilization Directorate	Code Section
Communications Section	Archives Section

INDEX